THE FORGOTTEN MAN

THE FORGOTTEN MAN
WALTER HINES PAGE,
NEW SOUTH VISIONARY

ANDREW R. PARNELL

The University of Georgia Press
Athens

© 2024 by the University of Georgia Press
Athens, Georgia 30602
www.ugapress.org
All rights reserved

Designed by Melissa Bugbee Buchanan
Set in Minion Pro

Most University of Georgia Press titles are
available from popular e-book vendors.

Printed digitally

Library of Congress Cataloging-in-Publication Data
Names: Parnell, Andrew R., author.
Title: The forgotten man : Walter Hines Page, new South visionary /
Andrew R. Parnell.
Other titles: Walter Hines Page, new South visionary
Description: Athens : The University of Georgia Press, [2024] |
Includes bibliographical references and index.
Identifiers: LCCN 2024029728 | ISBN 9780820367590 (hardback) |
ISBN 9780820367583 (paperback) | ISBN 9780820367606 (epub) |
ISBN 9780820367613 (pdf)
Subjects: LCSH: Page, Walter Hines, 1855–1918. | Ambassadors—United
States—Biography. | Journalists—United States—Biography. |
Southern States—Race relations—History—19th century. | United
States—Foreign relations—Great Britain. | Great Britain—Foreign
relations—United States. | United States—Foreign relations—1913–1921. |
Great Britain—Foreign relations—1910–1936.
Classification: LCC E664.P15 P37 2024 |
DDC 327.730092 [B]—dc23/eng/20240807
LC record available at https://lccn.loc.gov/2024029728

To my wonderful family,
Annie, Emily, Lucy, and Scarlett

In making an estimate of a civilization it is the neglected and forgotten man more than any other that must be taken into account.

WALTER HINES PAGE, "FORGOTTEN MAN" SPEECH, 1897

CONTENTS

Preface   ix

Introduction   1

PART 1. THE MAN

Chapter 1. Influences and Education   9

Chapter 2. America's "Best Editor"   30

PART 2. THE SOUTH

Chapter 3. "Wake Up, Old Land!"   59

Chapter 4. Racial Equality   77

Chapter 5. The Forgotten Man and Woman   91

PART 3. THE NATION

Chapter 6. Politics and Society   123

Chapter 7. "Watch That Man!"   142

PART 4. THE WORLD

Chapter 8. Starting His "Great Adventure"   163

Chapter 9. The Wartime Challenge of Neutrality   181

Chapter 10. The End of the Relationship with Wilson   203

Chapter 11. Vindication   218

PART 5. THE MYTHMAKERS

Chapter 12. The Myth of Neutrality   241

Chapter 13. Remembering Walter Hines Page   251

Notes   263

Bibliography   299

Index   305

PREFACE

I discovered Walter Hines Page (1855–1918) through Burton J. Hendrick's four volumes on the *Life and Letters of Walter H. Page* (published in the 1920s, and three of which won the Pulitzer Prize). What initially attracted me to Page was his ideas. Even more appealing, he communicated them so clearly, concisely, and persuasively. Probably most appealingly, he appeared to be promoting his ideas for entirely altruistic reasons, and often in the face of great resistance and criticism. He thought it was the right thing to do.

Determined to learn more about him, I researched and analyzed a vast range of sources, including letters, diaries, books, articles, papers, and newspapers, many of which were previously underused or unused. I took advantage of my extensive research and writing experience covering history, economics, politics, business, and law, gained at university and in my career. My qualifications include a bachelor of economics from the Australian National University, a master of commerce (First Class Honors) from the University of Melbourne, and I am currently undertaking a PhD in economic history at Monash University, Melbourne. These are three of Australia's leading universities. Over my career I have made significant contributions to a wide range of publications, projects, and reports, including currently as a senior analyst at the Australian Competition and Consumer Commission.

Researching Page's life from Australia presented challenges, though these were reasonably straightforward to overcome. The State Library of Victoria has all his magazines along with many relevant books, and I always found the staff very helpful. There are extensive resources on the internet. Particularly useful were JSTOR, the American Presidency Project, HathiTrust, ProQuest, Internet Archive, and Google digitization. I would like to especially mention the Library of Congress' excellent Chronicling America, which has thousands of newspapers from towns, cities, and states, digitized by universities and local organizations such as historical societies. I was able to spend a short time at Harvard University's Houghton Library where much of Page's archives are stored. The archives are easy to access, and I greatly appreciated all the assistance provided by the helpful archivists and staff.

I am extremely grateful to several people for giving me so much advice and most importantly, encouragement. Author Andrew D. Connell gave me the best advice a writer could get when he told me to write something every day—

it doesn't matter what it is, just write something. I followed this, sometimes not writing much or doing research, but it worked. To fellow-aspiring author Jo Townsend, with whom I spent countless hours talking about research and writing while we waited to pick up our respective children from school, your ideas and advice were always worth serious consideration and often adopted. My friend Simon Ville gave me great advice early on, which gave me the inspiration and confidence to change the direction of my work for the better. During more than four years working for Simon and his colleague David Merrett, two of Australia's preeminent business and economic historians, I learned from the best how to get the most out of archival research.

In recent years my supervisor and colleague at the ACCC, Sharyn Vaughan, gave me regular, sometimes daily, encouragement, willingly approving leave so I could do research and writing, and kindly, unexpectedly, gave me a copy of Booker T. Washington's inspiring autobiography *Up from Slavery*. To my friends, Justin Klvac and Philip Hayes, who have given me unstinting support: thank you, Philip, for taking the time to read an almost final draft and for your encouraging comments, and to Justin, who twice read drafts and gave such insightful feedback, thank you very much.

A huge thank you to everyone at UGA Press. Lisa Bayer, Elizabeth Adams, Rebecca Norton, and Laura Price Yoder for all your guidance, support, and faith in my work. Pat Allen originally saw the potential in my manuscript and gave me a second chance to submit a revised version. The anonymous reviewers provided extremely insightful and practical advice, which guided me in transforming the first draft and later giving the manuscript its final polish. As editor, I really appreciated Zubin Meer's thoughtful suggestions.

For the photographs, I am so grateful to Rebecca Freeburn for her professionalism, skill, and assistance at a crucial time. The staff at the State Library of Victoria were exceptional in the quality and speed of their work. William H. Brown and other staff at the State Archives of North Carolina were extremely helpful. I would like to give a special mention to Peggy Dillard at the Woodrow Wilson Presidential Library.

More than anyone I am grateful to my great friend James Holt. James has the ability to give the right advice at the right time. When researching and writing, in the back of my mind I knew James was vitally interested in my work, and often that kept me going, probing to learn more about Walter Hines Page.

I've saved the best to last. I cannot thank my family enough. My wife Anne and our special daughters Emily, Lucy, and Scarlett, I have so often been missing in the evenings, emerging only to talk endlessly about Page and his times. Despite this, you have given me unquestioning and unwavering support, and you have my complete gratitude.

Andrew R. Parnell
Melbourne, Australia
March 2024

THE FORGOTTEN MAN

INTRODUCTION

STANDING UP FOR HIS BELIEFS

On the morning of May 19, 1897, Walter Hines Page, the forty-one-year-old assistant editor of America's most prestigious magazine, the *Atlantic Monthly*, rose to speak to the graduating students of the State Normal and Industrial College for Girls in Greensboro, North Carolina. The message he gave them, and the state's leaders in the audience, was unequivocal: North Carolina—and the South—had forgotten the vast majority of its people by not providing them with an education.

Education had been provided for a minority, the powerful and wealthy, and certain religious people. However, the farmers and workers, and especially girls and women, were stuck in a cycle of poverty with no apparent means of escape. The solution, according to Page, was a universal public education system to be made available to all. He had spent his life standing up for the "forgotten man" and "woman." They were forgotten because they were poor and illiterate, because of their gender, or because of their race. They were forgotten by their leaders and by the rest of the world.

Through sheer perseverance, positivity, skill, and relentless hard work, Page had reached the pinnacle of his profession as a magazine editor. He used his national influence to do whatever he could for those who had been left behind, those who had been used as pawns in their leaders' fight for power. For daring to suggest such a radical idea as universal education, Page was criticized and ridiculed by leaders and in newspapers across the state. Yet his "Forgotten Man" speech set off a chain of events that transformed public education across the impoverished South.

Page was born and raised in North Carolina, and education made a major impact on his childhood. His mother was relatively well educated and passed her love of reading and learning on to her son, and she likely inspired his lifelong desire for greater opportunities for women. His father's side of the family were also strong believers in education, and, with no accessible public school system, they established several schools for local children over the years. Both his father and paternal grandfather focused on practical education and training.

From his paternal grandfather, Page learned about the Southern prosperity of earlier decades. Combined with what he observed in his formative years, Page became convinced that the source of the South's problems were the Southern leaders who had established a social and economic structure that entrenched their power, by enslaving an entire race and shunning education or any type of industrial or economic advancement. From his father, Page learned the importance of standing up for what he believed in, even if it was unpopular, and he would dedicate most of his life to standing up to these leaders. As a result, he was forced to leave the South, spending most of his career in New York and Boston.

This book introduces the concepts of the antebellum myth, the race-problem myth, and the myth of neutrality. As a prolific writer, newspaper and magazine editor, reformer (social, political, and economic), adviser to presidents, persuasive public speaker, and ambassador, Page stood up to the mythmakers.

The antebellum myth was the idealization of the pre–Civil War South, the antebellum period, as a perfect civilization. In the 1880s, Page was afraid Southerners would be seduced by the myth and aspire to the antebellum way of life, which in reality was dominated by poorly educated agrarian workers and families living in poverty while the North was booming. Realizing there was no reason why the South should lag so far behind the North, and lacking the parochial defensiveness of many Southerners, Page identified the leaders' *"trying to make a lost cause a living cause"* as the true problem. Working with his fellow progressive New South advocates, Page made a significant contribution to Southern economic and educational development and helped Southerners realize this was their future.[1]

Trying to defeat the idea that there was a "race problem" that threatened the futures of white Southerners was Page's greatest challenge in his attempts to develop the South. He saw this for what it was: an attempt by the "race politicians" to gain and retain power by taking advantage of white Americans' latent racism and fear of the unknown. Abandoned by most of his New South colleagues in the first decade of 1900s, many of whom were racist, he chronicled the losing fight for racial equality. Tragically, by then the myth that there was a "race problem" that threatened Southern society had become entrenched and Page's despair was palpable.

May 1913 was the start of Page's greatest adventure as ambassador to Great Britain. He was an internationalist, and this orientation came to the fore in this position. He advocated that America should take on a leadership role to bolster the nascent global democracy movement, which would provide opportunities for forgotten people around the world. During World War I, Page was up against the myth of neutrality, which was the idea that America could ignore the war in Europe as if it had no consequences for its future. It was a similar situation to that which Page had encountered all his life while working to develop the South: having to stand up to creators and perpetuators of myths.

Four biographies of Page have previously been published. The most high-profile and influential was Burton J. Hendrick's four-volume *Life and Letters*, published during the 1920s, after Page died. Hendrick had been an employee of Page's, and still worked at Doubleday, Page & Co. when he wrote the books. More than four decades later, in 1970, Ross Gregory's work focused on Page's ambassadorial period from 1913 to 1918. In 1977 John M. Cooper published a full biography; then in 1982 Robert J. Rusnak wrote about Page's establishment and editorship of the *World's Work* from 1900 to 1913.

Hendrick's narrative and interpretation of the letters presented Page in a largely uncritical light, leading to questions of accuracy, such as overstating his influence on President Woodrow Wilson and exaggerating his role in certain situations during World War I. The later three authors provided information and, in some cases, reacted to specific events, actions, or comments with either criticism or praise for Page. They appear to have tried to address the imbalance in Hendrick's work and create the impression of having set out to be critical when the opportunity arose. Yet readers could easily be confused by Page's role in history as these three authors understated or misinterpreted his roles in a range of areas.

One of these areas is Page's roles in the development of the South. For example, Cooper downplayed the role of Page's "Forgotten Man" speech in initiating the subsequent education campaign, implying that while it benefited him personally in his "self-appointed" role as an "intersectional ambassador," it was not a factor in the campaign. Further, this author stated Page was unlikely to have been a significant contributor. This understates the reality, as chronicled in this book and espoused by the people who worked with Page who believed the speech was the catalyst for the campaign and that he made a major contribution.[2]

It is widely accepted that Page wrote negatively in trying to change the South, to the point where authors make passing references to it without feeling the need for justification. Gregory, for example, stated that "Page goaded provincialism and backwardness, directed sharp jabs at the Daughters of the Confederacy and high officers of the Civil War" and criticized Page because it "hardly was the tactful way of reforming North Carolina." This is misleading as Page was overwhelmingly positive in his attempts to advance North Carolina and the South by encouraging industrial and economic development, campaigning for education, and advocating for racial equality.[3]

Page's position on racial equality is considered by most authors to be "complex"; they imply or state he was confused, partially racist, or an underlying racist who tried to cover it up. Cooper claimed Page did not know his own position on racial equality. Hugh C. Bailey, who in 1969 wrote a book about a number of New South reformers, imposed modern values on him by stating his personality was "complex" because he delighted in telling racist jokes despite firmly believing in racial justice. Further, Cooper implied and Bailey stated that Page believed in the superiority of Anglo-Saxons. Other authors claim he was soft in his criticism of lynching and that he accepted segregation in education. In her 2011 history of the *Atlantic Monthly*, Susan Goodman assumed Page was racist simply because his family had owned slaves and he once used the word "niggers." In the same book this author praises groundbreaking articles by two high-profile African Americans, though she does not mention they were published at Page's instigation.[4]

Rather than being complex, Page's belief was very simple: he believed in people as people regardless of race. This is crucial to understanding Page. His courage in standing up for racial equality has been understated; he knew it would be highly controversial, make him virtually unemployable in the South, and create difficulties with some friends and family members, including his wife. His advocacy of racial equality and his exposure of the race-problem myth as a political power play has not been given the prominence warranted for such a major issue in America and around the world. This is a part of Page's story that needs to be told.

The area where Page has attracted greatest criticism is as U.S. ambassador to Great Britain during World War I. The most serious and widespread criticism is that he was too pro-British and, in defiance of President Woodrow Wilson's orders and contrary to America's interests, relentlessly advocated entering the war in support of the Allies. It is claimed Page had become too enamored by the British people and allowed himself to be swayed by the British government. Wilson increasingly made this criticism as the war went on, and many authors took it at face value. This practice is so insidious that Wilson's biographers and chroniclers blame Page for the subsequent breakdown in Page and Wilson's relationship without even feeling the need for justification. Ray S. Baker and William E. Dodd refer to Wilson managing "to hold Ambassador Page in peaceful leash" and Arthur S. Link writes that by the end of 1915 Wilson considered Page "thoroughly unreliable and totally ineffective, because of his partiality to the British cause." Cooper asserts that "Page's confused political bearings helped create a gulf of misunderstanding between himself and Wilson," and August Heckscher claims that Page was so "crassly" pro-British that he hardened Wilson against Britain. According to Gregory, "there was little doubt that Britain's attitude guided Page's thoughts" and this eventually led to "the problem of Page" being discussed in Wilson's "inner circles." In his book *Rogue Diplomats,* Seth Jacobs gave numerous additional examples and himself claimed Page was one of "the most incorrigible rogue diplomats in the annals of American foreign relations," continually defying the president as he sought to influence U.S. foreign policy.[5]

This criticism is unwarranted. Extensive analysis of correspondence between Wilson and Page, combined with numerous other sources, reveals these authors misinterpret Page's arguments and misunderstand the relationship between the two men. The analysis shows that far from being pro-Britain, Page was looking out for America's interests. Page was being realistic and perceptive in the advice he was providing. He understood what was happening and how his nation should act to secure its long-term future. Previous authors have not noted that President Wilson effectively negated his own criticism because he ended up using similar "pro-Britain" arguments in his historic 1917 speech to Congress, embracing policies Page had long advocated. Nor did these authors recognize the very strong links between the strategy used in World War II by President Franklin D. Roosevelt and the strategy that Page advocated to President Wilson in World War I. All these factors are integral parts of the Page story; in refuting the claim that he was too pro-Britain, this book reveals that he was actually pro-democracy and pro-America.

Page showed remarkable foresight, borne from a great understanding of, and compassion for, his fellow man. When reading about historical figures, we are generally implored to remember they were persons of their time, reflecting the prejudices, values, and limitations of their compatriots and society. This is generally not so with Page; most of his beliefs were well ahead of his time. He was one of the few public and consistent advocates for racial equality, women's rights, and the need for America to take some responsibility in international leadership.

Democracy and freedom underpinned his beliefs, and from democracy and freedom, he believed, come equality, education, opportunity, and prosperity. More than anything, Walter Hines Page was interested in people, what they did, and how he or society could help them to live to their fullest potential.

PART ONE

THE MAN

\ 1 /

INFLUENCES AND EDUCATION

1855 TO 1883

EARLY LIFE AND INFLUENCES

Walter Hines Page was born on August 15, 1855, to Catherine "Kate" Raboteau Page and Allison Francis "Frank" Page. His birthplace was their two-story house Frank had built at "Page's," the unofficial name for the four hundred acres in Wake County, about eight miles west of Raleigh, North Carolina. Surrounded by pine trees, it was an isolated setting on the railway line with a quiet, barely used stop known as "Page's Station" with the occasional train passing through. In this idyllic environment Walter spent his childhood, and the three people who had a particularly significant influence on the young boy were his mother, father, and grandfather.[1]

KATE RABOTEAU PAGE

Kate's father, John Samuel Raboteau, was of French heritage and worked as a saddlemaker in Fayetteville, North Carolina. Kate's mother, Esther Barclay, was born in 1808 to a Scottish family in Barclaysville, a small town between Raleigh and Fayetteville. Married in 1828, John and Esther had eight children and lived most of their life in Fayetteville. Esther was remembered in the *News and Observer* after her death in 1901 as having led a "quiet and unassuming" life with "clear, good sense, sound judgement, honesty and sincerity of purpose" as well as "ready sympathy and winning simplicity of manner." Esther's parents, Kate's grandparents, were proprietors of the Half Way House tavern where stage coaches stopped to rest overnight and change horses. After her husband died Esther Barclay Sr. ran the tavern. In the early 1850s, pioneering landscape architect, author, and conservationist Frederick Law Olmsted was touring the South as a reporter for the *New York Times* and stayed at Barclay's tavern. He described being welcomed to a "cheerful and comforting" inn by "a nice, stout, kindly looking Quaker-like old lady" who was a "genius" with hospitality.[2]

Kate was born in 1831 in Fayetteville, John and Esther's second child and eldest daughter. Her education was better than many other girls of the time, attending Peggy Eastwood's girls' school in Raleigh and the Louisville Female

Academy, a seminary in North Carolina. As well as the standard education, which included needlework, Kate learned some French and algebra. Also highly unusual for a woman, Kate was a voracious reader of quality literature. She was rarely without a book, either inside or out doing household chores, even as a mother. Kate was a strong, noble, and smart woman. A devoted Methodist, she did not allow gambling, smoking, dancing, alcohol, or other improper activities in her house. She lived simply, though it was not an austere environment as she had a great sense of humor and was very affectionate. Driven by a sense of duty, Kate raised her children with a strong moral code.[3]

Josephus Daniels, a lifelong family friend, described Kate as "of the best type of old-fashioned North Carolina Methodist matron" with a "lively imagination" who knew what was right. When Daniels was editing a newspaper, she thanked him for not describing the outfits worn by young ladies at a social function, telling him, "It is nobody's business what young women wear."[4]

Kate and Frank were married in Fayetteville on July 5, 1849, and had eight children who survived to adulthood. They had a tough start, moving from one pine field to another making turpentine and lumber. Around 1854 they bought the land where Frank built their home, and in the same year the state-owned North Carolina Railroad, between Goldsboro and Charlotte, came through, passing nearby.[5]

Walter was their third child and the first to survive beyond infancy. He was born when Kate was just twenty-four. Indicative of the poor health that would afflict him throughout his life, Walter was a sickly baby and child. He required constant care in his first few years, and many times it was thought he might not survive. Mother and son were alone together most of the time, as Frank was often away on extended business trips, neighbors were few and far between, and his next sibling, Robert, was not born until four years later. Walter had memories of a young mother, telling her in a letter when he was twenty-one: "Do you know that I have dim recollections of a mother who was hardly more than a girl?"

Kate had a significant positive influence on her eldest son's development and in shaping his character. She took on Walter's schooling until he was ten, teaching him to read and write, filling him with a passion for reading and learning. She introduced him to literature such as the novels of Walter Scott and Charles Dickens. Walter portrayed their relationship in the same letter: "However we may seem to others, you are a young mother yet to *me*, and I am yet to you only the same little boy."

Their relationship remained close even after he left home, writing constantly, sometimes turning to her for support following setbacks, and sharing his triumphs. His Christmas 1893 letter captured her influence from those early years: "But wherever you are and though all the rest have the joy of seeing you, which is denied to me, never a Christmas comes but I feel as near you as I did years and years ago when we were young."[6]

Kate died suddenly at her home on August 21, 1897, at just sixty-five years old. She had been ill for several days, though appeared to be recovering so that Frank left her sitting on the front porch and spent the day in Raleigh. He was on the train coming home when she died. Walter did not realize how lonely his mother's death would make him feel as she "was a living presence" in his life and that of his children. Kate profoundly influenced her eldest son's lifelong belief in the power of education, especially for girls, and greater opportunities for women.[7]

ANDERSON PAGE

Anderson Page, Walter's paternal grandfather, was born in 1790 in Granville County, North Carolina. In 1820 he established a home, "Oaky Mount," in the wilderness about nine miles northwest of Raleigh in Kelvyn Grove, Wake County. He became a prosperous cotton and tobacco farmer, owning 1,200 acres and 30–50 slaves. Anderson married Mary Hayes, and they had eight sons and four daughters. As their family grew, Anderson added more buildings, and it became a revered family institution known as the "Old Place."[8]

A strong believer in education, in 1832 Anderson set up a primary school at the Old Place for his own children as well as those of neighboring farms. Then, in February 1839 he started a girls' school. It was initially advertised as simply a "Female School" offering two five-month sessions a year. Before the second session, it was readvertised as Oaky Mount Academy, offering additional services including tutoring in a wide range of subjects and boarding for ten to twelve pupils. One of his daughters was the teacher, covering "the different branches of an English education and Needle work." Later, during the 1850s and probably longer, Anderson was a member of a common school district committee.[9]

Anderson's interest in education extended to improving agricultural practices. In February 1852 he was a foundation member of the Wake County Agricultural Society, formed to work with farmers in surrounding counties to improve local agricultural practices. In 1869 Anderson was on a committee appointed by the North Carolina Agricultural Society to examine different reaping machines. They trialed two machines and recommended one due to its superior "perfectness of work," though they noted the other was at a disadvantage in the trial "owing to the inexperience of the driver and the unsteadiness of the team."[10]

Anderson was active in the local temperance movement and in 1853 was appointed delegate to the State Temperance Convention. The following year, at a local meeting on July 4, he was appointed to a committee that would prepare circulars and organize speakers throughout the county in an attempt to influence state elections in favor of candidates who favored liquor restrictions.[11]

Most of Anderson and Mary's sons and daughters received more than average education. Walter had a great deal of respect for Uncle Pascal, who was considered the family scholar, saying later, "He had the best head on his shoulders of any man I knew." Pascal ran a school for boys in a little house at the Old Place. Another uncle, Rufus, was a Whig leader before the Civil War and later North Carolina secretary of state for several years. Uncle John was a graduate from a medical school in Philadelphia who spent his career as a country doctor in Wake and nearby counties. A musician and reciter of poetry, his great talent was to bring Shakespeare to life in monumental impromptu plays for forty to fifty children at Old Place family gatherings.[12]

Walter had enormous respect for his grandfather. It was through him that he learned about the period before slavery defined the South, when there was a great unified American democracy. When Anderson encouraged Walter to serve his country, he was referring to the entire Union, not just the South as many would have implored. The profound influence on Walter was shown when he later said that his grandfather's thoughts were "the background of my life."

At the Old Place, Walter read American political literature, including speeches made decades before the Civil War and pamphlets on the war. He would say later this was a neglected area of American writing. Here was where Walter's love of literature, especially Shakespeare, flourished. It was the Old Place, its books, its visitors, and Anderson himself, that was the source of some of the most important ideas, values, beliefs, and interests that would shape Walter's character, life, and career. Walter regularly returned to the Old Place while he was a student, and in later years, often stayed for lengthy periods. In 1878, after having not visited for two years, he wrote to his mother's first cousin Sarah Jasper, with whom he had a close relationship: "You do not know how this old place always works strangely on me, and every year more and more strange seems the effect of its loneliness." Walter went on to identify the depth of his grandfather's influence: "He seems to speak to me back out of the far-gone forming elements that have made me." The previous night they had had a long talk about a range of things, and when his grandfather had finally spoken about his gradually failing health, Walter felt a profound sadness that divulged the extent of his feelings: "There is a nameless pathos in him for me."[13]

Anderson remained active into his nineties. He regularly went into Raleigh, where he spent his ninety-fourth birthday and, according to Walter, "jocularly assured his kinspeople that he expected to reach his one hundredth birthday." A few days later he was in Fayetteville and met eighty-eight-year-old William R. Poole. The two men hadn't seen each other for some time, though over many decades they had worked for the community, including on the Board of Wardens of the Poor and to improve agricultural practices. In the words of the Raleigh *Observer*, both were "sterling citizens, widely known and respected."

Several weeks later, on October 3, 1884, Anderson unexpectedly died. Walter was twenty-nine years old and wrote that Anderson's health had "been uncommonly good for a man of his age." For Walter, a tangible connection with the old South died with his grandfather. The extent of his respect, and the impact the old man had on his grandson, was shown by Walter's words written after his death: "It seemed to me that the history of the world fell into two periods—one that had gone before and the other that now began; for, when we buried him, we seemed to be burying a standard of judgement, a social order, an epoch."[14]

FRANK PAGE

Frank Page, Anderson's son and Walter's father, was born on August 30, 1824, at the Old Place. More settlers had moved into the area, though it remained a sparsely settled land of pine trees and sand with few roads or houses. Much of Frank's time as a boy was spent on hard physical work helping his father. Connected to his farm, Anderson had a transport business, taking produce from his and neighboring farms to Northern markets. Frank would go on this grueling journey, as Walter later described: "My father as a boy went with my grandfather's caravan of wagons, loaded with cotton, all the way from Wake County to Petersburg, Virginia, to sell it—over miserable roads, camping by the roadside at night and taking a week to make the journey either way."[15]

Unlike most of his siblings, Frank did not receive an academic education, and left home by the age of twenty to become a sawmiller and turpentine distiller. In the 1840s he was based in Fayetteville making a living from the pine trees, collecting sap and making lumber. He was a pioneer in developing North Carolina's pine industry, owning a lumber mill when it was widely considered to be a sure way to go broke. When he and Kate moved to Wake County he continued in the lumber business.[16]

Like his wife, Frank was a strict Methodist and did not swear, smoke, gamble, dance, or go to the theater. He passionately supported prohibition as he despised alcohol. Frank had a caring nature and a strong conscience, though he was also very practical. Hence while he abhorred slavery, he owned slaves; to him it was a labor supply system, implying he would have used another source if he considered it better. In 1860 he had four slaves: two men, a woman, and an approximately twelve-year-old boy named Tance, who was a constant companion for five-year-old Walter as they played and roamed together. Frank's lumber business thrived, and by the time of the Civil War he had built several sawmills in the area around his house to convert the pine trees into lumber and turpentine.[17]

Frank taught Walter the value of having his own opinions, even if they were not popular. In the 1850s he was a pro-Union leader of a local group that opposed the idea of slavery as a Southern "institution." Consequently, he did not support secession. He also believed the South had no chance of winning the Civil War. When it started, Walter later said, Frank discussed it with a North Carolina judge, weighing up the strengths and weakness of each side, and concluded "this is the most foolhardy enterprise that man ever undertook." Despite this, during the war Frank felt he should do the right thing by his family and friends who were all Southerners, and gave over his entire lumber production to the Confederate government. Walter's views on the Confederacy were in line with Frank's, rather than his mother's, family. Kate's views have not been recorded, though there were many supporters of the Confederacy in her family. Esther Barclay Sr., for example, was a passionate secessionist and had the Confederate flag painted across the gate to her yard.[18]

After the war the Pages struggled for several years. Frank traveled less and became involved in raising Walter. Families began moving to Page's, though growth was slowed by a provision Frank, who owned almost all of the property, put in the deeds requiring buyers to agree not to bring alcoholic drinks on to their premises. In 1871 a similar provision was in the charter when Page's was incorporated as a village that Frank named Cary after temperance campaigner General Samuel Cary of Ohio, who had recently visited Raleigh. In doing this Frank was standing up for what he believed in, even though it probably cost him and was unpopular. This is likely another example of Frank's influence on Walter, who throughout his life would stand up for what he thought was right, even when it was unpopular and came at a personal cost.[19]

In 1878 Frank moved his business, and they moved their home, to a pine forest in Moore County. Although pine forests were not considered valuable,

Frank took the risk and with two of his sons, Robert and Henry, established a highly successful lumber business, which started the town of Aberdeen. Frank retired after a few years and was succeeded by his son James. Another son, Chris, got involved and Frank built a railroad from Aberdeen into new pine forests. Their railroad was described in 1895 by F. B. Arendell, a North Carolinian newspaper editor who had a decade earlier worked with Walter, as "a well graded, standard guage [sic] highway with new locomotives, new coaches and a thorough up-to date equipment." Frank was a true pioneer as previously railroads of such length, nearly forty miles, had only been built by corporations or millionaires, and he inspired other citizens of Aberdeen to do the same.[20]

Although Frank was often described as a "lumber king," his activities were much wider; he became a rich man from operations that included factories, hotels, railroads, and the development of large areas of North Carolina. Josephus Daniels described him as "the best type of the lumber kings in the South, but he was much more than that." Frank was committed to the state's development, and following the failure of the State National Bank he promoted establishment of the Commercial National Bank of Raleigh, investing 10 percent of the $100,000 capital and contributing half the cost of the bank's building. He was a stalwart of the bank, becoming a director and securing other stockholders.[21]

Arendell's very apt description of Frank and his approach to life suggested his influence on his eldest son: "Mr. Frank Page is a big man, big in status, big of heart, and big in achievements. His undertakings have always been on a large scale, sometimes so large that they made his friends almost shudder at their magnitude. He has for half a century been a very busy man, and not all of his undertakings have been successful, but the failure of one has seemed only to stimulate him for a greater undertaking." Similar sentiments were expressed about Walter by his friends and colleagues throughout his life. His work ethic was similar, and, like his father, he would back himself in seeking jobs, opportunities, and trying to improve people's lives. While sometimes he failed, he was rarely deterred.[22]

In 1897 Daniels described the relationship between Frank and Walter as that of two men who had reached the pinnacle of their very different fields and had developed a strong mutual respect. Walter venerated his father's "great common sense, largeness of business view, sturdy integrity and Tar-heel directness and firmness." This was evident in the way Walter had emulated these qualities. Frank was proud of his son, who by that time was working in Boston effectively as editor of the *Atlantic Monthly*. In his biography Daniels wrote that Frank admired Walter's brilliancy, though he could not understand his son's apparent lack of interest in saving money. Walter wrote telegrams of three to four hundred words, up to three times a day, which Frank believed was an extravagant waste; he never sent one longer than ten words. This suggests Walter's creative side came from his mother, as Daniels perceptively observed: "the perspicacity and brilliance of the Page family" was from the Raboteaus, "while the practical business side came from the Pages."[23]

The contrasting parental influences on Walter were similarly observed by author Augustus White Long, who in the 1880s worked on Walter's newspaper and lived in his house. Long believed Walter was the only sibling who took so closely after their mother, and in 1939 wrote that Walter was "the only one with literary tastes and ambitions, which he inherited from his mother." Long went on: "His father was of the pioneer breed, bold, aggressive, dominant. Walter leaned to the feminine type rather than the masculine: he was feminine in the gentleness of his manner, his sensitiveness to impressions, and the generosity of his enthusiasms; but there was nothing in the least effeminate about him."[24]

Just over a year after Kate died, Frank moved to Raleigh, having bought the former home of the late chief justice, a mansion on N. Wilmington Street, to spend his retirement. Around the same time, in November 1898, Frank remarried. His new wife was Lula B. McLeod of Powellton, and his brother Rev. Jesse H. Page officiated at the ceremony.

Less than a year later, Frank died, on October 16, 1899. Walter had arrived from New York, where he was working, three days earlier and all his siblings were at their father's bedside. For Walter, it was what they had "been fearing for several years," and he was left "lonelier than I have ever felt before." It would have been particularly hard coming only just over two years after his mother's death. Frank's death was big news in Raleigh, where the *News and Observer* lamented him as "a man of ability of a high order" with "the genius of common sense, foresight and industry." He was "an honest and a just man, dealing fairly by his fellowmen and requiring all to treat him fairly. He was frank, outspoken and true to his convictions. He did not court popularity, though he loved the good esteem of his fellows." These were all qualities he passed on to his eldest son.[25]

EARLY SCHOOLING

School education figured prominently in Walter's formative years, which was highly unusual for a Southerner. Education was largely considered a private affair. Most families were poor, so it was not a priority and therefore their children generally had no schooling. In North Carolina primary schools were rare, predominately parish schools run by clergymen. Initially there were no schools in the Pages' area, which is why his mother Kate undertook Walter's early schooling. Sometimes parents with the financial means and desire banded together and employed a teacher to operate an ad hoc school in whatever room or building was available. Fortunately for Walter, this is what happened in his area. Adolphus Jones, a graduate of the nearby University of North Carolina, established a primary school in a small log building constructed for the purpose about two miles away from the Pages' home.[26]

So it was in 1865, just after the end of the Civil War, that ten-year-old Walter started school. He was very sociable, enjoying talking and laughing with his classmates. He was also happy with his own company and, like his mother, spent long periods walking in the woods, often by himself with a book. Although he would later be considered a very practical person, compared with his family in those early years he was the opposite, a thinker who would struggle to fit into a community predicated on men having practical occupations. His parents, especially his mother, considered it likely he would enter the Methodist ministry, a position held in high esteem by the community. With his love of books and learning, it seemed a logical career.[27]

In 1868 Walter moved to Bingham School, a boarding school in Mebane, forty miles away. Although short of money, Frank and Kate sacrificed to send Walter there at least partly because they thought he was destined for the ministry. Started in 1793 by a Presbyterian clergyman, William Bingham, it was very religious and military-like. Although one of the South's premier educational institutions, it was merely a collection of drafty, poorly lit log houses with rough bunks pulled down from the walls each night. Writing fifteen years later, an "Old Boy," likely to have been Walter, described the appalling conditions: "When, in 1868, I was led a trembling 'Prep,' to the shanty where Col. William Bingham slew himself by over-devotion to his books, and was assigned to 'No. 4,' the heart of a stouter lad than I would have sunk at the sight of the old stockade (very like that around the penitentiary.) It was not a comfortable day and my memory is above all things deceitful if 'No. 4' was a comfortable abiding place. 16x16 feet and four boys in a room!" The boys' fathers were mostly Confederate veterans who believed "rough fare was the normal condition of healthful men." The Old Boy himself saw some benefits: "While, therefore, I do not hesitate to confess that the back of my memory is yet sore from cob mattrasses [sic] and that my life there was not only rough, but very,

very rough, having escaped indigestion and grown to a vigorous manhood, I am not so sure after all that the old Spartan notion is wrong. At any rate, however uncomfortable the process, it made men!"[28]

High scholarly achievement was to be a common theme for Walter, and it was evident at Bingham. He thrived in the military-like environment, which reflected his hard-working, no-nonsense approach to life, and he was an outstanding pupil though his social status suffered because his father had not fought in the Civil War. Twenty-three years later, speaking at the University of North Carolina, Walter explained his predicament: "I recall now how greatly I suffered in my own childhood because at our foremost school (it was then just over the hills here) the boys rated one another according to the military prominence of their fathers, and my father was so unthoughtful as not to be even a colonel." Bingham was, he recalled, a very conservative environment, and consistent with the state's culture it "suppressed individual effort."[29]

Reflecting later on an event at Bingham attended by Confederate veterans, Walter wrote that it was these people, with their injuries, disabilities, poverty, and years of "ill-fed fighting" that "had borne the physical scourging of the nation for its error of slavery." These veterans "were blameless victims of our sectional wrath" who had "miraculously survived and crawled to barren homes from the clash and slaughter." Unfortunately, in their remaining years they had become subsumed by their experiences "which so filled their minds that thought on other things was impossible." His experiences at Bingham had a profound influence on Walter, including his ideas about what was holding back the South.[30]

In 1870, after two years at Bingham, Walter returned home to attend Cary Academy, a new coeducational institution cofounded by his father and Rufus Jones (brother of Adolphus) to accommodate the growth of Cary. It was a two-story building built with timber from the site and prepared at the Page sawmills. The leading teacher was an expert in Latin and Greek who had graduated from the University of North Carolina. Walter attended the school for a year.[31]

SECONDARY SCHOOLING

In the fall of 1871, sixteen-year-old Walter left home for the second time, to study at Trinity College in Randolph County, about fifty miles away. Trinity comprised a single brick building in disrepair with a few rooms and, having no dormitories, the students boarded in the houses of surrounding residents. He found Trinity's academic standards very low and was not intellectually challenged. Nor did he feel he had intellectual freedom, and his grades were nearly all 99 or 100%. He was at Trinity for just over a year, though it engendered a valuable legacy. Schoolmaster Braxton Craven continually preached the essential need for governments to provide education to all primary-age children; this became the cause to which Walter would dedicate much of his life.[32]

The importance of access to education was reinforced by another key influence on the young student: Thomas Jefferson. Walter studied and made copious notes in his copy of *The Life of Thomas Jefferson* by Henry S. Randall. He was inspired by Jefferson's ideas on equality of opportunity in a democracy, the value and self-respect of every individual in society, national unity, emancipation of slaves and, probably most importantly, public schools as the foundation of a democratic nation. Charles W. Dabney, who worked with Page on education campaigns and chronicled them in two comprehensive volumes published in 1936, believed Page made from Jefferson's ideas "a practical method of building up civilization through education."[33]

In January 1873 Walter took advantage of an opportunity to move to Randolph-Macon College in Ashland, Virginia, having been inspired by the president, Rev. James A. Duncan. Randolph-Macon was the nation's oldest Methodist school. Walter portrayed it in a letter to his mother as very religious: "We have a preacher president, a preacher secretary, a preacher chaplain, and a dozen preacher students and three or more preachers are living here and twenty-five or thirty yet-to-be preachers in college!" Yet in reality the school was tolerant of skepticism and encouraged independent thought. This was a remarkable approach in the 1870s, especially for a Southern religious college. Its faculties' academics were of very high quality, and Walter embraced the opportunity for intellectual freedom and personal development.[34]

Along with his teachers and friends, he questioned the role of the South in U.S. history, especially the Civil War. Former Confederate captain and graduate of the University of Virginia, John H. Chamberlayne addressed the boys, telling them the North won the war fairly and the South had stopped thinking and developing in 1830. Since then, Southerners had produced no books or ideas of interest to the rest of the world yet had claimed to be superior. Chamberlayne emphatically stated the South needed to end its obsession with "fondly turning back to the mythic beauties of a mythic past" and look to a future as part of one nation. The impact was lasting; for weeks the students discussed it with one another and their teachers. The address had a profound impact on Walter, and he had extensive discussions with his great friend Jack B. Wardlaw about how they could improve the South. Both boys decided they would do something practical with their lives to address the South's problems, and spent much of their leisure time together discussing what they could do.[35]

For Walter the influence lasted for decades, and it is likely to have been a key motivation in his lifelong mission to develop the South. In a 1904 speech at the Conference for Education in the South in Birmingham, Alabama, he reflected on Chamberlayne's speech and his subsequent discussions with Wardlaw. Tragically, his friend died several years after they graduated, and Page visited him toward the end. He recalled: "One evening at sunset he looked out of the window over the gullied fields (it was an endless waste of mistilled land) and he said to his mother and me: 'I love the old, red hills and we must show that men live on them yet.' A hint of death was already in his eyes, but an unbounded patriotism shone there too. He wrote me a little later: 'I do not mind dying, but I hoped to do something for the South before I went.' And he never wrote again. Our ambition is as great as his was, and—let us hope—as unselfish too. But even yet it is an unfulfilled ambition."[36]

For several years Walter went along with his parents' desire for him to enter the Methodist ministry. He wrote to his mother in April 1874 saying he had decided to be a minister and he indicated he knew they were keen for him to follow that path: "Of course I know that you and Papa would be pleased to see me become a faithful minister; but I have never had either of you to say what you think of *my* becoming one." Yet soon after Walter changed his mind and told his parents he was no longer interested in entering the ministry. A major argument ensued, and his father, who was suffering financial difficulties, tried to end Walter's time at Randolph-Macon. Walter did return for the 1874–75 year, though he was five weeks late "owing to the struggle I had with Father about going to college." He pretended he was going to be a minister, taking advantage of the college's policy of not charging fees to such students.[37]

Walter thrived in the environment at Randolph-Macon, academically and socially. In his first semester he was awarded certificates of distinction for Greek, English, and mathematics. A particularly impressive public speaker, Walter did well in speechmaking competitions. In the second semester, he and Wardlaw were the chosen orators for the Franklin Literary Society, the college's debating organization. In his second year Walter received distinctions for all his subjects, and his third year was even better. He won the prize for the best student in Greek and graduated early, receiving his bachelor's degree in less than three years, in June 1875. He returned in June 1876 to compete for the college's Sutherlin Oratorical Medal, which he won with his speech, "Our Professional Life—Its Tendency."[38]

Ironically it was a Randolph-Macon professor, Thomas Randolph Price, who gave Walter an alternative to the ministry: teaching. Price was a practical teacher, giving his English students tools to express what they learned in letters and other mediums. Walter saw teaching as a way of applying his love of learning to a practical occupation. He spent the second half of 1875 working for Price, who had been his Greek teacher. From early on Price had had an extremely high regard for Walter, writing on one of his first reports: "a young scholar of extraordinary promise." Price was also head of the English school and two or more times a week would have Walter to tea. These sessions vastly improved his understanding of Shakespeare, Milton, Wordsworth, Tennyson, and other great writers who would become his passion. Consequently, on Price's recommendation Walter was granted a fellowship to be part of the first cohort at Johns Hopkins University, founded in 1876 in Baltimore, Maryland.[39]

UNIVERSITY

Page had just turned twenty-one when he started at Johns Hopkins in early October 1876. It was a unique opportunity; for the first time in America a university was established to focus on learning for its own sake, rather than having a direct practical outcome. The university's faculty of eight comprised some of the most distinguished academics in America and beyond, including Basil Gildersleeve, America's premier classical scholar, and James J. Sylvester, considered Britain's greatest mathematician. Despite this, within two months of commencing Page was questioning his desire for an academic career. On November 30, 1876, he wrote to Sarah Jasper, who had become a confidant: "There is little encouragement in it, I confess; and I am sure that I have mistaken my work, or would mistake it, if I considered Greek-teaching my life work. In truth at times I am tempted to throw the whole matter away." He went on to emphasize his intensely practical nature: "In dead earnest, I have a strong mind at times to throw up all my scholarly plans, and go to work, go among men, I mean—go into politics, for example. Active work is worth tenfold more than book speculation. But what keeps me from such a course is an idea, that by all this I am gaining strength, and that there is time enough in the future for that."[40]

Page was correct in recognizing the benefits of his studies at Johns Hopkins. It gave him a greater understanding of how the world worked. Page informed a friend that Gildersleeve "makes me grow wonderfully" and he wrote to his mother: "Surely, it has opened up my eyes more than any year has done before." Page elaborated in 1900 when he wrote to Daniel C. Gilman expressing disappointment at his resignation after having been president for the university's entire twenty-five-year life: "It is especially bitter to men like me, who, coming out of a poor southern community twenty-five years ago, might never have got a wide view of the great world and of the great things in it in proper coördination but for the help that the university gave us."[41]

An experience that certainly opened his eyes was a four-month study trip to Germany in the summer of 1877. Their lecturers had so enthused about the German influence on what they were learning that Page and his friend William W. Jacques decided to go and see for themselves, using some of their Hopkins Fellowship stipend. Jacques later recalled Page wanted "to see how it seemed to live in a land not ruled by the people, and whether the Kaiser or we could best run a university." Page lamented the lack of other Southerners taking a similar opportunity, writing that he had visited "three of the great Universities" during the summer and found about seventy-five American students, though only about ten were Southerners. He dismissed the common excuse that Southerners were too poor to travel, criticizing their attitude: "Indeed to claim poverty as a serious hindrance to scholarship is to deny the whole history of scholarship. Never a nation rose to great culture through greater poverty than these very Germans. We say that we are poor. To say that, therefore, we cannot become scholars is as cowardly as it is untrue. The ail is otherware." This belief that poverty is no excuse for lack of education, or the provision of education, would stay with Page for the rest of his life.[42]

Page expressed surprise at how impressed he was with German universities in a letter to his mother from Berlin where he and Jacques were among about twenty Americans studying at Friedrich Wilhelm University: "There are in all 2200 students. Just think of that! They are from all the world, Japan, South America, Australia, and everywhere else. The University buildings are magnificent; and the Royal Library, which is under the supervision of the University professors, has 900,000 volumes in it. The great Peabody Library in Baltimore, which they make such a fuss about, has only 60,000." This may have been the answer to the question for which he came to Germany: "I am hardly in favour of kings, but when a kingly government does such things as that, I can't help saying 'hurrah.'" Page's approach to politics and education was pragmatic, caring less about ideology and more about the outcome.[43]

In his first known published writing, Page sent a series of letters to the Raleigh *Observer*. He compared Germany with America, including the lack of political freedom, and advocated North Carolina adopting some practices that he thought were working well. This included using German scientific methods in colleges and universities: "It is the lesson of scholarship, the lesson of education, the lesson of culture." Combined with the hard work of North Carolinians, it could have great results: "German accuracy wedded to such endurance as we show in many directions of labor might beget giants amongst us."[44]

In another letter home Page enthused about how much he enjoyed being in Germany and with the people: "I wanted to tell you something about how nicely I am fixed and how royal a time I am having. I am by dint of perseverance, and by the help of amusing incidents, getting into this colloquial jargon. I am Germanized as thoroughly as a fresh foreigner can well become in so short a time. And I was never happier in my life."[45]

Less than halfway through his second year at Johns Hopkins, in February 1878, Page fell ill and returned home. This ended his time as a student. While Page eventually used illness as an excuse to cease his studies, in reality he did not want to be an academic. He wanted to do "active work" "among men" as he had indicated just over a year earlier. This feeling would stay with Page for the rest of his life. Sixteen years later, a few months after being elected president of the New York Alumni of Johns Hopkins, he returned to the university and gave the commencement address encouraging universities to produce graduates with the practical skills required to excel in business, literature, and politics. He was at heart a practical man who was motivated by being with people, learning about their lives, helping them, and writing about them, rather than from studying subjects such as classical literature and undertaking scientific research, even in the outstanding scholarly environment at Johns Hopkins. He was interested in too wide a range of topics to remain focused on a narrow field of study. As Dabney, who was an eminent academic, observed, Page "was too much a man of action to be contented in a professor's chair."[46]

DECIDING ON A CAREER

After leaving Johns Hopkins, the twenty-two-year-old Page struggled to decide on a long-term career; he was not interested in physical work like his father, though was too practical for an academic career. It seems he thought writing or teaching could make a good middle ground. He soon had his first magazine article published, a review of the poetry of Southern poet Henry Timrod for the North Carolina–based *South-Atlantic*. Page did not think Timrod a great poet, though he praised Timrod's ability to recognize the poetic nature of the social aspect of the Civil War: "a passionate giving up to an all-enveloping cause."[47]

Page made attempts at establishing a teaching career. In June–July 1878 he spent six weeks at the Normal School run annually in summer by the University of North Carolina, the state's only university. As professor of English philology, he taught English literature, focusing on the works of Shakespeare and other great authors. He was about the same age as many of his students, men and women taking a short course before going out to teach in public schools. They appreciated, and were inspired by, his passionate and informal teaching style. Page saw it as a great opportunity to create enthusiasm for the subject, hoping his students would in turn inspire their students and help improve the culture of the state. Page aspired to join the faculty and continue teaching English, though he was not offered a position, probably due to the university's lack of finances. At about the same time he turned down an offer to head a Hillsboro boys' school, most likely because it would not have offered him the literary focus he was seeking. Then in August 1878 he was offered a position to teach English at the Boys' High School in Louisville, Kentucky, which he accepted. Page taught English grammar as well as literature, including Shakespeare and Chaucer. It was here that he would realize his future was not as a teacher.[48]

At the same time he took steps to become a writer. He registered with a literary agent in New York and sent a review he had written of *Prince Deukalion* by Bayard Taylor to the *Age,* a new weekly Louisville-based Southern political and literary magazine. It was accepted, and Page regularly contributed essays and reviews over subsequent weeks. As he became more involved, he wrote some of the editorials. Determined to have a writing career, in April 1879 he borrowed $1,000 to acquire half-ownership of the magazine. He wrote to his father that he would be "free from anybody's domineering," as it would be the "foundation of a life-time's independence." Unfortunately, despite Page's unstinting efforts, the *Age* folded less than three months later.[49]

Although "Prof. Walter H. Page" returned to the Normal School in 1879 to give the address "How Shall We Get to be a Reading People?," he had decided on his career goal, as he prophetically informed a cousin: "I am going to write—I am going to edit a magazine . . . And I am going to own the magazine that I edit." Journalism, Page strongly believed, was a worthy career. One *Age* editorial likely written by him stated "journalism is as much a profession as pleading cases or healing diseases, with as hard work in it as in the trade of blacksmithing or bootmaking." He saw out his first year at the Louisville boys' school and, though he had performed well, did not seek another year. He was going to focus on being a writer.[50]

Page wrote to all of North Carolina's newspapers, and some in Baltimore and

Louisville, seeking a job, though without success. He then advertised in the New York *Nation* in the fall of 1879, declaring with considerable exaggeration: "A journalist of experience desires an editorial position on a first-class journal. . ." His advertisement was successful; he received an offer that would launch him into his chosen career. In early February 1880 he started a trial as editor of the *St. Joseph Daily Gazette*, Missouri, an eight-page newspaper published six days a week. The twenty-four-year-old's role was to write editorials and manage the staff of five to six subeditors. Page believed editors of other small newspapers often focused on running stories that would get quoted in more prestigious publications, as he editorialized: "It is strange how persistently small calibre newspaper men will sometimes labor to secure the notice of a decent journal." By contrast he would concentrate on producing a high-quality newspaper: "A true journalist has neither time nor inclination to bother with such chattering newspaper parrots." For the rest of his long editorial career, Page would maintain the same approach. In mid-1880 he was promoted to editor in chief. It was clear from his editorials he was passionate about the South, especially education and racial issues. He argued that by far the biggest issue in the 1880 presidential election was "Southern education, the question of Southern thought."[51]

Willia Alice Wilson was born in Pontiac, Michigan, in 1858 and orphaned at a very young age. After the Civil War, with an older half-sister and her family, she moved to North Carolina and lived near the Page family on the Raleigh road. As a twelve-year-old, Alice attended Cary Academy at the same time as Walter in 1870–71. Soon after she returned to Pontiac to continue her education. Then in 1877 she returned to her old home in North Carolina. The following year, twenty-year-old Alice was a student at the university's Normal School where she attended Walter's classes and they became friends. It appears that in 1879, when Walter returned from the Boys' High School in Louisville, they became romantically involved, and soon after they were engaged. Walter wanted to establish some sort of financial security before getting married, and felt he had achieved this at the *Gazette*. Alice was an independent thinker with strong opinions and, while she and Walter shared many interests, she was a willing antagonist if she did not agree with him. She relished learning, and like Walter's mother she was well educated and a keen reader.[52]

On November 15, 1880, Walter and Alice were married at the home of one of his uncles in St. Louis, and, reflecting their precarious financial position, initially lived in a boardinghouse in St. Joseph. A sense of humor was shown by a neighboring newspaper, the *Kansas City Times*, noting that in the week following Page's nuptials his leading editorial's subjects were "The Necessity of Repose";

"Woman's Influence"; "Harmony"; "Is There a Hell?"; "Preparing for Death"; "Decay of Parties"; and "The Census of the Future." Walter and Alice would have four children: Ralph Walter (born in 1881), Arthur Wilson (b. 1883), Frank Copeland (b. 1887), and their only girl Katharine Alice (b. 1891). They were all well educated: the boys went to Harvard University, though Frank failed to graduate, and Katharine attended Bryn Mawr College, in Pennsylvania. Alice was an important part of Walter's life, including as a critic and adviser, though she was very modest and remained determined to stay in the background.[53]

A turning point in Page's career was when he had an article published in the May 1881 issue of the *Atlantic Monthly*. "Study of an Old Southern Borough" compared some parts of a fictitious borough, where the stifling pre–Civil War mentality persisted, with other parts where people had pushed past the social barriers that discouraged hard work to make the best of their situation. These people were helped by having opportunities to learn the practical skills they needed to improve the way they worked on farms, in factories, and in the providing of services. Reactions in newspapers were positive. The *New York Tribune* called it "a readable and life-like sketch," while an article printed in many other newspapers stated he wrote from "intimate personal knowledge" and "describes graphically and sympathetically former and present life in the South."[54]

Feeling confident after having this article published, Page took a year's leave from the *Gazette* to travel around the South sending weekly letters to leading Northern newspapers. Departing from St. Joseph in June 1881, his trip was very successful. Page targeted two key papers, the New York *World* and the *Boston Post*, as well as others. He wrote different letters to each, probably catering to differences in their readerships. Page later recalled: "I told them simply this: that I'd write letters and send them; and I prayed heaven that they'd print them and pay for them." He had about enough money to get to New Orleans and was delighted when his gamble paid off: "All the papers published all that I sent them and I was rolling in wealth! I had money in my pocket for the first time in my life."[55]

Page's timing was fortunate. There had been gradual moves in Northern magazines toward more sympathetically portraying what was happening in the South, rather than just coverage of the problems. The first was around 1865, when the *Nation* sent John R. Dennett to visit the South and published "The South As It Is," a series of articles describing and analyzing what he observed. The most significant was *Scribner's* abundantly illustrated series "The Great South" by Edward S. King in 1874–75. *Harper's Monthly* followed with a series, and the *Atlantic Monthly* had an article. Page's letters were the first time Northerners could read about the South from a Southerner. As news came through of the shooting of President James A. Garfield, Page was in Martin, a small Tennessee town. He reported in his first letter on July 2, 1881, that the inhabitants felt personally sad: Garfield's status as a former Union general was irrelevant, as these Southerners took it as an attack on their leader and their nation. This suggested sectional divisions might have been starting to heal.[56]

His letters contained problems and ideas, with his love and respect for the South evident. Writing from Martin, his affection for Southerners was clear, though he chided them for their slothful appearance and their apparent lack of interest in new ideas or the rest of the world: "This afternoon (Saturday) the town is full of country people. Too many of the men are of that cadaverous expression which on the seacoast has given them the name of 'crackers.' Yet they seem to be very happy, as indeed most Southern country people are, and they greet one another with a genuine welcome, always saying 'How's yer folks?'" His frustration was evident: "The people are apparently not interested in what is going on in the world. A new idea now and then is needed. The lack of animation is oppressive. Even a heresy, if it be fresh and bright, would be a relief. You feel as if you wished to see some sort of an effort put forth—a discussion, a fight, a runaway, anything to make the blood 'go pearter.'" Page sent letters reporting his interviews with famous people, including Jefferson Davis, who had been president of the Confederacy, and two Southern authors, George W. Cable and Joel C. Harris, the latter the author of *Uncle Remus*. His reports were published by other newspapers, such as the Washington, D.C., *Evening Star,* which referred to "the wandering southern correspondence [*sic*] of the *Boston Post*."[57]

NEW YORK *WORLD*

Upon finishing his Southern travels in September 1881, the New York *World,* one of America's preeminent newspapers, offered Page an assignment from October to November to cover the International Cotton Exposition in Atlanta, Georgia. Alice was expecting their first child, so she went to stay with Walter's uncle and aunt in St. Louis, and Ralph Walter was born on October 2. The same month, "The Southern Educational Problem" was published in *International Review,* Page's second article in a national magazine. After he finished his assignment, Page decided to resign from the *Gazette.* He unsuccessfully applied for a job at the *Atlanta Constitution* and was not sure what to do next. He was then unexpectedly offered a staff position at the *World* and moved to New York for the first time.[58]

Starting in December 1881, Page later downplayed his position as mainly writing literary reviews and occasional editorials. Most of his time was taken covering the tariff issue, going to Washington, D.C., for congressional debates and traveling through much of the country following the Tariff Commission. His reports on the commission, which was widely reported to have been established by tariff-supporting Republicans to neutralize the issue politically, indicated it was failing to have any sort of impact due to the commissioners' lack of interest. Other newspapers picked up his reports. The *Memphis Daily Appeal* reported: "The New York *World* says the Tariff Commission is bungling the job it has undertaken in a way gratifying to all who hate the tariff." The *Salt Lake Daily Herald* reported Page had hinted from time to time that the commissioners "were fast coming to the conclusion that the whole thing was a fraud."[59]

On September 22, 1882, while in Atlanta with the commission, Page first met Woodrow Wilson, who was unhappily and unsuccessfully practicing law. His partner was a former law classmate, Edward I. Renick. Page visited Renick, who was a friend, and got talking with Wilson. Impressed with his knowledge of the tariff issue and maybe seeing a chance to redeem the quality of the hearings, Page persuaded Wilson to address the commission. Wilson, who considered himself a Southern progressive, spoke on how the tariff disadvantaged the agriculture-based communities of the South and West. His presentation was praised by Page in the *World* as well as by the *Atlanta Constitution*. Rejuvenated by this chance to engage in politics, Wilson called together some friends so they could join Page and discuss the issue further. This likely had an influence on Wilson, who several months later decided to study politics, so he applied to the graduate program at Johns Hopkins University.[60]

Wilson was born in Staunton, Virginia, and studied law in that state. It highlights a difference in their personalities that Wilson set out on his path at Johns Hopkins where five years earlier Page had moved in the opposite direction and decided not to pursue an academic career. This first meeting led to a lifelong relationship between the two men. While Wilson often referred to Page as a friend, Page saw it more as a professional relationship. Both men were highly intelligent and had similar political and economic views that they wanted to develop and implement. They earned each other's respect, with Wilson seeking Page's advice and support, and Page asking Wilson to write for his magazines. Page was always keen to encourage and promote Wilson, whom he realized had the potential for high political office.

During this period Page also wrote for other newspapers and gave speeches on the South. In early 1883 he was contracted to write weekly letters for the

Boston Post, and in August wrote about North Carolina's development, which was reprinted in one of the state's newspapers. In April he commenced writing occasional reports for an Australian newspaper. The same month he gave a lecture in Boston on "The New South as Seen by a Southerner," arguing the South needed to embrace the process of evolving toward industrialization. In May, he gave a speech on the South's problems and some solutions to the Harvard Finance Club in Cambridge, Massachusetts.[61]

After one and a half years, after a takeover by Joseph Pulitzer in May 1883, Page resigned from the *World* and moved back to North Carolina. He left partly because, along with other serious journalists, he was concerned that Pulitzer would make it sensationalist. They were right, as Page wrote several months later: "Under its new management the *World* has become popularized but it has become vulgarized and carries the general and unfortunate tendency of the New York press to chronicle crime to a disgusting point." The other reason Page gave for leaving was he thought about getting into North Carolina politics. Although he had made reference to a political career seven years earlier, it would have been out of character for Page and not surprisingly nothing materialized. Instead, Page realized his real skills were writing and editing, often with the aim of initiating and facilitating change.[62]

\ 2 /

AMERICA'S "BEST EDITOR"

1883 TO 1913

THE *STATE CHRONICLE*

After returning to North Carolina at the age of twenty-eight, Page started the *State Chronicle,* a weekly newspaper in Raleigh. He was the editor, and it was published by the Chronicle Publishing Company, which had the financial backing of investors, primarily his father. Frank Page also helped his son by regularly advertising. Frank believed a newspaper should only print useful information. Years later he complained to Josephus Daniels, who had taken over as editor, that baseball news took up space that would be better used for advice about farming, religious sermons, developing the state's resources, education, and information to help people improve themselves. This is a good description of how Walter ran the *State Chronicle,* with the exception of religion, which suggests the influence of his father in his approach to editorship.[1]

When Page arrived in Raleigh, it was growing in its role as the state capital while transitioning from a regional city serving its rural surrounds to one with modern buildings, facilities, and a greater diversity of commercial activities. As he wrote a few months later, "the city of Raleigh has passed the period of its dependence on the Supreme Court, the Legislature and State conventions for its existence." A wide range of industries operated there, including wine-making; book and periodical publishing; the warehousing and selling of paper manufactured thirteen miles away on the Neuse River; cotton storage and trading; light manufacturing of sundries such as harnesses and saddles, clothing, candy, and jewelry; heavy manufacturing, such as of wagons and carts, and including iron foundries and tinsmiths; and a vast range of retail stores. Consequently, the Raleigh he encountered was a city of contrasts.[2]

Approaching the city a traveler would be impressed by the "gleaming granite" of the post office, a "magnificent edifice" built for more than $500,000. Next door was the new and "elegantly finished" Wake County courthouse, part of what Page proudly stated was $250,000's worth of building undertaken during 1883. Buildings completed during the year included the Leonard Medical College at Shaw University for the education of African Americans, and numerous businesses, most notably the new hardware store of Julius Lewis and Co. at 224 Fayetteville Street, backing on to Salisbury Street, which continued "the handsome block of three and four story buildings between Hargett and Martin streets." Other completed buildings included three churches, the county jail, the "North Carolina Insane Asylum," a number of commercial buildings, and some large residences. Buildings underway included the governor's mansion and the almost complete state penitentiary.

A feature of the city was the number and size of its trees on the capitol grounds, at the "Deaf Dumb and Blind Institution," and on the grounds of many elegant mansions. The city's female schools included the "attractive and prominent" Peace Institute and St. Mary's School, the latter surrounded by several acres of parkland. Page wrote: "If there is a city in the world as large as Raleigh that has a larger proportion of residences whereabout there are lawns and shade trees, what city is it?"[3]

At the same time there were elements of its former life as a village. Its wide streets were dirt and sometimes mud. There was no free delivery of letters by the post office, though during 1883 numbers had been added to the properties and signs with street names erected on corners in readiness for imminent commencement. It is likely none of the 2,025 houses or the businesses had electricity. Most of its 13,104 residents would see electric-powered devices for the first time a year later at the state exposition, after which they had "become so accustomed to the electric lights" that they were determined to introduce them to the city. Electric streetlights were installed in 1885.[4]

All this made Raleigh a confluence of elegant city, rural services, and commercial growth. One of the city's major recreation areas was, and still is, Moore Square, a parkland established in 1792. Also dominating that part of the city, just across Martin Street, was the massive stables of Mr. W. E. V. Jackson, built in 1880 and covering an entire block with a hundred feet fronting on to Wilmington Street. It contained 212 horse stalls and pens for eighty mules, and "steam apparatus for steaming and cutting food and pumping water." Under this enormous roof was also a "farmers' feed yard, comprising the best accommodation for horses and a sleeping apartment for men," with gas lighting, "heating stoves and other conveniencies [sic]." On the other side of Wilmington Street was Len H. Adams's "handsome and sightly" four-story building. A former leading cotton trader in city, Adams had expanded the grocery side of his business and did "a very large business in general merchandise, heavy and fancy groceries, boots, shoes and the like." Adams planned to install corn and wheat mills in the adjoining building, which he also owned.[5]

By this stage Page was respected nationally for his writing and speechmaking, so his venture attracted attention in other newspapers. In Utah, the *Salt Lake Daily Herald* anticipated great success referring to Page as "a brilliant writer and a clever gentleman, who will be a great acquisition to the journalistic profession in the south." In North Carolina, the Scotland Neck *Commonwealth* was confident that Page and his assistant editor Edward A. Oldham had "the editorial ability requisite to success." Daniels, who was editing the weekly Wilson *Advance*, felt a "thrill of pleasure" as Page brought "a new breath of fresh air into North Carolina journalism."[6]

Oldham was also the editor and publisher of the *Western Sentinel,* and an experienced and innovative newspaperman. Many years earlier he pioneered amateur journalism in North Carolina, publishing an amateur newspaper, and around the late 1870s was prominent in a state convention of amateur editors. Not long before the *State Chronicle* started, Oldham wrote in the *Sentinel* that Page's April 1883 Boston speech calling for an end to the anti-industrialization culture in the South "received very favorable comment." On July 5 Oldham presented an essay to the North Carolina Press Association on "North Carolina's Industrial Development." He wasn't with the *State Chronicle* for long, maybe just long enough to help Page get it established, though he remained a contributor from Winston-Salem and western North Carolina. Oldham continued editing the *Sentinel* and in 1884 married Page's cousin. He likely had a significant influence on Page, particularly reinforcing the thoughts and actions of Frank Page in pushing for state development.[7]

The *State Chronicle* was first published on Saturday, September 15, 1883. It was "its own master" as "a broadly Democratic State paper, containing more news, more timely discussions and more original matter than any other paper in North Carolina." Page appeared to have achieved his goal of editorial independence. Walter and Alice's second son, Arthur Wilson, was born in the same month. It appeared they could settle down in Raleigh.[8]

Newspapers of this era reflected the opinions, agendas, and influences of the editor. Editors of the major city dailies were granted a certain reverence; their newspapers were seen as impartially reporting the news. Smaller or less frequent papers reported primarily local issues and were seen to reflect provincial biases. Page's newspaper primarily fitted into the latter category with the content clearly reflecting the opinions and agendas of its editor, though in reality it was unlike any other with its statewide focus on industrial and economic development. There were three other newspapers in Raleigh: another weekly, *Farmer and Mechanic,* edited by Captain Randolph A. Shotwell, and two dailies, *News and Observer,* edited by Captain Samuel A. Ashe, and *Evening Visitor.*[9]

Page's focus was creating a grassroots publication and in doing so showed his love of people, interest in their work, and desire for them to have opportunities to improve their lives. The *State Chronicle* was a platform for spreading his ideas about developing North Carolina and addressing the chronic problems he saw in the state's politics and society. He went straight to the experts and other people, asking them for their ideas, opinions, and experiences. He declared early on "many of the best writers in the State—lawyers, teachers, preachers, farmers, manufacturers, miners, housekeepers, men and women of every calling, who know their business and know how to write about it—will write from time to time on subjects whereon they are authorities."[10]

Marking six months of publication on March 15, 1884, Page reinforced his intention: "The measure of its success depends not merely on the skill and industry with which it is conducted but also upon its identification with the people's interests. The notion that a newspaper is a teacher is much less correct than the notion that it is a servant." He reinforced his belief in an editor and newspaper actively engaging with readers: "The man who sits constantly in an editorial chair becomes a dull fellow at best. A useful newspaper must know its readers. It must know how they live, what they think, what they wish, what they do."[11]

Page's strong ideas about editorial ethics and the importance of being independent were other key factors influencing the *State Chronicle*'s content. He wrote in the first issue that it was "edited by Democrats who have never sought or held a public office, and who never expect to seek or hold one; who are trained journalists, and who have never had, have not now, and never expect to have any other occupation." He made a similar claim about the owners. Several months later he argued the state's newspapers had generally not been independent and therefore had not lasted long because "journalism is a jealous mistress. You can't serve her and anybody else." He went on: "The moment an editor becomes a special pleader for anything or anybody, the moment he allows a campaign committee to edit his journal, the moment he himself goes into politics, the moment he leaves his proper business to seek the State printing, for instance, or any other such thing, that moment journalism becomes a treacherous as well as a jealous mistress, and the delicate difference between failure and success leans towards the former." Page also took an ethical approach to advertising, as he outlined on October 20, 1883: "Every column of *The Chronicle* is edited; and, if a man imagines that he can publish for cash or credit or kind anything he may wish to publish in these columns, he is mistaken, as several vendors of medicines could testify."[12]

On February 24, 1885, Page resigned from the *State Chronicle* and moved back to New York. While he probably had a number of reasons for making such a momentous decision, the newspaper was struggling financially and Page was personally in severe financial difficulties. Frustration was the other major factor: while he had independence as editor, he was held back by the state's leaders. By playing on his status as a Southerner and a Democrat, he anticipated being able to point out problems with the state's culture, and be a catalyst for change, especially industrial and economic development. He had some success, for example, after reprimanding the university for allowing speakers at an event to criticize Northerners, a trustee responded: "You have shown by works and words that you are true blue Southern to the core; and you can, therefore, speak true words of criticism." Unfortunately, this success was not widespread. Not only was he continually attacked by other newspapers, as noted by Josephus Daniels in 1891, his main frustration was feeling unable to facilitate change. Just before leaving Page wrote in the *State Chronicle*: "The men and forces who rule society are opposed to intellectual progress. They do not welcome differences of opinion." A few months afterward he lamented in a letter to his father, "There is no use in my trying to do anything down South any more. It proved disastrous every time." He couldn't see how to affect change working in the South, correctly judging he was better off trying to do it from the North.[13]

F. B. Arendell, the business manager, took over as *State Chronicle* editor. Around June a merge with the *Farmer and Mechanic* was agreed, though Shotwell, who was editor and publisher, died shortly afterward. Daniels, keen to realize his "long-cherished desire to edit a paper in Raleigh," was given the stock for no charge. After finishing his law course Daniels became editor in October 1885, with Arendell as his assistant. He kept up many of Page's campaigns, especially education. Like Page, he struggled financially, working day and night trying to make it viable, and ended up selling it in 1892 solely due to insufficient income.[14]

BACK TO NEW YORK

Page moved back to New York in the same month he left the *State Chronicle*, February 1885, and, though it was not his choice, circumstances meant he never again lived in the South. Alice joined him after three months, and their two young sons stayed in Aberdeen with Walter's parents, Kate and Frank, for the summer. Alice and Walter moved into a small apartment in Brooklyn where Frank Copeland, their third son, was born in March 1887. Alice and their sons would regularly spend summer in Aberdeen during these first years. Walter often visited them, and in August 1888 they all stayed for a month. In October they returned for another visit. They passed through Raleigh on their way home, and Page, according to the *State Chronicle*, "was hurrying back to vote for Cleveland and Tariff Reform."[15]

Arriving in New York at the age of twenty-nine without a job was a gamble. Yet again he had backed himself, and again it paid off. Soon after arriving he obtained freelance work for the *Boston Post* and the *Brooklyn Union*. Before long he had a permanent position as editorial writer for the *Union*. This was followed by a short stint, February to September 1887, at the *New York Evening Post*. During this period he joined with Franklin Ford (former editor of the Wall Street *Bradstreet's* newspaper), F. W. Rollins (of the *Commercial Bulletin*), and later Lindley Vinton, to form Ford's Special News. This was a syndicating service with many influential newspapers and magazines as clients. Page had numerous articles published, predominately on Southern issues, increasingly arguing these were national problems that could not entirely be left to Southerners to fix. His clients included the *Atlantic*, *Harper's*, *Century*, and the New York–based *Independent*.[16]

Page also contributed regularly to the *State Chronicle*, to Daniels's delight: "Shortly after I became editor of the *State Chronicle* I had a letter from Page wishing me luck and offering, without charge, to write a letter for it every week. He may be said to have been the first columnist in North Carolina. The letters were fresh and interesting." Not surprisingly Page's letters "pleased many and offended others." In 1891 Daniels wrote that Page was "the most brilliant young man that has been connected with North Carolina journalism in the entire history of the State."[17]

For his efforts, Page was accused of being a "traitor to the South," and abused with derogatory names such as "yellow dog" and "nigger-lover." There was prejudice against Page by people who had never even seen his work. Regardless, he was the Orator of the North Carolina Press Association and returned to give the annual oration in Smithville on June 17, 1885. This ability to be geographically removed from the criticism, while being able to return readily, reinforced the wisdom of his decision to leave the South.[18]

INFORMATION REVOLUTION

There was another benefit of working in New York when Page decided he wanted to move from newspapers to magazines. In the South there would have been no suitable opportunities, because while more than twenty literary or general magazines had been established from 1865 to 1885, they did not reach the standards of Northern publications and most failed within four years. None existed when Page resigned from the *State Chronicle*. By contrast, New York had consolidated its position as the hub of America's magazine industry, accounting for a quarter of the monthly periodicals and two-thirds of magazines with a hundred thousand or more circulation.

Another factor in Page's favor was that there was a revolution under way. Previously, the magazine industry had comprised a small number of general monthly publications, containing high-quality literature including poetry, reviews, and fiction. While they were well respected, they targeted a small proportion of the population and so had low readership. This changed in the 1880s when innovative magazines emerged and reached out to the broader population. This suited Page as his aim as a writer and editor was always to spread his message to as many people as possible. It was how he had edited the *State Chronicle*, which was similar to the new magazines in structure, content, and accessibility. It was an information revolution in which Page would play a leading role. According to Pulitzer Prize–winning historian Frank L. Mott, "Some of the greatest editors in the history of American magazines were at work in the 1890's." This revolution was driven by three factors: increasing demand by consumers, significant reductions in cost of production and distribution, and entrepreneurial magazine publishers.

Consumer demand for information increased, driven by the increasing complexity of American life, with more social, economic, and political issues arising. Newspapers were well placed to provide information on these issues and had the great advantage of being low cost. Between 1870 and 1900, demand rose dramatically and circulation increased sixfold. Many changed their structure and content to be similar to magazines, especially the Sunday editions, which increased in number by 50 percent over the 1890s. Despite this, it was magazines that experienced the real boom as providers of information to the people.

During the 1880s and 1890s there were substantial reductions in costs for magazine publishers, allowing them to reduce their prices and compete with newspapers. Rather than buying magazines from street vendors, as they did with newspapers, most people took out a postal subscription. In 1885 the postal rate for magazines was reduced from three cents to one cent. Major cost reductions also came from technological improvements. During the 1880s American publishers led the world in the mechanization and automation of typesetting, previously a labor-intensive and time-consuming operation. They more than quadrupled productivity and dramatically reduced a range of other costs associated with the process. Around 1890 the development and commercialization of half-tones enabled a massive reduction in the cost of illustrations. By 1893 even *Century*, which used high-quality illustrations developed using wood engravings as a key selling point, used some half-tones costing under twenty dollars, well below the cost of engravings, which could be up to $300.

Taking advantage of increased demand and reduced costs were many entrepreneurial cheap general magazine publishers. Samuel McClure launched his abundantly illustrated monthly *McClure's Magazine* in 1893 at just 15 cents a copy or $1.50 per annum. It had fiction and quality literary articles, as well as current, entertaining, and journalistic articles. In 1895 *McClure's* dropped its price to ten cents, the price of many of the new magazines. These generally contained numerous good-quality illustrations, serious consideration of current issues, nonfiction articles with fresh perspectives, and coverage of many subjects including new ideas and how society was progressing.

All this led to a dramatic increase in readership. In 1885 there were four general monthlies with circulations over 100,000, a combined circulation of 600,000, and costing either 25 or 35 cents. In 1905 there were 20 of these high-selling general monthlies, with a combined circulation of over 5.5 million, and of these 16 sold for just 10 or 15 cents. This was the revolution: getting information to millions of people for whom it was previously unavailable.[19]

THE *FORUM*

Page joined the information revolution when in October 1887 he was approached by the *Forum*, a one-and-a-half-year-old magazine, edited by Lorettus S. Metcalf. Precursors were *Harper's Weekly*, *Frank Leslie's Illustrated Newspaper*, and, from 1869, *Appleton's Journal*. They were highly opinionated, with a range of illustrated articles across a number of categories, especially current events. The *Forum* was one of the new innovative magazines, though it was unusual as it published only nonfiction. It was one of the more expensive, at fifty cents a copy.[20]

Page was offered the position of business manager, which he accepted primarily to see if he could make it profitable. He had been told no profit had been made by a "dignified nonillustrated monthly either in England or in America," though, as he wrote to Metcalf, "I cannot bring myself to believe that the *Forum* cannot be made to pay." If he were successful, Page would know that magazines were a financially viable option for him, and the next step would be to seek an editorial position with the independence he so fervently desired, either at the *Forum* or at another magazine. Back in North Carolina, Oldham was confident he would do well, as he wrote in the *Western Sentinel*: "Thus it is that Carolina's sons go onward and upward. Mr. Page was known as the most facile, gifted writer in the State, and he will be a valuable addition to *The Forum*."[21]

In September 1890 Page briefly returned to North Carolina, visiting B. F. Long, an old friend from college, his parents, and his father's family. While he was there, both Raleigh newspapers referred to him as the "brilliant North Carolina journalist," though the *Watauga Democrat* harbored resentment: "It is a wonder to us that he would set his foot on N.C. soil, after his wilful misrepresentation of it, in the northern papers, a few years ago." By then Walter and Alice had decided to move to a home with more space and chose New Rochelle, about an hour's commute north of Manhattan. Soon after, in January 1891, their only daughter Katharine Alice was born. In early March Page again set foot in his home state. He visited Raleigh, stimulating the *State Chronicle* to acclaim, "He has won success and position in New York journalism," and "When he was editor of the *State Chronicle* there was no paper in the State that compared with it in ability, sprightliness, progress and true newspaper excellence."[22]

Page's first three and a half years as business manager were successful, substantially reducing costs and probably increasing income by attracting more and better advertising. After several months he had made a positive impression, earning praise from a senior manager and a $1,000 stock bonus (his annual salary was $3,000). It gave him valuable experience about running a magazine, and by early 1891 he was keen to take over the editorship.

In March 1891, after Metcalf resigned, Page was promoted to editor. There was praise in North Carolina newspapers. The *News and Observer* believed it was recognition of his abilities: "Mr. Page's merit is thus shown to be appreciated and we are glad to chronicle his success in this field of literary work for which he is so well fitted by education and natural parts." According to the *State Chronicle*, Page "won his promotion by his capacity and success in pushing the circulation of the *Forum* until, in every State in the Union, it holds a place side by side with the North American Review." Newspapers across the nation noted his promotion.

Page continued as business manager, as well as editor, and consequently was busier than ever, working very long hours. He took time in October 1891 to spend a few days in North Carolina where, with stockholders of the *State Chronicle*, he attended a dinner in his honor by Josephus Daniels, who was still editor, and visited his parents in Aberdeen. Alice and their children spent the winter there with Walter's parents, and he came down to visit in January.[23]

On February 29, 1892, Page and a few partners acquired the *Manufacturers' Record* from Richard H. Edmonds, who was suffering very poor health, and his brother William H. Edmonds. A Baltimore-based newspaper, the *Record* was established in 1882 to encourage industrial development in the South, especially through Northern investment. One of the first publications of this type, it inspired many others. It was highly regarded by many Southern newspapers, both for its financial success and for its contribution to Southern development.

All this would have been attractive to Page, especially the *Record's* statistics, facts, and other information about industrial development in Southern states. He had long believed this was the most effective way of encouraging industrial development; it had been an integral part of his strategy at the *State Chronicle*. Despite the mostly positive press, doubts were raised by some newspapers, including the Winston *Sentinel*, which thought Page would have known better. The doubters proved to be correct. From the start the partners disagreed over the direction the newspaper should take, which was exacerbated by a national economic depression. Financial losses mounted rapidly and in mid-1893 Page asked R. Edmonds, whose health had recovered, to return as editor. Edmonds agreed on condition he regained control. Page agreed, though, in 1896 after a dispute ended up selling Edmonds most of his shares, at a considerable loss.[24]

After two years as both editor and business manager of the *Forum*, Page wrote to a friend in April 1893: "I have worked nights and Sundays, hardly had a dinner at home in a month, have four drawers full of manuscripts, have gone two days at a time without seeing my children when one was sick." Later in the year when the New York *Herald* asked how he managed, he replied: "I'll tell you. I work. There is not much else to say. It is work here, and hard work." The problem was partly solved in 1894 when he employed Frank Presbrey as business manager. Presbrey was a former newspaperman and editor of *Public Opinion*, a moderately successful national weekly news magazine he founded in 1886 in Washington, D.C.[25]

Page sought to use the *Forum* to influence public opinion, believing that "the magazine in the United States is the best instrument that has yet been invented or developed or discovered for affecting public opinion in our democracy." He knew the editor needed to have a good understanding of readers: their needs, aspirations, and interests. He was highly approachable, as noted in the *Indianapolis Journal*: "He always received personally and with rare patience all who called." Writers had to present readers with appealing ideas and convincing arguments, as he advised George W. Cable: "In spite of the fiction that The Forum or any other publication is supposed to lead public opinion, the truth is that the best we can do is wisely to follow it, & may hope somewhat to guide it."[26]

To achieve this Page directly contacted the author he thought would best write about a certain matter, and as a result the *Forum's* authors were among the best in the nation, either as opinion leaders or experts. Famous and influential contributors included Theodore Roosevelt, Woodrow Wilson, Senator George F. Hoar, Professor William P. Trent, Professor Brander Matthews, and Professor John B. McMaster. This had been a key part of Metcalf's editorial strategy, as had the technique of authors with differing opinions "debating" one another in the magazine. Page used both these techniques, though his contribution to the character of the magazine should not be underestimated, as noted by Mott: "Page's editorship seems integral with Metcalf's, but it was more brilliant," and he produced "a more attractive magazine" by amplifying the *Forum's* "distinguishing characteristics" and insisting on timeliness of articles. Also, Page was better at promotion than Metcalf. Henry Holt, one of the nation's preeminent publishers, wrote in 1923 that when Page was at the *Forum* he was "the best editor that, up to that time, America had had."[27]

On October 7, 1893, the New York *Herald* published a two-column feature article based on an interview with Page. Asked about the policy of the *Forum*, Page replied it was "to provoke discussion about questions of contemporaneous interest, in which the magazine is not a partisan but merely the instrument." The *Herald* stated that in striving to achieve this goal of stimulating debate "he has probably accomplished more than any other one man." In North Carolina, Raleigh's *News-Observer-Chronicle*, with the formerly hostile Samuel Ashe still serving as editor, stated this was "high praise" and was pleased Page had "accomplished in this line more than any other living person." Praise also came from other previously extremely critical newspapers, including *Gold Leaf* of Henderson, North Carolina. The *Herald* article elicited responses from across the nation. An article published in at least four states focused on his success and unique editorial style, including what would later be known as investigative journalism: "His special studies have always been concerned with the large social problems of the day, and he had gained considerable reputation as a writer on sociological subjects before he assumed his present position."[28]

At least partly in response to the proliferation of cheap magazines, some of which were competitors, at the end of 1893 the *Forum* announced the cover price would be halved, from fifty cents to twenty-five cents. The change was noted positively by many newspapers. The *Jersey City News* noted the *Forum* was one of the cheapest popular magazines. An article in the *Western Sentinel* and other newspapers claimed it was "the cheapest by half of all great Reviews in the world."[29]

Page's editorial strategy combined with the price reduction led to a dramatic increase in readership. Circulation rose from 2,000 copies per month when he took over as editor, to peak at 40,000. Even when in 1894 it fell to about 28,000 due to the recession, the *Forum* had far more readers than any other magazine of its type in America, where the *North American Review* considered 18,000 a month to be successful, or in Europe where the illustrious English magazines sold about 6,000 to 10,000. This put the *Forum* in a very strong financial position.[30]

With this large, highly connected, readership as the foundation, the *Forum* was increasingly influential across the nation. According to Paull Fry of the *Birmingham Age-Herald*, "Among deep-thinking, earnest reviews The Forum, edited by Walter H. Page, always leads." In Salem, Oregon, the *Capital Journal* stated that while competitor *Harpers* remained leader, "The Forum under Walter H. Page is steadily striding forward to great national success." On August 4, 1892, North Carolina's *Western Sentinel* reviewed positively an article by Hoke Smith in the *Forum* on the impacts of a "force bill" on the Southern states. About two months later Smith, who was president of the Atlanta Board of Education, owner of the Atlanta *Journal*, and later a member of President Grover Cleveland's cabinet and governor of Georgia, had no doubt about the extent of Page's influence: "Page is a man of handsome, intellectual presence. He has made his mark as the leader in a field of literary merit of the highest order in New York city. He is sought after by all of the best literary clubs of the city. Going to New York simply as a reporter of a newspaper, he to-day exercises more influence in magazine circles than probably any man in the United States."[31]

Many newspaper editors used the *Forum's* content as the basis of their own articles and editorials, often briefly highlighting a point of particular interest or, sometimes, controversy. On August 17, 1893, Honolulu's *Pacific Commercial Advertiser* had an article on George Kennan's allegation in the *Forum* that "Russian secret police at St. Petersburg" opened and read letters received by U.S. diplomats, including the ambassador. Other articles used an issue raised in the *Forum* to frame a broader debate. San Francisco's *Morning Call* of March 10, 1894, for example, emphatically disagreed with a *Forum* article offering an explanation for, and a solution to, the significant financial difficulties of many railroad companies, and offered its own solution.[32]

In December 1894 Page asked Woodrow Wilson, a professor at Princeton University with whom he had been discussing issues for many years, what he thought about the magazine's influence. Wilson replied: "I have been little less than astonished at the number of persons I seem to have reached in the papers I have written for it within the last two years." He believed his February article "Calendar of Great Americans" had gained more recognition than anything else he had written. Wilson summed up: "If I wished popular notice and wide currency, I should certainly write for the *Forum.*" Then just over six months later he told Page that under his editorship he had "elevated it to a place of authority."[33]

In January 1895 Walter's parents, Frank and Kate, visited him in New York, staying for about two weeks. A few months later F. B. Arendell, Page's business manager and successor at the *State Chronicle,* noted the strong similarities between Walter and his father: "Like his father, success and growing reputation have only the effect of increasing his modesty and his usefulness to others."[34]

Despite his success, Page left the *Forum* in June 1895 after trying and failing to gain financial control. The *News and Observer* reported his brother Henry's claim that while at the *Forum,* Walter had received several offers of more lucrative positions which he declined in the hope of securing financial and editorial control. He had still not achieved the editorial freedom for which he yearned. Ironically the reason the existing owners fought to retain the magazine was that Page's decisions as business manager and editor had made it profitable.[35]

Page's departure "very much startled" Wilson and, according to the *Indianapolis Journal,* "occasioned considerable surprise in Gotham's literary circles." The *News and Observer* stated the *Forum* had attained a place of authority, "derived from the editorial perception of what questions were most worthy of discussion and what writers were best entitled to be heard upon them." In New York the *Outlook,* itself an influential magazine, stated, "Mr. Page had made the 'Forum' the medium of communication between the leaders of thought in this country." It eulogized a man who was at the top of his game and who had made the *Forum* "a publication which, although not faultless, commanded the widest respect, was rapidly obtaining the most influential constituency, and had become a genuine educational force in the community." The *Review of Reviews,* a major competitor, credited Page with reviving the *Forum*: "He has an incisive and lucid style, and commands respect whenever he chooses to express his opinions."[36]

THE *ATLANTIC MONTHLY*

Page's success at the *Forum* had been noticed by George H. Mifflin, CEO and part-owner of Houghton, Mifflin & Co., and Horace E. Scudder, editor of the company's flagship magazine, the *Atlantic Monthly*. Featuring quality literature with a strong New England focus, the *Atlantic Monthly* was the most respected magazine in America. Its problem was that like many venerated publications it had lost its way—and its readers; its circulation was too low to be financially viable. Mifflin and Scudder were torn; they knew change was necessary for the magazine to survive, though did not want to alienate their loyal readers. Page, they were sure, had the intelligence, people skills, and drive to turn its finances around, though they were uncertain if his approach and ideas would be compatible with its culture. Despite these concerns, they approached Page about working for the company.[37]

Page had concerns about working on a magazine that had a narrow focus in terms of both content and geography. Writing to Scudder to clarify the position being proposed, Page emphasized his desire to reorient the magazine toward articles relevant to current events. He went on to note "my work has been to know with as wide a horizon as possible, the directions and values of contemporary activity." His other concern was the potentially stifling culture of the organization, and he hoped "the way should be open to become, if I show the qualities that entitle me to become, one of the real forces in the institution."[38]

Scudder and Page discussed the offer, once in Boston, then again in New York, and on August 7, 1895, Page agreed. The forty-three-year-old Page was Houghton, Mifflin & Co.'s acquisitions editor and *Atlantic Monthly's* assistant editor. His position encompassed, for his first time, responsibility for trade (nonacademic) books. He was put directly under Scudder's supervision in an attempt to retain the magazine's culture, while Page would try to make the changes it so desperately needed. It soon became clear this would not work; with the magazine's precarious financial position and low circulation, they needed to give Page more freedom.[39]

Consequently, from mid-1896, though Scudder kept the title, Page was effectively editor. His strategy was, as he told a friend, to get the magazine "out of the New England rut" and remake it as a truly national publication. He took steps to make the articles timely, more reader-focused, and appealing to a broader readership. He was confident about being able to retain existing readers while exposing the *Atlantic* to a whole new readership. As preempted in his letter to Scudder a year earlier, Page actively sought articles from many authors from across the nation, covering a much wider range of topics and professions than had previously been published about. Page's successor as editor, Bliss Perry, continued with this strategy, which he referred to as involving "wild west feats of editorial chase, capture, and exhibition." Scudder and some of his predecessors were completely different; they generally waited for authors to send them work. Contemporary topics were Page's primary focus, moving away from the former core content of fiction, history, biographies of historical figures, literary criticism, and book reviews. He embraced personal accounts that humanized tragedies and social problems, such as Jacob Riis's "Out of the Book of Humanity." Page sought and encouraged contributions from women and from ethnic writers, including African Americans. It was a much more radical change than at the *Forum*; Page attempted a transformation. He was taking the *Atlantic Monthly* into the information revolution.[40]

Again, Page tried to use his magazine to influence public opinion. For example, in 1898 he asked James Bryce, British author of *The American Commonwealth* and later ambassador to America (1907–13), to write an article on the unity felt by British and American peoples. Page believed in developing and nurturing a strong relationship between America and Britain, which was the theme of this article. Bryce was confident America would come to Britain's aid if attacked by other European nations, and that such a move would have public support. The article was covered in the *American* and probably other newspapers, and would prove to be very relevant to Page less than two decades later. In the same year he published an article advocating America take a greater interest in international affairs, which was supported by the New York *World* in an article on the Spanish-American War.[41]

Not surprisingly, some of Page's changes caused ongoing conflict with his editor, especially the sidelining of literary content, which Scudder believed was integral to the magazine's reputation. In mid-1897, Scudder went to Europe for a year and Page was formally promoted to acting editor. During this time the volume of articles on current affairs—political, economic, and social issues—increased markedly. Scudder, writing from Europe, complained to Page that by giving greater prominence to current affairs articles he "by implication made the literary character of the magazine subordinate."[42]

In July 1898 Scudder returned and resigned; Page was then promoted to editor. He had reached the pinnacle of the editorial profession, and was the first Southerner to reach this position. This was no surprise to the Los Angeles *Herald*, stating it was "the fulfillment (sic) of a step anticipated by the public ever since Mr. Walter H. Page became associated with the magazine three years ago." Page's success as acting editor in making it a national magazine was widely recognized. The *Kansas City Sunday Journal* enthused: "No one who has followed the Atlantic for the past year would need to be told that there is a new hand at the helm of the conservative old craft. . . . Formerly the reader of the Atlantic scarcely knew in what decade he was living, and as to place, only that he was in the world of New England." His changes met with the Boston *Herald's* approval; the magazine had become a "broadly national periodical in its scope" while remaining "representative of the best Boston culture."[43]

In North Carolina there was considerable pride and, as happened when he was at the *Forum*, considerable praise from formerly critical newspapers. The *Semi-weekly Messenger*, previously one of his harshest critics, quoted the Rev. Dr. John S. Lindsay as saying Page was editing the magazine "with a capacity that has not been exceeded in all its honorable history" which this newspaper thought was "gratifying to North Carolinians." Another example was the *News and Observer*, which stated that Page had "made the Atlantic Monthly easily the foremost American literary magazine."[44]

In June 1899 he was conferred with an honorary Doctor of Laws by Randolph-Macon Woman's College in Virginia, and consequently was sometimes referred to as Dr. Page. This inspired the *News and Observer* to pronounce Page "one of the greatest men the South has produced in the era following the war," and the *Charlotte Observer* to declare him "the ablest man born in North Carolina in the last fifty years."[45]

For the second time Page turned around a struggling national magazine. Circulation rose from around 10,000 per month in 1895 to around 17–18,000 in 1899. More significantly for the financially stricken magazine, advertising revenue increased twentyfold, from $1,059 to $20,750 per month. In January 1900, an announcement was placed in many newspapers, likely by Houghton, Mifflin & Co., that the number of subscribers in 1899 was a record and public interest in the magazine grew faster "than at any time in its long history." As the *Kansas City Sunday Journal* noted, Page's changes made the *Atlantic Monthly* competitive with other American magazines.[46]

Throughout his life Page suffered from poor health, exacerbated by the stress he placed on his body from a stressful workload, excessive worrying, and heavy smoking. From around the time he turned forty, he would suffer regular bouts of minor illness and some more serious episodes. In January 1898, he had a serious eye condition, forcing him to stay in darkness for a week, and then in April 1899 he may have almost died from a severe skin infection caused by erysipelas. He eventually recovered and returned to work in mid-May.[47]

In July 1899, soon after resuming work, Page resigned from Houghton, Mifflin & Co. While the catalyst was an offer by Samuel McClure, Page was dissatisfied for a number of reasons. He did not see any hope of attaining shares in the company, which he believed was essential for personal financial security. Additionally, he wanted to be able to dedicate all his energies to producing a magazine; as editor he had retained responsibility for the company's books. Further, he could see no prospect of achieving his long-sought goal of editorial independence. Culture and literary traditions stifled the magazine, and even as editor Page was reminded of this by Scudder, who was still with the company. One of his successors, Ellery Sedgwick, noted Page felt constrained by its "high-culture, literary traditions." With this stifling of his editorial freedom, and compared to the *Forum*, he had very few articles on the wide range of issues he believed were vital. So despite his success, he was not achieving anything like his full potential.[48]

Following his resignation, newspapers across the nation carried praise for Page's achievements. In mid-August the *Semi-weekly Messenger* published an article recognizing his achievement and influence: "Northern newspapers thought Dr. Page added to the interest and value of the leading $4 monthly in America. We think that true. He made it really a superior monthly to what it had been for some years." The same article was published in newspapers across the North and West. New York's *Saturday Review* praised Page and looked forward to his return: "Magazine literature in New York will be distinctly a gainer when Mr. Page once more is somewhere at the helm." The *Boston Transcript* lamented the great loss to the city, the magazine, and the company. It believed "Mr. Page is a born magazine editor," who was able to make the *Atlantic Monthly* "very strong on its public and political side without sacrificing anything of its literary character." It had rarely been better.[49]

After he left, his successors and the company expressed their gratitude for his revival of the magazine. Mifflin wrote to him on November 1, 1901, saying: "We always think of you as having ploughed the way for a good and permanent future for the old magazine." In 1904 his successor, Bliss Perry, told Page he often wondered "by what extraordinary talent you rescued this magazine from perdition." Years later Perry's successor, Ellery Sedgwick, admired Page for pulling the magazine out of the past—and driving it into the future, with his "revolutionary and invigorating hands."[50]

THE *WORLD'S WORK*

The publishing partnership of Frank N. Doubleday and Samuel McClure, Doubleday & McClure, was attempting to take over Harper & Brothers, a New

York–based publisher of four preeminent magazines. This was where McClure had offered Page a position. Page thought he had the opportunity to achieve editorial independence, having been told by McClure in a letter that he would have the chance to "pick out your own planets to rule," though he was made head of the book department and could have nothing to do with magazines. To make matters worse, the proposed takeover struck severe financial difficulties. Page soon realized he had made an error in judgment.[51]

Soon after moving to New York in 1885 Page had met Doubleday, who was with Scribner's for sixteen years and had recently established a small publishing company before entering the partnership with McClure. The two men subsequently had dealings in 1898. Doubleday was having second thoughts about the partnership, so he and Page started having discussions about going into business together. In late November the proposed takeover was abandoned. The following month Doubleday left the partnership and Page left Harper & Brothers. On December 18, 1899, they announced the formation of publishers Doubleday, Page & Co. as a partnership with Harry W. Lanier, S. A. Everitt, and J. L. Thompson, with their office in New York. This was where Page was to achieve his career goal of editorial independence.[52]

Doubleday, Page & Co. had a successful start as book publishers, and Page thrived. He developed strong relationships with his authors, engendering great loyalty and respect. As he wrote in *A Publisher's Confession*, in 1905, "Every great publishing house has been built on the strong friendships between writers and publishers." Ellen Glasgow's relationship with Page, which started while he was at the *Atlantic Monthly*, is a great example of the strong friendships he liked to have with his authors. Page was keen to discover new authors from the South and increase the number of women writing for the magazine. Glasgow's first novel, *The Descendant*, was published by Harper & Brothers in 1897 when she was in her midtwenties and Page saw through its faults to recognize her potential. Their first project together was Glasgow's poem "The Freeman," which he published in the December 1897 issue.[53]

In the same month Page wrote to Glasgow reinforcing the advice he had given her in an earlier discussion to focus on publishing novels as too many aspiring authors write numerous short pieces diluting the impact of their work. He wrote: "Even if all the minor literature that they put forth be excellent of its kind, the public comes after a very little while to regard the author as a sort of 'professional' writer who turns up with poems or short stories, or essays and other things so often as to cause one to regard the writer rather as a 'literary operative' than as a person who is bent upon doing only great pieces of work." He gave her the respect she was searching for and had not received, especially as a Southern woman aspiring to be an author: "But with your seriousness of purpose and your high aim I cannot help believing that it would be a grave mistake for you to do anything except to drive forward with your greater efforts." He went on to say that once established as an author of great works, this reputation would not be harmed if she published "smaller things." She decided to take his advice, replying, "As regards my work I shall follow your advice in full. I shall write no more short stories and I shall not divide my power or risk my future reputation. I will become a great novelist or none at all. For which determination you are in part responsible."[54]

While working on her second novel, Glasgow wrote to Page to see if he might be interested in publishing it: "It is going to be worth my while and worth your while, and if I send it to you and you do not want it for *The Atlantic* you will be very blind and I shall be very wrathful." Page did not publish it, and later said it would have been better for her if she had burned the manuscript. The novel, *Phases of an Inferior Planet*, was published by Harper & Brothers in 1898. These first two novels were set in New York, and Page advised her to set future novels in Virginia, where she lived her whole life. She decided to follow this advice, writing in 1898 that the framework of her novels would be "a series of sketches dealing with life in Virginia." Both pieces of advice given by Page were to be proven correct.[55]

In early 1900, very soon after Doubleday, Page & Co. had been established, Page convinced Glasgow to move to the company, warning her of the financial trouble being experienced by Harper & Brothers. That year Page published Glasgow's third novel, *The Voice of the People*, which became a bestseller. She worked closely with Page and his colleagues, spending most of the winter of 1900–01 in New York so they could have regular meetings. In 1901 Glasgow spent Christmas with the Page family, "the pleasantest Christmas" of her life, and two weeks later was inspired to write to him: "When I hear—as I do now & then—of the many forms your amazing energies acquire, I begin, indeed, to regard you as a kind of animated Colossus, or a second Theodore Roosevelt."[56]

As well as Glasgow's publisher, Page became a personal friend and adviser. Glasgow told Page that having him as her publisher provided half the joy of writing. Extremely grateful for his support, in 1902 she wrote: "You have made it all seem worth while, somehow—the work and the struggle, and the going on to an aim, which in itself can be but a little thing. But in the highest sense you have given me encouragement, even when you did not dream that I needed it, when you did not know how bitterly I wanted to throw it away—and life with it." She wrote at least six more novels while Page was with Doubleday, Page & Co., and after he left remained with the company for almost another two decades. Glasgow became one of America's most popular authors and five of her twenty novels were bestsellers. She was awarded the Howells Medal by the American Academy of Arts and Letters in 1940, and her final novel, *In This Our Life*, published in 1941 received a Pulitzer Prize.[57]

Doubleday, Page & Co.'s partners soon decided that, having all had experience with magazines, they "must make a magazine, *must* for the sheer love of it." They gave Page the editorship and free rein to run it as if it was his own. When they were looking for a title, Rudyard Kipling, one of their authors, perceptively said to Page: "What you really want is a magazine that deals with the work of the world." Page immediately recognized what he was looking for, exclaiming, "There it is, 'The World's Work.'" He then extended it to *The World's Work: A History of Our Times*.[58]

The first issue of the *World's Work*, dated November 1900, was promoted extensively during October in newspapers across the nation. Page's long interest in people and their work, as shown at the *State Chronicle,* was to be the focus: "It is with the activities of the newly organized world, its problems and even its romance, that this magazine will earnestly concern itself, trying to convey the cheerful spirit of men who do things."[59]

There were differences compared with most other magazines. From the start Page decided, like the *Forum,* it would not publish fiction. This remained a radical departure from the norm though there were other precedents, including *Penn Monthly,* which started in 1870, and *International Review*, which started in 1874. While he believed literature was important, Page's real passion was learning and writing about people, and helping them if he could. He wanted to edit a magazine for all the people, get away from the "old straw" and on to topics all Americans could relate to, especially "the new impulse in American life, the new feeling of nationality, our coming to realize ourselves." Another innovation was the extensive use of photographs, while other magazines mostly used illustrations. More editorial comment was noted by some newspapers as a key difference, including the *Indianapolis Journal*: "The World's Work differs from the stereotyped magazine in containing much editorial matter, current events being commented on with clearness and decision."[60]

Page introduced each issue with an extensive editorial, "The March of Events," comprising comments and facts on the key American and international issues. He wrote practically all of them during his tenure as editor. This was followed by articles covering a vast range of topics such as the environment, industrial development, growth of cities, farming and rural life, and other countries and cultures. He had sufficient confidence in his opinions to be prepared to expose them to scrutiny and allow his readers to make up their own minds. In his editorials and articles he tried to educate and inform, often hoping that when people had the facts they would go along with his way of thinking. He wanted to showcase what Americans, both individually and as a nation, had achieved and its potential if everyone had equality of opportunity. Page sought and published articles from a wide range of writers, including those who had different opinions from himself. A practical man, he was interested in the exchange of ideas, realizing this could bring about beneficial change. In 1884 he wrote that while "the sweetest pleasure in life is the pleasure of maintaining one's theories" he would relinquish this pleasure "in order to bring practical results."[61]

There were similarities with the *Nation*, a weekly magazine also published in New York and edited by Wendell P. Garrison. It had been established in 1865 under the editorship of the innovative and groundbreaking Edwin L. Godwin. Page was aware of this magazine—it was where he had placed his career-changing advertisement back in 1879. By 1880 the *Nation* had only eight thousand subscribers, though it was highly influential. A high-quality journal of opinion, it covered politics, economics, science, the arts, and literature. Like the *World's Work*, the *Nation* embraced clear, concise writing, eschewing the heavy, cumbersome writing then characteristic of serious American magazines. Some of its key themes were similar to the *World's Work*, including the South: conditions, lack of public education, equality for poor white people, and improvement for African Americans. One key difference was style: the *Nation* was sometimes criticized for intellectual pride, seeming to think itself above concern for people's day to day lives. These were criticisms unlikely to be made of Page's forthright style and interest in people.[62]

Accessibility was the basis of Page's preferred style. Responding to questions from the American Library Association in 1902, he outlined the challenge for magazine writers and editors: "The truth is, our style must become better. We do most things better than we write. Effective style is changing. The somewhat leisurely style of a generation or two ago pleased the small circle of readers within its reach" though it was no longer appropriate. Just as the nation had developed, so had readers' tastes. Therefore, "the man who would write convincingly or entertainingly of things of our day and our time must write with more directness, with more clearness, with greater nervous force."[63]

Page made sure his staff took this accessibility approach. Isaac F. Marcosson, who wrote many articles for the *World's Work*, recalled Page emphasizing the importance of "writing for everybody," often saying, "Make your articles so simple and concrete that a Kansas farmer can understand them." Brevity was essential. Marcosson related Page's response to an academic who thought twenty thousand words was short enough for a proposed article: "Do you realise that the story of the creation of the world—the biggest thing that ever happened—was told in a single paragraph?" The author agreed to do it in three thousand words. Page's approach generated criticism from some other editors and journalists who claimed the trend toward shorter articles, illustrated with an increased number of photos, prevented serious discussion and encouraged mediocrity. For example, Bryon R. Newton, a well-known journalist, stated in *Era Magazine,* "No country in the world is so prolific in mediocre magazines as our own United States." This criticism missed Page's point: the writing and content remained high quality, just more accessible.[64]

Page was also very prescriptive about the content. For instance, on July 14, 1908, he wrote to Ray S. Baker asking him to write an article on wheat and corn, requesting examples, both written and photos, of people who would be considered typical men and had become great farmers. He exhorted, "I keep coming back to individual experiences. Everything interesting reduces itself to that at last—doesn't it?" After receiving an article Page generally edited it, sometimes quite extensively, according to what he felt was wanted by his readers. He outlined his approach in two letters to his friend and fellow education campaigner Edwin Mims during 1911, asking him to travel through the South writing a series of articles to commemorate the fiftieth anniversary of the start of the Civil War. These were to be historical and, ideally, also have literary value. Mims was requested to follow the approach Page himself would use: "You'd have to take some typical communities and study them thoroughly; some typical industries and do the same thing; some typical men and their careers; some typical institutions, too; you'd have to find definite typical opportunities and show that it is a land of opportunity." The challenge was then to "weld all these kind of facts into definite, attractive, cumulative form, and do a great piece of writing, using almost wholly facts." He summed it up in the other letter: "we have got to have stories. That may be regrettable, but nevertheless it is a fact. Essays don't do the trick."[65]

Despite being so prescriptive, or maybe because of it, as a magazine editor he engendered great loyalty and respect from his authors. As he explained in *A Publisher's Confession,* to be successful a publisher needs to believe in their authors, the quality of their work, and their ability to tell a story. It's likely they also trusted him. What he asked of his writers was typical of the way Page approached his own work. He did not use trickery or distortion; he knew that if he did his research thoroughly and based his writing on facts, then they would tell the story.[66]

The *World's Work* was an immediate success in terms of profitability and quickly became one of the nation's leading magazines. Its first print run was 35,000 and after six months had 16,000 subscriptions. At the time, circulation for an extremely successful general monthly magazine was considered to be 100,000 per month and the *World's Work* reached this in 1907. It rose to about 125,000 two years later, and was independently estimated at 126,500 in 1910. It was likely to have remained above 100,000 during the rest of Page's time as editor.[67]

Page made efforts to become personally familiar with many of the areas and people about which he was writing and publishing. As editor of the *State Chronicle*, he had traveled extensively around his newspaper's circulation area, and he did the same at the *World's Work*. As he wrote in 1913, along with his associate editors, he traveled all over the country: "The theory is that at least one editor of the magazine shall visit every section of the country at least once a year, and, of course, at times other countries also." One man's surprised comment, "Why, you really regard Wyoming and Louisiana as parts of the United States," was highly treasured by Page, highlighting the importance he placed on being in touch with his compatriots. In the second anniversary issue, Page had quotes from some of the "active people" who read the *World's Work* including the following: "It's a working magazine"; "It believes in the American man who does things"; and "It gives new energy to its readers." Page worked closely with his staff. Their ideas for articles were discussed, and in some cases demolished, at regular editorial sessions in his office. On most days informal lunches of staff and authors were held in a nearby hotel, Everett House in Union Square. Marcosson believed this "intimate personal companionship" was "one of the delights of magazine-making." It was this hands-on approach that gave Page and his magazines such success.[68]

For many years magazines had been criticizing government corruption at all levels, and then in the 1890s there was an increasing number of articles in magazines exposing the misuse of power by large companies and corporations. This investigative journalism came to be known as "muckraking," and took off early in the following decade with articles in *McClure's* on the Standard Oil Company and corruption in the cities. Involving thorough, time-consuming, and expensive detective work, it was most prevalent and effective in 1903 and 1904. There was another type of muckraking that was essentially taking advantage of the sensation and opportunity to increase sales, though without the hard work and expense. This became more prevalent after 1904 and undermined the process. It continued to be used by certain magazines, though with growing criticism and flagging interest from readers, the period of muckraking eventually ended around 1912.[69]

Page introduced investigative journalism to magazines when at the *Forum*, with a series on education by J. M. Rice during 1892 and 1893. It was followed by other series on education and local sanitation, and articles on local government, corporations, and railroad regulation. Even earlier he had undertaken this type of journalism at the *State Chronicle*, most notably numerous research-based articles on education. Page used investigative journalism relatively sparingly at the *World's Work*. During the peak he ran several series and articles, including a 1904 series on American schools by Adele Marie Shaw. In April 1906 he responded to ongoing insurance scandals with articles exposing abuses and corruption, and others advising how consumers could avoid being victims of the scandals by selecting the right life insurance. In May 1906 the *World's Work* had lead articles on the meatpacking industry, and Doubleday, Page & Co. released a book exposing the industry by Upton Sinclair. Page's efforts were a factor in the Pure Food and Drug Act of 1906 being passed by Congress.[70]

Page foresaw the decline of muckraking, writing in May 1906, "reform by shrieking exposure does at last become tiresome. It is another evidence of sanity that the people are showing some weariness with the literature of corruption." He preferred muckraking be used for positive purposes, such as improving education, rather than what he considered to be negative exposés. The practice did not necessarily lead to increased sales, with *McClure's* and other leading muckraking magazines not increasing circulation during the period, while that of the *World's Work* steadily increased.

Page has been criticized for not embracing muckraking, claiming he missed an opportunity to ensure it was entrenched and expanded. This misinterprets Page's intentions for the practice. He never intended it to be the foundation of a magazine's approach to journalism or to increase sales; he had used it as one-offs to focus on issues of particular importance to bring about positive change. Page's approach was summed up by the *Outlook*, in an article following his resignation from the *Forum*: "Discarding all sensational and cheap methods, he dealt with his opportunity with a statesmanlike breadth and sagacity."[71]

In 1911 Page summarized his ethical approach to editing, arguing that a magazine "must be uncompromisingly given to the public welfare and to no private or special or local or party interests of any sort." Page went to great lengths to ensure he did not use his influence for personal gain, even inadvertently. For example, he could have sought favors from the Cleveland administration given how strongly the *Forum* had supported his presidential campaign. He refused, even for his friends. And he had strong business ethics. In 1889, as business manager of the *Forum,* he was approached by the contracted printer of competing magazine the *North American Review,* John P. Dalton, offering to sell Page the list of its subscribers. Page advised the *Review's* owner, General Lloyd Bryce, who went to the police and Dalton was charged.[72]

Although he operated the *World's Work* on a commercial basis and needed to make a profit, he did not let this interfere with his desire to publish articles of public interest. For example, following the articles on the insurance industry, the magazine appeared to lose the Mutual Life Insurance Company of New York's advertising, as it suddenly stopped appearing. As at the *State Chronicle,* Page's ethics extended to advertising, claiming the *World's Work* never engaged in false or misleading promotion and that it never accepted advertisements from businesses about whose practices he was even slightly uncertain.[73]

Page spent 12 1/2 years editing the *World's Work* and it was by far the longest he spent in a position, which was not surprising. As he wrote in 1913: "It is a cheerful and exhilarating occupation; for we must keep an eye on all sorts of human activities and meet and learn from men of all helpful minds and callings." This was the intellectual independence he had craved since his college days; unlike at the *State Chronicle* he didn't have to contend with the negativity of the old Southern leaders. Page had achieved his career goal. For the first time, he had the freedom and a platform to express his opinions and allow others to express theirs.[74]

In 1913, Page left the *World's Work* to go on the greatest adventure of his life: leaving behind everything he knew and had worked for to become U.S. ambassador to Great Britain. It was the culmination of a thirty-year relationship with Woodrow Wilson, who had been elected president. This dramatic period of Page's life is covered in chapter 7 and part 4.

FAMILY MAN

Page's family was important to him, and he was a devoted father. From 1902 to 1909 the family leased a grand house with extensive grounds on Teaneck Road, in Englewood, New Jersey, which Page considered a quiet country area. Traditionally farmland, the district was rapidly becoming more residential. Over the period the Page's lived there the population more than doubled, from around 800 to 2,000. He was a sporadic diarist, and one of his attempts started on March 31, 1907, when he described a pleasant Saturday night: "I begin this book with this night's pleasing picture." "Brownie," his daughter and youngest child, Katharine, had been beaten in her basketball game, though "the glow of the contest" was in their home, and had "enlivened all the dinner-talk." After dinner Walter was writing an address to give to students at Richmond College, Virginia, and was inspired as he heard Katharine in the hall where she "played beautifully on the piano." When he kissed her goodnight, Walter told his daughter how much pleasure she gave him, and she replied, "It is a pleasure to give you pleasure, dear Daddy." He could hear laughter from the parlor where Alice ("Mother Bunch"), Arthur and "two of the Parker boys" were playing cards. Their house was not far from Manhattan, over the Hudson River, and their youngest son, Frank, had gone there to the theater with a friend. Arthur had been "steadily working this month at the 'make-up' desk of *The World's Work*." Their eldest son Ralph had written "cheerful nothings" from Harvard, where he was in the final year of his law course.[75]

Page was very proud of his sons. One afternoon several weeks later when two of them arrived home, he and Alice were full of admiration, later noting in his diary: "When they came home this afternoon, Ralph and Arthur—two stalwart fellows, each now a man, earning his living, I said to their mother as we watched them from the window: 'Do you realize that they are ours—these men?' And she said 'No.' And neither do I."[76]

Their father's character was evident in his face and in his laugh. Isaac Marcosson, who worked for him for three years until 1906, enthused: "Mr. Page was vitally human. There was something almost Lincoln-like in his rugged honest face. His eyes were fine and friendly; his voice rich and eloquent. Nothing about him was more characteristic than his laugh, which rang out like a joyous peal. It was the echo of a deep character." Ten years earlier he had been described in the *Charlotte Observer* as "tall, muscular looking, and the least bit awkward. His face is rugged, strong and shows determination and courage."[77]

PART TWO

THE SOUTH

\ 3 /

"WAKE UP, OLD LAND!"
STANDING UP TO THE ANTEBELLUM MYTH

SECTIONALISM IN THE ANTEBELLUM PERIOD

The antebellum period started early in the first decade of the 1800s and ended with the Civil War in 1861. In the first half of this period, the South occupied a prominent place in a unified nation. Southern politicians dominated federal government institutions, and Southern agriculture was a force in the national economy, accounting for the bulk of exports. These were Anderson Page's formative and probably most active years, and from them came his way of thinking that would have such a profound influence on his grandson.[1]

This period of Southern strength, and national unity, was not to last. By the early 1830s the North was developing and growing rapidly as it embraced industrialization. By contrast, the South had difficulty changing its dependence on agriculture and so was being left behind socially and economically. Southerners had many theories as to what was holding their "section" back, though the dominant feature of all the states was slavery. In 1820 there were 1.5 million slaves in the South out of a population of 4.3 million, and the average annual increase over the antebellum period was 2.5 percent; in the North slavery had virtually ended.[2]

By the 1840s the gap had widened significantly. The increasingly prosperous North was experiencing rapid change with fast-growing cities, factories, and infrastructure being connected by an expanding railroad system, combined with the changing attitudes of an increasing population. By contrast the South was largely unchanged since the previous century. Growth in industrialization, exports, income, population, and urbanization was well below Northern levels. It remained an agrarian economy with scattered populations living on farms and plantations, in small towns and a few cities. Page interpreted this life in an 1883 speech, as reported by the *Boston Post*: "Industrial activity, with the exception of agricultural activity, was not thought desirable." Southerners were totally opposed to the idea of being employed by someone else. A typical farmer lived "the life of one hundred years ago, and the railroad, the printing press, banks and trade, have no influence upon his life."[3]

As the gap between the two sections widened national unity fractured. Northerners regarded the agrarian South as an impediment to national social and economic development, as well as immoral for continuing with slavery. Southerners were shocked by what they saw as unwarranted attacks on their way of life while being confused and concerned by their comparative lack of development. It became the most extreme sectionalism in American history.[4]

THE ANTEBELLUM MYTH

In the 1830s when it was evident the South was stagnating, instead of looking for reasons why their section had not kept up with the North, Southern leaders responded with a defense of their agrarian social and economic structure. They did all they could to create the image of the South as a perfect civilization: the antebellum myth.

These leaders included the plantation owners who, along with political and religious leaders, had power and influence in the South. While family farms were common in both sections, in the South it was the export crops—cotton, tobacco, rice, sugar, and hemp— grown on plantations that dominated agriculture and the economy. The situation was described by Winston Churchill as an aristocracy with three to four thousand principal slave owners ruling the section "as effectively as the medieval baronage had ruled England."[5]

The leaders were committed to ensuring the status quo was maintained, especially slavery, which they claimed underpinned the viability of their operations. There were a number of arguments used to create the myth, and these changed over the decades. Initially they criticized industrialization, the characteristic of the North most unlike the South, claiming it involved labor exploitation. In the long term they were forced into increasingly convoluted and contradictory defenses of slavery. Slavery was claimed to be God's will, to help Southerners become better people, and to underpin the social fabric; a social order had evolved where everyone fitted well in society according to their class and race.[6]

In 1835 South Carolina governor George McDuffie claimed slavery was "manifestly consistent with the will of God" and was a "corner stone of our republican edifice." In 1849 William P. Miles, later a leading South Carolina politician and secessionist, claimed slave owners developed strong characters as many of the "highest, manliest and most admirable qualities in the Southern character have been preserved in their pristine strength" and therefore became respected leaders throughout the nation.[7]

Reverend Iverson L. Brookes's descriptively titled 1850 essay encapsulated many of its arguments: "A Defense of the South against the Reproaches and Encroachments of the North: in Which Slavery is Shown to be an Institution of God Intended to Form the Basis of the Best Social State and the Only Safeguard to the Permanence of a Republican Government." One of the most pervasive arguments was proffered in 1858 by former South Carolina governor, Democrat senator James H. Hammond: "In all social systems there must be a class to do the mean duties, to perform the drudgery of life." These people are "the very mud-sills of society and of political government," and the South had "found a race adapted to that purpose to her hand."

Southern leaders created the antebellum myth to defend the social and economic structure that entrenched their power; they were content to sacrifice the freedom of an entire race and their section's development to ensure their power base remained intact. It is impossible to know how many Southerners went along with their leaders' arguments, though the reality is a way of thinking came to exist in the South that was persuasive and powerful enough to inspire the Confederate soldiers and then endure for many decades after the Civil War as the romantic vision of a perfect society.[8]

PUSHES FOR INDUSTRIALIZATION

Starting in the mid-1840s, there were two types of pushes for Southern industrialization. The initial push was positive, aiming to enhance economic development and improve people's lives, though it was soon subsumed into separate pushes with the negative purposes of defeating the North and promoting the antebellum myth.

William Gregg led the initial push. Gregg was a former jeweler and silversmith who established a cotton mill in South Carolina that became the most successful manufacturing business in the state and was seen as a model for other operations. Gregg wrote a series of articles in the *Charleston Courier*, which he consolidated in an 1845 book, *Essays on Domestic Industry*, passionately calling for South Carolina and the South to commence manufacturing coarse cotton fabrics.[9]

Like Page would do forty years later, Gregg directly criticized the state's leaders for opposing manufacturing. He specifically attacked Langdon Cheves, a former Speaker of the House of Representatives, for advocating that "manufactures should be the last resort of a country." Gregg stated the current position was not sustainable. Soils had lost their fertility due to poor farming practices, so farms were full of abandoned fields, broken fences, and emaciated livestock. The state abounded with unpainted and dilapidated houses, and the population was "poor and half-starved." He contrasted this with the prosperity he saw on a trip to the North.

Gregg advocated cotton manufacturing to encourage local investment of capital currently sent outside South Carolina. He noted cotton had been the pioneering industry in Great Britain, continental Europe, and America, introducing and giving "an impetus to all other branches of mechanism." It would encourage the establishment of tanneries and blacksmiths as well as makers of shoes, wagons, carriages, and other goods in villages throughout the state. As Page would do decades later, Gregg implored residents of his state to work hard and "think less of their grievances," and politicians to encourage support for local industry, rather than "teaching us to hate our Northern brethren." He believed there was no shortage of capital; it was lack of will that was the problem. Meanwhile millions of dollars were being transferred to the North.

Addressing Southern prejudice against industrialization, Gregg wrote, "Surely there is nothing in cotton spinning that can poison the atmosphere of South-Carolina. Why not spin as well as plant cotton?" The people who made cotton manually could be taught to use a machine. He advocated using slaves for two reasons; first, they did not have to be educated and so were available "uninterrupted" from the age of eight years; and, second, there would not be the high turnover, which was a major problem with "white" workers in the North. This was where Gregg differed from Page's later arguments—he strongly opposed both child labor and slavery.

Using similar positivity as Page would use forty years later, Gregg stated, more out of hope than reality: "The period is fast approaching in South-Carolina, which shall produce a great change in these matters. Many persons are now looking to the subject of manufactures with intense interest, and it is believed that many men of capital would at once embark in this business, could this field for profitable enterprise, be laid open before our wealthy business men of Charleston, a host of whom can be found, with nerves that never tire, and as much forecaste and shrewdness as the merchant manufacturers of Boston."[10]

A vastly different motivation for Southern industrialization was led by barrister and publisher, James D. B. De Bow. Inspired by the 1845 Memphis Commercial Convention, which concluded that Southerners needed to "economize their capital, erect mills and factories of *all kinds,*" in 1846 De Bow commenced publishing what would become known as *De Bow's Review,* focusing on industrialization to end importation of goods from the North. De Bow built on advocacy by leading Southern radicals, known as "fire-eaters," for agricultural advancement to build up self-sufficiency. As a variation of the antebellum myth, often preparing the path to secession, these radicals were determined to convince Southerners that Northerners were doing all they could to ruin their society and make the South economically dependent on the North.[11]

In the 1850s the *Review* had the highest circulation of any Southern magazine, and De Bow's call to prepare economically and politically through industrial self-sufficiency was repeated by newspaper editors throughout the South. In 1851 De Bow proposed a program to ensure the South was prepared for "the invader" from the North, which included a Southern Manufacturing Convention to get the people "to manufacture at home every bale of cotton that we eventually consume and pay no more tribute to northern looms." It also advocated industrial diversification to minimize imports of other goods from the North, as well as building railroads and roads, educating children in the South, ending the practice of sending them to Northern universities, and encouraging Southern literature.[12]

De Bow continued his campaign throughout the decade and by 1856 appeared to be confident that the message was getting through: "Let the South but adopt a system of manufactures and internal improvements to the extent which her interests require, her danger demands, and her ability is able to accomplish, and in a few years northern fanaticism and abolitionism may rave, gnash their teeth, and howl in vain."[13]

This desire for self-sufficiency was a significant factor in the weakening in some centers of prejudice against industry, and there is evidence it accounted for a major part of the rapid growth in the value of Southern manufactures from 1850 to 1860. The value of capital invested increased by 73.6 percent and the value of labor employed rose by 25.3 percent. The largest increases were in industries competing with the North: woolen manufactures, boots and shoes, men's clothing, paper, coal, flour, lumber, tobacco, and iron.[14]

The distinction between the positive and negative pushes for industrialization is confused by some authors writing about this period. In his 1950 book, *Coming of the Civil War*, Avery Craven erred in including Gregg as one of the leaders whose purpose was self-sufficiency, when it was actually to improve the lives of Southerners. In a 1931 review of *De Bow's Review*, Herman C. Nixon noted that to encourage industrialization De Bow profiled cotton mills, cotton seed oil mills, turpentine factories, and other manufacturing operations. Page would later do this in the *State Chronicle* and the *World's Work*, though his purpose was completely misunderstood by Nixon who wrote that the *Review* could have become a "Southern *World's Work,*" which would have met Page's approval. As with Gregg, Page did it for the purpose of state development for the benefit of the locals living in a unified nation; this was the complete opposite of De Bow's sectionalism.[15]

RECONSTRUCTION

After the Civil War ended in 1865, President Andrew Johnson pardoned virtually all the Southern leaders. Their political rights and property, excluding slaves, were restored. Slavery was abolished with the Thirteenth Amendment and the federal government established the Freedmen's Bureau to assist the freed slaves. The new Southern state governments went in the other direction and enacted the "Black codes" that restricted African American's civil rights. Congress responded by not allowing elected Southern representatives and senators to take their seats, passing a bill to continue the work of the Bureau, and, most significantly, passing the Civil Rights Act 1866. The act gave the former slaves citizenship and guaranteed all citizens equality before the law. Soon after, Congress ratified the Fourteenth Amendment, which entrenched the principles of the act into the Constitution.[16]

In 1867, the Reconstruction Acts granted the vote to men of all races, transforming the South politically and socially. Most African Americans voted Republican, and by 1870 almost all Southern states were under Republican control. Hundreds of African Americans were elected to offices across the South—including sixteen in Congress, over six hundred in state legislatures—and to local positions such as sheriffs and justices of the peace. They developed social institutions, such as religious congregations, many of which remained after Reconstruction.[17]

Southern Republican state governments sought to implement nondiscriminatory policies and reforms, though they often failed in delivery. Their reforms included public school systems, greater bargaining power for plantation workers, more equitable taxation, and banning discrimination on public transportation and in accommodation. They funded the expansion of railroads and other businesses to develop a "New South" for both races. "Carpetbaggers," including former Union soldiers, teachers, Freedmen's Bureau workers, and businessmen, came from the North and while some assisted Reconstruction, others came to take advantage of the situation to their own benefit and engaged in widespread corruption and unethical behavior. "Scalawags," predominately white, small farmer operators who had not owned slaves nor supported the Confederacy, also tried to take advantage of the situation. It was common for businessmen and politicians seeking power and wealth to create monopolies and engage in unethical and illegal practices. Most notably, owners and operators of railroads and lotteries gained considerable power and influence in the South during the 1860s and 1870s. The actions of these people were so pervasive and corrosive that they often fatally undermined the good intentions of the governments' initiatives.[18]

On February 3, 1870, the Fifteenth Amendment was ratified preventing governments from denying the right to vote based on race, though the Republican national government's commitment to Reconstruction had waned. A number of Supreme Court decisions reduced the impact of the Reconstruction laws and constitutional amendments. White voters became disillusioned, and by 1876 only three states were controlled by Republicans. In the 1876 presidential election the results in those states were so close that they were disputed by both parties. Eventually the Compromise of 1877 was reached. The Republican candidate Hayes would be elected, and the Democrats would be allowed to regain control of the South. The federal troops were withdrawn, and that was the end of the national government's attempts to protect the rights of the former slaves. The "Solid South" of Democratic control was restored.[19]

The Reconstruction period was ultimately an uneven contest. At the start Judge William M. Dickson, a prominent Republican from Cincinnati, Ohio, had written to English (classical liberal) philosopher John S. Mill asking for his advice. Mill perceptively responded that it would take two generations to change the culture of the South, requiring strong federal leadership backed up by military force. The opposite happened, and the aspirations of often distant national leaders were defeated by Southern leaders determined to re-establish the old social order and return to positions of power and wealth. The vast majority of prominent Confederates, civilian and military leaders, returned to similar positions to those held during the peak of the Confederacy.[20]

NEW SOUTH PROGRESSIVES

The return of Democratic governments following the Compromise of 1877 led to the second phase of the antebellum myth, primarily perpetuated by Confederate leaders as well as the few surviving aristocrats of the antebellum period. One of their most pervasive techniques was re-creating images of a glorious era, a "golden age without shadows and the Confederacy as all dash, gallantry, and sacrifice." According to Waldo Braden, a leading scholar of Southern rhetoric, the antebellum period was described in terms of "the white-columned mansion, acres of snowy cotton, the coquettish belle, the genteel master, the crooning mammy, singing field hands, reckless young gallants, and a native chivalry."[21]

Soon after the Compromise, advocates for a "New South" emerged. Progressive young men, they wanted the South to catch up to the North. Most were conservative progressives: progressive because they wanted change, though conservative because they wanted to work within the political beliefs of the Democrats and other Southern leaders who had taken over from the Republicans. They were led by the dominant newspaper editors Henry W. Grady of the *Atlanta Constitution,* Henry Watterson of the Louisville *Courier-Journal,* and Francis W. Dawson of the Charleston *News and Courier,* as well as orators such as Daniel Augustus Tompkins of South Carolina. Looking to encourage investment from the North and the growth of large Southern enterprises, especially railroads, they promoted the South as a place of plentiful low-cost resources and vast business opportunities.[22]

By being conservative and not insisting on fundamental changes to the structure of politics and society, the efforts of these New South leaders were doomed to repeat the mistakes of the past. Large enterprises came to dominate the Southern economy, often benefiting Northern interests. Unregulated by governments, the businesses took advantage of their market power to engage in illegal and unethical behavior, spreading corruption throughout the South. Grady and others also stoked racial tension, claiming African Americans were inferior and held back Southern development. Seduced by the prospect of power and wealth like their predecessors of the antebellum period, and unimpeded by an uneducated and impoverished population under the spell of the myth, these New South leaders came to resemble the worst aspects of the Reconstruction. Page believed it was actually worse as they lacked the redeeming quality of striving for racial equality; the conservative New South leaders did all they could to return the freed slaves to their previous position of subservience.[23]

In the early 1880s a different breed of New South advocates emerged who were liberal progressives. They were progressive because they wanted change to address societal problems, and liberal because they wanted significant and fundamental changes, especially greater equality of opportunity. Many advocated public schools (government-owned, operated, and funded), industrial development from within the South, and innovation and education to develop agriculture. Some supported improving the lives of African Americans. This required challenging the existing leaders and defeating the antebellum myth.

Page was one of these as were former pupils from his Normal School teaching stint in 1878—such as Edwin A. Alderman, Charles B. Aycock, and Charles D. McIver—and others with whom he would work on education campaigns or whose writings he would publish, including Charles Dabney, Josephus Daniels, Edward P. Moses, George W. Cable, Alexander J. McKelway, Edgar G. Murphy, Booker T. Washington, and T. Thomas Fortune. Of these liberal progressive New South advocates, Page was the only one who advocated all the changes; the others generally focused on one, predominantly public education. He particularly stood out as one of the few passionate and outspoken advocates for racial equality. As Isaac Marcosson argued in 1919, "Wherever Walter H. Page hung his hat that place became automatically the unofficial capital of the New South—the South of progressive thought and intelligent labour, where education was the watchword and the Negro had an opportunity to make himself a useful and helpful citizen."[24]

An integral part of the mythmaking was to create an environment where it was accepted by as many people as possible. Southern leaders did all they could to make it unthinkable for the myth to be challenged; anyone doing so was criticized and had their patriotism questioned. Historians had a critical role to play, and in 1897 John S. Bassett, a teacher at Trinity College, claimed any Southern historian who questioned the glorification was "denounced as a traitor and mercenary defiler of his Birthplace." Page realized the danger facing the South if the antebellum myth was accepted by the people as a true representation of their history and as a way of life to which they should aspire. Robert D. Connor, who worked with Page on campaigns to develop the South, summed it up as follows: "The South of the 'eighties and 'nineties was in mortal danger of being strangled in the grip of a deadening sectionalism, and no voice was raised in warning so fearless, so far-reaching, and so stimulating as the voice of this Southern Nationalist [Page]."[25]

Page had long recognized this danger. He attributed the South's significantly lower standard of living to an obsession with thinking and talking about slavery. In 1883 he warned Confederate veterans against using their war record to seek votes as they would be defeated, "not because Confederate soldiers are not held in high esteem, but because there is no sense in trying to make a lost cause a living cause." In 1902 he stated: "Three influences have held the social structure stationary—first, slavery, which pickled all Southern life and left it just as it found it; then the politician and the preacher." The South was consequently "gagged and bound," holding the "people back from their natural development."[26]

DEVELOPING NORTH CAROLINA

In the early 1880s Page believed North Carolina was entering "the most notable industrial era in her history," though as a result of the inertia created by the antebellum myth it lacked the "commercial tension" required to attract Northern investment. Those investors were looking for the infrastructure, spirit of enterprise, energy, and wealthy customers they were used to in their home states. So while he encouraged Northern investment, local entrepreneurship was always Page's preference. He wanted North Carolinians to move on from the antebellum attitude of measuring prosperity by size, especially number of acres or slaves, and instead to start small and grow efficient, productive businesses: "The tradition that we were once all rich and that the war made us poor lingers unconsciously in our minds with such tenacity that we dream in capital letters. We unconsciously scorn any process of regaining our fortunes penny by penny; and our dreams of prosperity are too likely to fashion themselves in the shape of a syndicate or of a money-bag from Boston."[27]

Page's strategy to encourage local entrepreneurship was relentless positivity, and while he was editor more was written about developing North Carolina in the *State Chronicle* than any other topic. Manufacturers were encouraged to invest in and build up their businesses, farmers to improve their way of farming, and everyone to undertake education or training. On September 22, 1883, he editorialized that agriculture was more prosperous than ever, in contrast to the antebellum period when only the wealthy few prospered: "There are men that take pleasure in remembering the easy days of slavery who are inclined to deny so sweeping a proposition. But they are mistaken. Many men who were rich and prosperous planters before the war are less rich and prosperous now; but the mass of farmers is in better condition." Now more crops were being sown, yields were larger, and profits were greater; there were more crop farmers, cotton was being grown over a greater area, and the culture of tobacco farming had been transformed.[28]

During the initial months each issue of the *State Chronicle* had articles describing the progress and potential of a couple of towns, counties, or regions. Page wanted to show: "the numerous manifestations of progress and prosperity in nearly every town and village in North Carolina." On October 6, 1883, he published profiles of Newton and Smithfield. In Newton, according to the *State Chronicle's* correspondent, "our people are wearing better clothes, driving finer horses and riding in better buggies. The people are prospering." The town had a cotton factory "running night and day, humming

2,000 spindles," 11 brick stores, seven wooden stores, and a market where cotton, wheat, corn, flour, bacon, dried fruit, eggs, and chickens from across Catawba County were sold during fall. It was surrounded by fertile land where farmers bought a large range of implements including wheat drills, reapers, mowers, horse-rakers, and fine plows. On top of this, "the taxes are lower, the schools are run longer than any other county in this section, and we have a great many of them to run, there being seventy school districts in this little county of 375 square miles."[29]

On November 3, 1883, he published a profile of Cary, the area where he grew up, which had become a suburb of Raleigh. Page was the likely author and noted the two railroads to Raleigh that gave better access than any other suburb in the state. Many residents had hoped this would make it the site of "manufactories," though this had not occurred. One such person was "the founder of the town, Mr. A.F. Page, who built the large brick house which is the most prominent object in the village." As with other profiles, prominent local businesses were promoted, though there were not many in Cary. It was primarily residential, though there was "no reason in the world why it should not become a manufacturing town of some importance." In the meantime "the people are proud of their town and think that there is no other more desirable place to live in the State." This was an important part of Page's message; he wanted the people of North Carolina to feel good about themselves and their state, to give them the confidence to assert themselves: "What we need in North Carolina is self-assertion, only in a proper and becoming way, of course, but yet self-assertion; not by praise of our ancestors, but especially in politics and in business."[30]

While not his focus, Page encouraged Northern investment. In early August 1883 he had an article published in the *Boston Post* promoting North Carolina's exhibit, an almost $15,000 Department of Agriculture display, at the annual exposition of the New England Manufacturers and Mechanics Institute in Boston. Reprinted in the *Commonwealth*, Page's article emphasized the need for development, encouraging New England investors, manufacturers, and families to move to North Carolina, and increase everyone's prosperity. On January 12, 1884, he published the "Special Raleigh Edition." It was eight pages, double the usual size, about Raleigh and its progress; statistics, praise, and information on numerous businesses, the people who ran them, and the city itself. It was a great example of Page's interest in peoples' work. Ten thousand copies were to be distributed throughout the state as well as to New England and the Middle

States: "It will be the best advertisement of this city and this State that a North Carolina newspaper can make."[31]

Then on May 31, 1884, he published his most concerted attempt at state development, the "Tobacco Edition." Looking to lure farmers and investors from other states, there was extensive coverage of North Carolina's tobacco growing regions and businesses. Data showed it was the fourth largest producer in 1882, though production of the leading state, Kentucky, was more than six times greater. Despite this, North Carolina was the most profitable state to grow tobacco, with high returns also from cigarette manufacturing. Page claimed this edition was the largest newspaper, at twelve pages and with the largest print run, 25,000, in the state's history. It may not have been a coincidence that in the following decade, when the industry became mechanized, North Carolina became the nation's largest tobacco-producing state.[32]

On September 13, 1884, Page celebrated his newspaper's first anniversary with a very positive and comprehensive review of the significant events in the state. After enthusiastically outlining some of the industrial progress, he suggested the *State Chronicle* had had a positive impact on newspaper coverage, as "these days the newspapers of the State give five times as much space and five times as great emphasis to industrial progress as they did a year ago."[33]

On October 1, 1884, the North Carolina Exposition opened, and it was a testament to Page's practical approach to promoting development. He had initiated the idea in the *State Chronicle* a year earlier, after enthusing about the reported success of North Carolina's exhibit at the Boston exposition. Page continued to push the idea. After local businesses decided to go ahead, he relentlessly promoted it in the *State Chronicle* and became a secretary of the Vance County organizing committee. During the exposition Page profiled some of the counties' exhibits, including a feature on Forsyth County informing readers of its history and growth, soil types, topography, water sources, and main agricultural and industrial activities.[34]

Although its purpose was to attract Northern investment, most of the sixty thousand exposition attendees were North Carolinians and it raised their awareness of their state's achievements and potential. In the *News and Observer* Samuel Ashe editorialized that it "opened the eyes of North Carolinians to the fact that their State really has great actualities as well as great possibilities." For many, including Josephus Daniels, it was the first time they had seen electricity in operation. On the last day, November 1, the *State Chronicle* proudly lamented that "the visitors could'nt [sic] hide their regret at witnessing the close of the greatest month in onr [sic] recent history."[35]

DEVELOPING THE SOUTH

Not long after he moved back to New York in 1885, the *Boston Post* stated Page's efforts as a writer and speaker, including as editor of the *State Chronicle*, had made him "one of the most active forces in the development of the new South." This continued as magazine editor, where Page took advantage of opportunities to present the South, its problems and development, to a national audience. He published 13 articles on the South as editor of the *Forum* (about 50 issues), and 8 as editor of the *Atlantic Monthly* (21 issues). At Doubleday, Page & Co., he saw himself and the publishing operation as "tools to be used for furthering great purposes," one of the greatest being "the broadening of Southern development." He published 82 articles and wrote 141 editorials about Southern issues (across 151 issues) at the *World's Work,* significantly more than any other major American magazine. The main article topics were African Americans (22), agriculture (14), general Southern progress (8), education (6) and business and industry (4).[36]

The standout in Page's efforts to promote the South at the *World's Work* was the special "Southern Number" of June 1907 of which two hundred thousand copies were distributed throughout the nation. Edwin Mims, who had an article in the issue, believed "no such varied and comprehensive statement has ever been made of the intellectual, social, and industrial progress of the Southern states." Page opened the issue with a typically positive and inspiring editorial: "The present industrial awakening in the Southern States is the most important economic event in our history since the settlement of the West. Go where you will, the people are building homes, schools, and roads, and in the cities business buildings and factories." He wanted to convince people in the North to revise the "old notions about the South and the Southern people" and for Southerners to do the same, change "old notions" about themselves: "New economic forces" meant "every-day events contradict the conclusions that they also drew from the facts of the past." The issue was full of articles and editorials by Page and other Southerners. Page had traveled throughout the South for two and a half months, and he presented his findings in a comprehensive article rich with photos. He enthused that the most significant change he found was a spirit of cooperation. Southerners who previously were fiercely independent were working together and achieving significant benefits for the cities and rural areas.[37]

In June 1901 Page was pleased South Carolina Democrat senator John L. McLaurin had turned his back on part of the party's Solid South platform, seeing it as a possible catalyst for change: "it is a radical departure, by a man of character and influence, from the 'solid' programme of these 'solid' forty years;

for war, poverty, illiteracy, epidemics and tornadoes have done less hurt to the South than (be it said with respect to all men of breadth and tolerance) the politicians and preachers." They had taken away Southerners' intellectual freedom: "They have suppressed thought and prevented growth—these unscarred Colonels who wear long hair and white ties and frock coats, and these doctors of divinity who herd good women by the most stagnant waters of theology."

Page noted McLaurin was not criticized in the South as widely as a "'traitor' to the Democratic party" would have been previously, and it was similar for Page; considerable vitriol declaring he was slandering the South by criticizing its leaders, though in fewer newspapers. His message was getting through as Raleigh's *News and Observer* expressed frustration that he was so widely respected. It claimed politicians and preachers had contributed to the South's development, and it wasn't being held back as cotton production was higher than under slavery and more was being processed every year. Wilmington's *Semi-weekly Messenger* had numerous highly critical articles on Page's "very absurd and intemperate opinion." The newspaper hoped his admirers would reconsider their opinion, suggesting the editor was also worried about the number of people who listened to Page. Just over a year later Page lamented McLaurin's policies had been defeated by Senator Benjamin R. Tillman's "machine" and tragically the South would remain "solid."[38]

Page was optimistic about future industrial development of the South because the two great impediments since Reconstruction, the old soldiers as leaders and the Farmers' Alliance, were having significantly less impact. He noted that a feeling had arisen in the Democratic Party "against giving all the offices to old soldiers simply because they were old soldiers" and there were less of them as time went on. The Farmers' Alliance, of which the Populists were the political arm, had adopted the "free silver" policy of prominent Democrat William J. Bryan. Page believed tariff reform, industrial development, international trade, and other policies were more important for the South's future.[39]

PAGE'S RELATIONSHIP WITH THE SOUTH

The key to understanding Page's relationship with the South is that, unlike his fellow progressive New South advocates, he wanted to change the culture; change the way Southerners thought about themselves, about their society, about their history, about their future, and about their nation. He wanted them to break free from the antebellum myth, to stop seeing themselves as Southerners and see themselves as part of a great democracy that should offer every citizen the same opportunities regardless of race or gender. This was the most important change he was seeking and the one that would prove impossible for him to achieve while he was living in the South. The antebellum myth was so pervasive and so ingrained that he was seen as a Southerner criticizing his home and his own people. The leaders saw him as a threat and so tried to bring him down, while those who were taken in by the myth took it as criticism of their society. He could have acquiesced and gone along with the myth, though, like his father, it was not in his nature to accept something he knew to be wrong. So he moved.

Page was better off living in the North for a number of reasons. He was much more effective trying to change from outside as he was seen as less threatening, though more importantly he was a source of pride to Southerners, which gave him credibility, and was less likely to be criticized. Also, it was less stressful as he was physically removed from the criticism, and he was able to keep a better perspective on the problems he wanted to change. Additionally, it was much better for him professionally. Career opportunities were very limited for him in the South, even more so after he decided to move into magazines. New York publishing had a national approach unlike any other city. So Page was in the unusual position of being the most ambitious of the progressive New South advocates, wanting to fundamentally change the culture of the South, though being more effective by not living there.

In April 1883, when Page was living in New York for the first time, he gave a speech in Boston on "The New South as Seen by a Southerner" which captured the way he thought the South's future would pan out if the people changed their culture in the way he hoped (as reported by the *Boston Post*): "If this generation or the next, with the misfortune that are its inheritance, by the ambition that also is its birthright, from the ruins of an aristocracy and from the barrenness of ignorant citizenship and kindred prejudices, builds progressive States, it will be the strongest proof yet given of the steadfastness of our institutions and the noblest achievement of republicanism."

On the crucial question of how Southerners saw themselves fitting into the Union, he claimed, "Do they love their State more than they do the Union? Indeed they do. And State pride, being now forever made harmless against the Union, is a fine old virtue." Tellingly in the context of how his own life would pan out, Page went on to talk about the attitude of expatriates like himself toward their native region when he said: "And in this homeless age, when a man is most at home away from it, it is a pleasant idiosyncrasy." Page seemed ambivalent about whether he loved his state more than the Union, though he later was convinced that Southerners, himself included, should think of themselves as Americans first and Southerners second.[40]

It is unlikely Page ever thought of himself as a Northerner and was frustrated by their ignorance of the South. Some years after moving there he asked his friend Daniels: "Can you tell me how we can give the cultivated, progressive Northerner the truth about the South? He knows all about South America, the topography of the Transvaal, the possibilities of Alaska, but about the South he is densely ignorant. How can we reach that sort of man? He can read Greek, his knowledge is greater than ours, his information more varied, and yet he needs a missionary to tell him about the South and how can the missionary get his ear? It would do him good in every way to know about us, and if he knows the truth he would do the South good. How can he be reached?"[41]

Despite this, he was well entrenched in the North and had developed strong professional and social networks. As a successful New Yorker, he was asked and expected to join numerous organizations that he generally enjoyed, though he found them expensive. In April 1907 he lamented in his diary the expense of paying membership fees to the Arts Club, Barnard Club, Armstrong Association, Civil Service Association, North Carolina Society, Johns Hopkins Alumni, and about five other clubs that taxed "a man's public spirit and his—purse." He was continually declining election to more and called it "the decent blackmail of urban life." Regardless, he dismissed thoughts of getting rid of "the really useless ones" so he could afford a vacation, in case one of his good friends thought him "niggardly."[42]

Page's diary of May 16, 1907, gives great insights into his relationship with the South after over twenty years of standing up to the mythmakers. He had been asked to be a member of the Jeanes Fund board, which had been established with a million dollars to help primary schools for African Americans, though he hesitated. He felt it would make him unpopular, and the criticism was getting to him: "It is unpopular yet in the South to be too thoroughly identified with Negro education; and I do sometimes become tired of the constant and senseless criticism directed against men who try to help the Negro." His other concern was not being seen as an American: "I do not like to be regarded as a sort of 'professional' Southern 'reformer.' I am an American citizen, and not merely a 'Southerner.'" Despite these concerns he saw a great opportunity, and a duty, to be of service and so agreed to join the board.[43]

Ellen Glasgow was one of the first authors to reject the antebellum myth. On Page's advice she wrote a series of novels portraying Virginia's Civil War and postbellum social and political turmoil, and these novels focused on the reality of her characters' lives. Also unusual for a Southern writer, Glasgow espoused democratic values and rejected societal restrictions on women's independence, growth, and education. These were similar themes and ideas to those espoused by Page, who encouraged her all the way. They were extremely radical for the time when there was overwhelming pressure to conform, as she recognized decades later: "More than thirty years ago, I began my literary work as a rebel against conventions. I am still a rebel, but the conventions are different."[44]

It is likely Page's feelings toward the South were exposed in his only novel, *The Southerner*. Published in 1909, it was ostensibly a story about the life of the fictious Nicholas Worth, though his experiences often bore a close resemblance to Page's. The book was a means for Page to get his message across, to express his feelings about the South and how they drove his desire for change.

Describing how Worth felt when he returned after graduating from university in the North, which had been his first time leaving the South, there was a sense of hopelessness and waste. Dismayed, Worth thought how very different the South was compared with the North: "I had forgotten the neglected homes visible from the [railroad] cars, the cabins about which half-naked Negro children played and from which ragged men and women, drunk with idleness, stared at the train, the ill-kept railway stations where crowds of loafers stood with their hands in their pockets and spat at cracks in the platform, unkempt countrymen, heavy with dyspepsia and malaria, idle Negroes, and village loafers." Soon though, he began to feel at home and his sense of pride and affection took over: "I recalled my own impassioned description of the old red hills and of the pine barrens. 'They once bred men; they shall breed men again.' And at last a sort of patient pride swelled up in me that I, too, was a part of this land, had roots deep in it, felt it, knew it, understood it, believed in it as men who had come into life elsewhere could not." This gets to the nub of what drove Page— he wanted a homeland of which he and all Southerners could be proud, where everyone had the opportunity to achieve their potential.

Continuing his journey, Worth arrived in the capital and observed from his hotel window "a Negro boy spinning a top and five white men standing about him, resting heavily on their own trousers' pockets." He found the scene, which was "unchanged and unchangeable," both amusing and depressing. He had become "two men—one who knew this scene and contentedly took it for granted, and another to whom it now came as a revelation of despair." It is likely this is how Page felt when he returned to, and even thought about, his home. He remembered what he learned from his grandfather about the South before it came to be defined by slavery: actively part of the Union, positive, and full of promise.

Worth's creed poetically expressed how Page felt about the South and its potential: "I believe in this land—our land—whose infinite variety of beauty and riches we do not yet know. Wake up, old Land! I believe in these people—our people—whose development may be illimitable. Wake up, my People! I believe in the continuous improvement of human society, in the immortality of our democracy, in the rightmindedness of the masses. Wake up, old Commonwealth!"

Worth articulated the attitude that impeded Southerners' thinking and development: "When I hold an opinion that differs from the dominant formula, I am asked if I have forgotten that I am a 'Southerner.'" It was "this self-conscious 'Southerner' that must become a part of every public Southerner's self" that was deterring good people from the South from entering public life. It had driven Page from the South when he was editor of the *State Chronicle* and was a factor in keeping him away; he only had the freedom to be himself, to achieve great things, when he was away from the restrictive thinking that he was trying to change. Page believed the attitude of Northerners was also holding Southerners' back: "If you, you who live in New England in particular, would regard us who now live and work in these Southern Commonwealths as citizens of the Republic, your regarding us so would help to make us so. So long as we are regarded as a problem we must play the part of a problem, whether we will or no." This was the concern Page raised in his 1907 diary, though he had landed in the ideal position. As a Southerner speaking to a national audience from the North, he could simultaneously address the attitudes of people from both sections. He took advantage of this position to push for more change, across a broader range of issues, than any of his fellow progressive New South advocates, especially on racial equality.[45]

\ 4 /
RACIAL EQUALITY
STANDING UP TO THE "RACE-PROBLEM" MYTH

THE "RACE-PROBLEM" MYTH

It was widely accepted throughout the nation, especially in the South, that there was a "Southern problem," "race problem" or "Negro problem." This became increasingly prevalent over Page's lifetime and fundamentally changed the lives of Southerners. It was based on the premise of racial superiority: that African Americans were a problem, and that either they constituted a burden because they were illiterate and unskilled or, more insidiously, that there was a threat of them overwhelming or even attacking the white population. In a 1903 speech, Senator Benjamin R. Tillman of South Carolina said educating African Americans was more than a waste of time and money; it was dangerous. He believed the "race question" involved "the most complex, the most difficult, the most dangerous of all the questions which confront this Republic." Similar arguments were used by the next generation. Tom Heflin of Alabama, before the start of what would be a long political career, stated in 1901: "The negroes are being educated very rapidly, and I say in the light of all the history of the past, some day when the two separate and distinct races are thrown together, some day the clash will come and the survival of the fittest, and I do not believe it is incumbent upon us to lift him up and educate him and put him on an equal footing that he may be armed and equipped when the combat comes."[1]

Page accepted that there was a problem, but he did not accept that there needed to be a problem. If everyone were treated equally regardless of race, there was no reason why African Americans should remain disadvantaged in the long term, especially if there was widespread education and economic development. If there was any "race problem," it was the fault of white people. At the *St. Joseph Daily Gazette* in 1880 he argued slavery and the attitudes of former slave owners caused the problems facing the South, while the former slaves had been "working quietly along solving unconsciously the problem that vexed the wise so sorely." Mocking the idea of a physical or political threat, he later stated that the real racial problem was the ongoing fear campaigns by politicians who raised the specter of "Negro domination" and "Negro supremacy" whenever they were challenged: "The race-politician will never bring peace; he can only hinder it." He knew the idea that there was a "race problem" was a myth (though he did not use the actual word); it was perpetuated by existing and aspiring Southern leaders to gain and retain power. As their antebellum myth had lost its potency, they had successfully replaced it with the race-problem myth.[2]

The race-problem myth was significantly harder to defeat than the antebellum myth because it played on the racism, both latent and overt, of white people all over America. After 1890 a number of eminent writers used statistics to prove that African Americans were impeding Southern development and blamed them for their own predicament. These included Alfred H. Stone, Walter F. Willcox, Frederick L. Hoffman, and Raymond Pearl. Most of the progressive New South advocates who played a significant part in defeating the antebellum myth were racist. Aycock was a white supremist and assisted Senator F. M. Simmons in leading the push to disenfranchise African Americans in North Carolina. Josephus Daniels, who himself believed in white superiority, related how Page accused his friends Alderman and McIver of "Southern prejudice" when they refused to eat with Booker T. Washington and another African American, even though Page had invited them all to lunch in New York. Clarence H. Poe, an influential North Carolina newspaper editor and great supporter of Page in the education campaign and personally, advocated segregation of farming areas in the state.[3]

In the North, where most people would have dismissed the antebellum myth as a Southern quirk, racism was common. In 1892 the Nineteenth Century Club organized a debate on race relations between a Southerner and a Northerner and they were to be both white. Page convinced them the "opposing side" should be an African American, though not only did he have difficulty finding nonracist accommodation in New York, he also didn't invite the speaker to his house to eat as his wife had "a lingering race-prejudice in such matters." In contrast, his attitude was that he had "eaten and lived with 'em" all his life, so would have liked "nothing better." In 1896 he met Washington in Boston and invited him to dinner in a hotel. It was not so easy for the president. In October 1901 Roosevelt dined with Washington at the White House. It caused such outrage in Southern newspapers and from politicians that the president, despite denying he would be influenced by such behavior, did not do it again.[4]

This exemplifies the forces Page was up against. Because the race-problem myth was less parochial than the antebellum myth, it was more resilient and much more difficult to defeat. Page didn't fully appreciate how difficult it would be, though even if he had it wouldn't have stopped him from trying.

TRYING TO DEFEAT THE MYTH

Literally believing that everyone should be treated equally, Page didn't support the Civil Rights Enactment, which in 1884 had been declared unconstitutional by the Supreme Court, nor the Republican's civil rights policy of the 1884 presidential campaign: "The effect of the law was really to give a black man an advantage that men of no other race enjoyed." Not appreciating how potent the race-problem myth was, he thought African Americans would be more successful if they focused on improving themselves through education and contributing to society as individuals, rather than trying to obtain equal rights as a race. He made this point a number of times in the *State Chronicle*, such as in September 1883 when he wrote: "If the Negro insists upon consolidating his race as a race instead of accepting in an individual way his place as a citizen, the race problem will be made grievously worse." Instead: "What they need most to do for themselves is to work slowly and hard for their elevation and improvement precisely as white men or any other men work." Although this tragically turned out to be naive, it was consistent with his belief in equality.[5]

In the *State Chronicle* Page rarely published articles advocating racial equality. He knew he could lose a lot of readers and diminish the opportunity to sell his positive messages on education and development. Trying to be a subtle influence, he carefully expressed his opinions in a few articles. An article on abolition of segregation in New York City schools was headed "They Are Welcome," and another, "A Terrible Warning," argued that African Americans were not violent by nature, though they were sometimes provoked by white people. After moving North he became less circumspect and more directly tried to increase understanding of African Americans. Seminal examples at the *Atlantic Monthly* were "The Awakenings of the Negro" by Washington and "Strivings of the Negro People" by W. E. Burghardt Du Bois. The *World's Work* published significantly more articles about African Americans than any other major magazine. This was by far the most frequently covered Southern topic in the *World's Work*, and the authors of most of them were African American: Washington, Du Bois, and Robert R. Moton.[6]

In May 1901 Page published an insightful article by Du Bois, professor of economics and history at Atlanta University, "The Negro As He Really Is." Du

Bois visited and wrote about Albany, a town two hundred miles south of Atlanta "in the heart of the Black Belt" segregated by its broad main street, with "whites usually to the north, and blacks to the south." He aimed to increase Americans' understanding of African Americans, "their daily lives and longings, of their homely joys and sorrows, of their real shortcomings and the meaning of their crimes." Du Bois was very clear about their predicament; though they lived in a resource-rich region where cotton had made many people very wealthy, African Americans lived in appalling conditions, worked hard for little reward, and were often in perpetual debt. Individuals lived in cabins that were the same as the slaves,' while families lived mostly in sparsely furnished homes of one or two rooms. Few owned a home or farm; they effectively existed as serfs. The greatest problem was ignorance. Du Bois's message was that despite their ignorance and poverty, an African American was a person just like every other American with hopes for the future, and "looks in vague and awful longing at the grim horizon of its life—all this, even as you and I."[7]

Daniels noted that Page was "the first journalist born in the South who took a cosmopolitan position with reference to the Negro," for example adopting the unusual practice of showing respect for African Americans by using an upper-case "N" for "Negro." This was also advocated by Washington, who in 1911 wrote to the editor of the New York *Evening Post* forcefully, though unsuccessfully, requesting the newspaper adopt the practice. In some ways, Page was a man of his time. After he moved North he frequently told what he called "nigger stories." Concerned about his audience of New Englanders being "somewhat solemn" at an alumni dinner in Durham, New Hampshire, he wrote in his diary, "I, therefore, told two or three old nigger stories. The crowd roared." At the *Atlantic Monthly*, his colleague Frank Garrison, son of prominent abolitionist William Lloyd Garrison, supported equality for African Americans and was annoyed by Page's stories, though it's likely Page used them to break down the stuffiness of the Houghton, Mifflin offices. When Page first said "nigger," a former colleague recalled, Garrison admonished him: "Mr. Page, we have never used that word in this office," to which Page responded, "Well, we do now." Despite this difference, the two men often talked about racial issues. Page could not understand the attitude of many Northerners, like Garrison, who did not transfer their support for equality to other races. Isaac Marcosson believed Page "did more for the real advancement of the coloured man than half a dozen decades of New England 'sympathy with the black man.'" Page believed in people as people regardless of race and struggled to understand the vast majority who thought differently, and he likely thought everyone of any race or nationality was fair game for "stories"—jokes or ridicule in the right spirit.[8]

When Page wanted to promote understanding on an important issue, he often advocated research so that the facts could tell the story. In his speech at the inauguration of University of North Carolina president George T. Winston in October 1891, Page suggested establishment of a *seminarium* of social science," aimed at improving the lives of African Americans through wide-ranging research into their sociology and problems. In January 1892 President Winston announced it would probably be set up in the form of a chair of social science though it did not proceed, and the university's Department of Sociology was not established until 1920. If it had gone ahead, it would have been one of the first such positions in an American university.[9]

RACIAL VIOLENCE

Throughout his editorial career, Page generally tried to be positive, even regarding violence. This was particularly true at the *State Chronicle* where, unlike other North Carolinian newspapers, he virtually never reported lynchings, other murders, or any other violence. It would have undermined his message of positivity: he wanted locals to feel good about their state and contribute to its development, and to encourage investment and migration into the state. Further, he believed that to report lynching would merely serve to encourage others, writing in 1903: "Men are lynched for an increasing number of crimes, for lynchings spread by example. One suggests another." He hoped that as the state developed and society became more civilized the number of race-related barbaric and murderous acts would decline.[10]

After moving to the North, Page was more direct in criticizing racial violence, though he tried to remain positive. As *Forum* editor the only article to which he put his name was an appeal to a sense of community to end lynching, "The Last Hold of the Southern Bully." Using a typical Southern town to expose this "grave social danger," he argued a whole "pleasant county-town of comfortable homes and intelligent and kindly people" is demoralized by lynching, as "acquiescence is surrender." Even worse was the danger to civilization itself if both races went "down to the vengeance-taking level." People needed to respect the institutions underpinning society and "fortify us against the vengeance-taking temper of the savage." Turning the tables, the "bully" is called a "savage," a derogatory term used against African Americans. He wanted businesses, newspapers, churches, and political parties to publicly state their opposition.

Then "public sentiment would soon actively shape itself into such condemnation of mob-violence that it would cease."[11]

Page was doing what he had done at the *State Chronicle*: He did not launch an all-out attack on lynching, knowing it would be ineffective in trying to change public opinion. By focusing on the impact on community morale and calling on their leaders to step up, he was trying to end the practice in the most effective way he knew. Newspapers' reactions were mixed. Virginia's *Richmond Dispatch* agreed with Page's arguments, though it stated they were not new, and the article would alienate the average Southerner. Another Southern newspaper, the *Atlanta Constitution*, had a lengthy article denying the existence of the "Southern Bully"; Southerners were fundamentally kind, which was why crime rates were higher in the North, and the South needed to be defended from Page's "slanderous assertions concerning its morals." By contrast, in the North the *Indianapolis Journal* published a positive summary of Page's argument.[12]

By the beginning of the 1900s, Page was still advocating civilization and enlightenment as the long-term solution to lynching, though he had given up on it working in the short-term and believed the law had to take drastic action. After an African American was horrifically murdered by "a mob of 2,000 persons" in Winchester, Tennessee, in 1901, he was pleased that many sheriffs were firing on or threatening to fire on such mobs. In Wetumpka, Alabama, lynchers had been handed life sentences, and Page made his opinion very clear: "The only way to get rid of that type of man and of his demoralizing influences on ignorant communities is the Alabama way of sending him to the penitentiary and not the South Carolinian way of sending him to the United States Senate."

In the first half of 1903 there had been about fifty lynching deaths, almost all involving African Americans, and Page had given up on a legal solution as it would require commitment throughout the system, from juries to prosecuting attorneys, and this had not been evident in the past. Further, Page's assessment was that a man was a different person while in a mob compared with as an individual. So "as soon as a mob that has killed a prisoner has dispersed, the real murderer is gone." He concluded that it was a problem affecting the whole nation and encouraged everyone to support the people in the South who were standing up to the criminals and mobs. He had lost confidence in the solution he proposed a decade earlier, when he hoped the growth of civilizing influences would end the murderous practice. Consequently, he reluctantly supported sheriffs and other law enforcement officers using lethal force against violent mobs. Again, Page underestimated the pervasiveness of the race-problem myth, as many Southern leaders were doing all they could to encourage lynching.[13]

DISENFRANCHISED AND SEGREGATED

After the Compromise of 1877, local governments in Southern states implemented various means of preventing African Americans from voting. In the *State Chronicle* Page exposed how this was happening in North Carolina. Then, starting with Mississippi in 1890 and ending with Oklahoma in 1910, twelve Southern state governments enacted measures to formalize disenfranchisement. Literacy tests and property ownership were the two most common methods. Concern was raised that vast numbers of illiterate, poor white people, some of whom had fought for the Confederacy, would be disenfranchised, so various amendments were tried unsuccessfully until the "grandfather clause" was agreed upon at the Louisiana convention and became the template for the other states. This allowed someone to vote if they, their father, or grandfather was eligible to vote on January 1, 1867. Page opposed the "grandfather" clauses because they were racist. He approved of preventing illiterate people from voting or a "tax-paying qualification," as with Massachusetts, which had both. Like Page, Washington and J. L. M. Curry, a fellow education campaigner, believed in such restrictions on voting that applied to both races.[14]

There was not united support for disenfranchisement. Some states had whites-only conventions on disenfranchisement constitutional amendments, and the minutes reveal considerable angst and concern among the delegates. Newspapers were often hostile; in Mississippi virtually all the leading newspapers, and many others, opposed the new constitution. Fearing it would not be accepted by the people, the Mississippi convention decided to ratify it themselves, so the amendments were never voted on by the electorate, a precedent followed by all other states except Alabama. In this state, as Page grimly explained in the *World's Work*, the previous governor, Democrat Joseph F. Johnston, stated that the majority of white people voted against the amendment and that it only passed due to widespread electoral fraud. This supports claims made regularly by Page in the early years of the *World's Work* that disenfranchisement did not have the support of the majority of white people. After disenfranchisement there was a campaign of repression against those still advocating for equality, even subjecting some to violent attacks, until ultimately the Solid South prevailed.[15]

Relations between the races deteriorated dramatically as a caste system evolved that led to segregation. From February to March 1899 Page made an extensive tour of the South to examine the racial situation, especially the position of African Americans. He was astonished by the extent of segregation—for example, in New Orleans, African Americans were banned from the main public library, even if they were university professors. The way they were treated outraged and frustrated him: "You know, it has all come over me that we are dealing with a case of caste, pure and simple—just as Telang has in India."[16]

In February 1901, Page wrote a highly critical assessment of democracy in the states where African Americans had been disenfranchised. It was a structural change in Southern politics that would not be reversed for a very long time, as it was "the definite and final and deliberate action of the dominant Southern sentiment." Political change was not going to come from within the South; it needed to come from external encouragement or pressure, and he was doing what he could. Later that year he lamented race relations had deteriorated over the previous decade, though he remained confident the problem would be overwhelmed by the industrial development and training that was taking place in the South. Page was continuing to be too optimistic because, and though these improvements were factors in the demise of the antebellum myth, he underestimated the extent to which the race-problem myth had become entrenched.[17]

In October 1902, Page's hopes of a move toward racial equality were finally dashed when the North Carolina Republicans excluded African Americans from their convention: "The elimination of the Negro from politics has been somewhat more than tacitly approved—it has been applauded—by the Republican State convention in North Carolina." He was particularly disappointed because disenfranchisement and segregation now dominated the less racist political party in one of the least racist Southern states. By the end of the year African Americans had been excluded from Republican conventions in several other states, and the rest of the South would soon follow. It was the inevitable outcome of disenfranchisement and was effectively the end of African Americans' involvement in Southern politics: "There is nothing left for the Negroes to do but to refrain from political activity or to make a political party of their own." He overoptimistically thought that they would "reappear in politics" as they became educated and accumulated wealth and so could vote.[18]

Page wrote no more sympathetic and touching editorial on the predicament of African Americans than in January 1903. President Roosevelt had proposed an African American as Collector of the Port of Charleston, South Carolina, leading to a widespread public outcry. Page was no longer his optimistic self, accepting public opinion had turned: "White public sentiment in the South almost unanimously declares that a black man's skin should debar him, that such an elevation of a Negro disturbs the whole social and political status of Southern society, that it encourages 'Negro supremacy,' and that it gives the support of the Federal Government to a principle that Southern society will never admit." On the other side, the president had made it clear he would not discriminate between American citizens by skin color. African Americans could only hope that eventually "a humaner [*sic*] and more tolerant public opinion prevails among the Southern whites." In the meantime, "there is no more pathetic figure in modern life than the educated and capable Negro of high character. He has the white man's civilization, and he has the white man's responsibilities as a citizen; but he may not, in the dominant Southern opinion, indulge in the white man's aspirations nor open doors of opportunity that to the white man are flung wide. The National Government is his only political hope." It would be a forlorn hope.[19]

Page was particularly disappointed that segregation was happening when Southern prosperity was generally increasing. In March 1903 he editorialized that people from the two races were increasingly working in jobs together, African Americans were buying property, becoming influential in their communities, and state government support for their education was the highest it had ever been. He believed industry and education, and the resulting personal relationships, would overcome the political controversy that was setting the race and sections against one another. Page lamented that the controversy was holding Southerners back: they were overwhelmed by the "Negro problem." Young people were missing out on being part of the most dramatic industrial growth of any country in history, while the productivity and morale of even the hardest-working and smartest people was reduced as they were isolated from the "stimulus of a strong national feeling." He hoped the next generation could solve the problem; maybe even by then it would have worked itself out. Page was clearly confused and frustrated by such a tragic outcome.[20]

In June 1903, after a U.S. Supreme Court ruling effectively legalized disenfranchisement, Page postulated that the only solution was military force. John S. Mill had also recommended this at the start of the Reconstruction period. Slavery's legacy had held back the South since the Civil War, as he explained in his 1883 speech, and the same thing was happening again in 1903. In their quest to retain power the Southern leaders had replaced the antebellum myth with the race-problem myth.[21]

In 1907 Page had another long Southern tour and was pleased with progress in most areas, the significant exception being the plight of African Americans, which remained abysmal, and he could only see further decline. His despair was captured in letters to Alice in February 1907: "They will not train him fast enough, nor tolerate him untrained. He will disappear faster

& faster." A few days later he wrote: "I don't know where he'll go; but he will never be given a fair chance and he will get the worst of the economic pressure." Consequently, he editorialized less and less in the *World's Work* about disenfranchisement and segregation, and in his final years as editor barely mentioned the topics at all. By April 1909 African Americans, largely resigned to their fate, were focusing on improving themselves and their prospects as a race. Always trying to be positive, Page wrote, "Race friction has apparently passed into the stage of work and toleration; and good men of both races are to be thanked for it."[22]

Page continued to publish articles by African Americans, especially Washington and Du Bois. In May 1909 Du Bois wrote about their success in creating a large pool of savings and property investments, though he lamented the lack of a savings bank for the race. Like Page, it seemed Du Bois had reluctantly accepted segregation and was making the best of it. Washington had numerous articles, including "How to Help Men with Most Money—Educate Six Million Negro Children" in June 1910 and a year later compared Denmark's rural high schools with African American schools. He contrasted the way they integrated with the rest of the education system, unlike in America. Most significant was a series of six articles, from October 1910 to March 1911, forming the continuation of his autobiography, *Up from Slavery*.[23]

ACADEMIC FREEDOM AND THE RACE-PROBLEM MYTH

In July 1902 the Reverend Andrew Sledd, a professor at Methodist Church–owned Emory College, Atlanta, wrote an article in the *Atlantic Monthly* stating that African Americans, though an inferior race, had certain "inalienable" and "fundamental" rights and should not be discriminated against because of their color. He went on to be extremely critical of lynching, saying the state of mind that allowed such a practice to persist was a blight on all Southerners, and in the process denied the accepted defense that it was necessary to protect white women from attacks by African American men. While similar critiques of lynching previously made by Northerners had been ignored, Sledd's article was savagely attacked by W. H. Felton, an influential and powerful Georgian whose husband was a federal and state politician. After an outcry from some newspapers and leaders, the college forced Sledd to resign. Page was appalled. Although he did not agree with all Sledd's opinions, he passionately supported his right to express them; public opinion in Georgia, including a "shrieking ghost of a dead era" as he referred indirectly to Felton, should not determine an academic's employment.

Page suggested a member of the college board should have had the courage to stand up and say, "We can listen to temporary and local clamor, made by persons who have not perhaps even read Mr. Sledd's article, and we can dismiss him; or we can pay no attention to it. If we pay no heed to it, we may lose a few students this year—a very slight loss, and we shall keep the respect of the whole academic world. But, if we dismiss him for this reason, we shall do the college an irreparable injury; for our action will be interpreted as notice that we do not wish freedom of opinion here." Other Northern magazines were also critical of Sledd's treatment.[24]

Sledd left the South and in late August, as he was preparing to leave, wrote "I want to get away, I feel alien and wronged. I am cramped and stunted by the atmosphere that prevails. I had thought to be able to bring about a better state of things; but the people and the College will have none of it." Page had had similar feelings when he left the South almost twenty years earlier. By contrast with Page, Sledd returned to the South soon after leaving, though never again writing an article on racial issues. By working in the North, Page could not be reached by those perpetuating the myths, so unlike Sledd he was not at risk of losing his job and being silenced.[25]

Always trying to dispel the race-problem myth by greater understanding, in response to Sledd's treatment Page suggested a Southern college or university undertake a "scientific investigation." It would involve asking African Americans about their property ownership and education and the impact of these factors on their family life and place in the community. He believed this would be immensely valuable "for the Negro himself and for the ruling class and for all students of the race problem." Page was keen for such work to be done by students as in a few years they would be influential in the South. He noted similar work had been started by Du Bois at Atlanta University and also at conferences of African Americans in Tuskegee and Atlanta.[26]

In October 1903 John S. Bassett, a history professor at Trinity College, North Carolina, wrote an editorial in the *South Atlantic Quarterly*, a journal he had founded in 1901, stating that racism had got worse over the previous five years. It was and had "been for a long time a political matter" and was due to "the contempt of the white man for the negro." Bassett declared Washington to be the "greatest man, save General Lee, born in the South in a hundred years." Led by Josephus Daniels, who by then was editor of North Carolina's leading newspaper, the *News and Observer*, Bassett was widely attacked by Southern newspapers for placing an African American on so high a pedestal; some demanded he be fired.

Page was furious, writing in a letter that it was "simply the cry of prejudice—a blind howl by those who think they can rule North Carolina and do gross injustice to men who differ with them—by simply howling 'Nigger.'" Bassett did offer to resign, though the administration and faculty refused to accept, a decision that made Page so happy he said it extended his life by ten years. He greatly regretted not having been part of the fight as the pleasure of this victory would have been the greatest of his career. In January 1904 Page published his version of this "notable victory" as the leading article in the *World's Work*. As a nationalist keen to bring the sections together, he wanted people living in the North to be aware of this positive development in the South. Although not mentioning Daniels by name, Page did not hold back when describing his former friend's role, saying his newspaper was full of "appeals to sectionalism, partisanship, religious bigotry, and personal enmities." Most other North Carolinian newspapers followed, "and they indulged in vituperation, invective, and scurrility not surpassed since the days of reconstruction." Page stated it was Senator F. M. Simmons, "the political source of Negro disfranchisement," and most of the Methodist clergy who demanded Bassett be dismissed. It was board members from business and industry, "the men who are moving forward," who voted against accepting Bassett's resignation. Page's anger remained in 1912 when he referred to the newspapers' behavior as an "inquisition" led by Daniels as its "vicious mouthpiece."[27]

EDUCATION AND RACIAL EQUALITY

In his October 1881 article "The Southern Educational Problem" Page approved of racial separation in schools as "manual labor" was most suited for African Americans. This was one area where Page changed his opinion. Later, such as in his 1902 article "The Rebuilding of Old Commonwealths," published in the *Atlantic Monthly*, he intentionally did not distinguish between the races. In 1903, Charles Dabney noted, Page appeared to indicate that white people should have priority, though it's likely he was being pragmatic. Page's priority was to get a public school system established in the South and judged that advocating for equality would stymie any progress. Similarly, he was a great supporter of colleges for African Americans, because otherwise they would be unlikely to get an education, and certainly not one of such quality. While he eventually accepted the inevitability of it being segregated, he was one of the few education campaigners who spoke out against it. In *The Southerner*, published in 1909, he made his position clear: "In any proper scheme of education, there are no white men, no black men—only men."[28]

Washington was one of the people Page most admired; they had very similar views on racial equality and the best ways for it to be achieved, most significantly through education. Washington was principal of the Tuskegee Normal and Industrial Institute in Alabama. In a letter to Alice he enthused that it taught African Americans practical skills in a way Page felt constituted a "level of academic achievement." In 1899 Page referred to Washington as "by far the greatest constructive mind his race has produced, & one of the most useful men now alive. *His institution could be spared less well than any university or school of any sort that we have in America.*" On December 4, 1899, at a fundraiser for Tuskegee in the Madison Square Garden concert hall, Page was the first speaker and, as reported in the *New York Tribune*, "spoke at length on the needs of the institute and the condition of the black race." In the same month he arranged to publish Washington's autobiography, even though it had not been written and Doubleday, Page & Co. had not opened its doors. *Up from Slavery* was published by Page in 1901.[29]

Washington was the *World's Work*'s second-most prolific author on Southern issues (just behind Page himself, and triple the next author). The most prolific authors were Page (13 articles), Washington (12), Poe (4), Edwin Mims (4), Du Bois (3) and Moton (3). Washington's July 1901 article "The Salvation of the Negro" praised achievements of the Hampton Normal and Agricultural Institute, Virginia, which had been established to train young African Americans "to meet conditions as they existed in the South." The aim was to change the way the freed slaves thought about manual labor; now they were no longer "being worked" it could be possible for them to value "working." During the month Page spoke at a function in New York to raise funds for Hampton.[30]

With African Americans disenfranchised in the South, Page could see no other solution other than his long-held belief that for democracy to function the people must be educated: "The problem is to make a democracy possible there. That task can be done only in one way, and that way is to train the people to a higher level of economic life. There is no other radical solution. A democracy must be based on economic efficiency and general intelligence. It cannot be superimposed on ignorant masses. The foremost patriotic duty of our time, therefore, is to educate the southern masses of both races to economic efficiency."[31]

Page passionately argued for racial equality in education in a widely acclaimed speech to the 1904 Conference for Education in the South in Birmingham, Alabama. Before his speech Page asked "heads of several Negro schools" to compare pupils' incomes before and after training. Washington provided the responses of a few schools showing that trained workers were earning significantly higher wages. Page argued: "Now in the face of such facts, any able-minded Negro who does not train himself is a fool; for there is a greater economic difference between an income of 70 cents and $2.50 per day than there is between $3,000 a year and $30,000. Now if a Negro be a fool not to train himself, what shall be said of a white man? He, too, is a fool."[32]

Addressing the widespread notion that if everyone was trained there would be no one to do the menial tasks, in this speech Page explained how a trained man is more likely to be innovative: "A trained man would drive his scoop to your dirt, attach it to an electric wire and shovel your dirt more accurately, more quickly, more cheaply than any Negro in Alabama can do it." Such thinking, he said, had revolutionized industries from shoemaking in towns to iron-ore mining on Lake Superior. And the benefits had spread throughout the community as work is done more cheaply and workers have higher wages to spend in other businesses.

Page then led his audience to the next logical step: a public education system funded by the community because the community would reap the benefits, which went beyond economic. It would solve most of the South's social problems—Page noting it was rare for there to be racial tension between well-trained people—and strengthen democracy: "In an untrained democracy low minds will lead, and an organized howl will lift demagogues to power." Page concluded with a new declaration of rights that included the statement: "We hold these truths to be self-evident; that all men should have equality of opportunity; that they are endowed by our institutions with inalienable rights; and that among these are free training and free opinion." It was a radical as well as a powerful speech: a passionate plea to use proven means to give African Americans the opportunity to improve their lives.[33]

Page (*right*) with Wilbur F. Tillett (*left*) and John B. Wardlaw, his two closest friends at Randolph-Macon College, in 1875. His extensive discussions with them, especially with Wardlaw on developing the South, had a lasting impact on Page.

From Hendrick, *Earlier Life and Letters*, reproduced by Rebecca Freeburn.

Willia Alice Wilson in 1879, the year before her marriage to Walter.

From Hendrick, *Earlier Life and Letters*, reproduced by Rebecca Freeburn.

U.S. Electric Light Company exhibit, provider of lighting at the North Carolina Exposition, 1884. Many North Carolinians saw electricity in operation for the first time at the exposition, which Page initiated and heavily promoted in the *State Chronicle*.

Courtesy of the State Archives of North Carolina.

The Atlantic Monthly

FOR JULY

Will contain two articles of great interest and timeliness,
Arbitration and our Relations with England,
By Hon. E. J. Phelps, *ex-Minister to England, and*
Some Disappointments of Democracy,
Apropos of Mr. Lecky's newly published "Democracy and Liberty," by E. L. Godkin, *editor of* The Nation.

The fourth paper on Race Characteristics in American Life will discuss
The Germans and the German-Americans.

There will be further installments of
The Old Things, *by* Henry James,
Letters of D. G. Rossetti, *by* George Birkbeck Hill,
The Country of the Pointed Firs, *by* Sarah Orne Jewett,
A continuation of the delightful sketches of Maine life, which have appeared in previous issues under the same title.

The Atlantic is taking up
The Whole Subject of the Public Schools,
And the Practical Problems Presented by Them,
and is discussing them with first-hand information, in the way most directly helpful to the public and the teacher.

In this number will appear
The Confessions of Public School Teachers,
in which a number of superintendents, principals, and teachers, men and women, in different parts of the country, frankly tell their hindrances and disappointments, as well as their satisfactions, and point out the lessons of their own experience.

This group of confessions throws a direct and most instructive light on the actual work of schools and on the teachers' life.

The practical problems of public school work, the duty of the community, the methods of developing and strengthening the force of the teachers, will be discussed for the rest of the year.

Thirty-five cents a copy. $4.00 a year.
HOUGHTON, MIFFLIN & CO., Boston.

Advertisement in the *Atlantic Monthly* promoting articles based on a survey Page conducted of thousands of public school superintendents, principals, and teachers in early 1896.

Atlantic Monthly, June 1896, accessed through ProQuest.

Page as editor of the *Atlantic Monthly*, ca. 1899.

From Hendrick, *Earlier Life and Letters*, reproduced by Rebecca Freeburn.

Ellen Glasgow, who Page nurtured and mentored, was a great example of the strong friendships and professional relationships he had with his authors. Glasgow became one of America's best-known novelists and received a Pulitzer Prize in 1941.

World's Work, November 1902, p. 2793, reproduced by the State Library of Victoria.

"A Negro School Near Albany, Georgia: Where Children Go after 'Crops Are Laid By.'"
W. E. B. Du Bois, "The Negro As He Really Is," *World's Work*, May 1901, p. 851, reproduced by the State Library of Victoria.

"An 'Outdoor' Lesson in Arithmetic: Calculating Amount of Lumber Required and Cost of Construction of a Green-House" (Hampton Institute). This is the type of education Page and Booker T. Washington encouraged.

Washington, "The Salvation of the Negro," *World's Work*, July 1901, p. 968, reproduced by the State Library of Victoria.

THE WORLD'S WORK

SOUTHERN NUMBER

JUNE 1907

VOLUME XIV
NUMBER 2

The Arisen South

THE present industrial awakening in the Southern States is the most important economic event in our history since the settlement of the West. Go where you will, the people are building homes, schools, and roads, and in the cities business buildings and factories. "There is a crying need of more houses in this town"—a headline like this appears in most of the newspapers from Virginia to Texas. The trains are crowded with people. The railroads cannot haul the freight. On one day lately, 100 freight trains passed through the first capital of the Confederacy; and Montgomery is now a city of beautiful homes and modern business methods. The very streets of Mississippi River cities were filled with cotton last spring, for there were not enough boats and trains to move it. The income from the very cabbage and lettuce fields of South Carolina is greater than the revenue of the state was when it seceded. There are new hotels in most of the towns, and new and old alike are crowded. Several Southern States have commissioners of immigration in Europe seeking men. Emigration has stopped, and you may read in the newspapers of the Northwest advertisements for farmers to go South, where fertile lands and good markets await them.

A young man who inherited a farm in Georgia left it ten years ago and went to Atlanta, thence to New York. After a few years of successful work in New York, he went back to Atlanta; and now, after successful work in Atlanta, he is going to return to the farm. He has made every one of these moves along the line of the greatest profit.

The newspapers are prosperous; fine school-houses are replacing old and smaller ones. Thousands of farmers who used to be in debt now have cash in banks that did not exist five years ago. The people are cheerful and they look at life from a new angle.

The South has worked out three fundamental tasks which all the world may profit by:
(1) How to teach the farmer who is now on the land to double his crop;
(2) How to teach boys and girls practical trades while they are "getting their education";
(3) How to govern cities without politics and without graft.

Most of the old notions about the South and the Southern people that have been held in the North must now be revised; for every-day events contradict the conclusions that were drawn from facts of the past.

Most of the old notions likewise about the South and the Southern people that were formerly held by the Southern people themselves must now be revised; for every-day events contradict the conclusions that they also drew from the facts of the past. New economic forces are at work.

It is these changes that are explained and emphasized in this number of THE WORLD'S WORK, because there is nothing in our contemporaneous life more interesting or more important than this rise of the people in these states, eager to the task of their own development and of the development of this richest region of the Union. This work has now been begun with such vigor that it will go on indefinitely; for natural forces have come into play and the land of "problems" has become a land of progress.

Copyright, 1907, by Doubleday, Page & Co. All rights reserved.

Wallace Buttrick (*left*), Secretary of the General Education Board. Page's great friend and neighbor, with whom he regularly discussed "what more we could do for the happiness and well-being of our fellow-men."

From John D. Rockefeller, "Some Random Reminiscences of Men and Events," *World's Work*, April 1909, p. 11010, reproduced by the State Library of Victoria.

"Farmers Inspecting the College Demonstration Field at Athens, GA." The State College of Agriculture of Georgia practiced the successful demonstration techniques of Seaman A. Knapp, which transformed Southern agriculture. One of the previous year's graduates became a Demonstration Farm agent in an adjoining county.

From Edwin Mims, "The South Realizing Itself," *World's Work*, November 1911, p. 44, reproduced by the State Library of Victoria.

The hookworm exhibit at the North Carolina State Fair, 1911, part of the campaign by the Sanitary Commission for the Eradication of the Hookworm Disease. Initiated by Page, the campaign ran from 1909 to 1914 and was one of the most successful in Southern history.

From W. H. Page, "The Hookworm and Civilisation," *World's Work*, September 1912, p. 518, reproduced by the State Library of Victoria.

Arriving "home for a personal conference"; Page on board the S.S. *Philadelphia* upon arrival in New York, August 11, 1916. The visit turned out to be a disaster, and Page decided to resign as ambassador.

Published by Bain News Service, 1916, from the George Grantham Bain Collection, accessed through Library of Congress Prints and Photographs Online Catalog (source: Flickr Commons project, 2014). Quote from Page, letter to Wilson July 21, 1916, Page Papers.

Page in April 1917, the month America declared war on Germany.

From Hendrick, *Life and Letters*, vol. 2, reproduced by Rebecca Freeburn.

Ambassador Page (*left, standing*) giving a speech at Plymouth, England, on August 4, 1917, the third anniversary of the start of World War I.

Published by Bain News Service, 1917, from the George Grantham Bain Collection, accessed through Library of Congress Prints and Photographs Online Catalog (source: Flickr Commons project, 2015).

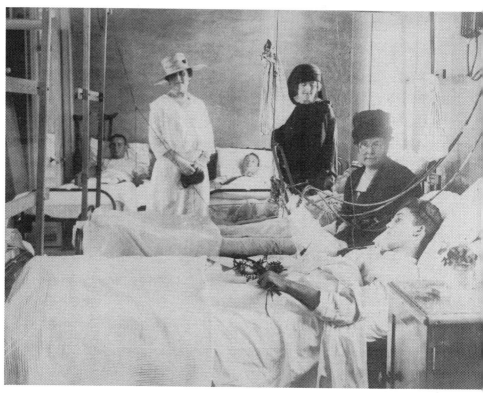

Alice visiting an American soldier with a wounded arm at Dartford Hospital, near London, 1918. Dartford and other large hospitals around London were regularly visited by "American woman members of the visiting committee of the A.R.C." Alice was a founder of the American Red Cross' London Chapter and had "a lot of friends among the men at Dartford, friends who will remember her visits all their lives."

Quoted and cited from the American Red Cross photograph collection, accessed through Library of Congress Prints and Photographs Online Catalog.

Alice saying farewell to convalescing American soldiers, in 1918: "The American wounded soldiers in the hospitals around London will lose one of their best friends in the departure for America of Mrs. Walter Hines Page, wife of the retiring American Ambassador." Alice was one of the most regular American Red Cross "Care Committee" members to visit soldiers at the American hospital in Dartford, near London.

Quoted and cited from the American Red Cross photograph collection, accessed through Library of Congress Prints and Photographs Online Catalog.

President Wilson and King George V outside Buckingham Palace, December 28, 1918. It was Wilson's sixty-second birthday and he was on the way to treaty negotiations at Versailles. Page wanted America to present this image to Europe when war was brewing in mid-1913, hoping that if Germany thought America would support Britain war could be avoided.

Courtesy of the Woodrow Wilson Presidential Library.

\ 5 /
THE FORGOTTEN MAN AND WOMAN
SOUTHERN EDUCATION WAS PAGE'S
LIFELONG PASSION

"THE SOUTHERN EDUCATIONAL PROBLEM"

Given the significant influence of education in Page's childhood, adolescence, and into his twenties, it was not surprising that, starting with those first articles sent from Germany in 1877, education was the dominant theme in his writing, and the focus of his speeches and extensive volunteer community service over many decades. Education had three interrelated benefits: giving people the knowledge and skills to achieve their potential; reviving democracy in the South by making voters more informed and circumventing disenfranchisement using literacy tests; and underpinning Southern economic, social, and cultural development.

The antebellum way of life mythologized by Southern leaders did not include public education. They did not want their positions, nor the prospects of their sons, threatened by an educated populace. The leaders discouraged debate on the issue, and there was little push from the people for education. Most Southerners lived on small family farms, and illiteracy rates were high. Children were needed to help on the farm, and sons were expected to follow in their fathers' footsteps and daughters to help in the home. There was a widespread belief the only education they needed was a practical one, and this was received at home and on the farm. So formal education was considered a waste of time. There was strong resistance to taxation for schools, especially a public school system to educate other peoples' children. Incomes were low and there was a strong sense of self-reliance, so education was seen as a private matter. The farmers were locked in a vicious cycle where they were continually working for their survival.

Page brought this debilitating problem to national attention in his October 1881 article "The Southern Educational Problem." Money was desperately needed, as well as a focus on systematic and practical approaches to education and training, and significantly greater public support. An article in a number of Northern newspapers, including the *Connecticut Western News*, stated Page showed "how far behind Northern ideas education has been at the South, but suggests better prospects for the future," though the response in the South indicated what he was up against. Misconstruing his argument, the *Charlotte Democrat* proclaimed Page had betrayed his roots: "It is an ill bird that befouls its own nest." It claimed to be shocked that a Southerner would "affirm, falsely, that the ignorance of the South is a contented ignorance" when they were doing all they could in straitened circumstances to "extend their common schools throughout all their borders, so that every one, black and white, may learn to read and write."[1]

Education was one of the major issues covered in the *State Chronicle*. Page often contacted educators and others asking opinions on their areas of expertise. Articles by himself and his correspondents were relentlessly positive, trying to undermine the antebellum myth and change attitudes by highlighting improvements in education across the state. On September 29, 1883, for example, his correspondent wrote about the region at the junction of Wake, Nash, Franklin, and Johnston counties: "In this section the people are giving more attention to education than ever before. In nearly every house you find during study hours children pondering over what seems to them complicated lessons, while the old folks are reading from good periodicals, (*The Chronicle* for instance) the news of the day." He subtly attacked the antebellum myth and prevailing antieducation culture of the state. On December 8, 1883, under the heading "A Mediaeval Heresy," he published a clipping from the *Goldsboro Bulletin*: "In conversation with a gentleman the other day he unhesitatingly announced himself as opposed to educating the masses; for, says he, 'educate a man and he will not do drudgery; he will feel himself above it.' This is gospel truth, every man will admit it." This was exactly the attitude Page argued was holding the state back.

Page delighted in presenting good news on education. On May 30, 1884, at La Grange Collegiate Institute, in Lenoir County, he gave the commencement address, one of the first of many he would give over his lifetime. The following week, the *State Chronicle*'s "correspondent" (almost certainly Page) enthused about schools being built in the county: "The people are king. Long live the people! And when the people of any community take a problem in hand it is quickly solved; and the building of schools in Lenoir county has proved it." The enthusiasm and support of the community for education was praised and the county had "common schools and High schools—where it had neither before; and so many and so flourishing are they that Lenoir claims to be the foremost county in the State in educational work."

Following in the steps of his grandfather, Page regularly encouraged agricultural education and innovation. While farmers should be "learning all they can from books," practical experience "is the best teacher." He was particularly pleased to hear about two agricultural clubs, the Montpelier Agricultural Club and the Pioneer Club. They had a maximum of twelve farmer members, with the aim of learning as much as possible from one another. Members' farms were evaluated in turn by other members, meetings were held at the farms, and the evaluators reported on what the other members could learn and supplied suggestions for improvements. The Montpelier Club even conducted experiments, like Anderson Page had done three decades earlier. Page wished them "long life and great usefulness" and encouraged other farmers to form similar clubs.[2]

STATE OF EDUCATION IN NORTH CAROLINA

Page saw a way of changing Southern attitudes to education when in the 1880s Republican Senator Henry W. Blair introduced a bill requiring surplus federal funds to be provided to the Southern states to aid primary and secondary schools. The bill was passed in the Senate three times, though it was never presented to the House of Representatives and so did not become law. While this was happening, on April 9, 1884, Raleigh's *Farmer and Mechanic* warned, "If passed, it will make many changes. Whites and negroes must be put on the same footing regardless of numbers, colors, or needs . . . it will hasten the fast-coming day of African Equality, and State extinction."[3]

Page countered this attitude by asking the public school county superintendents for their opinions on Blair's bill. On April 26, 1884, under the heading "North Carolina Favors It," in the *State Chronicle* he published letters from thirteen counties and eleven were in favor. The common theme was that money was desperately needed as the schools were in dire straits. Edward Wootten from Iredell County referred to "the necessity of additional aid to North Carolina to enable her with her slender and wholly inadequate means to educate the poor illiterate children of her soil." The biggest concern was retaining control, with seven letters emphatically stating they did not want the federal government being involved in running schools. John W. Starnes, from Buncombe County, summed it up: "A man at the National capital could no more dictate for a school in one of our extreme Western counties than I could regulate operations upon a farm in New York, a place unseen, to me." Two superintendents noted education's importance in a functioning democracy; B. W. Hatcher from Johnston County wrote, "We need National aid, not as a charity, but as citizens of a government, the prosperity and safety of which depend upon the intelligence of those who direct it." The resistance of some of the old Southern leaders and others was raised by Jas. Murray of Wilson County, a teacher for forty years: "We have in our midst many that are opposed to the measure, and who are in reality against public schools in any form."[4]

On July 26, 1884, Page reported in the *State Chronicle* on a survey he had conducted of private schools and colleges in the state asking about teachers, students, and resources. Of the forty-two responses, including the university's, thirty-three had enough data from which to draw conclusions. From these, Page editorialized that while growth in good private schools since 1880 was greater than in the antebellum period, and principals and teachers were generally positive, their greatest concern was the "meagre supply of school apparatus and of libraries." Consequently, pupils were being taught the fundamentals, though they were missing out on "the enticing experiments and demonstrations which make the difference between a routine book-learning pupil and a child whose intellectual life is awakened."[5]

Similar comments were made by Professor H. E. Shepherd from South Carolina, following visits which included the normal schools at Wilson and Chapel Hill, and Bingham School. Probably an expert in teaching, he wrote an article with his observations on October 25, 1884. He was very impressed with the progress since a previous visit, with improved discipline and greater teacher commitment, though he warned of the danger of the increasing tendency toward rote learning rather than true understanding. It was exercising "pernicious fascination" over some of the teachers.[6]

In April 1884 the Wilmington, North Carolina, *Banner Enterprise* reported 1880 census data showing the state's illiteracy rate for people aged 10 and above had increased over the previous decade, with 38.3 percent unable to read, up from 31.7 percent in 1870, and 48.3 percent unable to write. Page did not report these statistics, which was either an oversight or lapse in judgment for someone so committed to the truth, though in June he optimistically wrote they had "caused a public awakening to educational work that is unprecedented in our history." Trying to be positive, he went on: "We are educating more children by at least 33 1/2 percent; and our instruction is at least a third better than ever before. And in spite of the meagerness of our school funds, the work of the public schools is going forward with hardly less rapidity than the work of our high schools and colleges."[7]

Strongly supporting teacher education and improvement, on June 14, 1884, Page congratulated the North Carolina *Teacher* for organizing the Teachers' North Carolina Chautauqua at Waynesville. A summer workshop with a "most attractive intellectual programme," Page encouraged teachers to attend. He sent a staff correspondent and gave the event extensive coverage. Papers included three by female teachers on the following topics: "The Necessity of Self-Culture among Teachers"; "The Dignity of the Teachers' Calling"; and "The New Education." After it ended, Page praised the two-week event and hoped it would be held every summer: "The organization is regarded as permanent, and next year 700 or 800 people will be expected, and some of the most distinguished lecturers in the Union will be there."[8]

TRAINING WORKERS AND THE "MUMMIES"

In his response to Page's survey of superintendents on the Blair Bill, Superintendent B. W. Hatcher called for the establishment of "technical or industrial schools." The following week the *State Chronicle* published letters about a lack of formal training that had led to a shortage of genuinely skilled workmen in the South and lower wages compared with the North due to lower productivity. Soon after, on May 26, the Watauga Club was formed in Raleigh to, as their constitution would later state, "promote the material interests of this community" and the state. Page was among its twenty-four members, all young men aged under thirty. Charles Dabney, a prominent club member, believed Page was a "leading spirit" and the *State Chronicle* was its "unofficial organ."[9]

At the second meeting, as noted later by the chairman William J. Peele, a paper was presented on "*Industrial Education* and the feasibility of establishing an Industrial School in North Carolina." The *State Chronicle* then announced a competition with prizes for the female teacher who wrote the best essay on "Recent Educational Progress in North Carolina" and for the male teacher who wrote the best essay on "The Most Practicable Plan for Beginning Industrial Education in North Carolina." For the rest of the year, Peele noted, other papers were presented and discussions held on "the most practical plans for establishing such [a] school." At Page's suggestion they put forward a case to the state legislature to establish an industrial school, which was successful, and An Act to Establish and Maintain an Industrial School became law in March 1885. The Watauga Club, according to charter member John W. Thompson, was "elated." This was around the time Page moved back to New York, so he would have departed confident the industrial school was going to be established.[10]

Unfortunately, it soon became obvious that was not the case because there was no funding and no time limit placed on the board of agriculture to seek proposals from cities and towns. This did not happen until October 15. To move things along the club held a public meeting, likely at Page's suggestion, on November 26. It was a great success and resolved that an industrial school should be built in Raleigh, that it would have public support and a committee be appointed to prepare a report for the board. Two months after the meeting there was a major setback when in January 1886 the board rejected as inadequate proposals submitted by the three cities of Raleigh, Charlotte, and Kingston. Public reaction was immediate, with considerable, and sometimes lively, debate in some of the state's leading newspapers.[11]

The most prominent and spirited debate was instigated by Page in his famous "Mummy Letter," written from New York. Published in the *State Chronicle* on February 4 by Josephus Daniels, a fellow Watauga Club member, Page equated the state's leaders with Egyptian mummies, leaders of dynasties whose time had passed: "They don't want an Industrial School. That means a new idea, and a new idea is death to the supremacy of the mummies." Consequently, North Carolina's most talented people sought opportunities in other states and: "Not a scientific discovery has been made and worked out and kept its home in North Carolina that ever become famous for the good it did the world." He believed "the dead weight of these provincial and ignorant men" was demotivating "thousands and thousands" of North Carolinians, though they were afraid to speak out for fear of being branded disloyal by the mummies. Without new ideas the state could not develop: "Are we to sit down quietly forever and allow every enterprise that means growth, every idea that means intellectual freedom to perish, and the State to lag behind always, because a few amiable mummies will be offended?"[12]

For publishing the Mummy Letter, Daniels was accused of being "ignorant," "prejudiced," "malicious," "an upstart," and "other such complimentary names." Despite this, as he pointed out to disgruntled reader "Capt. X" who had canceled his subscription, in the week following the letter the number of subscribers increased from 3,100 to 3,126. Page was accused of being a traitor and encouraging young men to leave North Carolina. Meeting his critics head on, he replied: "I have never said that men, young or old, had no chance in North Carolina. Never!" His point was that "a man, young or old, infant or centennarian [sic], has less intellectual stimulus, less chance to win by intellectual work, less opportunity for mental growth, less encouragement to mental work in North Carolina than in any other State I know of—less than in South Carolina, or in

Tennessee, or in Georgia, or in Virginia, or in Kentucky, or in New York." He challenged his critics to "address yourself to it. Find out the cause. If you remove it, you will do what no man has yet done, and very brave fellows have tried it for about a hundred years." Page believed the industrial school was the solution: "The idea of the Industrial School is to give men a chance—to give mechanical workers an opportunity to put thought and taste into their work." The mummies were the cause: "They will misquote, misconstrue, argue, argue, argue, accuse you of saying things you never said, till they die." On February 26, Charles Aycock, who would later be known as the state's "education governor," wrote to Page stating that regardless of the "abuse heaped upon you by the various editors of the State," he was supported by three-quarters of the population. Aycock wished Page could return and, with Daniels, publish a daily newspaper.[13]

There were subsequently numerous letters, including another from Page, articles, and editorials in the *State Chronicle*, right up to a board of agriculture meeting on April 21, 1886. At this meeting the city of Raleigh increased its proposal and the board voted in favor of establishing an industrial school in the city. Before building started, however, the state's farmers, led by Leonidas L. Polk, pushed for increased funding and more land so that it could also be an agricultural college. After the Watauga Club agreed, Dabney and other members prepared a bill that was supported by the board of agriculture, Polk, and farmers' organizations across North Carolina. Page, who was visiting North Carolina, and other club members actively lobbied the legislators to support the bill. It was passed by the legislature on March 3, 1887, establishing the North Carolina Agriculture and Mechanic Arts College. On August 22, 1888 Peele made an address at the laying of the College's cornerstone, and declared Page one of the "principal actors" in its establishment and whose name "will always be indissolubly connected with this institution."[14]

The college opened on October 3, 1889, and was a great success. A year and a half later the *Western Sentinel* published an article asking whether Page was "the Galileo of the nineteenth century," as he had dared to question the accepted wisdom and was proven to be correct. In 1896 a new building was opened and christened "Watauga Hall," and the College's subsequent dramatic growth was chronicled in the state's newspapers. In 1914 college president D. H. Hill recognized the groundbreaking achievement of the Watauga Club and the college in turning around public opinion. The college is now North Carolina State University, and in 1975 the Watauga Medal was established as the university's highest nonacademic award featuring images of Page, Peele, Polk, and Justin S. Morrill.[15]

INAUGURATION OF PRESIDENT WINSTON

After he moved to the North, Page expanded the scope of his writing, editing, and speechmaking to address national education problems, though his priority remained the particularly dire situation in the South. One of his best speeches was at the inauguration of University of North Carolina president George T. Winston on October 14, 1891. It was extremely positive, full of praise for the university and hope for its, and the state's, future. He continued his earlier criticisms of slavery and the inertia it created in farming practices, and the "tradition that somehow education is a thing for a particular class," which led to a "slumber of the people."[16]

The report by the *State Chronicle's* correspondent indicated Page had been redeemed in at least some sections of North Carolina; his audience accepted the praise and criticism. It is hard to imagine a more ringing endorsement: "He received a perfect ovation and it was several minutes before he could speak. His address was a model of literary excellence, original thought, bold utterance and broad vision. It was a vivid and masterful production. It was compact. The ideas bristled in every paragraph, and the words were vascular. If you had cut them they would have bled. There was beauty, but not the mere beauty of rhetoric, but the beauty of strength that lent a charm to elegant diction. The speech was literally punctured with applause. It is not too much to say that no speaker at the university ever received more cordial greeting, and that no speech was ever productive of more real enthusiasm."[17]

Outgoing president Kemp P. Battle was particularly impressed, and in his history of the university specifically noted Page's appeal to the new president and his colleagues: "We charge you to remember that this is the peoples' institution. Renounce forever all servitude to ecclesiasticism and partyism and set out to be the ruling and the shaping force among the energies that stir the people and are making of the old fields a new earth, of our long slumbering land a resounding workshop."[18]

Page's speech was praised a few months later in the newspaper that had previously been one of his harshest critics, the *Charlotte Democrat*. It noted Page's earlier efforts had led to "a howl" going up, though everything had changed: "He is now invited back to the State, and at its brightest seat of learning repeats and reiterates the profound thoughts and convictions of his mind. The faculty and officials approve, and the students in a body have gone to work to organize and train themselves along the line of research and development indicated. Here is true intellectual inspiration."[19]

"FORGOTTEN MAN" SPEECH

In 1897 Page was invited by Charles D. McIver to give the first commencement address at the State Normal and Industrial College for Girls in Greensboro, North Carolina. McIver was a good friend, and founder and president of the college. Page replied that he planned to provide "a campaign document that would be serviceable in the great work you are doing." Just over two weeks later he wrote again, saying, "I should be prouder to say something that would help this fight along than I am of anything that I have ever done in my life." According to Dabney, McIver's school opened 1892 with the purpose of giving "young white women a fundamental education upon which to base training for teaching, and also training in the industrial arts suitable for their sex."[20]

His speech was well timed as public school education across the South was worse than it had been before the Civil War. There had been a revival in the early 1880s, and advocates had undertaken some groundbreaking, arduous, and sometimes successful campaigns, though little progress had been made toward a public school system. These disparate efforts desperately needed a unifying force. They also needed someone who was able to draw publicity, which had previously been lacking. For example, in June 1892 Rev. L. E. Busby addressed the literary societies of Newberry College, South Carolina, on "The Educational Problem in the South—a Plea for the Education of the Masses." The speech received coverage in the *Newberry Herald and News*, including more than half the front page seventeen months later, though it received little other publicity and appears to have had no impact.[21]

There was a sense of anticipation with the state's newspapers announcing more than a month in advance that Page would be giving the commencement address. A few days beforehand the *News and Observer* reported that "Mr. Page has written President McIver that the subject of his address is 'The Forgotten Man.'" This newspaper conveyed a palpable sense of excitement about the three days of commencement exercises, writing of the opening day, Monday May 17: "The commencement exercises of the Normal and Industrial school have opened in a blaze of glory. Every train brings more visitors, and Tuesday and Wednesday will be red letter days." Then on the big day it advised readers that Page had arrived in Greensboro on Monday night, as had Josephus Daniels, who would be introducing him.[22]

In the audience as Page rose to give his speech on the morning of Wednesday May 19, 1897, were the graduating young women, many of them future teachers, many of his extended family, and, according to Daniels's *News and*

Observer, "distinguished men from all sections of the State, who had come to greet the brilliant North Carolinian who had returned home with many honors." Most important for Page, Daniels believed, was his father, who had made a special effort to be there for his son's address because he was "proud of his scholarly son, making his way from the Cary home to the centre of the most learned society that environs Harvard." So all was set for the speech that Page had spent fifteen years writing and many more reflecting. It was a speech from a man who spoke with conviction. Daniels called him "the clearest and freshest talker North Carolina has produced in this generation"; a man driven by common sense, who despised deceptions and who "speaks his mind with utter disregard as to what Col. This or Judge That may say about it." Dabney described him as a "ready and forceful speaker, clear, direct and virile" whose thoughtful and passionate speeches reflected the extent of his convictions.[23]

Page did not disappoint, sending a very powerful and unequivocal message: North Carolina's most underdeveloped resource was its people, in particular its forgotten and neglected people who had been failed by a society that not only discouraged people from undertaking education and training; it had also failed to provide the necessary resources. It was a speech about equality of opportunity and the importance of education in engaging the people in the democratic process. Strengthening democracy through education strengthens the community and, in the process, gives everyone the opportunity to achieve their potential. All people are equal, so therefore "in making an estimate of a civilization it is the neglected and forgotten man more than any other that must be taken into account. When you build a house, you make the foundation the strongest part of it, and the house, however ornate its architecture, can be no stronger than the foundation."[24]

Education in North Carolina was not democratic as it was accessible only to the rich and upper class, who considered education a luxury or privilege, and the ruling class, the only people for whom it was considered a necessity. Consequently, there was no provision to educate the vast majority of the population: They were forgotten. The lack of state-funded education was a hangover from the societal structures of previous generations. Page attacked the "aristocratic system of education" that had existed during the antebellum period, stating, "It did not touch the masses. They had no part in it. They grew up with the idea that education was a special privilege: they did not aspire to it . . . They remained illiterate, neglected, forgotten." Religious schools had slightly improved the situation over the previous fifty years. While this "ecclesiastical system" was notionally more accessible than the aristocratic system, proclaiming a goal of general education, in reality the schools were just for members of specific religions: "universal free education, was not on their programme."

The entrenching of these two "systems" and the associated lack of progression toward a public school system was due to two factors: a culture of very low taxation and very strong resistance to government paying for education. As a result of these influences, "there was no substantial progress in broadening educational opportunities in North Carolina from the time of the colony till the beginning of the civil war, except the noteworthy and noble work that was done just before the war to develop a public school system."

He argued if only certain small groups of people are strong, intelligent, wealthy, and healthy there will be a low level of engagement in the democratic process. For democracy to work and for individuals and the community to function fully and achieve their potential, everyone needs to have the opportunity for a formal education: "In proportion as any community in the organization of its society or in the development of its institutions lays emphasis on its few rich men, or its few cultivated men, it is likely to forget and neglect its very foundations. It is not these small classes that really make the community what it is, that determine the condition of its health, the soundness of its social structure, its economic value and its level of life."

This was Page building on his criticisms over many years of the state's leaders and the way they had denied people access to education, perpetuated the antebellum myth, and entrenched their own power. In "Study of an Old Southern Borough," published in 1881, he referred to an "*ante-bellum* gentleman" who heartily supported the perpetuation of antebellum institutions while strongly opposing public schools. This gentleman would never change his mind regardless of the "number or strength of arguments."[25]

Having made these points, Page became characteristically positive. Over the previous decade great work had been done toward a public school system in North Carolina. It was an educational revival, which he doubted had been seen in any other state. Towns had started levying taxes to pay for the schools, and there was momentum, which he attributed to new educational leaders in the South: "These old educational systems having failed here, as they have failed in other States, the public-spirited, far-sighted and energetic young men, chief among them your own President [McIver] and the President of the University, who came into activity ten years or more ago, began seriously to develop a public school system, first of course in the towns." This momentum was the most important event to occur in North Carolina since the American

Union was formed, and it would lead to a public school system reaching every child in the state.

He was trying to be positive so as to instigate change and motivate the South's new leaders and other advocates of public education. He knew they still had a long way to go if the state was to develop a public school system. Even with this significant growth in the previous ten years, North Carolina's public school expenditure per pupil per annum was the second-lowest in America. Taxes were also relatively low. Taxpayers in North Carolina paid less than a quarter of that paid in "poor" Maine, less than half that of those in Virginia and Florida and less than one-seventh the amount paid in Iowa. One in eight people born in North Carolina had immigrated to another state. Almost all had moved to states with higher taxes, though offered more and higher-quality schools. The other states were not necessarily richer, and they certainly didn't have as much potential as North Carolina, but they provided people with opportunities.

While this became known as Page's "Forgotten Man" speech, it was a misnomer in line with the convention of the time, as the education of girls and women were his main concern. As he explained to his audience of young women, "I have thus far spoken only of the forgotten man. I have done so to show the social and educational structure in proper perspective. But what I have to come to speak about is the forgotten woman." While the aristocratic and ecclesiastical systems had looked after the education of "the fortunately born and the religious well-to-do," all other women had been forgotten. He continued his argument from "Study of an Old Southern Borough." While poverty was the lot of the forgotten men and women, it was women who were trapped in poverty: "Some *men* who are born under these conditions escape from them; a *man* may go away, go where life offers opportunities, but the women are forever helpless."

A system of public education was the solution, though the state's culture was the hindrance. The people of North Carolina needed to change their attitude to education and appreciate its ability to develop the forgotten man and woman: "We pay for schools not so much out of our purses as out of our state of mind." He summed up his appeal by enunciating a platform upon which a campaign could be run: "*A public school system generously supported by public sentiment, and generously maintained by both State and local taxation, is the only effective means to develop the forgotten man, and even more surely the only means to develop the forgotten woman.*"

The next steps, Page believed, were high schools, colleges, technical colleges, and universities. These were the natural progression and essential if the forgotten men and women, and the state as a whole, were to achieve their full potential. The South was significantly behind the rest of America. In one example he compared North Carolina's university and denominational colleges with those of the other twelve original states, stating they were inferior to those of Virginia, New Jersey, New York, Connecticut, and Massachusetts. He expressed confidence they would be built, though was concerned that the factors that had for almost a hundred years stood in the way of a public school system being built would also hinder the secondary and tertiary systems being developed.

Page was advocating a revolutionary approach to Southern education. It was completely contrary to the way the social, political, and education systems of North Carolina and the rest of the South were operating at the time. For Page, though, it was the culmination of the arguments he had been making publicly for many years. He built them into a powerful analysis of why education was so undervalued in North Carolina and the South, what was the cost, both for individuals and the states. Most importantly he gave the South a positive and motivating message for the future, one which the new leaders could rally around.

North Carolina's newspapers praised and criticized Page's speech. The *News and Observer* published it in full the next day with an introduction by Daniels, who praised his friend, stating, "He did not come a thousand miles to utter platitudes. He would have remained in Boston if he had not felt that he had a message for his people." Several days later the *Western Sentinel* summarized a speech by McIver in which he referred to Page's "remarkable address" and the urgent need to stop the state's most productive citizens from leaving. The *Progressive Farmer* noted Page's "eloquent speech" had been "highly praised."[26]

By contrast, the *Semi-weekly Messenger* seemed annoyed that it was the "most read, most talked about, most overhauled" commencement address, and proceeded to attack him personally, saying he "seems to have been Germanized as to the Bible and Yankeeized as to North Carolina and the south." The *Charlotte Democrat* reported favorably on an address by Superintendent Graham at Providence Academy, which it claimed rebutted Page's arguments, though ignored Page's substantial argument about the need for a public school system. About a week later the *Messenger* had another go at "Page's over-much ventilated attack upon North Carolina" as "a land of intellectual poverty, and darkness," claiming it would deter migration to the state. Previously, this newspaper had for years offered generous praise for Page's achievements and lamented that he had left North Carolina.[27]

In September, Clarence Poe, who had taken over as editor of the *Progressive Farmer*, looked back and gave perspective to the criticism: "No commencement address delivered in the limits of Tarheeldom this year attracted so much attention as that of Mr. Walter H. Page at the State Normal and Industrial College. Nor has any speech been so much criticised, for when Mr. Page came back to his mother State he came to tell her of her forgotten sons and daughters—of her neglect of them—and those who had expected from Mr. Page only fulsome and valueless praise were disappointed." In October the *News and Observer* reported that "copious extracts" had been published in the *North Carolina Journal of Education*.[28]

Meanwhile the South's leaders continued to perpetuate the antebellum myth about a way of life in which education for the vast majority of the population was not necessary. Just over a month later Tennessee governor Robert Taylor gave a speech to Confederate veterans in Nashville lamenting the demise of the antebellum South, which had been "the high tide of earthly glory" and doubted people would "ever see another civilization as brilliant."[29]

Page saw past the criticism and mythmaking to articulate the true predicament of the vast majority of the population of North Carolina, which was widely seen as a proxy for all the Southern states. He presented the reality as he saw it, and for every problem he identified a solution. He tried to unify leaders of the New South movement and galvanize the campaign for education in the South. Some campaigners had been prepared to compromise and accept a partly taxpayer-funded school system until Page put forward such an uncompromising and forceful argument for a fully taxpayer-funded public school system. The campaign became united behind this idea. As Josephus Daniels wrote: "He believes so firmly that the doctrine he expounded is based on eternal truth that, having sown the seed, he will await with confidence the day of harvesting." Two months after the speech McIver wrote to Page saying he believed "the educational effect of this campaign will be tremendous." According to Charles Dabney, the speech became "the gospel of the campaign that followed." Connor summed up its powerful and widespread impact: "When the cause began to lag, it was Page who furnished its rallying battle cry—'The Forgotten Man'—which lived in the popular mind and summed up, in a way that a thousand speeches could never have done, the great purpose for which the best people of the state were striving."[30]

CAMPAIGN FOR EDUCATION IN THE SOUTH

Following his "Forgotten Man" speech, Page did what he could to maintain the momentum through his writing, editing and speechmaking, though he was constrained by the cultural and literary traditions of the *Atlantic Monthly* where he had just been appointed acting editor. Consequently, the few education-related articles he published were focused on teaching, literacy, and the English language, topics hardly relevant to the South without a functioning public school system.

CONFERENCE FOR EDUCATION IN THE SOUTH

In 1898 a new conference, the Conference for Christian Education in the South, was held in the small and remote town of Capon Springs, in West Virginia. Then two more annual conferences were held, renamed the Conference for Education in the South and focused on African American education. Page was invited to speak at the second conference in 1899, though he had to decline due to illness and work commitments. These three conferences were largely ineffective, mainly attended by about a hundred invited, eminent, and educated Northerners. As noted by Dr. George S. Dickerman, the agent of the conference, there were few school representatives and minimal Southern press attendance, so the gatherings were hardly heard of in the South.[31]

The turning point was at the third conference when New York businessman Robert C. Ogden, though he was unable to attend, had a paper presented that so impressed the attendees they unanimously elected him president. Realizing the conference needed to attract a much broader attendance, Ogden and the other leaders moved the fourth conference in April 1901 to the more central and commercial, manufacturing and educational city of Winston-Salem, in North Carolina. Ogden's leadership was to give education the professional and public prominence Page had advocated. He was so prominent that people often named the campaign after him, including Page, who referred to it in his diary as "the Ogden movement for education in the South."[32]

The conference was given extensive coverage in Southern newspapers. From New York, Walter and Alice Page traveled in a train chartered by Ogden with about sixty other people interested in education. It was, the *News and Observer* reported, a ten-day return trip in "five Pullman cars, dining car, and every convenience." They visited major educational institutions along the way, with promotion by local newspapers. In Alabama, the *Birmingham Age-Herald* proclaimed, "PROMINENT PARTY TO VISIT TUSKEGEE—Fifty of North's Most Distinguished Citizens Will Come South This Month." Page was among the most eminent education speakers on board and gave a speech at each institution, which was reported in Southern newspapers' regular updates of the trip. With this lead-up there was a great sense of occasion, a feeling that it was an important event in Southern history. The *News and Observer* dedicated most of its front page to the conference on the first day, and on the last day summed up its achievements.[33]

The conference started on April 18, 1901, and went on for three days, with Page playing an integral role. He was one of the principal speakers and elected a vice president. Importantly, the recommendations of the Committee on Platform and Resolutions, of which Page was a member, were adopted, the key one being to conduct "a campaign of education for free schools for all the people, by supplying literature to the newspapers and periodical press, by participating in educational meetings, and by general correspondence." The conference would conduct a practical, grassroots campaign for the provision of education regardless of race or gender.[34]

Not everyone was happy with this development, and some used it to perpetuate the race-problem myth. Governor Allen D. Chandler of Georgia was quoted in Southern and Northern newspapers telling the "Yankees" to mind their own business: "I do not believe in the higher education of the darky," because they will get jobs in factories and offices which "will cause dissatisfaction between the two races and such things might lead to a race war." In response, Dabney noted, some Northern newspaper editors asked other Southern governors for their opinions and all respondents opposed Chandler's view.[35]

Annually over subsequent years the conference brought together for a week the North's leading philanthropists and others wanting to improve education, as well as the South's experts and school workers. For example, in 1903 in Richmond, Virginia, over 2,000 people attended, including 112 from the North by Ogden's train. Among the 37 college and university presidents were Francis Venable (University of North Carolina), David F. Houston (Agricultural and Mechanical College of Texas), Laura D. Gill (Barnard College), Ira Remsen (Johns Hopkins University), and M. Cary Thomas (Bryn Mawr College). There were also 39 college professors including Wickliffe Rose (University of Tennessee), James H. Kirkland (Vanderbilt University), Edwin Mims (Trinity College), and Walter B. Hill (University of Georgia). By far the most attendees at this and other conferences worked in the state education systems as superintendents, principals, and teachers. Dickerman noted that "many of the speakers came there directly from the campaign work in which they had been engaged in different parts of the South" and that it "was like the focalization of the best thought and feeling now coming into vigorous expression everywhere."[36]

Page gave speeches at most of the conferences, and probably his most inspirational was on April 27, 1904, to the conference in Birmingham, Alabama. He addressed patriotic Southerners who would give their work and lives "to restore the thought, the character, and the influence of the South to the commanding position that they held a hundred years ago." This was an "unfulfilled ambition that has given a deep seriousness to our lives." It was an ambition of all Southerners as they had been left behind "in the life, in the thought, in the conduct of the republic, we have not a share as large as they had. In our own fathers' house, we are practically disinherited." Page knew most Southerners' fathers or grandfathers would have told them about this period of power and prosperity, as Anderson Page had told him.

Why, he asked, when America was more than ever the land of opportunity, had Southerners been left behind? The answer was lack of training: "The secret of the unrivaled progress of the United States—the secret of the swift forward movement in our time that puts all preceding social advancement to shame, is the training of the mass of the people." It was training "that has made the world a new world, that has vindicated Democracy, that has opened the door for opportunities as fast as we can seize them—opportunities not only industrial and diplomatic, but intellectual and moral also." With words that, as Mims later wrote, rang "with the challenge of a great task," Page called on conference attendees to do all they could to end the South's educational disadvantage: "Those that sit in soft places and discuss academic propositions (and mistake self-indulgence in criticism for the intellectual life) are welcome to their ease. We would not swap birth-rights with them. If we have a rough task, it is a high task. When it is done we shall leave the world better than we found it; and, while we are doing it, we shall have the joy of constructive activity. We look forward to a golden age that we may surely hasten, not back to one that never was."[37]

Page's speech was widely reported and acclaimed. Writing to Page a few days afterward James H. Kirkland, chancellor of Vanderbilt University and founder of the Southern Association of Colleges and Secondary Schools, stated the speech made him feel "as if a spell were on me," which remained for some time. Fellow campaigner William H. Baldwin was unable to attend the conference, though he felt the impact when he read the speech. He wrote to Page: "Your Birmingham speech was just you as I know you. I would that I had been there to feel it with the audience—and to watch the faces of some hearers, who even inside these surroundings dared not give sign of approval." Dabney believed this "powerful address" was a "frank discussion of the economic and educational errors of the southern states." Sarah D. Lowrie from Hampton Institute's *Southern Workman* was inspired by "Mr. Walter Page's ringing sentences," and Clarence

Poe published most of the speech in the *Progressive Farmer*. Poe thought Page's speech so worthy the following week he republished four of what he thought were the key points under the heading "Worth Remembering."[38]

SOUTHERN EDUCATION BOARD

The 1901 conference resolved to appoint a board, which Ogden organized in November. This became the Southern Education Board (SEB). Its role was to support and encourage conference attendees and others involved in providing education in the South during the year, between conferences. The *Richmond Times* quoted two members, Page and Albert Shaw, explaining that the SEB's role was as follows: to "gather facts, distribute information, and wage a deliberate and continuous propaganda in favor of educational progress. It will do everything in its power to persuade communities to tax themselves for schools, and it will interest itself in plans for the provision of competent teachers."[39]

Page gave numerous speeches supporting the SEB's work. A standout was on December 11, 1901, when he gave the commencement speech at the State Normal School in Athens, Georgia, with the provocative title, "The School that Built a Town." His fundamental point was the foundation for the South's development had to be a public school system that had "ceased to be regarded as schools for the poor." They needed to be "the best schools," used by "almost all the people." Upon this could be built industrialization, entrepreneurship, agricultural innovation, further educational institutions, libraries and cultural centers, and many other enterprises and services. In Georgia, the *Savannah Morning News* called it an "Able and Unique Address" that "drew a comparison between the old and the new ideas of education, the old that a few should be educated, the new that all should be educated; the old a selfish idea; the new a patriotic idea; the old which merely played with education; the new which turned out trained men." Page's ideas about education were becoming more widely understood and accepted.[40]

GENERAL EDUCATION BOARD

During its first year the SEB realized it needed to get involved in the funding and building of schools. It appointed a committee, which included Page, to determine how money could be raised for Southern schools. Fortunately for this committee, John D. Rockefeller Jr. had been at the pivotal 1901 conference. He and his father, John D. Rockefeller Sr., had over a number of years become very aware of the need to improve education in the South and were impressed with the work of the SEB in its first months. Rockefeller Sr. proposed to a group of seven SEB members, including Page, that they incorporate a new board to manage and disburse money for projects that would benefit education across the nation, especially in the South. Page and other SEB members developed the structure of this new board in early 1902, in conjunction with the Rockefellers and their representatives. On March 1, 1902, Rockefeller Sr. pledged $1 million "to promote education in the United States of America without distinction of sex, race or creed," initially focusing on the South. This new organization was called the General Education Board (GEB) and started operations on April 1, 1902. While the conference and the SEB focused on sharing and disseminating information, the GEB's role was financial. It worked with local communities to jointly fund education projects that were needed and would be used, maintained, and developed by the community. Its structure accorded with the requests and concerns of the school superintendents Page had received at the *State Chronicle* back in 1884 regarding the Blair Bill for federal funding of public schools. This suggests their ideas were influential, with Page as the conduit. The GEB filled the gap caused by the failure of Congress to pass the bill. As noted by researchers J. A. Jenkins and J. Peck, federal government funds were not provided for public schools until President Lyndon Johnson signed the Elementary and Secondary Education Act in 1965, the year after the GEB was wound up.[41]

While providing education regardless of race was ostensibly the aim of the conference (and by extension the SEB) and the GEB, this proved to be too ambitious in the segregated South. Charles Aycock, the "education governor" of North Carolina was one of their greatest supporters. He believed white people should have priority and, if it ever happened, they would educate African Americans. As Ogden wrote in a letter to Page, "The southern Democratic politician still has use for the sectional issue [racial prejudice], and that fact constitutes one of the difficulties to be overcome." The campaign realized any improvement in education was a great achievement. If they had insisted on racial equality, it was likely the campaign would have failed given the political climate, with the race-problem myth having turned public opinion. So the campaign accepted the reality of segregation and most resources went into white education, though it did make substantial contributions to education for African Americans. For example, state agents for African American schools, which Page advocated in 1910 and who Dabney believed were the "pioneers" in advancing their education, were supported by the SEB and the GEB. For decades after 1914 the GEB's largest grants were to pay these agents' salaries and their expenses.[42]

Page's commitment to the education campaign through speeches and writing was relentless. A snapshot appears in a letter to Wallace Buttrick, the GEB's secretary and executive officer. Page outlined some of his planned activities in case any could "serve the Board." On June 13, 1902, he planned to dedicate the new Trinity College library and address the North Carolina Teachers' Association on "Education towards Freedom of Speech." On June 17, he was giving the commencement address at the Jacob Tome Institute, in Maryland. In July he was to speak over a week at the inaugural Summer School of the South for teachers, which was organized by Dabney with funding from the GEB and other sources, and used facilities provided by the University of Tennessee. He was planning to publish "The Rebuilding of Old Commonwealths," a book incorporating his *Atlantic Monthly* article and his "Forgotten Man" and "School That Built a Town" speeches. Page intended to pay for the printing, then "give away to anybody who will read it."

He planned to publish editorials and articles to support the campaign in the *World's Work*, and had commitments to write editorials or articles for *Outlook* and newspapers across the nation. He planned to follow up his *Everybody's Magazine* profile of Booker Washington with a similar article, and write an article in the *Atlantic Monthly* on "The Political Side of Southern Education." Page concluded his letter to Buttrick: "Whatever I can write, wherever I can get in a word, or wherever at any time I can go and do anything for the cause—these are my tools and channels and ways of doing it; and I am at the service of the Board for field-work, pen-work or tongue-work—all, of course, and always at my own expense."[43]

On May 20, 1903, Page gave the commencement address at the North Carolina Agriculture and Mechanic Arts College, which he had been so instrumental in getting established more than a decade earlier. Page made an impression with Clarence Poe, who declared in the *Progressive Farmer*, "no other commencement address delivered in North Carolina this year has been so widely discussed," and a week later published extensive extracts.[44]

In his speech, Page challenged the widely accepted theory that society needed uneducated people as they were needed to do menial tasks for low wages. He compared North Carolina with Iowa, both agricultural states of similar size and population. Many more people born in North Carolina had left than had arrived, while in Iowa more had arrived than had left. Homeownership was much higher in Iowa. The difference in education was stark: "Of children from 5 to 9 years of age North Carolina has 39 per cent at school; Iowa has 67 per cent. Of children from 10 to 14 years North Carolina has 63 per cent; Iowa 91 per cent."

Farm workers in Iowa were much more efficient than those in North Carolina: "although we have more farm workers and very nearly as large an area, their farm products are every year worth more than four times as much as ours are worth," and farm property was worth eight times more. Appealing to his audience, he asked, "What has caused this difference?" It was not geographical—North Carolina had "rich land." It had "a greater diversity of soil than the Iowans," was just as close to markets, and could grow some staples Iowa couldn't, such as cotton, tobacco, and rice. The difference was "the men behind the plows." Their wages were more than four times higher; an average of $146 per annum for farm workers in North Carolina, compared to $611 in Iowa. Workers were more than four times more valuable to the farmers, and that was "the whole story." Iowa had superior training in agricultural schools and even public schools; therefore, "they till the soil better; they know it better. They use more machinery; they use more intelligence."

This was his critical point: North Carolina had fallen into the slavery-era trap of believing that the goal was cheaper labor, when the secret was actually well-trained, more efficient, and better-paid labor. His message to the graduates from the state's first agriculture college was this: "Here comes your opportunity—you who are the first generation of men in North Carolina that has had a chance to be trained to scientific agriculture. You have the high duty to make the man behind the plow an efficient man. In doing this you will do more than add incalculably to our wealth. You will bring also a better view of life."[45]

PAGE'S IMPACT ON THE CAMPAIGN

Page made a significant contribution to the education campaign of the conference and its two connected boards for thirteen years (1901–13). In Ogden's judgment, Page was responsible for "furnishing a large proportion of the brains of the campaign." According to Dabney, Page's "counsel weighed heavily in these bodies." Buttrick believed Page's opinions were "prophetic" and that he contributed more than any other GEB member to its work. The two men became great friends and were neighbors after Buttrick moved to Teaneck Road. They spent countless hours together, often walking in their neighborhood that was transitioning from rural to residential, and talking about education, particularly in the South. As well as his direct contributions, Page had a pivotal role in persuading, facilitating, and motivating people in many areas of the campaign. Connor, who was secretary of the Education Campaign Committee in North Carolina for three years, thought Page was the SEB's "most active worker." Connor believed the experts involved in the campaign would agree "their work in its fullest scope would have been impossible but for the influence, moral and financial, which Walter Page was largely responsible in bringing to their support." Abraham Flexner, who had served as Buttrick's assistant secretary at the GEB, and was secretary from 1913 to 1928, believed that "Page was one of the real educational statesmen of this country, probably the greatest that we have had since the Civil War."[46]

While the old Southern leaders did all they could to discredit Page and his "Forgotten Man" speech, they failed. In 1919 Edwin Mims, one of Page's fellow campaigners, professor of English literature at Vanderbilt University and former joint-editor of the *South Atlantic Quarterly*, reflected that, "despite the criticism of newspapers and publicists and preachers, North Carolina for the past twenty years has been doing the very things pointed out by him in that address." Mims went on to illustrate how the "Forgotten Man" speech had changed people's way of thinking about education: "Many of its sentences and phrases have become the slogans of forward-looking men. Who does not say now that the greatest undeveloped resource in any state is the untrained masses of the people, that a democratic society must be based upon such training, and that 'a public school system . . . is the only effective means to develop the forgotten man, and even more surely the only means to develop the forgotten woman'?"[47]

AGRICULTURE-DEMONSTRATION METHOD

Southern rural poverty was quickly identified by the GEB as the biggest impediment to developing a public school system. The only solution was to improve the local rural economies, and the best way to do this was to improve agricultural efficiency. The problem was, as Page had been saying for over two decades, the slavery-era culture of self-sufficiency; there were plenty of methods available to improve yields, but the problem was getting farmers to adopt them. Buttrick visited agricultural colleges throughout America and Canada seeking solutions and by coincidence was at a college in Texas when Seaman A. Knapp was presenting his farm-demonstration method of disseminating information.[48]

Knapp's method was to approach a well-regarded farmer and ask if he, as a respected farmer in the area, would like a demonstration of a "carefully selected" cotton seed that would more than double their yield. If the farmer agreed, Knapp would methodically and simply explain the correct method of planting and cultivating. When the farmer produced a good crop, as usually happened, their neighbors became interested in using the method. It spread over regions and states, transforming the lives of vast numbers of previously destitute, struggling farmers. In Texas farmers using the demonstration method had been able to recover from Mexican cotton boll weevil infestations, which in 1895 had been called one of the nation's most dangerous pests and had devastated farms across entire counties. Even better, Knapp's method had led to production being higher than in the years before the pest attacked.[49]

Buttrick introduced Knapp to Page, and not surprisingly he embraced the method. It was like his grandfather had done and Page had been advocating it since his days at the *State Chronicle* when he wrote about "scientific agriculture" and praised the agricultural clubs. In 1903 he enthused over the Canadian method of getting results of experiments directly to dairy farmers "by model dairies and curing rooms, by traveling dairies" and numerous other means. Page strongly encouraged the GEB to finance expansion of the method to other areas, and he was successful. The GEB signed an agreement with the Department of Agriculture on April 20, 1906, under which the board would fund extension of the demonstration method to areas not infected by the weevil. Knapp was invited to speak at the 1906 Conference, held about two weeks later, and completely captured the interest of his audience.[50]

Page promoted the program enthusiastically, through articles in the *World's Work*, in speeches, in correspondence, and in any public forum he could. In July 1906 he published an article by Knapp, "An Agricultural Revolution." In May 1908 he gave an endorsement and summary of its work: "No more important work is going on anywhere in the United States than the 'farmers' cooperative demonstration work' in the Southern States, under the direction of Dr. S.A. Knapp, of the Agricultural Department at Washington." He explained: "148 agents, or traveling teachers of good farming, go to the farmers and 'demonstrate' on their own land (the farmers themselves doing the work, under the agents' directions) the benefits of right methods." Later in the year when he was appointed by President Theodore Roosevelt to his Commission on Country Life, Page extensively promoted Knapp's program. The farm-demonstration program transformed the rural South, making vast tracts of previously unviable land prosperous. It was expanded to Northern states and is still being used today all around the world.[51]

After successfully increasing interest in agricultural education for farmers, the next step was to do the same for children. This led to the establishment of boys' and girls' clubs to train them in agriculture and home-related work, funded by the GEB. These clubs played a key role in increasing acceptance for education. As noted by J. S. Lambert from the Alabama Department of Education in 1935, a criticism of schools had been that they "educate children for 'white collar jobs' that do not and may never exist." Now known as 4-H Clubs, they flourished into a worldwide organization.[52]

Page regarded Knapp as a "really great man," and they became friends. Knapp died on April 1, 1911, and at his funeral Page declared his friend had been inspired by love for the forgotten people, and his work had helped improve the welfare of the South more than anyone of his generation. A year later, on April 1, 1912, Page traveled by night train to Nashville, Tennessee, for the Southern Commercial Congress. He spoke on "The Democracy of Finance for the Farmer" and had a busy week of social engagements, though almost certainly Page's focus was on April 9 when he presided over a session memorializing Knapp and his work. Buttrick and Clarence Poe gave speeches, followed by each state that had benefited. That night Page left for New York with Buttrick, Wickliffe Rose, and others, and the next day traveled through the "very beautiful" countryside of east Tennessee and south-west Virginia.[53]

"VIGOROUS AND EFFICIENT" PUBLIC HEALTH

In November 1908, as a commissioner with the Commission on Country Life, Page was traveling on an early morning train from Goldsboro, North Carolina, to a public hearing in Raleigh. With him was Henry D. Wallace, a fellow commissioner and good friend, and Dr. Charles W. Stiles, the commission's medical attaché. Their train stopped at a small rural station, and on the platform they saw an anemic, listless, miserable-looking man. Shocked by his appearance, Wallace asked what was wrong. Stiles later recalled Page's lament that he was "a typical example, though an extreme one, of our poor tenant whites." Remarkably, Stiles had the answer—the man on the platform was suffering from hookworm disease, which could be cured very simply for about fifty cents and a few weeks rest.[54]

DR. CHARLES W. STILES

Dr. Stiles was a highly educated, internationally respected medical expert. He had spent five years studying in Europe's best medical schools. In 1888 while at the University of Leipzig he had read a book about human hookworm disease in France, Italy, and southern Germany. This work suggested the affliction also existed in the American states on the Gulf of Mexico, which led Stiles to strongly suspect many Southerners were suffering from hookworm disease. For decades people living in large areas of the South had suffered from what was thought to be "chronic anemia" or "continuous malaria" and there was no known cure. As well as the physical symptoms, which included stunted growth, ongoing weariness and lack of energy sapped the ability to think or work.

On his return to America in 1891, Stiles sought to find either a specimen of this hookworm or reference to it in the medical literature. Although unsuccessful, Stiles knew environmental conditions in the South matched those required for the hookworm to thrive, so he was certain it existed in the region. He had limited opportunities to pursue his theory, as his time was taken up as a zoologist in the Department of Agriculture's Bureau of Animal Industry and as the custodian in charge of the National Museum's collection of parasites.

Over subsequent years Stiles was able to find time to undertake further research. He became convinced that hookworm disease was widespread among Southerners and took every opportunity to promote this theory. He unsuccessfully tried to garner interest among the medical profession. For example, he encountered considerable skepticism and disbelief at a meeting of medical professionals at Johns Hopkins University, with some considering Stiles's theory an attack on the competence of Southern doctors, none of whom had diagnosed or reported a case of hookworm infection. It was not until September 1902, when he was teaching medical biology at the Army Medical School in Washington, D.C., that Stiles had the opportunity to travel to the South to study the condition. In Columbia, South Carolina, he was able to get two local doctors to assist him and he established America's first hookworm clinic. His study of local people soon confirmed they were suffering from hookworm infestations.[55]

Hookworms had been transmitted to America from Africa in people brought in as slaves. They are internal parasites that infect the small intestine and absorb nutrients from their human host's blood. The eggs leave the body in feces and need a warm moist climate to hatch. The climate and environment in the South were perfect. Poor sanitary conditions were common in homes, and often schools, churches, and other public buildings lacked hygienic toilet facilities. Southerners' common practice of not wearing shoes gave newly hatched hookworms opportunities to enter peoples' bodies. It is highly contagious, so entire families were often infected. The infection becomes a disease when the host shows symptoms of lethargy and anemia; the latter can in rare cases be so severe as to be fatal.[56]

Based on his research Stiles prepared a report highlighting the damage being done by the disease, and emphasized how simple and cheap it was to cure and prevent. Patients could kill the worms with one or two doses of thymol, then cleanse their body with a drink of Epsom salts. Stiles estimated this would cost just fifty cents per person. They could avoid reinfection by wearing shoes. Stiles's report, which the public health service published as a bulletin, stated there was an urgent need for a national campaign for eradication. It all seemed so straightforward, Stiles expected, "that the country would be stirred, an aroused country would galvanize Congress, and Congress would provide the sinews for the kind of war contemplated tons of thymol and Epsom salts, and flying squads of sanitarians."

Tragically this never happened. Not only was Stiles's report ignored by Congress, his findings were subjected to public ridicule, along the lines of having discovered "the germ of laziness," so it was almost impossible to get anyone to take it seriously. So the illness debilitating the lives of millions of Southerners was ignored for another six years.[57]

"SLANDERING" THE SOUTH

All this changed once Page became involved. With his encouragement, Stiles announced at the Raleigh hearing an estimated 35 percent of school children in the state were anemic due to hookworm. When challenged by a doctor at the hearing, Stiles replied "that there were four well marked cases of hookworm disease in the room at that moment." Some leaders were still perpetuating the antebellum myth, so both men were accused of disparaging their native region (Stiles was also from North Carolina) and defaming the South. In the *News and Observer*, still edited by his former friend Josephus Daniels, Page was strongly attacked, and the long lives of both his father and grandfather given as proof that people living in North Carolina were the healthiest in the nation. There was severe criticism of the commission, especially Stiles, from the North Carolina governor, Robert Glenn. His attack backfired when he tried to support his criticism by demanding the state board of health release the facts about hookworm in the state. As Stiles noted, it had the opposite result: "One of its officers immediately came out with the statement that the assertions which I had made . . . were exceedingly conservative and . . . below the statistics of the State Board of Health."[58]

Page's reaction to what Stiles was telling him would have been a great sense of relief. He had been long horrified by the behavior of Southerners. This was shown on his writing trip in 1881, then on his 1899 tour when, as he wrote to Alice, he was appalled and dismayed by the laziness, dirtiness, and inefficiency of many people: "The sorry white man in the South is the real curse of the land." They did not deserve to be the people "for whom Southern civilization sacrifices itself." It was not just poor people. In Jackson, Mississippi, he was appalled that when he visited one of the state's top lawyers in his filthy office, he was unkempt and unwashed, and simply ripped pages from a law book rather than copy them. This was in direct contrast to Page's understanding of human nature: that people would take advantage of opportunities to better themselves. Knowing that the reason for Southerners' behavior was primarily medical and not their nature would have restored the fifty-three-year-old's faith in human nature. This was borne out in research, published in 2007, comparing North and South, which estimated hookworm disease caused about half the literacy gap and about a fifth of the income gap at the time.[59]

AN EDUCATION CAMPAIGN

Page and Stiles spent hours discussing the problem and used the rest of the commission's hearings to promote Stiles's diagnosis. By coincidence earlier that year Page had emphasized the importance of a grassroots campaign when he wrote in the *World's Work* regarding changes being made to public health and disease prevention: "But such changes never come without individual as well as coordinated effort. Laws are of value only in proportion to the active public opinion that is behind them. One of the first duties of citizenship—individual duties—is to see to it that your own household and your own neighborhood live up to the light of hygienic knowledge. However competent and efficient and untiring your local health-officer may be, his permanent success in enforcing the laws is dependent upon the sentiment of the community."[60]

Upon being told Stiles had just lost a financial backer for his plan, Page thought of the Rockefellers. He was convinced that, given their satisfaction with the education campaign, they would be the ideal people to back a grassroots hookworm campaign based on Stiles's recommendations. Ignoring the negativity and parochialism of the mythmaking leaders of the South, who would see any campaign as a threat to their leadership, Page realized the campaign needed to be instigated and funded away from these people, and taken straight to the sufferers. As soon as he could, Page got Buttrick, secretary of the GEB, and Stiles together. After talking with Stiles, Buttrick met with Frederick T. Gates, manager of Rockefeller philanthropies, who after extensive research presented the proposal to the Rockefellers and obtained their approval. The intention was to run the hookworm campaign along the same lines as the successful grassroots work of both the education boards.[61]

On October 26, 1909, primarily as a result of Page's persuasion, the Rockefeller Sanitary Commission for the Eradication of Hookworm Disease was formed. The Rockefellers had granted $1 million dollars to be spent on an "aggressive" five-year campaign. This was the largest private donation for a public health campaign in American history. Six commission board members, including Page, were also on the Southern Education Board and it was run by the administrative secretary, Wickliffe Rose. Page was jubilant, writing that evening: "The one greatest single cause of anaemia and stagnation in the South will by this fund be ultimately removed, and 2,000,000 inefficient people be made well." He enthused: "It is the largest single benefit that could be done to the people of the South." The grassroots focus of the campaign was reflected in the commission's bylaws, which stated the purpose was "to bring about a cooperative movement of the medical profession, public health officials, boards of trade, churches, schools, the press and other agencies for the cure and prevention of hookworm disease."[62]

While ostensibly a health campaign, Page and the rest of the board knew it was actually an education campaign, and the first step was a cultural change to get the people and their communities to embrace the need for better public health. Skepticism and outright opposition had to be overcome, including from newspapers. The commission's plan to implement its campaign through existing local, county, and state agencies was challenged by the very poor state of public health services. Board members saw this as an opportunity to give them a shot in the arm.

The campaign was successful in encouraging community leaders including health officials, school principals, doctors and other medical professionals, and newspaper editors to become key supporters and participants. People had to be educated about symptoms, cure, and prevention. Integral to this was making the importance of hygiene part of the curricula in public schools. Achieving this became a source of pride for communities, as shown in the *Putnam County Herald* of Cookeville, Tennessee, when it declared on December 5, 1912, "The Cookeville public school bears the distinction of being the first school in the state, if not the South, to institute a regular course in hygiene and sanitation." It went on with great pride: "This fact is receiving the favorable comment of many throughout the state, and should be a source of pleasure to every citizen of Cookeville." This needed to be combined with intensive awareness and education efforts. The worms remained in the soil for many months, and longer if some people remained infected, so to eradicate hookworm the campaign needed to be as comprehensive as possible, ideally curing and educating the entire population of each area. Health centers were made as attractive and enticing as possible with testimonials from fellow community members, singing and refreshments to balance the less attractive activities of examination and treatment. Recent studies in developing countries have highlighted the importance of changing behavior to prevent reinfection. Often only in schools rather than the whole community, these campaigns were unsuccessful in their attempts to increase school attendance rates.[63]

Page played an important role promoting the campaign. In May 1909 he published an article by Frances M. Bjorkman on "The Cure for Two Million Sick," which praised Stiles's work and quoted the *Atlanta Constitution* saying hookworm was "more costly, threatening, and tangible than the Negro problem." In a September 1912 article in the *World's Work*, Page hailed Stiles's discovery as "the most helpful event in the history of our Southern states" because "its eradication will contribute more than any other event to the well-being and to the mental and moral life of at least 2,000,000 persons and, therefore, to all the rest of the population." While the issue was also covered by other high-profile writers in national magazines, according to Rose, it was articles published by Page that led to the most inquiries to his office.[64]

The hookworm campaign was integral to the success of the work of the SEB and the GEB. Children had by far the highest infection rates and benefited the most from the campaign. During the first four years of the campaign, 892,000 people were examined at random in 488 counties across 11 Southern states. While 34 percent of these people were infected, among school-age children the infection rate was 40 percent. Children cured of hookworm regained the energy to take advantage of the increasing number of educational opportunities becoming available in the South. There was a dramatic increase in school enrollments and regular attendance, and literacy rates, as a result of the campaign. In Mississippi the state supervisor of rural schools, W. H. Smith, firmly believed the state's economic and educational development was primarily a result of the significant reduction in the rate of hookworm disease.[65]

"THE MOST EFFECTIVE CAMPAIGN"

In his September 1912 article, Page looked back to when it all started at the November 1908 meeting in Raleigh. He noted that despite the criticism, the campaign had made remarkable progress in such a short time: "A local newspaper declared that the Commission was slandering the community; the Governor gave out an interview in praise of the health of the fair land that he ruled over and denouncing its slanderers. Sketches of the lives of aged men of the neighborhood were published, to prove the healthfulness of the community, and much other such nonsense and ignorance was put forth. That was less than four years ago. Now the organization for eradicating the disease in North Carolina is one of the most vigorous and efficient in all the South."[66]

The Rockefeller Foundation had provided funding for five years, so the commission's campaign in the South ended in 1914. By this time the severity of hookworm infestation was significantly reduced, which was remarkably rapid progress by historical standards. An estimated 64 percent of infected people were treated. According to Charles W. Eliot, president of Harvard University, it was "the most effective campaign against a widespread disease which medical science and philanthropy have ever combined to conduct." As Page had predicted on the day it was established, it had one of the greatest positive impacts on the lives of Southerners in history.[67]

PART THREE

THE NATION

\ 6 /

POLITICS AND SOCIETY
PAGE STOOD OUT AS A CLASSICAL LIBERAL PROGRESSIVE

A CLASSICAL LIBERAL PROGRESSIVE

As outlined in chapter 3, Page and the New South advocates with whom he worked were liberal progressives for whom public education was the priority. Page stood out because the changes he advocated were greater in number and broader in scope; he wanted to change the culture of the South. As well as this, he had numerous policies that also applied nationally. Key among these were tariff reform, civil service reform, controlling abuse of power by monopolistic conglomerations and labor unions, public education, women's rights, and the protection of the environment. These policies, as well as his belief in racial equality, were broadly consistent with those of British classical liberal philosophers such as Adam Smith and John S. Mill. A fundamental belief of classical liberals is maximizing individual freedom and minimizing the role of government, except where something is poorly provided by the private sector, such as education. At the same time classical liberals in Britain sought a lesser role for government, bureaucracy, and mercantilism, Page was seeking to take "feudalism" out of the South and replace it with a modern, productive, efficient, educated, and democratic society. It is important to clarify that "classical liberal" has a different meaning to "liberal," which over the centuries and in different countries has been claimed by politicians and others from a wide range of the political spectrum. Today in America liberals advocate a more extensive role for government compared with classical liberals.

Page summed up his philosophy in his "Forgotten Man" speech, stating: "The doctrine of equality of opportunity is at the bottom of social progress, for you can never judge a man's capacity except as he has opportunity to develop it." This is classical liberalism. He expanded on this at the 1912 Conference for Education in the South, stating social and economic progress could only be achieved if everyone had the same opportunities as one another. Referring to the difficulty some Southern farmers had with getting credit from banks, Page stated they were being judged on their status, position, or class in society. Using himself as an example, Page said he and some of those farmers unable to borrow money would be in similar financial positions, though Page would have no trouble getting credit due to his position in society. Democracy needed to extend beyond equal opportunity in politics, government, and even education: everyone needed to have the same "economic chance."[1]

In 1903, Page stated he did not support the immigration of people whom he thought would not fit into American society. He was particularly concerned about the "coaching" of European migrants who would have been refused entry for reasons of disease or poverty, to enable them to pass U.S. immigration checks: "These miserable people are so instructed before they leave home that they manage to pass through the immigrant office when they land here." Page was concerned they were not fit enough to move to "new land in the West nor to unsettled places in the South," and ended up in the already overcrowded slums in large cities. While this appears inconsistent with classical liberal philosophy of equality regardless of race, Page was trying to be pragmatic.[2]

Page was appalled by the use of child labor. In 1901 he published an article by Irene M. Ashby exposing the "abominable system," the cruel and exploitative use of child labor in Alabama and in other Southern cotton mills. Page stated in 1902 it was conservatively estimated that more than twenty thousand under-fourteen-year-olds were working in cotton mills in just four Southern states, and some were working all night. Laws to forbid what he called the "most heinous crime of civilization" were urgently needed. He encouraged readers to contact Edgar G. Murphy, chairman of the Executive Committee on Child Labor in Alabama, for a pamphlet which could be distributed. In 1907 Page called on consumers to speak out against "a dark side of Christmas." An investigation by several New York City charities and philanthropic organizations revealed that women and children were working in inhumane and dangerous factories to produce Christmas goods; and the only dubious benefit they received from the season was overtime work.[3]

POLITICS AND PRESIDENTS

Although Page leaned toward the Democratic Party, he supported individual candidates and their policies rather than political parties. In making an assessment he was interested in their character, especially frankness and honesty, as well as what they believed in and whether their policies would be good for the people. At the *St. Joseph Daily Gazette*, Page praised James A. Garfield's nomination by the Republicans, saying he was "assuredly one of the strongest men the party could have selected." Page wrote: "He is a statesman of eminent ability,

POLITICS AND SOCIETY / 125

and his record as a public man justifies us in saying that he has been by far more consistent and honest than many other noted Republican politicians who have occupied exalted positions in the American Republic."[4]

Grover Cleveland was the first president Page met. Invited to the White House to discuss the president's concerns about negative attacks by editors and politicians following his nonpartisan civil service appointments, Page, who had strongly supported Cleveland in the *State Chronicle,* offered reassurance that his policies had majority support. Page's beliefs in democracy and the importance of looking after the poorest people in society were very much in line with those of Cleveland. They both believed the government had a direct role in ensuring everyone had equality of opportunity, and in 1904 Page stated that he believed Cleveland was "one of our greatest Presidents."[5]

Page had known Theodore Roosevelt before he became president in September 1901, having published his articles in the *Forum* and the *Atlantic Monthly.* After a visit to the White House shortly after Roosevelt's inauguration, Page wrote a charming assessment of what a visitor might expect as his *World's Work* lead editorial in December 1901. His admiration is evident: "Every visitor to the White House receives a shock—an invigorating shock of frank earnestness . . . Mr. Roosevelt comes into his audience room alert, earnest, with the air of a man who has something to do. There's a spring in his step. There is candor in his manner and a natural cordiality, but his quickness of motion and of mind gives a new sensation." If the visitor has prepared a speech, there will be no time to give it: "During a three-minutes' interview he has time to rush you forward with your story, to take in and digest all that you meant to say, to laugh, to look you in the face squarely, to give you an answer, to shake your hand cordially; and you are gone with your speech undelivered, but he has perfectly understood you and your errand."[6]

The day after his controversial dinner with Booker Washington in October 1901, Roosevelt met with Page as he was concerned Washington's standing in the South would be damaged. Subsequently, Page was periodically called to the White House for advice on a wide range of matters, including treatment of African Americans and conservation of the environment. Sometimes it was not so formal. In a letter to Alice on December 9, 1906, Page related how, at the 1906 Gridiron annual dinner, Roosevelt had asked him to the White House to discuss lynching, to which Page replied it was an area in which he had no experience! They had a meeting the next day that Page considered successful. Despite this relationship and their similar gregarious and action-orientated personalities, they did not become close and Page was not a confidant. He generally gave

Roosevelt strong support in the *World's Work*, though even when he was critical, such as over Roosevelt's support for tariffs or failure to entrench a strong Republican Party in the South, it didn't seem to affect their relationship.[7]

Page's support in the *World's Work* for Republican William H. Taft was the first time he had openly supported a presidential candidate. Supportive articles commenced in October 1906 and continued after they became acquainted through serving on the Jeanes Fund together. Taft's ability and experience was regularly lauded in editorials, and in 1907 Page ran a series highlighting his qualifications for the presidency. Taft's previously low profile benefited greatly from this publicity. Page was also motivated by his passionate dislike of Bryan, the Democratic candidate whose policies and abilities had regularly been subjected to editorial disdain in the *World's Work*. Taft won the 1908 election and initially Page was happy to be called for advice, as he had been with Roosevelt. Despite some early promising signs that he would rejuvenate Southern Republicans and break the "Solid South," often with Page's encouragement, Taft proved to be a great disappointment in this and many other policies. During 1909 Page wound back his relationship. In September 1910, after visiting Taft at the White House, Page wrote to a friend: "I feel sincerely sorry for the President. He's a mighty nice man and a mighty poor President . . . he has no political sense." Page became focused on supporting a Democrat for the White House (his relationship with Woodrow Wilson is the subject of the next chapter).[8]

TARIFF REFORM

Tariffs were one of the most controversial national economic policies of Page's time. While they had originally been in place to protect emerging manufacturing, the increasing strength of these industries compared with their counterparts in the rest of the world was making tariffs harder to justify, as exports of manufactured goods rose dramatically in value during the 1870s, and continued to rise in the 1880s. Classical liberals argue tariffs can only be justified in certain circumstances, including to protect emerging industries that have the potential to be internationally competitive: once established, protection is no longer required.[9]

Page believed tariffs to be an inefficient tax that discriminated against the South. Southerners paid higher prices for the imported products upon which tariffs were levied, without having a large manufacturing base to receive the benefits in terms of higher profits, incomes, and employment. This was contrary to Page's sense of justice and fairness; it was also contrary to his belief in good policy as it reduced the incentive to work hard and innovate. On the other side of the debate, the manufacturers and regions in the North that benefited from tariffs had considerable political influence and public support.

Tariff reform was covered extensively in the *State Chronicle*. The first issue had an article on the 1883 New England Manufacturers and Mechanics Institute exposition in Boston. It was essentially a show of "the best specimens of foreign-made things which have a sale in this country" because the "exorbitant" tariff had failed to establish American manufacturing as a world leader. Subsequent research published in 1975 indicates Page was correct. At the end of the nineteenth century the fastest growing industries were not the ones with the highest tariffs. On December 8, 1883, Page published a number of articles, primarily stimulated by the election of a tariff reform supporter, John G. Carlisle, as Speaker of the U.S. House of Representatives. His front-page article compared the responses of "the tariff reform wing of the Democratic party" who supported a revenue tariff to raise necessary government revenue with those of "Protectionist Democrats" who supported the protectionist tariff that disadvantaged the South. In another article he stated the battle for reform was between the people, who would benefit from tariff reform, and the monopolies that wanted to keep the protectionist tariffs as they prevented competition from imports.[10]

The push for tariff reform received a boost from President Cleveland's third annual message on December 6, 1887, which committed the Democratic Party to comprehensive reform. Speaking passionately against tariffs, he proposed removing tariffs from goods that did not compete with American manufacturers and reducing them for goods considered necessities. Nine days later the Reform Club was formed by former members of the New York Free Trade Club to support Cleveland's policy, and the president worked closely with the club. Page was a member, and later vice president and chairman of its press committee. Page was active in its activities, which included sponsoring speakers, distributing pamphlets, surveying farmers about the impact of tariffs, and assisting in Cleveland's 1888 re-election campaign. Countering this campaign were the arguments made by businesses benefiting from tariffs, especially trusts, and other vested interests who often successfully lobbied politicians who were keen to be seen as supporters of local industry and jobs.[11]

To Page's disappointment, Cleveland lost the 1888 election, though he sent a strong message of support to the February 1889 American Tariff Reform League conference in Chicago, at which Page was elected one of the secretaries. In June 1889 the Reform Club had a survey published in newspapers across the nation asking farmers to, among other things, indicate the impact of tariffs on the condition of farmers in their community. Page was nominated as the person to send responses to, and it is likely he was an instigator given his belief in getting information directly from those affected by an issue.[12]

In 1890, Republican Representative William McKinley sponsored the Tariff Act, which raised tariffs to record levels. In the *Forum*, Page published articles supporting tariff reform at pivotal points in the subsequent debate from 1892 to 1894, including the 1892 presidential campaign. Cleveland won the election and tried to reduce tariffs, though to Page's great disappointment he was unsuccessful.[13]

At the *World's Work*, Page continued to raise tariff reform as a major issue. In the first issue he published statistics showing the extent of America's superior production. Estimates of the value of manufactured goods in 1900 prepared for the *World's Work* were $125,000 million, which was $450 million higher than that of Britain and Germany combined. Bureau of the Census data shows that two years earlier the value of exported finished manufactured goods exceeded imports for the first time. This confirms Page's argument; there was even less need for a tariff to protect American manufacturing industries from international competition.[14]

In January 1908, Page contrasted the pro-tariff view of President Roosevelt with Cleveland and the practical view from a manufacturer, H. E. Miles, president of the National Association of Implement and Vehicle Manufacturers. Roosevelt believed America was committed to tariffs and predicted "widespread industrial disaster" if it was reformed. Page wryly noted Roosevelt's view would have certainly met with "the approval of the majority of business men." Cleveland told the *World's Work* that he believed his speech of 1887 remained relevant and tariff reform "should certainly be possible without disastrous shock to any interest." Miles had explained in a recent issue of *American Industries* how businesses had exploited the system to make "a double profit": "When Congress gave us 45 per cent., we needing only 20 per cent., they gave us a Congressional permit, if not an invitation, to consolidate, form one great trust, and advance our prices 25 per cent., being the difference between the 20 per cent. needed and the 45 per cent. given." As Page had argued over the years, with these higher profits largely concentrated in the manufacturing North, tariffs harmed the agricultural South.[15]

CIVIL SERVICE REFORM

With Southern politics dominated by the Democratic Party, many of its leaders, the "bosses," took advantage of the opportunity to advance their own power, influence, and wealth. The bosses ensured the party put up candidates who, once in office, would look after them and their supporters with the "spoils" of office: appointments to lucrative positions, the awarding of government contracts, and benefiting from favorable policies. Although considerably weaker, Republicans had a similar desire for spoils, ensuring a paucity of ethical candidates to challenge the Democrats.

At the *State Chronicle* Page stood up to the bosses in North Carolina by exposing their self-serving tactics, poor policies, and negative impact on the state's development. He hoped to turn the people against these leaders, reducing their power and influence. He believed the U.S. Civil Service Reform Act of January 16, 1883, was essential to reducing the bosses' power. The act was aimed at stopping political interference in filling government jobs so that they would be filled on merit rather than as spoils of office. Page's only long-term concerted attack against an individual for a single action was in 1883 against Republican colonel Isaac J. Young, who had directly undermined civil service reform by sacking a civil servant for political reasons at the request of a congressman. Page challenged the Republican Party to take action, though Young was too powerful and when he escaped reprimand Page concluded civil service reform in North Carolina was dead for the foreseeable future.[16]

In the 1884 presidential campaign, Page praised Cleveland's actions as governor of New York to support civil service reforms and oppose "spoilsmen" and Democratic Party bosses. Page thought highly of Cleveland because he focused on having the best people for the job, not because of who they were or who they knew: "The jocular Colonels and briefless lawyers, therefore, in the South, who look forward to his election as a deliverance from poverty, and who hope for services rendered to eat from the table of Government patronage, will remain hungry until they go to work like honest men, if their feeding depends on Governor Cleveland."[17]

In November 1885 Page had an article in the *State Chronicle* reporting public condemnation of a clear case of spoils in New York, where he was living, and called on the people of North Carolina to do the same. He criticized the Democratic Party politicians and public officials who engaged in it, and the party members who expected appointments: "men who cannot earn a living or do not, and all sorts of riff-raff that every other profession or business excludes—

come up after an election and claim the offices, and often get them!" Two weeks later he described the reaction from the editors of Democrat-supporting newspapers: "All these fine discharges of slabbering gabble come from Democratic editors in North Carolina, and I seem to have provoked it for no other offense than for standing up as bold as I can in my little way for the first Democratic President that has been in the White House for 25 years and the greatest one that has been there since Jefferson."[18]

Page published several articles supporting civil service reform in the *Forum*. In July 1892 Charles F. Adams praised Cleveland, the Democratic presidential candidate, for having previously stood up to "severe pressure" from Democrats who were "simply ravenous for spoils" after twenty-eight years of Republican administrations. Later that year Page published five articles on the topic, including two looking back over a decade of reform. Lucius B. Swift was critical of Cleveland as lack of planning meant his reforms were only partly successful, though he was scathing of his successor President Benjamin Harrison and his embracing of spoils: "Cabinet officers were so busy making removals and appointments that they had no time to attend to other business." Cleveland's reforms were "swept away." John T. Doyle took a more detached view of how the merit system had evolved under different presidents, believing it had improved the quality of public officials and the peoples' perception.[19]

By 1904 Page believed that the appointment system was shameful and needed an overhaul. A senator had been "indicted by a federal grand jury for selling an appointment to a post-office," which was only possible because the system was so open to abuse and corruption. Page outlined how it worked: "It is perfectly well known that if Senator So-and-so desires the appointment of a certain man to an office in his State—especially if the Representatives from that State and the State machine all favor him—he is appointed, provided he seems to the President to be a fit person." Page's solution was for politicians and party bosses to be "stripped of this power"—and the president only making the most important appointments, such as those for judges, ambassadors, and key army and navy positions.[20]

"TRUSTS" AND LABOR UNIONS

During Page's period as magazine editor there occurred the rise of monopolistic conglomerations through the use of "trusts," the growth of large, industrywide labor unions, and two great strike periods. Page's approach to these was consistent with classical liberalism, arguing that society was undermined if there was abuse of power, including by large corporations or unions. While large corporations were generally beneficial as they often led to increased efficiency and lower prices, problems arose if they formed monopolies using trusts. The companies in the trust could agree on prices paid to suppliers and charged to consumers, maximizing profits and minimizing quality. Page believed in freedom of association; therefore unions had an important role to play in society, though they needed to respect the democratic freedoms of companies and the rest of society.

The great strike period of 1892–94 had more strike participants than any in American history and involved a series of major disputes in different industries that included workers at the Homestead steel mill in Pennsylvania, workers at the Pullman company in Chicago and on the railroads, and coal miners. Like the *North American Review* and some other magazines, the *Forum* aimed to portray both sides of the arguments. Page published about eight articles presenting the issues from a few different perspectives. His author selection had a clear bias toward the companies, the only person sympathetic to the unions' actions being Carroll D. Wright, inaugural head of the U.S. Bureau of Labor, first U.S. commissioner of labor, and later chair of the commission appointed by President Cleveland to investigate the Pullman strike. Wright, who was also an eminent statistician, conducted studies and wrote articles about the plight of workers. Despite this bias, most authors recognized the predicament of the workers, especially their weak bargaining position and, for some, appalling conditions. They tended to focus their criticisms on the potential for society and democracy to be undermined as a result of the strikes and the accompanying lawlessness such as violence, trespassing, and other actions.[21]

The Standard Oil Trust was formed in 1882 as a combination of numerous oil companies to form a monopolistic conglomeration. This was the first "trust," and was based on an idea constructed by its attorney Samuel C. Dodd. In the *Forum* Page published articles presenting different ideas on trusts, including those he did not support. In 1891 Aldace F. Walker argued that "unregulated competition" had failed and proposed governments control prices charged by merged entities. Standard Oil was the subject of most articles. In May 1892 Dodd had an article defending Standard by comparing it to any other form of business structure, and claiming the trust had led to strong competition, lower prices, and higher wages. Two months later Roger Sherman, a lawyer assisting independent refiners and producers trying to compete with Standard, published a critical response. He claimed the trust was illegal. Sherman argued it had become strong entirely due to extremely favorable railroad freight rates, which had sent its competitors out of business, and was expanding into oil fields after having depressed their price by driving down the cost of crude oil, as virtually the only buyer.[22]

In 1899 there was a boom in trust formation that led to the merging of unions in the major industries and a dramatic growth in union membership from 1900 to 1903. The link between these events was described in the *World's Work* by William Z. Ripley, Harvard University professor of economics. As monopolies grew larger, they could increase prices; as prices went up, especially for staples, workers had incentives to join a union in order to seek wage rises. With few or no competitors, trusts could be able to afford to pay higher wages by passing the cost on to consumers through higher prices. Page pointed out that as unions grew, this provided incentives for even more large companies. Significant resources were needed to negotiate with the large and powerful unions, especially to survive strikes. Smaller companies were better off merging, as a large corporation "can longer endure a siege, and it can make it harder for the labor union after the fight is over." There was the danger of an industrial-relations arms race with bigger and bigger corporations and unions at war with each other, with smaller businesses and consumers the biggest losers.[23]

The second great strike period occurred at the start of the twentieth century. Page and other authors wrote extensively in the *World's Work* on trusts, labor unions, strikes, and the impacts on the rest of society and the economy. One of the most instructive, both in terms of the story it tells and how it illustrates Page's way of communicating with his readers, was in October 1901. He published a case study by Michael G. Cunniff on the W. Deeves Wood sheet-steel mill in McKeesport, Pennsylvania, showing the similarities between corporate monopolies and large unions, and the devastating impact "an ill-managed and unnecessary labor-war" could have on a community. The local residents were the forgotten victims, and the future of their city was uncertain.[24]

In October 1901 Page took a classical liberal position when he explained the unions' inherent weakness: "they put every workman on a level with every other one; and that level must be the level of the mediocre man and not of the strong man. A capable and ambitious worker must take and keep the pace of the duller and slower one. He may not work longer hours, he may not receive larger pay, he may not regard his work as the primary thing in life for him." Consequently, it destroyed ambitions and entrepreneurial spirits. Unions were restricting freedom by putting each worker in a class, exactly what the American democratic principle of freedom was conceived to prevent. He was unsure how this weakness could be addressed, though it was worth trying because employers and employees could not always be trusted to deal fairly with each other. Leadership might be the answer—for example union leaders could help workers to improve themselves, and not lock them into a "class."[25]

Also in line with classical liberalism, in 1903 Page supported checks on corporate power as he was concerned it would be the people who suffered if trusts kept growing. The "very foundations and instruments of prosperity" would be owned and controlled by a few large corporations and men, which would end in disaster. An unexpected event, such as a bad crop, would cause an economic downturn and subsequent radical government intervention, and the value of people's assets would fall. Therefore, the following year he commended President Roosevelt for taking on large corporations and attempting to restrain monopoly power by establishing a Department of Commerce and Labor with the power to compel corporations with interstate operations to "answer questions about their organization and conduct." Page thought it was part of a gradual process to answer "the question [of] whether the corporations or the people are the masters."[26]

In 1909, Page wrote that the Sherman Antitrust Act of 1890 was essential to protect consumers and smaller businesses: "In so far as the great trusts have used their power, gained through combination, to oppress, to rob, or to destroy by unjust means, or to practice extortion through high prices, they should not be exempt from punishment." Despite this he agreed with criticisms made by President Roosevelt and others that the act did not discriminate between mergers that were and those that weren't anticompetitive. Page was therefore very pleased with two 1911 Supreme Court decisions using the act to dissolve the Standard Oil Company and the American Tobacco Company. He stated the outcomes had been "accepted by the general business world as satisfactory, and have been received by the people as a victory over monopoly." Page believed the decisions gave more certainty as the law would now only apply to conglomerates that would restrict competition, and so each one would be assessed on its merits. He was full of praise for Roosevelt for having the "aggressive temperament" to have initiated the cases while he was president. Page concluded that conglomerates would continue to exist, though they would have to be accountable to the law and to public opinion: "The monopolizing trust that defies law and scorns public opinion is hereafter impossible."[27]

Page believed the underlying problem for unions was poor leadership. He provided numerous examples, such as the National Cash Register Co., in Dayton, Ohio, which one employee described as a "regular paradise," though the union continually quibbled over minor matters and eventually called a strike when six workers were made redundant. The factory closed and had not reopened when the July 1901 *World's Work* went to press. More significant was the 1901 steel strike, called by the Amalgamated Iron and Steel Workers in an attempt to get the entire U.S. Steel Corporation, a recently formed conglomeration of union and nonunion mills, under union rules. The union was unsuccessful, and Page did not hold back, saying it was a mistake, badly managed and did not have the support of the workers. He summed up his position on the quality of union leadership when he referred to 1903 as the worst for industrial unrest in American history. There was always public sympathy for a worker "struggling for a better position," though this had fallen over the year through union belligerence, pointless struggles, and illegal activities including extortion.[28]

Voluntary conciliation and arbitration had been proposed, and it received varying degrees of support from Page, in several articles and editorials. In May 1902 he enthused about the National Civic Federation's new Industrial Department, which in four months had "settled or averted" six labor disputes. This included the National Cash Register strike, which had been "amicably settled" following "concessions from both sides." A difficulty with undertaking this process was that formation of employer associations was proceeding slowly, and more than a year later Page noted there was still only a "somewhat general movement toward counterorganizations of employers."[29]

Page also noted good union leadership. He believed that the late P. M. Arthur, former chief of the Brotherhood of Locomotive Engineers, was possibly America's most successful long-term union leader. He served in that position from its establishment until his death, and Page had three characteristics to explain his success. First, the union made membership conditional on whether they believed an applicant was fit to join, and it did not "scour the earth for members." Second, it only used strikes as a last resort, so small groups of members with a grievance could not escalate it into a major dispute, and, third, it did not engage in "sympathetic strikes" by taking on causes on behalf of other unions. This meant it won real victories for its members, "measured by increased wages, fair hours of work, and considerate treatment" that exceeded those of any other union in the nation.[30]

NATIONAL EDUCATION PROBLEMS

Education was the most frequently covered topic in the *Forum* while Page was editor, averaging almost one article per issue. Investigative articles were one of his most significant editorial innovations and, as at the *State Chronicle*, this was how Page hoped to foster change: identify a problem, involve one or more experts to get an informed opinion and the facts, and then present to the public with solutions. Education was the focus of his most comprehensive investigative undertaking. J. M. Rice was commissioned by Page to study the nation's public schools. Rice was a doctor who had studied psychology and pedagogy, and over the previous two years had studied education and visited schools in Europe. The *Forum* placed no time or geographical constraints on his study; Page wanted him to do a thorough job, and he did.

Rice spent over five months visiting the public schools in 36 cities across 13 Northern and Western states and the District of Columbia, studying and documenting the practices of over 1,200 teachers. Based on these studies he wrote eight articles that Page published from October 1892 to May 1893 with a summary in June. Rice was very clear about the many serious problems, which included ineffective teaching methods and superintendents, schools' poor condition and management, and extensive undermining by political patronage. He was horrified by the "mechanical" teaching method he observed in almost all the schools, meticulously describing examples of the deadening impact on pupils' interest and motivation. A school in New York City, where the principal had been graded "excellent" for twenty-five years, was the worst he had seen: "In no single exercise is a child permitted to think. He is told just what to say, and he is drilled not only in what to say, but also in the manner in which he must say it." Rice's articles diligently offered suggestions about how these problems could be addressed. He believed children learn better when they find education enjoyable and practical: "there is an abundance of evidence to prove that the life of the child is rendered happy by natural methods, while the mechanical render it burdensome and miserable." According to the New York *Herald*, Rice's articles led to a "revolution" in how American schools were organized.[31]

Soon after commencing at the *Atlantic Monthly*, Page started planning for a major series on public school education, the topic being Scudder's suggestion. In early 1896 Page sent surveys to thousands of public school superintendents, principals, and teachers, asking questions about the teaching profession. These covered the ratio of teachers to students, the rate teachers left the profession, the proportion aged over thirty-five, the extent of improper external interference, remuneration, qualifications, and opportunities for promotion. The covering letter, likely written by Page, explained that the purpose of the survey was to gather facts about teaching with the aim of improving the dignity and reward of the profession, which would flow on to enhancing the public school system.

Well over a thousand responses were received, analyzed, and summarized.

Page and Scudder had selected three education experts to write articles based on the responses: G. Stanley Hall, president of Clark University and pioneering adolescent psychologist; Fred W. Atkinson, principal of the high school in Springfield, Massachusetts; and L. H. Jones, superintendent of schools in Cleveland, Ohio. Page contacted each one to ensure they understood what the project was about and the topic of their article. These were published in the March, April, and June issues, followed by an article in July in which six teachers were invited to give frank assessments of their careers, and to draw any conclusions about how the status of teachers and public schools may be improved.[32]

GIVING WOMEN "THE CHANCES THEY DESERVE"

Growing up in an extended family of women who were educated, like his mother, and independent, like his maternal great-grandmother, it was not surprising Page believed from an early age that women needed to be given the opportunities to achieve their potential. As he stated in his seminal "Forgotten Man" speech, fundamental to this was education and significantly greater occupational choices for the "forgotten woman."

In "Study of an Old Southern Borough," his first nationally published work, he strongly supported women receiving an education and becoming more independent. Page was appalled by their predicament; he felt women were trapped, unable to leave their home, let alone the South. He lamented, "The intellectual training that they receive is indeed insignificant and in the main worthless. They are never trained to think in good earnest, and they learn nothing thoroughly in literature, in art, or in science. The whole structure of society is opposed to their being made able to support themselves. They are taught exclusively to look to doing the offices of wifehood." Women of wealthy families did have opportunities to be trained as teachers. Unfortunately, "very few have had sufficient training to be very efficient teachers; and thus the general educational advancement is hindered." Many women unconsciously induced their brothers and sons to leave the South so they could achieve "wonderful things." Page concluded, "The women are the power and the hope of this society," if only they could be educated. This was extraordinarily progressive for 1881.[33]

On February 2, 1884, he wrote approvingly in the *State Chronicle* of a proposal by Major Robert Bingham of the Grand Lodge of Masons to establish an orphanage that would be run and almost entirely staffed by women. Page saw this as a move in the right direction, increasing the opportunities for Southern women to do a wider variety of work: "One difficulty that we suffer in these latter days is the difficulty of so adjusting our society as to permit our women to earn their living in as many ways as women can and do most honorably in other communities." The South had been held back by women's work being "circumscribed" to social activities, and consequently "we have never given our women the chances they deserve." Ending on a positive note he was confident that "we see a wider horizon than our fathers ever saw."[34]

Later in 1884 he gave a remarkable tribute in his lead editorial to the late William H. Walker, a modest man who kept a low profile, though had been "one of the most useful citizens of Raleigh." Page thought so highly of Walker because he and his brother employed "as many as one hundred and fifty women, nearly every every [sic] one of whom is poor" at their clothes manufacturing business, Walker Bros. Page eulogized: "If this is not a real service to such a community as this, where unfortunately poor women have so few opportunities to earn any money at all, it would be difficult to say what a real service to the community is."[35]

By contrast with the *State Chronicle*, other North Carolina newspapers reinforced the traditional roles of women. For example, on April 4, 1884, another of the state's major papers the *Charlotte Home-Democrat* had two articles on the front page, "Domestic Duties" and "Common Sense," focusing on the importance of wives looking after their husbands and homes.[36]

In the *Forum*, Page frequently published articles on women's issues, covering a wide range of topics. In terms of stimulating debate, he was the best editor of the time, as noted in the *Herald* feature on Page in October 1893. A good example was in July 1892, when he published two articles arguing for a different role for women. M. G. van Rensselaer argued for women's education so they would be better wives and mothers. By contrast Carroll D. Wright, U.S. commissioner of labor and chief statistician, strongly advocated for women's "industrial emancipation" so that they could be independent of men. This was made harder as they were paid less than men for equivalent work. Society's attitude needed to change before this was fully addressed, though women could take action to reduce the pay gap by obtaining technical education, joining trade unions, and moving their focus away from matrimony to developing a career. While recognizing a career would generally end upon marriage, many women would be freed from the need to seek a husband for financial security, which was probably "the worst form of prostitution that exists." Wright knew his argument was controversial, though he believed there would be significant personal and societal benefits.[37]

In June 1904, Page used national census data in the *World's Work* to show the number of women doing jobs traditionally thought too "arduous." These included stock raisers and drovers (1,947 women), fishermen (1,805), miners (1,370), and hunters (1,320). He concluded that "women as workers are, very evidently, versatile and ubiquitous." To illustrate his point, he gave an example of a woman who had built up a highly lucrative commission-based business as a coal agent in New York. The following month Dr. Lyman Abbott, editor of *Outlook*, had an article in the *World's Work* describing how there had been a significant widening of occupations, so women could try most jobs. Abbott was pleased women could become financially independent and be released from the "odious compulsion" to get married for financial reasons. Supporting this, women's tertiary education had relatively recently been introduced to America and demand had been high. The previous year, as noted in an article by J. M. Taylor, president of Vassar College, women accounted for nearly 30 percent of students of the "really important colleges," and about 20,000 had graduated. Page was concerned that the expansion of women's work could lead to exploitation by making them work excessive hours in factories and sweatshops, and so was pleased when in 1908 the U.S. Supreme Court permitted the states to limit their hours of machine work.[38]

Writing about female suffrage in February 1884 Page was candid but restrained: "Southern society is very conservative in this as in most such questions—so very conservative, indeed, that it is like old Akriel Matthews's trees which were so straight that they leaned the other way." In 1909 Page reported Colorado judge Lindsey's opinions on the pros and cons of fourteen years of women voting in that state. Page noted that in reality such an exercise was irrelevant because "the ballot for women is not regarded as an experiment" in Colorado; it was a question of women having the right to vote. Introducing it in the Eastern states would be harder due to cultural barriers that meant both men and women resisted such a change. Page was confident it would spread "as fast and as far as the mass of women demand it." He noted woman had the vote in three other states as well as in Australia and New Zealand. He was confident "sooner or later" that it was likely to happen in the Eastern states. Three years later women could vote in nine Western states, and obtained the vote nationally on August 26, 1920.[39]

THE ENVIRONMENT

Page had a strong belief in preserving and enjoying the natural environment. As a child he spent countless hours with his mother, and by himself, reading and appreciating their surroundings in the nearby woods. This engendered a love of nature that he carried into adulthood. In the summer of 1901 the *News and Observer* noted that he organized a hike with two of his brothers, who were living in Aberdeen, "through the most romantic parts of the mountains of North Carolina." The party compromised fifteen: Walter and his brothers Henry and Chris; two of his sons, Ralph and Arthur, and eight of their friends; "Uncle Isaac," a Page family ex-slave, who went along to "drive a pair of strong mules to a wagon" with the tents and provisions; and a local chef, also an African American. Visiting Asheville, Hot Springs, Linville, and many other places, they planned to walk for thirty days, and "Mr. Page expects to get great benefit from this vacation, spent among the splendid mountains in the isothermal belt of his native State."[40]

It was several years later that he enthusiastically wrote how he felt about the environment: "When a man once comes to understand the whole commercial, economic, agricultural, sanitary, and aesthetic value of a stream and of a tree, he becomes a changed man; and nothing can throw his life and his thought back to the old, careless level of indifference to them. He sees a higher reach and a greater breadth of life for a people who preserve and wisely use them." Despite the significant man-made problems facing the South, Page remained positive and a big part of this was his appreciation of its natural environment.[41]

As editor of his different publications, he often took opportunities to encourage people to appreciate nature. The *State Chronicle* often mentioned local natural beauty when profiling a town or region and occasionally had a feature. Mt. Mitchell, about thirty-two miles east of Asheville, was described by a "Special Correspondent" who recounted the adventure of riding mules with three others, complemented by rarely used photos. As they rode along the Swannanoa River, they admired the laurels growing on the bank and the "reflection which its pink blossoms and green leaves cast in the clear, sparkling stream, was just too lovely for any use in this prosaic world." At the top they spent the night sleeping outside by a campfire, and in the morning enjoyed the beautiful sunrise: "We could sit under our rock, enjoy the good fire, and look out towards the east and enjoy all its glories. At first, the horizon in every direction was deep crimson, and then it gradually grew paler, and then the crimson faded away into old gold."[42]

At the *Forum* he published a few articles on the environment, though they tended to be about explorers and adventurers. In August 1891, he published Fridtjof Nansen's "A New Route to the North Pole," and in June 1894 "The Antarctic's Challenge to the Explorer" by Frederick A. Cook. Theodore Roosevelt's "Big Game Disappearing in the West" appeared in August 1893; primarily about game hunting, he advocated it being done responsibly and incidentally provided extensive information about America's natural environment. In the *Atlantic Monthly* Page published several articles, including on Yosemite and Yellowstone national parks, and "Wild Parks and Forest Reservations of the West," all by John Muir, as well as "Illustrations of North American Butterflies."[43]

It was at the *World's Work* that Page had free rein to indulge his passion. He regularly published photos, editorials, and articles with conservation messages, promoting parks and other vegetation to beautify cities, and encouraging readers to visit America's national parks and other natural places. Among the opening photos in the May 1910 issue, for example, were four illustrating the importance of preserving forests on mountains to prevent avalanches. A dramatic photo of a destroyed house was accompanied by the caption: "A dwelling destroyed by such a catastrophe as lately carried away a Great Northern Train near Wellington, Washington, and killed many people." Two photos showed resplendent intact forests, and the other illustrated how vulnerable mountainsides became after their protecting forest was destroyed; avalanches destroyed the young trees trying to replace them. In June 1903 Page's editorial encouraged busy city people to spend time in the country getting "close to Nature." In the same issue he published a series of lavishly illustrated articles encouraging readers to experience the natural environment by vacationing in natural recreation areas such as lakes, beaches, forests, and mountains, as well as going camping, trying fly-fishing, and photographing nature.[44]

One of Page's key themes was sustainable forestry. In 1904 he published an article by James W. Pinochet, whose family had established the Yale Forest School in 1900. As well as training professional foresters, the school had a summer program for large-scale landowners, such as farmers, interested in sustainability, and educators, such as schoolteachers, interested in changing public sentiment away from exploitation. Pinochet was the father of President Roosevelt's Forest Service chief Gifford H. Pinochet, himself a contributor to the *World's Work*. Keen to show what was happening internationally, Page published articles about forestry practices in other countries. For example, an article about the management of German forests argued there were lessons for America, and another about forests in the Philippines expressed optimism the massive forests would be harvested sustainably.[45]

Likely inspired by President Roosevelt's conservation work, coverage of environmental issues in the *World's Work* peaked in 1908. In January Page enthusiastically supported Roosevelt's planned conservation conference with state and territory governors in May at the White House. He believed Roosevelt had the best group of environmental administrators in American history, and that the nation was making more economical use of, and better preserving, its natural resources. A few months later Page, who advised Roosevelt on conservation, believed the "systematic preservation and reclamation of the natural resources" being undertaken across the nation was "likely to be remembered longest and most gratefully" of anything from the start of the century. It was the start of a multigenerational change in the way Americans thought about the environment: "A new attitude of mind toward the earth and the culture of it and the enjoyment of it as a home for a saner, richer, life, to say nothing of its larger yield, its more healthful qualities, and the incalculable addition to our wealth."[46]

In 1909 Roosevelt's "long series of services to the land" climaxed in his calling of an International Conservation Congress at The Hague, which Page thought might be the most important outcome of his presidency. Advocating taking advantage of scientific advancements, Page used language about caring for the environment that is used today, though it is highly unlikely it was widely used at the time: "We may save much that our predecessors wasted for lack of knowledge; and the physical world is only one world, after all, and the only world we have." He was concerned Asian countries lacking this knowledge were suffering environmentally, and that millions of people were enduring starvation. He hoped the outcome of the Congress would be an international effort to preserve natural resources and increase the fertility and yield of the soil. Page believed in caring for the environment both for its enjoyment and to cultivate for food to avoid widespread starvation.[47]

\ 7 /

"WATCH THAT MAN!"
LIFE-CHANGING RELATIONSHIP
WITH WOODROW WILSON

A MUTUALLY BENEFICIAL RELATIONSHIP

From the time they first met in Atlanta in 1882, Page and Woodrow Wilson realized they had common political interests. Three years later Wilson indicated the nature of the relationship that would develop between the two men. Replying to Page's suggestion that he would like to discuss many of the topics raised in Wilson's recently published book, *Congressional Government,* he wrote, "I thank you very much indeed for your appreciative reference to my book, and I am sincerely glad to hear that you have a special appetite for serious political and economic study." It was 1885, Page had returned to New York after leaving the *State Chronicle,* and Wilson had just started at Bryn Mawr College, a women's institute in Pennsylvania which Page's daughter Katharine would later attend, as head of the economics, politics, and history department. Grasping the opportunity to have a political and economic discussion with Page in any of these areas, Wilson went on: "Here I have no associates who are more than mildly interested in the topics I care most for, and I assure you that the conversation you wish for, about 'half a hundred topics' suggested by 'Cong. Govt' would delight me beyond measure. It would give me a chance to let off some of the enthusiasm I am just now painfully *storing up* in enforced silence. I am afraid that I cannot often find time to get away to New York; but I shall take pleasure in looking you up, should I go there." Wilson then told Page he would "take great pleasure in mentioning your name for membership" of the newly established American Economic Association. He was on the association's Committee on Local Government and asked Page if he had any thoughts in that area. He concluded, "But, whether you have or not, I shall be glad to hear from you whenever you can write to me."[1]

Over subsequent years their relationship developed. They often discussed issues, by letter and in person. After Wilson became a professor at Princeton University in 1890, Page regularly visited his home, though it's unlikely Wilson was a regular visitor to Page's home as Alice did not meet him until April 1913. They developed great respect for each other. Wilson sought Page's views across a range of areas, and as a contributor to the *Forum* and the *Atlantic Monthly* Wilson was keen to comply with Page's requests even when he had other commitments. Wilson took advantage of Page's extensive personal network. In June 1899 he asked for Page's help in suggesting someone for a chair in politics. Wilson wanted a candidate who had "culture, scholarship, power without acidity, tolerance for the accomplished fact." Then in October he was looking for someone to give a series of lectures "on the administration of tropical dependencies." Wilson was thinking of Alleyne Ireland and asked Page if he could "put me on the track of learning something of his character, training, antecedents, and personality?" In the same letter, Wilson wrote he was glad Page had moved back to New York, to start at Harper & Brothers, because: "perhaps I shall now have more chance of seeing you." On June 9, 1902, Wilson was elected president of Princeton. The next day Page wrote a letter of congratulations, and Wilson's respect was evident in his reply: "I do not know of any man whose backing and confidence I would rather have than yours in the difficult thing I have now undertaken." Wilson had Page as one of his guests at his inauguration ceremony on October 25, 1902.[2]

NEW JERSEY GUBERNATORIAL CAMPAIGN

From the early days of their relationship Page had marked Wilson as someone with the potential to reach high political office, telling his friends, "Watch that man!" In 1907 there was talk of him being nominated for the U.S. Senate or the presidency though, to Page's disappointment, nothing happened. In January 1908 Page published an article on Wilson in the *World's Work* by Robert Bridges, portraying him as an intelligent and engaging person. "Stimulating" speeches were considered a great strength, and he was in demand. Bridges prophetically considered it was not surprising that Wilson had "been spoken of as the right man for political offices of the highest dignity—Governor, United States Senator, and President."[3]

On January 19, 1908, Wilson made a pivotal decision, setting himself on the path to seeking the presidency. Seeking the guidance of a close friend, he confided: "My friends tell me that if I will enter the contest and can be nominated and elected Governor of New Jersey, I stand a very good chance of being the next President of the United States." After discussing it for a while, he decided to go ahead. He did not make his decision public, wanting to be drafted to run for Democratic Party nomination, and was determined not to be beholden to the party bosses. During the 1910 nomination campaign, Page sent Wilson a letter, to which he replied, "We are having a hard tussle here and the victory is by no means yet won, but I cannot tell you how much it puts heart into me to know that men like yourself see what is involved and lend me your approval." On September 15, 1910, Wilson was nominated as the Democratic candidate for New Jersey governor.[4]

During the gubernatorial campaign Wilson espoused the range of policies and ideas that he and Page had in common and had likely discussed over the years. Most significant was opposing tariffs, specifically the Payne-Aldrich tariff, which President Taft had just signed into law, and reducing party bosses' power. Wilson stood up to the bosses who believed he owed his nomination to them, writing on October 24 that he was "pledged to the regeneration of the Democratic party" by removing the power of the bosses and their system of favors, graft, and cozy deals that were rampant in New Jersey. This dramatic reform had been long advocated by Page. Wilson won the election on November 8, 1910, in a landslide. The same day Page sent him a letter of congratulations, to which Governor-elect Wilson replied saying it gave him "the deepest pleasure." By then he considered Page a friend, writing: "The praise is stronger than I deserve, but I accept it gratefully as a token of generous friendship."[5]

CAMPAIGN FOR PRESIDENTIAL NOMINATION

The next step in Wilson's plan for the presidency was campaigning for nomination as the Democratic Party's candidate. Again, he insisted on being drafted rather than putting himself forward.

On February 8, 1911, Page wrote, half-jokingly, to Wilson saying there were some "bad omens" in some newspapers' comments about him. Page proposed William B. Hale, a journalist, spend a week with Governor Wilson and use the information gained as the basis of an article for the *World's Work*. Wilson agreed, his reply on February 10 indicating the extent of trust he had in Page: "It will be a novel experience to have a man like Mr. Hale spend a week seeing how I go through the paces, but he is most welcome and I am most happy to have a plan set afoot which may serve to keep the witches off. It is certainly generous of you to wish to have this done in the World's Work."[6]

Wilson had many political supporters including former students and friends from the Princeton board, though of most interest to him were a group of former Southerners who were organizing to get him nominated. Wilson was concerned about their ability, so on February 10 he wrote another letter to Page asking for assistance. The leader was Colonel James S. Sprigg, supported by other

"Southern friends" of Wilson's in New York, including a former student, Walter McCorkle. Wilson was concerned Sprigg did not seem to be wise or practical, and so was "a little uneasy" about his ability to organize such an ambitious venture. Wilson advised Page: "I have, therefore, taken the liberty of advising him to send Mr. McCorkle and others interested to you for hard headed advice. I hope that you will not mind my taking this liberty."[7]

Page needed little prompting. After so many disappointments with Democrat and then Republican presidents he had supported, he felt at last there was a person who not only believed in the same major policies as he did, but his track record as governor of New Jersey indicated he would actually implement them. Page was particularly encouraged as Wilson had stood up to the corrupt Democratic Party bosses in New Jersey, and hoped he would do the same as president where it was so desperately needed in the South. Governor Wilson had also got antitrust legislation enacted in the state to reduce the power of monopolies.

Page played an integral role in getting Wilson's nomination campaign started. On February 24, 1911, he met with McCorkle and William F. McCombs at the Aldine Club, in New York, and developed a preliminary campaign. A key action was to appoint a publicity manager, which Page did in early March. He chose Frank P. Stockbridge, a journalist and writer for the *World's Work*. Then on Thursday, March 23, Wilson wrote to Page saying, "I shall be at your house by ten o'clock on Saturday morning," and at this pivotal meeting Page, McCorkle and McCombs persuaded him to agree to the plan.[8]

Under the plan, Wilson first did an exploratory speaking tour of the West to test the extent of his popularity and gain support. Using $3,000 raised by Page, McCorkle, and McCombs and organized by Stockbridge with Page's oversight, Wilson set off somewhat reluctantly in early May and over the month visited 12 cities and delivered 24 speeches. Eight thousand heard him in Atlanta and he gave the commencement address at the University of North Carolina. He was determined that the tour appear nonpolitical, though it did not always work out that way. In Denver, for example, he gave a speech on "The Bible and Progress" to an enraptured audience of 12,000. The *New York Times* reported a Rockies resident saying, "The town is wild over Woodrow Wilson and is booming him for president."[9]

Supporting the campaign Page published numerous editorials and articles in the *World's Work*, the scope and effectiveness of which was probably unmatched in American political history. In the May 1911 issue, Page called Wilson's governorship of New Jersey a "revelation," and praised him for standing up to the party bosses. By preventing the Democrats from "sending a rich corruptionist to the United States Senate" and forcing through direct election laws, Wilson was taking "the organization of both parties in New Jersey out of the hands of bosses" and restoring "people's rule." Page concluded Wilson was "equipped to carry out the high responsibilities of the Presidency, if his party have the progressive courage to nominate him and act wisely enough to elect him." The same issue had very positive coverage of Wilson's tour and contained Hale's article "Woodrow Wilson—Possible President," based on his week with the Governor. Hale praised Wilson as "a man who represents a new phenomenon in American politics." Written after he had been governor for six weeks, it was extremely positive covering Wilson's style of leadership, intelligence, speechmaking, and "vitality." Hale enthused: "No one can listen to Woodrow Wilson and see the emotions of the audiences of earnest men who hang upon his words, without feeling that he is witnessing the beginning of a political revolution, and that its prophet and captain stands before him."[10]

In his May 1911 editorial, Page presented "A Programme for the Democrats," which was intended for members of Congress to take up with a view to victory in the 1912 elections. Page clearly and methodically laid out the policies he believed would be good for the country. He would have had an eye on paving the way for Wilson, who he knew supported most, if not all, of them. They were policies grounded in the ideas he had been developing and espousing for decades: tariff reform; negating the monopoly power of large corporations; banking and currency reform; curtailing the influence of big business and other vested interests on politicians; reforming the political system to give the people a more direct say in who represents them (ending control by the party bosses); introducing a process for methodically determining how to spend on public infrastructure; and cutting pension fund frauds. Most importantly, the policies needed to be explained to the people to gain their confidence and support, and then implemented well.[11]

In June 1911 Page wrote to Wilson suggesting his nomination campaign needed more structure, including the appointment of a manager. Wilson replied saying he was wary of appointing a manager "of large caliber who would direct attention to himself," as had happened with the manager of another candidate, Judson Harmon. This would "create some very unfavorable impressions." Despite this, he did not rule it out and was keen to talk further with Page about what he felt was "all too complicated a matter." In the meantime Wilson thought Stockbridge could coordinate the campaign through a "bureau of information and co-operation" in New York City.[12]

To assist the nomination campaign, Page made use of his extensive connections. Most importantly from Wilson's perspective, he persuaded his influential Texan friend "Colonel" Edward M. House, whom he had known since 1909, to throw his support behind Wilson's nomination. House was living in New York and had strong support in Texas where he had been one of the most influential advisors to state governors since the 1890s. Although House was irrelevant to the campaign, soon after their meeting he became Wilson's close adviser. Page also used his New York connections, persuading his friend Henry Morgenthau to donate funds, and he subsequently became one of the campaign's biggest donors.[13]

As Page did not have independent wealth like McCombs and some others on the campaign, he lacked the time to lobby for Wilson, though he continued to offer advice. Wilson's gratitude was shown two days after one letter, when he replied, "Thank you with all my heart for your frank and generous letter of July third. It breathes the true spirit of a friend and a wise man." On July 16, Page again suggested more structure for the campaign and on August 21 Wilson requested he talk with William G. McAdoo. Wilson thought McAdoo of similar ability and character to Page and was keen to have him involved. Wilson was instinctively "against having a real political campaign manager," but concluded his letter: "I need not tell you how it warms my heart to have you constantly thinking of me as you do." Then in October McCombs became campaign manager and with McAdoo gave the campaign structure largely in line with Page's suggestions. During the campaign Page met about once a week with McAdoo to consider ways of advancing Wilson's prospects. McAdoo was "struck with the incisiveness of Mr. Page's mind." In October 1911, when newspaper editorials started questioning the sources of donations to the campaign, Page advised Wilson to make the donations public, both to blunt the criticism and to encourage more donors. Wilson agreed and wrote how much he appreciated Page's "kind thought of these things." A few months later after Page had given advice on another matter, Wilson wrote to him, "I value your judgement and trust your powers of observation as I do those of few other men, and then it is always delightful to hear you put a thing."[14]

From October 1911 to March 1912 Page published a six-part series, "Woodrow Wilson—A Biography," also written by Hale. Resplendent with flattering photos, some obviously personal, the articles focused on his positive traits as a lecturer and president at Princeton and as governor of New Jersey. The series clearly laid out why Wilson was the ideal presidential candidate, concluding with an article titled "The Presidency Looms Up." This article was full of support for Wilson's reforms as governor, again praising him for standing up to the bosses and powerful corporations which had previously made New Jersey one of the most corrupt and poorly governed states in the country. The series was supplemented with supporting editorials and articles by Page. Combined, these took up a considerable amount of space, and it would have been a significant boost for Wilson's nomination campaign to have such a volume of friendly coverage in one of the nation's most influential publications.[15]

Wilson was nominated by the Democratic Party at the Baltimore Convention, in June–July 1912. When the news was announced on the *New York Times* building electronic news ticker, Page was standing watching with Stockbridge, who recalled Page's words: "Well, Stockbridge, it looks to me as if we started something." McAdoo referred to his work with Page on the campaign as "the happy fruition of our great adventure." A few days later Wilson told Page how grateful he was, writing: "Your friendship and your generous faith in me are a source of cheer and of strength to me all the time." Then later in July he mockingly scolded Page: "Never do it again! Never go by without invading my office if I am not otherwise accessible." He was about to start writing his acceptance speech, which would take all his time, though afterward he would be free to catch up: "Let me know by telephone or telegraph when you are coming this way again and we *must* hit it off." Wilson accepted the party's nomination on August 7, 1912.[16]

PRESIDENTIAL CAMPAIGN

Page was not directly involved in the presidential campaign, though he continued with his incisive and in-depth commentary and articles in the *World's Work*. Additionally, Page's influence on the campaign was there for everyone to hear. Wilson's speeches espoused many of the views and policies the two men would have talked about over many years, and had been articulated in Page's "Programme for the Democrats." Trusts and monopolies are a great example. Page had encouraged the Democrats to consider how the antitrust law needed to be amended "so as to make it effective to prevent the abuses of monopoly; and to limit it so that it will not prescribe legitimate business." He had also advocated "fair but effective regulation" to deal with the railways. During the presidential campaign Wilson made the same points, speaking out strongly against businesses that had constructed monopolies, primarily by amalgamating into trusts, shutting out small business and pushing up prices. He was concerned they had extended their influence and control throughout the industrial, financial, and political systems.[17]

Wilson won the presidential election on November 5, 1912, and on the same day Page congratulated him, enthusing they had entered the "Era of Great Opportunity." Wilson replied, "Just a line to thank you for your splendid letter. As I have told you more than once, you always set me thinking, and along fertile lines. I deeply appreciate your friendship, and your thought of what I must be thinking about as well of what I am doing." Page was rightly proud and excited. After years of knowing Wilson and watching him develop, discussing issues and advising him, publishing his articles and promoting his virtues, and finally helping initiate and drive the campaign, there was a real prospect all they believed in could finally be put into place.[18]

ASPIRING PRESIDENTIAL ADVISER

After the election Wilson had the important decision of appointing the ten cabinet secretaries to lead the federal government departments, and initially received and sought the advice of several people, including Page. On Thursday November 14, 1912, Page had a Rural Life Conference in the morning, then in the afternoon drove with his son Arthur to Princeton. Taking advantage of the short period when he knew Wilson's "political managers" would have left him alone, Page had asked Wilson for a meeting. He was keen to advise him of his "Big Chance" to restore rural life through the "Knapp Demonstration method," building quality rural schools and "agricultural credit societies." At their meeting they discussed these ideas, touching also on conservation, and Wilson asked, "Who is the best man for Secretary of Agriculture?" Page asked for time to look into the question. Taking the chance to try and influence policy in areas he'd long had an interest, he offered to prepare briefs for Wilson on "the Agricultural Department, the Bureau of Education, the Rural Credit Societies, and Conservation." Wilson replied, "I shall be very grateful, if it be not too great a sacrifice." Walking out of the president-elect's house Page was struck by Wilson's situation: "I stepped out on the muddy street, and, as I walked to the Inn, I had the feeling of the man's oppressing loneliness as he faced his great task. There is no pomp, nor circumstance, nor hardly dignity in this setting, except the dignity of his seriousness and his loneliness."[19]

Page was aware of a significant push for him to be secretary of agriculture. His support was especially strong in North Carolina, including James Y. Joyner, state education superintendent, and Clarence Poe, who was still editor of the *Progressive Farmer*, the state's major agriculture paper. After his meeting with Wilson, Page drafted a letter in a notebook that, though it may not have been sent and was in rough form, gives an indication of his thinking at the time: "I must make one remark even at the risk of making it wrong. Since I saw you, some of my friends have begun to talk of me as a possible Secty of Agrical. I think I've stopped it & probably you'll never hear of it. But I wish you know that I have never had this thing nor any such thing in mind and shall never have."[20]

In reply to Wilson's question regarding the agriculture secretaryship, Page suggested David F. Houston, chancellor of Washington University, in St. Louis. A close friend of Page's, Houston was elected to the Southern Education Board in 1906 and was a fellow charter member of the Rockefeller Sanitary Commission Board. Houston believed the big challenge for the Department of Agriculture was to improve the economic viability of farms and rural areas so that people would live there: "I knew that the task was one of the conservation of men and women and boys and girls in our rural districts." This was an issue about which Page was particularly passionate and had regularly covered in the *World's Work*.[21]

By now Page had developed a modus operandi where he put his ideas forward to the person or people that he thought would be best placed to enact them, then after stepping back to see where they went, he would take on a guidance or advisory role. This had worked very effectively for him in many areas, most prominently education, farm demonstration, public health, and Wilson's presidential nomination and election campaigns. Now he was following the same practice, though he became frustrated by Wilson's lack of substance in his responses. On December 23, Wilson wrote he was going to urge the New Jersey legislature to pass legislation "in favor of agricultural demonstration work" and asked Page if he could "put your hand on a suitable bill under which a beginning could be made, or could you have such a bill drawn up for me?" Several days later Page explained his feelings in a letter to his friend Alderman: "I sent him some such memoranda. Here came forthwith a note of almost abject thanks. I sent more. Again, such a note—written in his own hand. Yet not a word of what he thinks. The Sphinx was garrulous in comparison."

Page was ready to go to the next stage, whatever that might be, though felt he was being held back by a lack of direction. He went on in his letter to express doubts about Wilson's ability to work with people, a skill so essential if he was to translate his undoubted brilliance, honesty, and ideas into good policies: "Wise? Yes. But does he know the men about him? Does he really know men? Nobody knows. Thus 'twixt fear and hope I see—suspense." Two days later, Wilson wrote to Page from New Jersey asking if he could visit in the next few days as he was very keen to see him: "I wonder if you could find time to run down here on Monday the sixth, or Wednesday the eighth? I am sure I could find an hour on one or the other of those days, and I want very much to see you." While the outcome of the meeting is not recorded, it is unlikely to have provided Page the direction he was seeking.[22]

As Page had stepped back, the way was clear for House to step in. He had ingratiated himself with Wilson, building on the rapport developed in their initial meeting where, House wrote in his diary, after just one hour they felt there was the basis of a "fast friendship." According to House, they found themselves "in such complete sympathy, in so many ways, that we soon learned to know what each was thinking without either having expressed himself." Reverend Stockton Axson, Wilson's brother-in-law, believed House presented an image of being disinterested in personal gain, of wanting "nothing for himself," and hence he could be a valuable, impartial adviser. Wilson wrote later, on August 28, 1915, that House was "capable of utter self-forgetfulness." House had successfully portrayed himself as giving advice for the greater good rather than to promote his own influence. Ironically it was Page who was interested less in his own influence and more in the interests of his country. Most importantly he could offer the pertinent, well-researched, and sometimes contrary advice that is so valuable to an incoming president. Although he had envisaged an unofficial advisory role for himself, his natural reticence and lack of self-promotion lead to him being sidelined, and House ended up having by far the greatest influence on the composition of the cabinet.[23]

House's remarkable achievement was illustrated later when, in response to a query from another politician as to whether a comment by House had represented him, according to House's account, President Wilson replied, "Mr. House is my second personality. He is my independent self. His thoughts and mine are one. If I were in his place I would do just as he suggested . . . If anyone thinks he is reflecting my opinion by whatever action he takes, they are welcome to the conclusion." Josephus Daniels, who was a member of Wilson's cabinet for eight years, explained that House accomplished this feat by asking cabinet members what the president was thinking about a specific issue before meeting with him: "What is the Old Man thinking about so-and-so." House then repeated what he had heard as if it was his own opinion and, as Daniels recounted, "Wilson was astounded to find that their minds ran in the same channel, and that made him think that he and House were almost one man in their thoughts." Axson, who was Wilson's closest and longest-lasting friend, was also skeptical of this apparent closeness of minds, observing that House seemed "never to say anything rememberable" and on the rare occasions when he spoke was "deferentially in agreement with everything W.W. said." House became Wilson's most trusted presidential adviser, though he never held an official position.[24]

As the cabinet-selection process continued, in early January House sent Wilson a list of possible members that suggested Page and Houston, who was also House's friend, as secretary for the Interior or for Agriculture. Wilson and House then met several times to discuss cabinet appointments. House ended up advocating Houston for Agriculture and prevailed. When House emphatically offered the position, saying "You *must accept*," Houston turned it down mainly for financial reasons. Then, as House noted, Page "in his characteristic way" privately raised enough funds, a guaranteed $30,000 per annum over four years, to allow Houston to accept the appointment. Further, Page supported Houston when Henry Wallace and others in the agriculture sector expressed skepticism. In a letter to Wallace on March 11, 1913, Page encouraged him not to criticize Wilson's cabinet before they had started their work: "Don't damn Houston, then, beforehand." Ironically, Houston wanted Page to be secretary. He wrote in his autobiography that "Walter Page was fully aware of the nature of the problem [of needing to make it economically viable for people to live in rural areas], and, therefore, I wanted to see him appointed to the position, and said so." Houston believed the role "would interest Page more than any other man," and was disappointed when Page missed out, writing, "I wish I had been able to prevail."[25]

Houston shared Page's concerns about Wilson's people skills: "The only doubt I had about Mr. Wilson at the time was as to the extent of his executive ability, particularly his capacity to see a great many things in a short time, to dispose of them promptly, and to do team work." Just after Wilson's nomination, Houston had "had some apprehensions about his executive ability" because as president of Princeton, "he had created unnecesasry [*sic*] friction and had finally failed to carry his point except with resulting disorganization." Houston was concerned that Wilson would behave the same way as U.S. president.[26]

Contrary to the impression created by some of his biographers and other authors, Page did not want a cabinet position. He was hoping to be a voluntary unofficial presidential adviser. He also wrote in the rough draft letter to Wilson following their meeting of November 14: "It would be a waste of material to put me in any official place, for my help and my judgement (if they can ever be of value) are at your service & at the service of the gov't for the pleasure of doing. Whatever I can to further these big purposes." This would have allowed him to semiretire to the sandhills of Pinehurst, North Carolina, while still having opportunities to get his policy ideas enacted. Since 1908 he had been structuring his work to allow him to spend less time there, most importantly by surrounding himself with reliable and dependable people. In 1911 his son Arthur, who had been working at the *World's Work* since 1905 and had his first article published in January 1906 on the Southern cotton industry, had become managing editor.[27]

Page wanted to expand his voluntary activities, especially in education and public health, which he found particularly rewarding. On January 23, 24, and 25, 1913, he had consecutive meetings: the Southern Education Board, the General Education Board, and the Rockefeller Sanitary Commission's annual general meeting. Having enjoyed the work, the next day he wrote to Alderman, who was laid up with tuberculosis: "This has been 'Board' week as you know. The men came from all quarters of the land, and we had a good time. New work is opening; old work is going well; the fellowship ran in good tide." He was keen to get more involved: "We are trying to get the country school task rightly focussed. We haven't done it yet; but we will. Buttrick and Rose will work it out. I wish to God I could throw down my practical job and go at it with 'em. Darned if I couldn't get it going!" That's what he was really looking forward to doing.

After his "Board week," Page was going to continue putting his plan into action, as he told Alderman: "I am going down there to-morrow for a month, one day for golf at Pinehurst, the next day for clearing land with an oil locomotive, ripping up stumps! . . . It's a pretty good world, whether seen from the petty excitements of reforming the world and dreaming of a diseaseless earth in New York, or from the stump-pulling recreation of a North Carolina wilderness." On January 28, he noted in his diary, he left New York for South Carolina where he gave two speeches including one on "rural credit" to the Charleston Chamber of Commerce, and then on "Sat[day] Feb 1—We arrived at the little cottage at Pinehurst for a month's vacation." This was where he was planning to build a bungalow in the sandhills for, as he wrote to his friend Henry Wallace, "winter and old-age."[28]

Page's trip to the "wilderness" was when he knew Wilson would be trying to contact prospective appointees, which is what happened. While he was away, Wilson decided to offer Page the position of secretary for the interior and asked House to contact him and see if he was interested. House telegraphed Page on February 22 asking him to return for discussions. Before Page could get back, House and Wilson's secretary Joseph P. Tumulty persuaded the president-elect to change his mind using the argument that a Southerner should not head the department responsible for Civil War pensions for veterans of the Union army.[29]

154 \ CHAPTER SEVEN

That was Page's last chance for a cabinet position as Wilson finalized positions before his inauguration on March 4. House had intervened twice to ensure Page had not been offered a position, despite it having been Page who encouraged him to get involved with Wilson. House acted against Page and other highly qualified potential appointees, such as Louis D. Brandeis for attorney general, for fear of losing his influence over Wilson. House knew he would not be able to match their contributions to policy development, as Wilson himself recognized two and a half years later when he wrote, "Intellectually he is not a great man. His mind is not of the first class. He is a counselor, not a statesman."[30]

If a cabinet position had been offered, Page would have accepted out of his sense of national duty and support for Wilson, though he would have found himself continually pushing against the constraints of government decision-making. He would not have been able to publicly criticize decisions and operate within the boundaries of the public service. Page was much more at home asserting his opinions and raising his ideas directly in public forums. In his letter to Wallace on March 11, Page indicated he was pleased not to have been included in the cabinet, "Now I'll break stones before I'd have a job at Washington now." He wanted to see how the new appointees performed, though he was keen to "get on the job and tell 'em how." Several days later House told him how close he had come to the position, and Page expressed amusement rather than disappointment.[31]

Page was slipping into his envisaged advisory role. On March 20, along with Gates, Buttrick, and Houston, he met with President Wilson and, as Page noted in his diary, "explained the plan to develop country life." This would have been based on the policies advocated by both Page and Houston for the departments of Agriculture and Education to drive rural development with an education focus. Page wrote that Wilson "readily assented" and the "General Education Board made grant of money." This was the perfect role for Page and one in which he was ready to excel.[32]

APPOINTMENT AS AMBASSADOR

Page's plans were turned on their head when just a few days later President Wilson decided to offer him America's most prestigious diplomatic position: ambassador to the Court of St. James's (Great Britain). Wilson, House noted in his diary, "thought that Walter Page was about the best man left for Ambassador to Great Britain." While others, such as Alderman, had been advocating for a diplomatic position for Page, it was House's suggestion that held sway. On March 17, House mentioned it to McAdoo. They then commended the idea to Wilson three days later on March 20, who came to his decision on March 25.[33]

"Good morning, Your Excellency," Page heard when he answered the phone early on the morning of March 26, 1913. House was at the other end, and Page thought he was having some fun, writing later: "I thought his politeness was jocular." Wilson had authorized House to offer the position to Page, who had returned to New York from Pinehurst and was at his office desk. Page was incredulous and made a time to visit House that afternoon to discuss the offer. That night he discussed it with his wife Alice, who "didn't know enough about it" and son Frank, who was "enthusiastic." One of his other sons, Arthur, was not in favor, arguing everything his father was interested in was in America: "I would be thrown among people whom I did not know and would have duties that I cared little about." Page outlined his thought processes, including his doubts about being able to measure up in the job, the next day in a letter to Alderman: "Our friend in the White House pays me the high compliment and imposes on me the high duty of going as Ambassador to England. After wrestling with my fears of my ability to do such a task with distinction, I have let the spirit of adventure, which, I find, stills stirs in me, lead me on."[34]

The next day, March 28, Houston, who was visiting New York, called Page and asked him about rumors he was to be appointed ambassador. Page was taken aback, saying he had not heard anything directly from the president. Houston explained in his autobiography: "I told him I had been in the Cabinet for a number of weeks, and had seen the President a number of times, and that I had not yet had any word from him about my taking the position." According to Houston, Page was incredulous, responding, "Do you mean to tell me that he did not write you asking you if you would take the position and that he has not said a word directly to you about it?"[35]

The same day, Wilson wrote to Page formally asking if he would be willing to accept the position: "I am writing to ask whether you are willing that I should send your name in to the Senate when it meets again, as Ambassador to Great Britain." He went on to write about Page's characteristics he thought would be valuable in the role: "I hope with all my heart that you are. It would give me the deepest satisfaction to have in London a man whose character and ability and tact and ability to comprehend a situation and the men who formed a part of it I could so absolutely rely on; and it would be of the greatest advantage to the country and to the party. Pray say yes and make me content!"[36]

Page was surprised to have been offered the position, and it went against what he believed. In 1902 he wrote that too many ambassadors were appointed on the basis of political contributions rather than experience, so it became like a revolving door in line with election cycles: "The men who have had experience are recalled, and a new group, without experience, are sent abroad." He advocated a permanent, experienced diplomatic corps. Notwithstanding this, as Page thought about it, he felt an overwhelming sense of duty and began to relish the challenge offered by the president: "I had confidence in the President's character and purposes. He had a right to command the service of any man who was in sympathy with him. Did any man have a right to decline to do an important public service unless there were some insuperable private reason? I knew nothing about the duties; but should I shrink from a great adventure merely because of such ignorance? A man who should do that, would never have a great adventure."[37]

As he thought more about the position and the possible impacts it might have on his family, the fifty-seven-year-old Page was concerned, as they had lived in the "country," Alice had had a lack of social life, and Arthur, whom he had groomed to take over as editor of the *World's Work*, "would be overshadowed" if his father hung around. Katharine was about to graduate from Bryn Mawr and would have a great experience living in London with them. He had pleasurable thoughts about mixing, conversing, and making acquaintances with important people: "But I had worked so long in the trenches that I had had little time really to cultivate people; and I had associated too little with important persons: I had had dealings with them and had gone back to my trench again." He had "a sort of vague purpose to leave off active work at 60," though "this diplomatic task would bring change, obligatory social duties and I could test myself against men of consequence."[38]

After a few days Page wrote to Wilson accepting the position. Wilson was very pleased, replying, "Hurrah! I knew that I could count on you! Your letter of yesterday has made me deeply content." Wilson expected the position to be a sort of semiretirement, having previously offered it to two retired men in their late seventies, Richard Olney and Charles W. Eliot. Page was aware of this, though had no such intentions, as quoted on the front page of the New York *World* on the day his appointment was announced: "I shall go to Great Britain as a working Ambassador." Page took the chance to learn about the U.S. embassy in London. On April 4 he met with Henry White, a highly regarded career diplomat who had earlier been first secretary in the U.S. embassy in London, at the

Knickerbocker Club in New York where, as Page wrote in his diary, he "kindly coaches me about London Embassy." Then two days later he met with William Phillips who had been first secretary for about three years until late 1912.[39]

In his congratulatory letter of November 5, 1912, Page had urged Wilson to call Congress into session as soon as possible to "revise the tariff." Page stated it would give Wilson a "great tactical advantage—you can the better keep in line those who have debts or doubts before you have answered their importunities for offices and for favours." Page had long thought the practice of sending the president's message to Congress unsatisfactory, writing in 1883 that it had "come to be almost as uninfluential a thing as the Queen's speech to Parliament." Therefore he encouraged Wilson to address Congress personally: "The President reads (or speaks) his Inaugural to the people. Why not go back to the old custom of himself delivering his Messages to Congress? Would that not restore a feeling of comradeship in responsibility and make the Legislative branch feel nearer to the Executive? Every President of our time has sooner or later got away with Congress."[40]

Although the last time a president had addressed Congress was John Adams on November 22, 1800, in a move credited as the precursor of today's State of the Union addresses, this is exactly what the new president did. At midday on April 8, 1913, he interrupted his cabinet meeting to go to the capitol and address a joint session of Congress. Wilson used words similar to Page's, making it clear the purpose of personally addressing Congress was to leave the impression that "the President of the United States is a person, not a mere department of the Government hailing Congress from some isolated island of jealous power . . . he is a human being trying to co-operate with other human beings in a common service." As Page had suggested, Wilson stated his intention to honor his election promise to reduce tariffs, reflecting the fact that American companies no longer needed "protecting."[41]

At the time Walter and Alice were spending several days in Washington for social engagements. On April 12 they had lunch at the White House, when Alice met the president for the first time. Page also had meetings to prepare for his duties in London. As he emerged from meeting with Wilson and formally accepting the post, House met Page and asked, "Have you seen Bryan?" It dawned on Page that he hadn't "once thought of the Secretary of State!" Wilson had appointed William J. Bryan to the position, and as ambassador Page would report to him. He went over to the Department of State and the two men spent just ten minutes together and Page received no instructions.[42]

FINAL CONFERENCE FOR EDUCATION IN THE SOUTH

Page took a break from his ambassadorial preparations to travel to Richmond, Virginia, for the Conference for Education in the South from April 16–18. Ogden was too ill to attend so, Vice President Page presided. This was effectively the last conference as Ogden died in August 1913 and Page was his obvious successor to continue the transformation of education in the South. With him heading off to London, this never happened.

With the loss of Ogden and Page, the conference lost its grassroots focus. In this and subsequent years, the conference was run by the Southern Educational Association, which Charles Dabney believed, "departed entirely from the original purpose and ideals of the Southern Conference." What had been an informative and inspirational gathering that motivated, stimulated, and spread ideas among education experts and practitioners from the North and South was overwhelmed by a "multitude of new meetings for deliberative purposes on educational, economic, and industrial questions." The Southern Education Board was wound up in 1914, its remaining work transferred to local and other associations and societies.[43]

Page's legacy continued through the General Education Board that began to wind down in 1953, finally ending in 1964, and funded entirely by the donations of $187 million from the Rockefellers plus over $136 million in investment income. After Page had left, Buttrick wrote, "you planted seeds that are probably bearing fruit in these convictions which are coming over the rest of us." There was a significant cost to Southern education from Page leaving, an opportunity lost for further educational improvement and development.[44]

"FAREWELL TALK WITH W.W."

After the conference, Page returned to Washington and spent several days studying recent correspondence between the American and British governments, which seemed "very dull stuff" and made him wonder if it was "really worth a man's while." Despite this, he still felt it was an honor to be granted the position. A North Carolina member of Congress and others gave Page a dinner, presided over by his brother Bob. Secretary of State Bryan, who gave the only speech, "pumped Bob all through the dinner to find out the meagre facts of my life" and used them in his speech "with a genuinely kindly touch."[45]

On April 30 Page had, as he noted in his diary, a "Farewell talk with W.W." Although he had not expected to receive any direction from Bryan, he had anticipated obtaining instructions from Wilson and was disappointed when there were none. Wilson, according to Page "knew no more about the task that awaited me than I knew. Of course, the secretary of state knew nothing; his ignorance was taken for granted. But the president seemed to have in his mind only this idea—that he wanted somebody in London whom he knew and upon whose judgment he could rely. That was complimentary, but it lacked definiteness. The upshot of it all was that I had no idea what I was to do, where I was to live, nor what it would cost me." As Page reminded Wilson later, his only real advice was "go, and be yourself." While this was extreme in terms of poor communication, Page probably shouldn't have been surprised given his and Houston's earlier experiences.[46]

As he emerged from the White House, Page ran into Houston and they shared a joke between themselves about the unreality of the situations they found themselves in. It revealed something about Page's character. As Houston later told the story, "A few days after his confirmation by the Senate, as I was walking on Pennsylvania Avenue in front of the White House, I met our new Ambassador to the Court of St. James's, in the person of my old friend, Walter Hines Page. He was just coming through the gate from the White House grounds. As he came toward me, he was smiling. He gave one of his characteristic chuckles and said: 'Doesn't it beat the devil?' I asked him what the joke was. He replied: 'I am. Did you see that fellow come out of the White House grounds a few seconds ago? Did you notice the people staring at him? Did you see me among them looking at him with my mouth open? They tell me I am that man—that I am the Ambassador from the United States to the Court of St. James's. It isn't true. It's a dream. It's worse; it's a joke. I can't get used to this sort of show.'"[47]

Despite the lack of guidance from his president, the new ambassador was looking forward to the challenge. He had high expectations of interesting times, especially with his knowledge of, and interest in, what was happening in Europe.

PART FOUR
THE WORLD

\ 8 /

STARTING HIS "GREAT ADVENTURE"

PREWAR PERIOD—1913 TO 1914

ARRIVAL IN LONDON

Page and his son Frank left New York for London on May 15, 1913, aboard the *Baltic*, and they arrived on May 24. Alice stayed behind until Katharine graduated and to finish packing. They traveled on, as Katharine wrote, "the good old ferry-boat 'Adriatic.'" Feeling somewhat lonely 'Pagie' spent some of the trip writing an article for the Bryn Mawr 1913 yearbook about how she and her good friend Amy Gordon Hamilton spontaneously wrote many songs together after a "chance meeting on the campus." They arrived at the end of June, and Alice was horrified by the situation: Walter was living at the Coburg Hotel because there was no ambassador's residence, the embassy was downtrodden and there was nowhere near enough funds to cover expenses. House, who was with them, wrote in his diary: "She sees financial disaster staring them in the face." He went on to note Alice said she would not have agreed to Walter taking the position if she had known the true situation. Their precarious financial position was to cause Page increasing concern over his first year.[1]

The Pages arrived in time for the "season," the highlight of the social calendar, which ran over the summer from May to July. Aristocrats and other notable people descended on London from their country homes, from the empire, and from the rest of the world. Page wrote a letter to Wilson that captured the nature of the festivities and how much he enjoyed it: "The rich and the high and the climbing exercise on the social ladder and trapese; the Ambassadors dine one another and other great folk; American ladies come over to be presented; hundreds of people drink Mrs. Page's tea every Thursday afternoon (on July 4 they come 3,000 strong and knock a month's wages into a cock^d hat in 2 hours!); and we are supposed to have lots of fun; and the funny part of it is, we do!" He particularly enjoyed the socializing, having dined "with everybody, from the King to the newspaper man."[2]

When Page arrived in London it was the most important city in the world. It had the largest population of any city in history, over seven million people. New York and Paris had only three-quarters of this population and Berlin just over

163

half. It was the center of global finance and the busiest port, though both positions were about to be taken by New York. Its importance also stemmed from being the capital of the largest empire the world had known. International diplomacy was centered in London, with the foreign secretary, Sir Edward Grey, taking a leading role in efforts to maintain world peace. The experienced Grey had been in office since 1905. Classical and imposing, the Foreign Office dominated King Charles Street and was a short walk from the U.S. embassy at 123 Victoria Street. Also close to the embassy was the newly renovated Buckingham Palace, residence of Britain's ceremonial head of state, King George V. As Britain was a constitutional monarchy, the nation was ruled by a democratically elected government led by the prime minister, Herbert H. Asquith.[3]

One of the consequences of America's lack of international focus was the state of its diplomatic facilities in London. After three months at the Coburg Hotel, Page rented a house at 6 Grosvenor Square. Years later a story was related in the *Indianapolis Times* about him being "accosted by a London policeman in a park late one night and ordered 'to go home.' Page turned and exclaimed: 'Home? I have no home. I am the American ambassador.'" Compounding this, as he told Wilson, the embassy was located in a "cheap shopping street" with an entrance "the same as to the cheap flats above" and "once in a while I have met immodest-looking women in the hall." Consequently, around September 1914, Page moved the embassy from "the obscure and undignified and dirty-beyond-cleaning old hole" to Grosvenor Gardens. For no more rent than the old premises, they had a whole house, which gave them three times the space. As he told Wilson, "It will be the first dignified offices we've ever had in London."[4]

"ONE OF MY OLDEST AND BEST FRIENDS"

In his first fourteen months he thrived performing the ceremonial, diplomatic, and official duties required of the U.S. ambassador in London. This was not surprising for such an aficionado of English culture, literature, and history who believed a strong relationship was essential for both nations. On December 21, Page wrote to Wilson giving him an idea of his activities: "During the last month I have made almost a speech a day—most of them after-dinner speeches before such bodies as The Royal Society, the Economic Section of the University of London, The Authors' Club, the Worshipful Company of Mercers, the Navy League and the like; and I have tried to present one idea in each little speech that sh^d give the company one clear-cut notion of some part of the work of our great Democracy." He was enjoying his adventure: "If the King lives as long as I've toasted and sung him in my hopes of long life to him, he'll be immortal. He must have got some inkling of it, for he sent me two brace of pheasants the other day." Page was keen to promote his president. His Authors' Club speech was "President Wilson as a Man of Letters," and in it he enthused, "I am most thankful to say that Mr. Wilson happens to be one of my oldest and best friends, and I cannot divest myself of his friendship." He went on to describe Wilson's life, achievements, and popularity, concluding with gratitude to Wilson for appointing him ambassador. Page then said: "I owe him, also, the intellectual stimulus and companionship of more than thirty years."[5]

Not long after, he stayed at Windsor Castle where he had dinner with the king, followed by a private discussion. He wrote to Wilson: "Before I lie down in the King's bed, I jot down for you the conversation we have just had, chiefly about Mexico." Page concluded that although the conversation "lacked definiteness," the King was "frank and friendly and well-informed—very much better informed than most Americans imagine, and very much more of a man than he has got credit for being outside his own Kingdom."[6]

On September 9, 1913, Wilson's tariff reduction bill passed Congress and, from Skibo Castle in Scotland, Page sent congratulations: "Score one! You have done a great historic deed and demonstrated and abundantly justified your leadership." He had been telling the editor of the *Economist* "that the passing of commercial supremacy to the United States will be dated in the economic histories from the Tariff act of 1913." Wilson replied, recalling his own short stay at Skibo, and agreed with Page: "I do know in my mind that what we are accomplishing with regard to the tariff is going to be just as epoch-making as you indicate and in just the way you foresee."[7]

This was the issue that had brought them together and had come to a very satisfactory conclusion. On October 3, Wilson signed into law the Revenue Act of 1913. It was the largest reduction in tariffs for fifty years. By 1920 it would lead to by far the lowest levels of tariff revenue as a percentage of imports for at least a hundred years, falling from 18 percent in 1913 to 6 percent in 1920. The act sought to compensate for this decline in tariff revenue by introducing a federal income tax. This was a much more efficient tax—spreading the tax burden across the population more broadly, rather than concentrating on selected products and impacting only on the people and businesses which purchased them. It was potentially the first step in changing the way Americans thought about protection for their manufacturing industries. All this was particularly satisfying to Page.[8]

"YOUR LETTERS ARE A LAMP TO MY FEET"

Page had the embassy operating smoothly. He broke the practice of previous ambassadors and had regular staff meetings, as he told House: "I have organized my staff as a sort of Cabinet. We meet every day. We go over everything conceivable that we say or try to do. We do good team work." Page inspired great loyalty. Edward Bell, the second secretary brought in after Page had the incumbent transferred, later told Page's son Arthur: "How I wish I had even a small fraction of your father's talent for getting work out of his subordinates without asking for it. We were all ready to tear our shirts to accomplish anything he wanted."[9]

Dealing with the State Department was the greatest source of frustration for Page. The biggest problems were lack of responses to letters or telegrams, being kept in the dark regarding the government's positions on issues and policies, and the leaking of confidential communications to the press. In his letter to Wilson of December 21 he noted it had been the same for previous ambassadors, and U.S. embassies on the European continent were having similar problems. Page was having doubts about the usefulness of his work as "the vast silence across the ocean and the rhetorical indefiniteness at the other end of the line give a feeling at times of a vast vagueness." Wilson's letters were "the only definite things I get." Page sent other complaints to Wilson as well as to Bryan and House. He lamented to House, "Washington is a deep hole of silence toward Ambassadors." It was a great concern to Wilson, and he made this evident to Page on numerous occasions. On January 6, 1914, he wrote, "Back of the smile which came to my face when you spoke of the impenetrable silence of the State Department toward its foreign representatives lay thoughts of very serious concern. We must certainly manage to keep our foreign representatives properly informed. The real trouble is to conduct genuinely confidential correspondence except through private letters, but surely the thing can be changed and it will be if I can manage it."[10]

Wilson took action and in May hoped Page was getting "something like systematic information," which he had requested be provided by the State Department. Before this he had advised Page more than once to write to him directly, such as on February 24, 1914, when he wrote, "If there is anything in particular you want information about, do not hesitate to write to me directly and I will see that it is supplied to you." Later in the year there was a significant problem with Page's correspondence being leaked from the Department. When Page cabled Wilson to complain, his response was that he and Bryan were "chagrined."

STARTING HIS "GREAT ADVENTURE" / 167

They had been trying to find the source of the leaks and were "going to take thorough-going measures."[11]

Page certainly needed no encouragement to get around the problem by writing directly to Wilson and also to his friend House, who had become the president's unofficial chief adviser. He wrote prodigiously. Many of his letters were largely written as if he was editorializing at the *World's Work*. He wrote about his opinions on a wide range of issues, as well as impressions of London, England, and continental Europe. He was particularly observant and perceptive regarding culture and politics. Other parts of the letters were imparting important and confidential information. To Wilson, Page was always respectful, though he still made his opinions on specific issues very clear. Wilson greatly appreciated them, writing, "Your private and confidential letters to me are invaluable," and "Your letters are a lamp to my feet. I feel as I read that their analysis is searching and true."[12]

Wilson gave an example of how he used Page's letters on February 24, 1914: "I not only appreciate your letters but I profit by them, profit very much. They supply me with the impressions and the information which make my persuasions effective when I meet the Foreign Relations Committee of the Senate. You have a great faculty for making things real about which you write and I feel after I have read one of your letters as if I had been in London and seen the people you are dealing with and received the same impressions that you, yourself, have received from what they do and say."[13]

Page's ability to frankly describe key people and their opinions letters helped his president understand the importance of personal contact in diplomacy, as Wilson wrote on April 2, 1914: "I have come to see that the real knowledge of the relations between countries in matters of public policy is to be gained at country houses, and dinner tables, and not in diplomatic correspondence, in brief, that when we know the men and the currents of opinion we know more than foreign ministers can tell us, and your letters give me in a thoroughly dignified way just the sidelights that are necessary to illuminate the picture."[14]

One of Wilson's cabinet secretaries told Alice that after quoting from one of her husband's letters in a cabinet meeting, the president went on to enthuse: "Some day, I hope that Walter Page's letters will be published. They are the best letters I have ever read. They make you feel the atmosphere in England, understand the people, and see into the motives of the great actors." Houston stated in his autobiography: "I heard him [Wilson] say more than once that Page was the best letter writer he knew, and that, when his letters appeared at the proper time, they would make the most interesting contribution to the story of the period." A 2020 paper by the State Department's History Office noted the relationship between Page and Wilson was a "unique element" of the ambassadorship, leading to direct communication that circumvented the Department and the secretary of state.[15]

INTERNATIONAL ISSUES AND POLICIES

With his extensive understanding of international issues, Page was well suited for his policy-related duties. Over his editorial career he had published numerous relevant articles, and the *World's Work's* international coverage was the most extensive of all the major American magazines, including Page's wide-ranging editorials on international events. He had a great understanding of America's place in the world and its relationship with Great Britain, as well as interest in relations between Great Britain and European countries, especially Germany. A number of his editorials could be seen as prescient, including in May 1903 when he recognized German "restlessness" as a threat to European peace.[16]

He had the good fortune to arrive at his post when Britain was looking to develop an alliance with America. Britain had supported America or conceded to it on a number of key issues including the Spanish-American War (1898), the second Hay-Pauncefote Treaty on building the Panama Canal (1901), and the border between Alaska and Canada (1903). On November 2, Page advised Wilson the British valued the U.S. government's goodwill and would only risk losing it if there were more important domestic implications to consider.[17]

Despite this, when Page took up his position there were two issues causing diplomatic tension and testing relations between the nations: Panama Canal tolls, and a Mexican presidential assassination and coup.

PANAMA CANAL TOLLS

Before taking up the ambassadorship, Page had published articles in the *Forum* on the Panama Canal and written many editorials in the *World's Work* about the dispute with Britain. In December 1900 he wrote the Panama Canal was "one of the inevitable and necessary great tasks that must be done by the United States Government," and stated it was important to settle "Great Britain's rights and interests on the Isthmus." The 1901 Hay-Pauncefote Treaty gave construction rights to America on condition the canal "be free and open" to ships "of all Nations . . . on terms of entire equality." It stated, "such conditions and charges of traffic shall be just and equitable." In 1912 Congress had passed a bill exempting

American ships engaged in domestic trade from paying tolls, which was signed into law by President Taft. Britain considered this law to be a violation of the treaty that would affect shipping, one of their major industries, and protested to the U.S. government.[18]

In February 1913 Page had pointed out in the *World's Work* that the treaty did not allow such discrimination in the charging of tolls between ships of different nations. He stated that, as America had ratified the treaty, "good or bad, it stands; and the main question is the sacredness of a treaty." He went on to say one of the negotiators, Joseph Choate, had recently stated that the U.S. had explicitly waived its right to discriminate between nations on tolls." Page believed the new law was simply a subsidy to American shipping lines, which he thought a bad idea, though if it had to be done then do it without "the repudiation of an international covenant."[19]

On April 15 President Wilson had raised the issue in cabinet, as Houston noted, "He had been giving much thought to the matter" and that he was "inclined to be against the existing exemption of American ships on both economic and moral grounds." While Wilson wanted to act immediately to repeal the exemption, there were complications: his party's 1912 election policy was favorable treatment for American ships, Bryan opposed Wilson's position, and, probably most significantly, it was unlikely the Senate would support such a move. Congress had justified the law by arguing America had undertaken construction and the exemption did not give an advantage to American ships competing with those from Britain or any other nation engaged in international trade. The law had strong support from most Republicans and the public. So it was left in abeyance.[20]

Page took the initiative to sort out the dispute, though his biggest hurdle was trying to generate political interest in America. After discussions with Sir Edward Grey that commenced in June 1913, Page took the first steps to stirring the U.S. government into action by writing to House in August about the negative impression hesitation was creating. If America repealed the exemptions, Page stated, it would have significant influence over Britain: "We can command the British fleet, British manufacturers—anything we please," though if it was not repealed they would "regard us as mean and stingy and dishonourable on occasion and, therefore, peculiar and given to queer freaks." The next month he wrote to Wilson stating, "We made a bargain—a solemn compact—and we have broken it."[21]

Wilson agreed with Page. Although he did not like some aspects of the treaty, he believed it should be honored. He did not again discuss it in cabinet, though by March 5, 1914, he felt he had enough political capital and addressed Congress in an attempt to persuade them to go against public opinion and repeal the exemption provision of the law. He used words similar to Page's: "We consented to the treaty; its language we accepted, if we did not originate it"; and just because America had the power to interpret the treaty as it pleased that did not justify it doing so if no other nation had the same interpretation: "The large thing to do is the only thing we can afford to do, a voluntary withdrawal from a position everywhere questioned and misunderstood."[22]

There was a slight hiccup when Page inadvertently made comments in a speech on March 11 indicating British business, as the biggest shippers, would most benefit from the canal. American opponents of repealing the tolls capitalized on this, using it in their campaign. Although it was politically motivated to get at Wilson, Page was horrified, apologizing to Wilson numerous times and offering to resign. Wilson did not accept, writing on March 25, "You may be sure that none of us who knew you or read the speech felt anything but admiration for it." He blamed Democrat senators for creating "artificial difficulties" and "Mr. Bryan read your speech yesterday to the Cabinet, who greatly enjoyed it." Wilson reassured Page: "I want you to feel constantly how I value the intelligent and effective work you are doing in London. I do not know what I should do without you." Then a week later he wrote insisting Page not distress himself about the speech. He agreed with Page that it was a mistake to raise the matter "while it was right hot," though he fully agreed with the speech as there "can be no rational objection to it." He again assured Page, stating: "pray realize how thoroughly and entirely you are enjoying my confidence and admiration."[23]

The repeal passed Congress on June 11, 1914, after which Page sent a telegram to Wilson offering "hearty congratulations" and enthusing "there are expressions of gratification on all sides."[24]

"WILSON DOCTRINE"

On February 18, 1913, President Francisco Madero of Mexico was assassinated on the orders of General Victoriano Huerta, who took over as president. As this occurred during the final days of the previous administration, President Taft had left the question whether to recognize the new government to his successor. President Wilson refused to accept Huerta's legitimacy, declaring he would not recognize a leader who had come to power by "arbitrary or irregular force." Britain had recognized the new government, it was thought by Wilson and many others, to protect its citizens' business interests, especially oil wells that were the Royal Navy's main source of fuel.[25]

STARTING HIS "GREAT ADVENTURE" / 171

While this merely caused awkwardness in the initial months of Wilson's administration, it became strained with the appointment by Britain in July 1913 of an anti-American ambassador to Mexico, Sir Lionel Carden. This was compounded by allegations Lord Cowdray's Mexican Eagle Oil Company, owner of the oil wells, was dictating British government policy on Mexico. Page had to convince Grey, during a series of meetings in October and November, how serious it was for the U.S. government.[26]

On November 2, Page wrote to Wilson recognizing the significance of his stance: "Out of your insisting on a moral basis of government for Mexico must emerge a real policy for all the volcanic states in Latin-America; and it will emerge, as all right policies do, from proper and courageous action on a concrete case and not as a mere abstract doctrine. That's the value of it." The problem, he explained on November 22, was trying to convince the English, whose main concern was that order was kept in Mexico, regardless of who led the government. Page related how he had explained to Grey many times "how the policy that we all too easily have followed for a long time of recognizing any sort of an adventurer in Latin America had, of course, simply encouraged revolutions." He had assured Grey that "he need not be greatly concerned about the successor to Huerta; that this is primarily and ultimately an American problem." Grey was concerned it might take two centuries before Mexican self-government, and Page replied: "Well, the United States will be here for two centuries." He congratulated his president on "the historic Wilson doctrine."[27]

Page organized meetings in America between House and acting British ambassador Sir William Tyrrell. Page had spoken with Tyrrell in London before he left for Washington. Tyrrell then had meetings with Wilson, who on December 6 wrote to Page that he appreciated these "absolutely frank talks" and "you had laid the ground out in exactly the same terms I would myself have used."

In January 1914, Grey confirmed Britain would be guided by the United States on matters in the Western Hemisphere, and decided to transfer Carden. Wilson wrote to Page on January 6, 1914, crediting Page's urgings and reassurances with resolving the matter: "it is indeed a most fortunate thing and I feel sure is to be ascribed to your tactful and yet very plain representations to Sir Edward Grey" and stated "I congratulate you with all my heart on his transference." After this Mexico ceased to be an issue in American-British relations. Page's response was typically low-key in describing his contribution. He knew he had not solely resolved the matter, though he had played an important part, writing on December 28, "An abler man would have done it better; but, as it was I did it."[28]

He still had some work to do countering public opinion, writing to Wilson on February 22, "The feeling is strong here (I encounter it in London, in Leeds, in Newcastle) that our Government wishes to prohibit European financial adventurers from exploiting Central and South America because we wish to exploit them ourselves!" He had difficulty convincing the British of America's approach, moving away from the European practice of "the parcelling out of the world" to create colonies, to focusing on "popular government and popular welfare." Wilson sent replies a few months later. In one of these he wrote, "It seems to me that you are handling our critics, one by one, most admirably." He wanted them to understand the true situation, which vindicated the U.S. position: "There has been less disorder and less danger to life where the Constitutionalists have gained control than there has been where Huerta is in control."[29]

"SOCIAL HAPPY-HUNTING-GROUNDS OF RICH MEN"

On April 7, 1914, Page most reluctantly wrote a letter to Wilson that he had been putting off as long as he could, lamenting he could not afford to remain as ambassador unless his allowance was significantly increased. In his ignorance he had planned to live on $22–25,000 a year, with about $5–7,000 of this from his own funds. He now estimated it would be $45,000 in his first year and of this $28,000 "out of my own pocket." These figures indicate Page had an allowance of $17,000. The rent on the embassy offices at 123 Victoria Street had been raised from $1,500 to $5,000 per annum, rent for his house was $10,000, and he had used his savings to keep the embassy running. Page was disappointed no one had warned him of this, not even a previous ambassador, Joseph Choate. Otherwise, he said, he wouldn't have taken it on. To cover future shortfalls, he would have "to dispose of a part of my interest in the publishing house or borrow money to be paid in subsequent years." Such was his commitment to the job he did not begrudge the spending of his own limited funds, "but I do not think a man at my age ought to go in debt for such a thing—or for anything."[30]

Wilson replied on May 18 noting a bill was before Congress which included "$15,000 for the payment of the rentals at London." Page believed this was not enough and was forced to write again. On June 5 he sent an eleven-page letter comprehensively explaining the problem, reiterating some of the points from his previous letter. Having spent over $30,000 of his own money, he had been forced to go into debt. It was "so much more than I can afford" that his initial reaction was to ask to be recalled, though instead he decided to explain the situation and see if it could be resolved. He calculated $45,000 to $50,000 a

STARTING HIS "GREAT ADVENTURE" / 173

year was needed to run the embassy, supporting his claim by extensively outlining the demands on the ambassadorial finances. Much was entertainment of embassy visitors and guests, and travel: "Not a day passes but I am making speeches or taking journeys, short or long, by rail or by motor, trying to interpret our institutions and our life." He believed these activities were essential to improve understanding of America among British people. He was grateful for the $15,000 noted by Wilson, though Page calculated it would only be an $8,000 increase in his current allowance. Using the above calculation, this suggests an increase to $25,000.

Page emphatically made his point: "For we have gone on in this shabby fashion so long that perhaps no conceivable Congress can be made to understand what an Embassy is—or ought to be—we have gone on making them the social happy-hunting-grounds of rich men and continually lowering our own standing in English eyes at least; and this is one reason why our Government is held in contempt here, cordially as they regard our people and our nation." Without a further increase in his allowance, it would not be viable to remain ambassador. He would resign so the president could "find a man of fortune for this post." He clearly felt ashamed to be representing a country so embarrassingly unable to present a positive image in "the centre of the world." [31]

Wilson responded with an additional annual allowance of $25,000, which would have taken the total amount to Page's required $50,000, so he stayed. The funds were from a private benefactor, so it was merely a temporary solution. Page was also instructed by Wilson to renew the lease on his house, though again it was only short-term. This indifference to international diplomatic relations had been a long-term concern for Page, believing America needed to have a permanent diplomatic service. For example, in 1909 he strongly criticized Congress' practice of "underpaying ambassadors" and "neglecting to provide permanent and proper houses for embassies." For Page, this was indicative of America's unreadiness to take its place on the world stage. [32]

AMERICA THE UNREADY

Soon after arriving in London Page realized that, unless something was done to prevent it, a war in Europe was inevitable; and it would be a war between democracy and autocracy. While he was confident democracy was the future, he believed Europe's autocratic monarchies would try to survive by conquering other countries to shore up their power, and only America could prevent this happening.

For decades Page had argued America needed to start taking on a world leadership role, as its growth in economic and industrial power had significantly increased its influence and importance in international affairs. He believed President Cleveland's 1887 commitment to tariff reform was a move away from isolationism. In 1900 he argued the people had recognized their nation should take a larger role in international affairs when they re-elected President William McKinley: "There is no mistaking the larger meaning of the Presidential election. The events of the last four years have indicated the passing of the period of our international isolation; and the people have shown their understanding and approval of the change with an emphasis that they have not used since they expressed their understanding and approval of the war to preserve the Union." America had moved from its period of procuring, exploring, and settling land, which necessitated a "narrower economic and political vision." The 1898 war with Spain had lifted the nation's horizon to see "more clearly the place that we had won in the world." After McKinley was assassinated on September 14, 1901, Page lamented he had stood for the end of isolation, with a program to increase American engagement with the rest of the world. Writing a year later, Page praised McKinley for acting as a leader should by "leading the thought of his country and of his party to a wider and higher policy." He had not let himself be led by popular opinion, acting on the strength of his convictions and communicating directly with the people with speeches that "made a profound impression." Page believed the move away from isolationism was reinforced by subsequent presidential election results and events.[33]

"COMMERCIAL, POLITICAL AND INTELLECTUAL" WORLD LEADERSHIP

Page's concept of American world leadership was very different to the traditional approach of creating colonies. Unlike many other influential men of the time, he had developed a broad view of America's role in the world through his practice of obtaining facts and data before making decisions or forming opinions. Consequently, he understood the magnitude of American engagement with the rest of the world. American trade was vital to some countries' military strength, as he wrote in 1900: "What with our ownership of one-half of the coal area of the world, and furnishing at the present time one-third of its total production, the day is no longer distant when we will furnish not only food for the industrial and military armies of some of our chief competitors, but also the fuel by which they are supported." Page went on to provide data proving the commercial supremacy of America over the European powerhouses of Germany and Great Britain.[34]

America's leadership was "commercial, political, and intellectual." It was taking markets from the "Old World" by doing things better, "our knack of doing things." This was enabling greater political influence. Page reinforced this point in 1904 when some Central and South American countries were suspicious of U.S. intentions to invade and colonize them: "While conquest and annexation are worse than absurd—for no sane man in the United States desires it and no administration or party that should propose it could survive—yet in the course of time these countries must and will come more and more under our influence. But this influence will be won in the peaceful ways of trade." Using "peaceful and helpful methods," the United States would, Page believed, play a pivotal role in the advancement of civilization and development of stable government in Central and South America.[35]

Page saw American involvement in China in 1904 as further evidence of his nation taking on a leadership role to restrict the colonialist tendencies of military powers and promote peace. On February 8, a Japanese attack on the Russian navy at Port Arthur in the Chinese province of Manchuria led to significant losses. Page stated American policy was to prevent a war occurring that might lead to the dividing of China; it indicated to Japan, China and the "other powers," including Russia, "that China must be kept intact." Page optimistically believed this was a turning point for American foreign policy: "These events prove that we must now and hereafter play so important a part in the world that no government can take any serious action without indirectly consulting us. Our trade, our treaties, our great granaries, our vast supplies, our money market—every chancellery in the world consults these great facts before it dares declare war or to think seriously of changing the map even of the most remote part of the earth." He believed there had been a change in public opinion, to be more outward looking and confident.[36] This had been America's attitude regarding Mexico in 1913, and Page believed it was now time to look further afield and take on this role in Europe.

DEMOCRATIC WORLD LEADERSHIP

For people living in Europe under autocratic monarchies that tightly controlled the press and restricted freedom of speech and association, America was like a beacon: Millions had migrated across the Atlantic seeking the freedom, equality, and opportunities that come with democracy. The American example showed people could rule themselves, that they did not need hereditary rulers with their accompanying privileged aristocracy. In 1864, on the eve of Abraham Lincoln's re-election, Professor Edouard Laboulaye from the College de France, in Paris, expressed the feeling across the continent: "So long as there shall be across the Atlantic a society of thirty millions of men, living happily and peacefully under a government of their choice, with laws made by themselves, liberty will cast her rays over Europe like an illuminating pharos." During the Civil War there was a real danger that if America failed, this beacon would have been extinguished and the ruling classes would have been more powerful than ever. President Lincoln recognized its international implications when he said in his Gettysburg Address the war was testing whether America "or any nation so conceived" as a democracy could endure. In 1900 Frederic Emory, chief of the Bureau of Foreign Commerce at the State Department, identified in a *World's Work* article that this influence was one of the most profound impacts of America as a nation: "It is a well-established fact that the destinies of nations within the past century have been largely controlled by the example of the United States."[37]

Page believed America was leading countries toward democracy: "Its influence has broadened the thought of the Old World, and is now felt in the Oldest World. It is liberalizing kings toward their uncrowning, and softening class distinctions, and it is making all artificial authority obsolete." This idea was accepted throughout the nation, illustrated by comments such as those in a local Iowa newspaper in 1905 that referred to America as "the great country of which the oppressed European dreams and which means to him liberty and life." It was also what Wilson believed. On October 13, 1910, he concluded a gubernatorial campaign speech by stating the nation's destiny was to "do the thinking of the world" that would be "ruled by our passions." America, he said, "is not a piece of the surface of the earth. America is not merely a body of towns. America is an idea, America is an ideal, America is a vision." Then later as president, he proudly stated that "America stands for opportunity. America stands for a free field and no favor. America stands for a government responsive to the interests of all."[38]

Most of his life Page had recognized democracy in America was flawed, especially in the South where millions had been disenfranchised and segregation was becoming more entrenched. Women were only allowed to vote in several states and political corruption was rife. Despite this, Page remained hopeful for the future for a number of reasons. America did have varying degrees of transparency and accountability in different jurisdictions, it lacked "fixed classes and hereditary privileges," illiteracy was declining, and importantly there was a free press, as Page himself had shown.[39]

MISSED OPPORTUNITIES TO AVOID WAR

With America indirectly a world leader, the time had come, Page believed, to openly take the side of democracy by working with Britain and its democratic former colonies to ensure peace. Having been saying to his friends, he would like "the President of the United States and the King of England stand up side by side and let the world take a good look at them!" On July 20, 1913, he wrote to Wilson suggesting he visit England. He reinforced this move with a letter to House on August 25, saying he had written to Wilson encouraging him to visit England and asking House if he would "do the pushing," because if the president visited "the old Earth would sit up and rub its eyes and take notice to whom it belongs." Old Europe would be forced to face up to the shifting of power away from their tired, warring autocratic monarchies to democracies supported by America's economic and industrial power. It might "prevent an English-German war and an American-Japanese war."[40]

At a practical level, if President Wilson had stood with King George, Germany might have been deterred from declaring war and facing the prospect of losing its main source of food and other essential supplies such as copper and cotton. In 1903 Page had noted in the *World's Work* that England and Germany had become dependent on America to feed their populations and would remain so for the foreseeable future.[41]

The most pressing argument for his idea, Page reasoned, was that in a war for democracy America would end up supporting Britain if it looked like it would be defeated, rather than risk a world dominated by autocracies. Therefore, America would be better off avoiding a war altogether by siding with Britain before it started. On September 11, 1913, Wilson responded by agreeing with Page's suggestion, though lamenting that as president he should focus on domestic affairs: "As for your suggestion that I should, myself, visit England during my term of office, I must say that I agree with all your arguments for it, and yet the case against the President's leaving the country, particularly now that he is expected to exercise a constant leadership in all parts of the business of the government, is very strong and I am afraid overwhelming. It might be the beginning of a practice of visiting foreign countries which would lead Presidents rather far afield. It is a most attractive idea, I can assure you, and I turn away from it with the greatest reluctance."[42]

A key aspect of the Monroe Doctrine, enunciated by President James Monroe on the advice of Thomas Jefferson and others in 1823, was that America would not get involved in European affairs. Successive presidents had followed this practice, and a sitting president had never traveled to Europe. The first president to travel internationally was Theodore Roosevelt, when in 1906 he inspected Panama Canal construction. William Taft traveled for the same purpose in 1909, and later the same year visited President Diaz of Mexico. Ironically, Wilson became the first president to visit Europe when he traveled to the Versailles Peace Conference in 1918, and during 1919 became the most traveled president in history. This travel record was only surpassed by the next wartime president, Franklin D. Roosevelt (1933 to 1945).

While Wilson's reasoning was consistent with this practice, Page believed that era was over: America no longer needed to act as a colony, unsure of itself in international affairs and deferring to other nations, especially European, for leadership. During the political controversy over his speech on the Panama Canal tolls, he was accused of "truckling to British opinion." Page expressed frustration that American leaders did not realize their nation was so strong and powerful there was no need for their ambassador in London to "truckle": "Why doesn't some man who knows tell the whole truth, if it can be told without boasting—that we are so big and strong and rich, that the economic and political future of the world so clearly belongs to us that it is impossible for any business man who sees the nations in their proper proportions and relations to fear or tremble or imitate or 'truckle to' or to ask any improper favours of any nation on earth—that the 'trucklers' are those that kick up all this dust—they and only they?"[43]

Wilson was conscious of his nation's inexperience in international relations. On December 6, 1913, he wrote to Page regarding the lack of communication and coordination with him by the State Department on the Mexican dispute: "We have, I fear, a somewhat amateur hand in doing these things as yet and may leave you uninformed when we have no intention of doing so. We will get down to systematic business by degrees as our inexperience wears off." He appeared as frustrated as Page about the lack of American engagement in international relations, writing on January 6, 1914: "I long, as you do, for an opportunity to do constructive work all along the line in our foreign relations, particularly with Great Britain and the Latin-American states." He went on to say the most constructive work, "aside from definite acts of policy," was the diplomatic work Page was doing in London. Wilson's focus was on matters which directly affected America, such as the Panama tolls, rather than the true international perspective Page was advocating.[44]

Just over a year after Page made his suggestion to Wilson, in July 1914, Russian Foreign Minister Sergius Sazonoff used the same logic, the main difference being that he based his argument on geography while Page had focused on democracy. Trying to persuade Britain to join the Russian-French alliance, Sazonoff argued that war would be avoided if Britain, France, and Russia stood united against Germany and Austria-Hungary. He stated that if Britain did not stand now the war would start and Britain would be drawn into it anyway. Britain declined to join the alliance, Grey told the French ambassador (France had also tried to pressure Britain into joining) in London: "If Germany became involved and France became involved, we had not made up our minds what we should do; it was a case that we should have to consider." Prime Minister Asquith recognized Europe was headed for "Armageddon," though he told his king: "Happily there seems to be no reason why we should be anything more than spectators." British chancellor of the exchequer David Lloyd George told a journalist "there could be no question of our taking part in any war in the first instance."[45]

Germany was essentially an autocracy as Kaiser Wilhelm II had ultimate power over foreign and military decisions. His most powerful adviser was the chancellor, Theobald von Bethmann-Hollweg, an unelected public servant. The kaiser's military advisers, unelected military commanders, reported directly to him; they were not under the chancellor's control and were not accountable to the public. They were extremely influential and exercised considerable control over the Kaiser. There were elements of democracy as Bethmann-Hollweg, for reasons undefined at the time, had to take account of support from the Reichstag, whose members were elected, and public opinion.[46]

The U.S. government was looking at other ways to prevent a European war. In December 1913 House outlined in a letter to Page a proposal he had put to Wilson. House would travel to Germany and try to persuade the kaiser to agree to the "naval holiday" proposed by Winston Churchill. In March 1913, Churchill, then first lord of the admiralty, had proposed Britain and Germany stop expanding their navies for twelve months. Germany replied that it could not depart from its "naval law" requiring fleet expansion, so Britain responded it would build two ships for every one Germany built. In this environment, House proposed America would act as a mediator.[47]

Over the next few months, the plan developed into a proposal from Wilson and House for a pact between America, Britain, and Germany for permanent cooperation. House arrived in Berlin as the president's personal representative around May 22, 1914, and soon after had long talks with the political leaders, except Bethmann-Hollweg (whose wife had died). House came up against the power of the military leaders and they treated him poorly, in some cases with contempt, and almost prevented him meeting with the kaiser. Despite this, they eventually met on June 1. Although House wrote to Page that this meeting had been "satisfactory," he was not confident war could be averted because of the kaiser's weak leadership and subservience to the military.[48]

Page referred to House's plan in two letters to Wilson on July 5. In the first he appears to have accepted House's version, writing, "House has, I am sure, written you of his success and of the letter he is writing to the German Emperor." Page naively indicated the plan had succeeded and a protocol was in place for friendly negotiations between the three nations to resolve almost every issue. His second letter was more realistic, noting that though he was keeping House's idea in front of Grey, the British did not trust the Germans. Page knew House was wasting his time. A few months later he told Wilson that he had drafted a letter to House explaining the "utterly futility" of his plan, though he burned it, not wanting to discourage House.[49]

Page knew it was a lost opportunity. For House's plan to work Wilson and House needed to have shown leadership and forced the issue, though they failed to understand how much potential their country had to wield power. With the era of European supremacy and empire-building coming to an end, Page realized it was time for America to step up to the plate. Later in July war broke out between Austria and Serbia, and Page wrote to Wilson: "Monarchy and privilege and pride will have it out before they die—at what cost! If they do have a general war they will so set back the march of progress in Europe as to set the day forward for American leadership."[50]

Therefore it would be for the good of Europe and the rest of the world for America to be a leader with the support of the other democracies. To his great disappointment it didn't happen before the war; and wouldn't happen until the end of World War II, more than three decades later.

\ 9 /

THE WARTIME CHALLENGE OF NEUTRALITY

WORLD WAR I—1914 AND 1915

"CRAZY MEN AND WEEPING WOMEN"

"The Grand Smash is come" wrote Page in a personal memorandum on Sunday August 2, 1914. The previous night the German ambassador in St. Petersburg had handed the Russian government a declaration of war. Page was reluctant though unwavering in his belief that Britain had no choice but to become involved, otherwise Germany would "take Belgium and Holland, France would be betrayed, and England would be accused of forsaking her friends." He and Alice were, as he had written to Wilson earlier, in a "pretty little country house" twenty-five miles from London, where they had planned to spend "the quiet" three months. Page returned to London and that night wrote to the president saying Britain's and France's involvement was inevitable. Page immediately thought about what America could do, though "they don't want peace on the Continent—the ruling military classes do not." He was confident America would have a role when they did want peace, which he told Wilson would be "*your* opportunity to play an important and historic part."[1]

When Britain declared war on August 4, it was officially due to Germany's violation of the Anglo-French-Prussian treaty of 1839, which guaranteed Belgium's neutrality, though Page was correct in believing there were broader considerations. As Grey told him soon after, "The issue for us is that, if Germany wins, she will dominate France; the independence of Belgium, Holland, Denmark, and perhaps of Norway and Sweden, will be a mere shadow; their separate existence as nations will be a fiction; all their harbours will be at Germany's disposal; she will dominate the whole of Western Europe, and this will make our position quite impossible. We could not exist as a first class State under such circumstances." This realization by Grey and Britain that its prewar neutrality was a fiction vindicated Sazonoff's argument of deterrence, just as Page's argument against American neutrality would be vindicated much later in the war.[2]

America was officially neutral; it did not support either the Allies (led by Britain, France, and Russia) or the Central Powers (Germany and Austria-Hungary). On August 9, Page sent a letter to Wilson with ten pages of graphic and colorful descriptions of the previous week. He and his staff at the embassy had dealt with a vast number and variety of people: "Crazy men and weeping women were imploring and cursing and demanding—God knows it was bedlam turned loose." He described how America was asked by Germany to take over their embassy, and feared the German ambassador, who tried to prevent the war, "might literally go mad." The remarkably raw reactions of that man and other leaders in London made a great impression on him: "I shall never forget Sir Edward Grey's telling me of the ultimatum—while he wept; nor the poor German Ambassador who has lost in his high game—almost a demented man; nor the King as he declaimed at me for half-an-hour and threw up his hands and said, 'My God, Mr. Page, what else could we do?' Nor the Austrian Ambassador's wringing his hands and weeping and crying out 'My dear colleague, my dear colleague.'" Soon after, Page also took charge of the Austria-Hungary embassy after being requested by their government. This trend continued and by the start of 1917 America represented the embassies of all belligerent nations, except Bulgaria.[3]

Neither Britain nor Germany expected America to join the war, or even be a factor in how it played out. This was particularly so in the early months when it was universally anticipated to be a short conflict. In America, there was little political will or financial imperative to support either side. Most leaders and public opinion overwhelmingly supported having nothing to do with the war. At the same time a clear majority, Wilson estimated 90 percent, were sympathetic to the Allied cause. This seemingly contradictory stance was apparently not seen to be a problem.[4]

On August 19, President Wilson told the American people as they were "drawn from many nations, and chiefly from the nations now at war" he wanted to avoid friction between them. Therefore, he declared, "We must be impartial in thought as well as in action, must put a curb upon our sentiments as well as upon every transaction that might be construed as a preference of one party to the struggle before another." Page believed this interpretation of neutrality was unrealistic, as he wrote to his brother, "A government can be neutral, but no *man* can be." Page's argument was the same as that used by the nation's next wartime president, Franklin D. Roosevelt, when World War II started: "This nation will remain a neutral nation, but I cannot ask that every American remain neutral in thought as well. Even a neutral has a right to take account of facts. Even a neutral cannot be asked to close his mind or his conscience." Page believed Wilson's statement demanding personal neutrality was a breach of his liberty. Being told how to think was completely contrary to his belief in the democratic right to freedom of thought and speech. Further, it was completely against his character not to say what he thought about an issue; consequently, Page would find it very mentally and emotionally taxing.[5]

In a letter to Wilson on September 22, Page's exhaustion was evident: "It bears down on one very hard. There comes a kind of weariness that drives one to long sleep, w[h] [which] is the only way to get away from it." He summarized for his president how he saw the work of his three embassies, including the mutual respect that had developed between him and the British foreign secretary: "The diplomatic work betwixt G't Britain and our country is, as you know, not difficult: they play the game squarely; they are wholly courteous and sincere and even more than ever they value our friendship and sympathy. But I see Sir Ed[w] Grey four or five times a week; he gives me his confidence; and we have only to keep strictly neutral. That is not hard to do here. Nor does the work of the German and Austrian embassies cause difficulty—it is, on all sides, only the large volume of work, not its difficulty." The war had a profound mental effect on Page, too. On October 15 he grimly pondered how he often found himself at night, when he "ought to be in bed, sitting alone silently looking into the dying fire, not thinking but dumbly brooding on it, wondering in what world I live."[6]

In early October, he told Wilson a quirky story about how he made one exception to his refusal to use the embassies to facilitate letters being sent between citizens in Britain and Germany: "The Queen is very fond of an old German aunt, or great-aunt; and they keep up a correspondence by unsealed letters, through [U.S. ambassador in Germany James W.] Gerard and me; and her Majesty is very grateful. I said to myself: What Englishman will hold me guilty if his own Queen sh[d] give away secrets in a concealed cipher?"[7]

On 18 October 1914, Page asked Herbert C. Hoover, who had very successfully organized the return home of over a hundred thousand Americans, to help millions of starving people in German-occupied Belgium. It would not be an official U.S. government operation. Hoover accepted the challenge, though requested that the ambassador provide "full support and protection," to which Page agreed. Hoover's Commission for Relief in Belgium was one of the success stories of the war. According to Hoover, over four years it raised a billion dollars to provide ten million Belgians with five million tons of food, saving them from starvation. He recorded his gratitude to Page: "Our most intimate supporter was the American Ambassador in London."[8]

184 \ CHAPTER NINE

GERMANY AND ENGLAND

During these early days of the war Page thought a lot about the relationship between the main rivals and came to the conclusion that war had been inevitable. On September 6 he wrote to Wilson that he had given serious study to "the general subject of the German—English rivalry, which has fast become Prussian hatred and English distrust these ten years." Several years previously he had read the "literature of Prussian militarism" and concluded "Italy, Spain, France, Holland, and England had each had its day of primacy in Europe, and that Prussia would not content itself till it, too, tried." This opinion was confirmed after he arrived in London, "and little by little I got knowledge of the Prussian bureaucracy's methods—got glimpses from other than British sources." The German government's "recent diplomacy has been—simply a lie, all bent on making ready themselves and on keeping other nations from getting ready." Consequently, Page believed Germany was to blame for the war, was behaving reprehensively, and could not be trusted.[9]

On September 11, Page sent a confidential telegram to Wilson describing reports he had received from reliable sources about the German military: "Accounts of atrocities are so inevitably a part of every war that for some time I did not believe the unbelievable reports that were sent from Europe, and there are many that I find incredible even now. But American and other neutral observers who have seen these things in France and especially in Belgium now convince me that the Germans have perpetrated some of the most barbarous deeds in history. Apparently credible persons relate such things without end." At the same time he made it clear to Wilson any American peace efforts would be a waste of time as the Allies were determined to defeat German militarism, writing on September 8: "I see by this morning's papers that the Allies declaration, that none of them will make peace without the consent of all, is understood by the American press. As I regard it, this makes the result of the war certain—there will be no compromise with the German system. England will fight and starve the Germans out if it takes years to do it—to a complete defeat."[10]

From the time he visited Germany as a student at Johns Hopkins, Page had had a soft spot for Germans. He believed they were being held back by their system of government. He wrote to Wilson saying how he regretted the impact the German government's military ambitions had had on the people with whom he was so impressed when visiting thirty-seven years previously: "The Germans, when as a boy I went to Berlin, were a philosophical, studious, mystical, musical folk with a simplicity of mind and with no ambition to conquer the earth—to win a place in the sun. Their great war-machine and their war-party and their 'cult of valour' were just beginning. Their writers who have completely changed their thought and aims—or expressed this change of thought and aims—were just beginning to write. It is a frightful thing to think how a war-party may change a whole nation in three decades."[11]

In March 1912 he wrote an editorial extolling Germany's achievements and praising the kaiser's ability, though stating the time was right for him to step back and become the titular head of a democratic government. Page believed if Germany went down this road to democracy it had the potential to be even more progressive and prosperous, the envy of all other nations: "What a pity it is that the Emperor, with all his ability and brilliancy, is not sufficiently alive to the movement of the age to throw off the trammelling superstition of 'divine right,' break the shackles of bureaucracy, and put himself at the head of the popular awakening which has suddenly made Germany, despite its Mediaeval government, one of the most progressive and prosperous of modern nations, and which might make it, under democratic rule, led by an Emperor as sympathetic with the aspirations of the people as he is bold, energetic, imaginative, and magnetic—the most enviable of all!"[12]

Page was a democrat who believed the time had come for European monarchs to empower their people so that they could all have the opportunity to prosper.

Despite his belief in the German government's guilt, Page was conscious of his role as a neutral ambassador as well as officially representing Germany and Austria-Hungary. As he told Wilson, "I have tried in my own mind to detach myself from the English and from the English point-of-view." Focused on his nation's interests, Page stated that if Britain won America would have to treat it with firmness if it became arrogant. He used this as another argument in favor of enhancing American diplomatic representation in London and around the world.[13]

DECLARATION OF LONDON DISPUTE

America claimed that neutrality meant the freedom to trade with any country without being attacked or impeded in any way. It was keen to meet rising demand for its exports from the warring nations. The government saw nothing wrong with taking advantage of the situation to benefit their economy. America's position was based on the 1909 Declaration of London, which exempted neutral countries' exports from seizure as contraband. This included copper, cotton, rubber, and food, all of which were essential for the German war effort.

As Page noted in his letter to Wilson on September 22, all the British military people he spoke to thought the war would be won "quite as much by starving the Germans as by fighting them." Other goods exempted were raw textiles, hides, and nitrate, which was ostensibly fertilizer though could be used for explosives.

Until the war only America had ratified the Declaration, and almost as soon as the war started it asked the combatants to do the same. Germany agreed as it suited that country perfectly; it would have unhindered access to American supplies, putting it on an equal footing with the Allies. Britain declined as it felt ratifying the Declaration would have left it with little hope of winning the war. It needed to take advantage of its geographic position, allowing its powerful navy to control access to the North Sea, stopping American goods getting to the ports of Germany and neighboring neutral countries. Britain's dilemma was that it had an underlying policy of maintaining good relations with America; so it had to perform a balancing act of stopping as much as it could without excessively antagonizing America.[14]

Consequently, relations between the two nations became strained. On October 15, 1914, Page wrote to Wilson challenging the president to put himself in the shoes of Grey or any other British leader who was "listening lest the very pillars of civilization give way and the last crash come—in comes a telegram from Mr. Lansing [State Department counselor] about a cargo of copper or of wheat, saying that the Declaration of London is the furthest limit our Government can go in permitting this or that." In Washington, a "peaceful, happy land," the Declaration may seem important, though not in a country which was fighting for its very existence. As the controversy continued and relations deteriorated, Page despairingly wrote to House on October 22 and tried to put America's demand into perspective: "England is going to keep war-materials out of Germany as far as she can. We'd do it in her place. Germany would do it. Any nation would do it." He went on to expose the pointlessness of his nation's demands by stating America could claim damages against Britain for any goods confiscated from its ships regardless of whether that country ratified the Declaration. Page stated that Britain had given "four flat and reasonable rejections" and if he was asked again to request Britain sign the Declaration he would resign. Unbeknown to Page the controversy ended on the same day he wrote to House when America withdrew its demand that Britain ratify the Declaration. Britain was left to draw up its own list of contraband.[15]

The controversy caused Page enormous stress. On October 28 he advised Wilson that for the first time since the war had started "my appetite disappeared and my digestion went bad; I didn't know the day of the week nor what month it was—seeing these two Governments rushing towards a clash." Page felt it was unnecessary: "It seemed to me that we were about to cause a serious rupture, without sufficient warrant or reward." Not realizing the impact on Page's health or the potential damage to the relationship with Britain, Wilson played it down in his reply of November 10: "I am glad that the situation has been as much simplified as possible by our no longer insisting on the Declaration of London. Any mistakes that were made then can now easily be forgotten."[16]

Unfortunately, this was too optimistic and the U.S. government's attitude toward trade with Germany meant this was only a temporary solution. Ambassador Page was to bear the brunt of ongoing serious tension between the two nations.

LEADERSHIP LETTER

On October 6, 1914, Page sent his Leadership Letter to Wilson. In what could have been a seminal piece of writing, Page suggested plans to use neutrality-based leadership to end the war in the way most preferable to America. After considering various outcomes of "this vast tragedy" and concluding all would leave Europe under the control of military power, he purposefully pondered: "I have my moods when I wonder if we oughtn't to step in and end it on a definite programme of the reduction of armaments and the restriction of military authority and to make the acceptance of our programme a condition of our refraining from action. I am not yet sure; and I don't know what bad results this might bring us, who have at least the temporary happiness of being out of it. But this is a world-changing war."

The war, he wrote, is "between England's power and position and Germany's ambition to rule the world by sheer military strength." If Britain won without American assistance, it would "dictate the terms of peace"; there would be no limitation on its military power. Page believed America would be greatly disadvantaged by this outcome: "And the U.S. will have no voice in the terms of settlement—and England will keep building her mammoth navy and Russia will keep her innumerable army."

Page's strategy was for America, maybe in conjunction with other neutrals, to limit the amount of armaments available to all European nations: "But, if we were now to call high Heaven to witness this unspeakable result of armaments and war-preparations and call on all neutral nations to join us in a demand that they shall cease—Italy, Spain, Holland, the Scandinavian States, the

South-American Governments, and, if we sh^d say militarism must be rooted out of the system of every one of you—perhaps they'd all agree; but they w^d agree only as the price of our helping conquer Germany." This would be America acting in a truly neutral way to end the war.

Alternatively, if America wanted to support democracy and act to defeat autocracy it could end neutrality and cease all exports to Germany while continuing to supply Britain: "Or, if we alone sh^d do that—say to England: 'Now, you wish to end militarism? Very well, we'll recall our neutrality, we'll sell you guns and ammunition; we'll sell nothing to Germany; if necessary, we'll let our citizens volunteer in your army; you may have our navy if you need it: now what abridgement of armament will *you* make after this war, if we thus help you end it?'" If America went the other way and only supplied Germany, it would not solve the problem as "we sh^d only strengthen militarism in Germany and consequently everywhere else; and the same race in building armies and navies w^d go on as before."

The attraction of both Page's suggestions was that America would dictate the terms of peace without having to become militarily involved. Even more critical was Page's assertion that American leadership was essential to prevent another such war: "There's no important influence we can have on the terms of peace by any mere offers of mediation. The Allies will not consider peace till one side or the other be crushed. If they did, they w^d not be rid of the menace of German militarism long." He reinforced this message in the last paragraph, reiterating that America needed to take a leadership role or peace talks would not work: "A treaty is a scrap of paper. Nobody can stop it [the war] by 'good offices' or mediation—by talk or reasoning. It can be stopped or ended quickly only by us, and we can do it only by actions and threats. If that be impracticable, they must fight it out to the bitter end." As a footnote to his Letter, Page summarized the great opportunity available to their nation, inviting Wilson to join in a discussion on how the war could be ended on American terms and without becoming militarily involved:

The formula runs thus:

(1) If Germany were to win, the war-lord, the war spirit and armaments w^d remain, all around—fiercer and bigger than ever.

(2) If the Allies win, the armaments of Germany will be limited, but not of G't Britain, nor Russia, nor Japan; and probably Germany w^d not be left a fair chance for legitimate expansion.

(3) If the neutral nations sh^d join the Allies—not to fight but to supply arms

and to starve Germany out, millions of lives might be saved and the Allies might now agree to a far more satisfactory policy concerning armies and navies and concentrated executive war-power.

But I am not commending—only trying to think the thing out.[17]

There is evidence Page's ideas would have had a major impact. Germany was not prepared for a long war and quickly became reliant on America and other neutral countries for supplies. Its plan, the Schlieffen Plan, had been to invade Belgium as a means of getting to France, conquer that country within six weeks, and then concentrate on Russia. This was quickly exposed after Britain entered the war. On August 8, 1914, Walter Rathenau, a leading German industrialist, met with Colonel Scheüch, head of the General War Department, and pointed out the country did not have the resources to fight a long war. Rathenau was subsequently put in charge of a specially created War Raw Materials Department and, remaining there "for a long time," became well known to U.S. ambassador to Germany, James W. Gerard.[18]

How Germany obtained supplies through neighboring neutral countries, especially Denmark and the Netherlands, and circumvented the Allied blockade, was explained by Robert Lansing, U.S. secretary of state for most of the war, in his memoirs: "While the German ports were sealed to commerce, the blockade was, however, only partly effective, because goods could be shipped to Denmark and the Netherlands and from those countries transported overland across international boundaries into the German Empire." This is supported by trade statistics showing massive increases in food exports from neutral countries to Germany in the two years following Page's Letter. The Netherlands, for example, exported significantly higher volumes of cheese, meat, butter, eggs, and fish to Germany in 1915 and 1916 compared with 1914. It exported 56,526 metric tons of cheese in 1915 and 75,984 tons in 1916, compared with 19,108 tons in 1914; and 66,986 tons of meat in 1915 and 47,008 tons in 1916, compared with 14,061 tons in 1914. It was not only food at stake: for example, cotton was not declared contraband for fear of offending America, as noted by Page in his Letter. Ambassador Gerard confirmed this in 1917: "It was a long time after the commencement of the war before Great Britain declared cotton contraband. I think this was because of the fear of irritating the United States, but in the meantime Germany secured a great quantity of cotton, which, of course, was used or stored for the manufacture of powder."[19]

Page's foresight was confirmed in 1952 when George F. Kennan, one of the nation's preeminent foreign policy advisers, stated that the U.S. government ignored its own security interests by not taking enough interest in Europe before World War I started. It then could have used its power and influence to end the war as soon as possible by ignoring the "nonsensical timidities of technical neutrality and used our influence to achieve the earliest possible termination of a war that nobody could really win."[20]

Page was looking for some response and maybe debate from the man with whom he had had policy discussions for over thirty years, though Wilson did not respond. Wilson's reasons were probably revealed in a letter of October 28 regarding the dispute over the Declaration of London. Grievances related to the war could cause conflict between Americans of German, British, and other backgrounds, so Wilson believed he had no choice but appeasement through neutrality: "More and more, from day to day, the elements (I mean the several racial elements) of our population seem to grow restless and catch more and more the fever of the contest. We are trying to keep all possible spaces cool, and the only means by which we can do so is to make it demonstrably clear that we are doing everything that is possible to do to define and defend neutral rights." Page could not understand this approach, believing it was the president's job to lead, not follow, public opinion.[21]

So with his president focused on placating American public opinion and with little interest in foreign affairs, Page's perceptive and nuanced suggestions in his Leadership Letter went nowhere. This could have been a turning point; they had the potential to form a plan for America to end the war relatively quickly and on its own terms.

NEUTRAL COMMUNICATION

Not only did Wilson turn down this opportunity to enter a discussion with Page, two months later he effectively ended any chance of it ever happening when he asked House to contact Page and request that he be neutral in all future communication. On December 4, 1914, House wrote to Page, "The President wishes me to ask you please to be careful not to express any unneutral feeling, either by word of mouth, or by letter, and not even to the State Department. He said that both Mr. Bryan and Mr. Lansing had remarked upon your leaning in that direction, and he thought it would materially lessen your influence. He feels very strongly about this, and I am sending the same message to [Ambassador] Gerard."[22]

This set the scene for the rapid breakdown in communication between the two men that would eventually end their relationship. On the one side there was the ambassador, with extensive knowledge of international affairs and used to being able to freely express his opinions, being told he could no longer be frank in his letters and other communication. On the other side was the president telling him that he and others in the government did not want these opinions or advice unless they were neutral.

Less than a month earlier Wilson had responded to a letter in which Page confessed he had "a mortal fear of wearing you weary with my letters" with an emphatic request to keep writing: "My dear Page: You may be perfectly sure that you do not weary me with your letters. They give me an intimate view of men and things which I could not obtain without them and are invaluable to me. I cannot have too many."[23] Despite this, it was Wilson's neutrality edict that Page took to heart. He significantly cut back the volume of letters to the president, instead mostly writing to House, friends, and relatives.

On December 15 he bluntly replied to House's letter. Clearly unimpressed about being accused of acting unneutrally, he stated Americans and English had accused him of being pro-German. He encapsulated how he approached his job, and how it would be undermined if he took the approach he thought Wilson had instructed: "I'll ask you a question: Is an Ambassador a man sent to keep another Government friendly and in good humour with your Government so that you can get and give all sorts of friendly services and make the world better? Or is his business to snap and snarl and play 'smart' and keep 'em irritated—damn 'em!—and get and give nothing?" Page sent this letter "as my Xmas greeting" through Alice, who went back home for Christmas on the steamship *Lusitania*. Arriving on December 23 in New York she was met by two of their sons, Frank and Arthur, and spent the holidays with them in North Carolina. For Walter, this gives a personal aspect to what happened to the ship just over four months later.[24]

In a letter to Wilson on January 12, 1915, Page showed waning enthusiasm for the post and indicated he would resign when the war was over. The State Department was withholding vital information from him and leaking confidential information he sent them—the worst of both worlds. He wrote, "As soon as this war-job is passed and conditions come when I can be relieved, I shall be glad to escape the constant danger of this situation and of the continual leaking of confidential information." He only got by "with the most active 'intelligence' system" and only sending to the Department what was strictly necessary. Being forced to be neutral in his communications to the President was likely the last straw.[25]

HORROR OF THE FRONT LINE

In this letter of January 12, which was twenty-three pages long and marked "Confidential to the last degree," Page presented a fascinating, moving, poignant, dramatic, and historic description of the front line. Britain's secretary of war, Horatio H. Kitchener, had given the embassy's military attaché, U.S. colonel George O. Squire, permission to visit the British and French armies in France, including the British commander-in-chief, General French. This was a highly sought after opportunity, which was only provided to Squire; even soldiers from other Allies did not get such access. Page wrote, "He lived with the officers and men (in every English corps) for five weeks and nothing was concealed. He went in the trenches. Bombs missed him [by] only a few yards time and time again." Squire, for whom the British military had great respect, had just returned and was sworn to secrecy until the end of the war.[26]

Page believed Squire's report would be "a military document of very great value," and proceeded to give his President a confidential preview. He noted how warfare had fundamentally changed since the American Civil War due to the "new big guns," airplanes, radio communication, and trenches. Forts had become useless because it "helps the big gun of the enemy: when it is blown to pieces every piece of it becomes a missile." This lesson was likely learned early, as Page remarked: "Look at the big, strong forts of Belgium." The guns therefore needed to be hidden, which was made trickier by airplanes and radio communication: "The thing to do with a big gun now is not to put it in a fort, but to hide it. They put them in carriage-houses on farms, in dense thickets, in the shallow cellars of houses—anywhere to prevent discovery from aeroplanes. Once discovered, move it quickly. Else an enemy battery 5 or 6 miles off will presently hit it, its shots ranged by wireless reports from an aeroplane." Instead of forts there were trenches, and Page foresaw the stalemate the western front would become: "The zigzag trench with laterals at short intervals with a reasonable number of men can hold back a large army. When both armies have trenches, it looks as if war may be prolonged indefinitely. Neither army in France has really moved appreciably since they got into trenches nearly 3 months ago."

Soldiers were being killed, "some days many thousands of them," with improvised hand grenades containing "anything the soldiers can pick up—rusty nails, stones." They also did bayonet charges, sometimes practically wiping out whole regiments. That was one of the few things reminiscent of the Civil War. As Page noted, "Except for the noise of the guns it's a silent war. No bugles, no music, no shouted commands." Officers gave orders "by silent motions: nobody speaks," "just deadly, silent, grim striving to death." Commanders were no longer on the front line as they were too easy a target for the planes: "The greatest ingenuity is required to conceal the officers' headquarters, miles back from the front." And they constantly had to be moved, like everything, in darkness. They dressed the same as their soldiers as "even a strip of red on the collar is too good a target."

Page went on to make it absolutely clear to his president what was happening. It was not fighting for "glory" like in the Civil War: "The horror of this thing outruns all imagination. Yet somehow nobody seems to realize it—men marched into the trenches to as certain slaughter as cattle when they are driven into the killing house in a stockyard. There's no chance to escape—so nearly no chance that it need hardly be counted. There's nothing of the old 'glory' of war—the charge, the yell, the music, the dash and the giving way of one side or of the other. That's all gone. When they bayonet one another to death, more men come from the rear and fill the same ditches."[27]

While Page's motive cannot be known, he made it very clear that the war was already a stalemate that could go on for years, and maybe he was reminding his president of the opportunity for America to stop supplying the warring nations and therefore the trenches.

ONGOING TRADE TENSION

Although the Declaration of London dispute had ended, Page was continually involved in dealing with American complaints of British interference in trade with Germany. In November 1914, Britain declared the entire North Sea to be its "military area" in which they would lay explosive mines and the only safe way for neutral ships to get through was to stop at a British port, be searched for contraband, and then escorted to their destination port. The following month Bryan sent a telegram, likely jointly prepared with Wilson, directing Page to pass on America's "growing concern" and "deep regret" that Britain was impeding trade between neutral countries. Ships carrying American goods were being detained, sometimes for weeks, despite warring nations having no right to seize ships unless they had evidence of contraband being carried. America wanted to continue trading as if there was no war: "Not only is the situation a critical one to the commercial interests of the United States, but many of the great industries of this country are suffering because their products are denied long-established markets in European countries, which, though neutral, are contiguous to the nations at war."[28]

Still facing the dilemma of the Declaration of London dispute, Britain's policy was, as Grey admitted after the war, to push America as far as they could in terms of goods listed as contraband without threatening the two nations' relationship. In October 1914 the number of items listed as "absolute contraband" was more than doubled and, according to Lansing, the reaction in America was explosive; the State Department was inundated with protests. During 1915, many neutral ships voluntarily docked to be searched, though an average of two ships a day were intercepted by the Royal Navy and taken to a British port where any contraband was seized. Trying to keep the issue in perspective, Page realized it made commercial sense for American cotton farmers, miners, businesses, and other exporters to demand access to European markets. It was not their role to see the bigger picture of international relations or world leadership. This fell to their nation's leaders, who Page felt should be concerned about the greater threat to civilization. Therefore, though he has been criticized for acting inappropriately for the ambassador of a neutral country, he supported the British government's right to stop and inspect neutral ships. As he wrote in a letter at the time: "When I am asked to inquire why Pfister and Schmidt's telegram from New York to Schimmelpfenig and Johann in Holland was stopped (the reason is reasonably obvious), I try to picture myself the British Minister [ambassador] in Washington making inquiry of our Government on the day after Bull Run, why the sailing boat loaded with persimmon blocks to make golf clubs is delayed in Hampton Roads."[29]

Regardless of his private thoughts, Page diligently carried out his duties and confronted Grey with each new inquiry from the Government or exporter's complaint from the State Department. Page strongly believed his close relationship with Grey had ensured the two countries continued to sort out their issues. In December he wrote to his daughter, "When we have come to sharp corners in the road, I have known that whatever happens we must travel in the right general direction—that no temporary difference must be allowed to assume a permanent quality."[30]

Page was looking after the long-term interests of his country. He realized the trade protests were short-term problems and dealt with them as best he could while maintaining good relations with Grey and Britain.

A NAIVE PEACE PLAN

On January 30, 1915, House departed for England on the *Lusitania* on a peace mission. On January 18 he had written to Page explaining his reasons for the trip: "The President and I find that we are going around in a circle in dealing with the representatives in Washington, and he thinks it advisable and necessary to reach the principals direct." Page could not see how the trip could succeed, though he tried to be positive. On January 24 he wrote to Alice, who was still in America: "I guess he wished to look the ground over to see if he can find any peace-doves' nests. Well I hope he'll succeed. I can't see any way out by keeping on this fighting."[31]

House's heart probably wasn't in it, as he largely agreed with Page. About two months before leaving, on November 25, he expressed concern in his diary that if Germany won, they would look to invade South American countries, precipitating the U.S. getting involved. Then on December 14 he wrote he would not push the Allies into peace talks, as "I feel they are determined to make a complete job of it while they are in it, and I also feel in my heart that it is best for Germany, best for Europe and best for all the world, to have the issue settled for all time to come."[32]

House arrived in London on February 6 and in early March left for Paris and Berlin. He returned to London in late April, then, having had no success, returned to America in June. The attempt at peace failed as it had no strength behind it, only the weakness of neutrality. Page noted in his diary on March 11, 1915, that Prime Minister Asquith referred to House's peace talks as "the twittering of a sparrow in a tumult that shakes the world." From early in his ambassadorship, Page had consistently advised on the pointlessness of trying to talk peace without taking leadership. He clearly made the point in his Leadership Letter, then a week later compared a peace resolution from the Pan-American Union to a Sunday-school in Kansas requesting "cruel Vesuvius to cease its eruption, which destroys villages of innocent people."[33]

GERMAN SUBMARINE CAMPAIGN

From the end of 1914, Chancellor Bethmann-Hollweg had been under intense pressure from senior naval officials, the Navy Minister, other leaders, and the public to commence a U-boat (submarine) campaign. This was triggered by a desire to counter the Royal Navy's dominance of the sea and by a few lucky strikes against British ships in September. Bethmann-Hollweg was not concerned about a possible negative American reaction, confident that Wilson's insistence on neutrality and the trade tension with Britain would ensure relations between the nations remained good. He was worried that other neutrals including Italy, the Balkans, and northern European countries might turn against Germany. Despite this he ended up yielding to the pressure, and on February 4,

1915, Germany announced it would use submarines freely in the water around the British Isles.[34]

Germany warned U.S. ambassador Gerard and other neutral countries that their ships might be accidently attacked. Wilson responded with disbelief that Germany would "declare or exercise a right to attack and destroy any vessel entering a prescribed area of the high seas" without first confirming it was not neutral and that its cargo was contraband. Such an act would be "an indefensible violation of neutral rights," which was incompatible with friendly relations. The German government could appreciate, Wilson hoped, America would have to hold it accountable for the actions of its submarines and would "take any steps it might be necessary to take to safeguard American lives and property and to secure to American citizens the full enjoyment of their acknowledged rights on the high seas." Bethmann-Hollweg immediately realized the danger of a breakdown in relations with America, which would be disastrous for Germany: not only the loss of supplies but also the potential turning of other neutrals against Germany. He tried to halt the campaign, without success.[35]

Page's initial reaction to this response was optimism that Wilson would take action against Germany if American lives were lost, though there were numerous German submarine attacks leading to such losses and America did not respond. Consequently, by April the German government was less concerned. It considered American foreign policy to be dictated by public opinion, which was potentially quite malleable, so they thought it unlikely America would get involved. The German ambassador to America, J. H. von Bernstorff, wrote to Foreign Minister Gottlieb von Jagow: "Our diplomatic situation here has significantly improved in recent days . . . , commercial circles begin to realize that England menaces American trade more than we, and, conclusively, commercial interests are always decisive here." The next day Bethmann-Hollweg made an observation about American leaders that illustrated the German government's loss of respect for the U.S. government: "The United States of America would be able to play an influential role if imaginative and strong men were at her head. That is not the case. The American politicians limit themselves to paper protests even against Japan in order that their businessmen may enrich themselves. American public attitudes toward Germany have improved but without attaining influence on policy."[36]

This was the point Page had consistently made: America was in a position of strength and could control the direction of the war. It would miss this opportunity if it made threats and didn't follow through: it would lose the respect of all the warring nations and with it any chance of broking a peace deal. He thought America would lose the ability to protect its own citizens as Germany would keep pushing as far as it could with its submarine campaign and, when it went too far, just pulling back enough to keep America from breaking relations. On May 2, he wrote to Arthur: "If a British liner full of Americans be blown up, what will Uncle Sam do? That's what's going to happen." Tragically he was right.[37]

Five days later, on May 7, 1915, the British Cunard Line's RMS *Lusitania*, carrying 2,000 passengers and crew, was torpedoed and sunk by German submarine U-20. Of the 1,198 who were killed, 128 were Americans. Ambassador Gerard made preparations to be recalled from Berlin, while from London, House and Page sent telegrams to the president. House's telegram declared America should immediately demand Germany provide "assurance that this shall not occur again." Declaring war might be the only option as he thought "we can no longer remain neutral spectators. Our action in this crisis will determine the part we will play when peace is made, and how far we may influence the settlement for the lasting good of humanity." Page's telegram conveyed what he thought the British people were thinking: "The freely expressed unofficial feeling is that the United States must declare war or forfeit European respect. So far as I know this opinion is universal. If the United States come in, the moral and physical effect will be to bring peace quickly and to give the United States a great influence in ending the war and in so reorganizing the world as to prevent its recurrence."[38]

Page did not express his own opinion in his telegram, as Wilson noted two days later to Bryan: "After all this* does not express Page's own opinion, but what he takes to be public opinion at the moment in Great Britain. It is a very serious thing to have such things thought, because everything that affects the opinion of the world regarding us affects our influence for good. Faithfully yours, W.W. *Page's dispatch about the *Lusitania* which I find I have burned."[39]

Page erred by not reiterating his idea, outlined in his Leadership Letter, that America could influence the peace without joining the war. Not only did he miss an opportunity to influence Wilson, but it also led to misunderstandings. His friend David Houston, who was still a cabinet member, criticized Page for encouraging Wilson to join the Allies. Houston believed Wilson would have had "hard sledding" with "a large element in Congress against him and no such unity in the Nation as he did have when we did enter the war."[40]

While Wilson believed that if he asked Congress to go to war it would have supported him, he told his secretary Joseph Tumulty that he was worried about the people's response to "all of its horrors and bloody aftermath." So, instead on May 13, 1915, he sent the First *Lusitania* Note to the German government making clear the ongoing attacks on civilian ships either owned by Americans or with Americans on board constituted "a series of events which the Government of the United States has observed with growing concern, distress, and amazement." Such actions were "absolutely contrary to the rules, the practices, and the spirit of modern warfare." Wilson was unequivocal: "American citizens act within their indisputable rights in taking their ships and in traveling wherever their legitimate business calls them upon the high seas, and exercise those rights in what should be the well-justified confidence that their lives will not be endangered by acts done in clear violation of universally acknowledged international obligations, and certainly in the confidence that their own Government will sustain them in the exercise of their rights." He was not interested in excuses, such as advertisements in newspapers "purporting to come from the Imperial German Embassy at Washington" warning Americans not to travel in the war zone. The U.S. government expected the German government to renounce the actions, compensate the victims as far as possible, and "take immediate steps to prevent the recurrence of anything so obviously subversive of the principles of warfare." Wilson concluded by warning that the U.S. government would protect its citizens; it would not "omit any word or any act necessary to the performance of its sacred duty of maintaining the rights of the United States and its citizens and of safeguarding their free exercise and enjoyment."[41]

Bryan believed the president was acting unneutrally in blaming Germany entirely for the sinking, and on June 5 resigned in protest. While this note was the catalyst, Bryan had been unhappy about being sidelined by the president for some time. Having made his decision he confronted Wilson, with the charge that "Colonel House has been Secretary of State, not I, and I have never had your full confidence." Robert Lansing replaced Bryan as secretary of state and Lansing was instructed by Wilson to send two subsequent notes.[42]

Page was increasingly frustrated by the failure of his nation to show leadership when he believed it was so urgently needed. He expressed this frustration, and reiterated the point he made in his Leadership Letter to Arthur after the first note was sent: "We are caught on this island, with no chance of escape, while the vast slaughter goes on and seems just beginning, and the degradation of war goes on week by week; and we live in hope that the United States will come in, as the only chance to give us standing and influence when the reorganization of the world must begin."[43]

On August 19, less than a month after the Third *Lusitania* Note, the unarmed British cruise liner *Arabic* was torpedoed by a German submarine with the loss of forty-four lives, including three Americans. America protested to Ambassador Bernstorff, who sent a message to the German government: "I fear I cannot prevent rupture this time if our answer in the Arabic matter is not conciliatory." Concerned about this threat to American relations, Bethmann-Hollweg was able to outmaneuver the senior navy officials and force a suspension of the submarine campaign.[44]

In a letter to Wilson on August 19, Page perceptively noted "from what I hear and can infer we had as well prepare our minds and our plans for a long war yet." He then reiterated the futility of trying to put forward peace proposals: "If the Allies make a peace that leaves the Germans really victorious, they'll have to fight again, perhaps with fewer of them united than now." Reinforcing his report from Colonel Squire on the intransience of trench warfare, he noted the ongoing hopelessness on the western front: "The report (private) here is that a little while ago the French, with half-a-million men, tried to break through the German line, that they advanced about five miles and had lost more than two hundred thousand, and that they then gave it up."[45]

On August 4, 1915, Walter and Alice had reason to celebrate, with the wedding of Katharine to Charles G. Loring, an architect from Boston. While constrained by wartime considerations it was still a major social event, held in the Chapel Royal of St. James's Palace at the insistence of the king and queen and attended by Asquith, Grey, and other senior leaders as well as famous Americans who were in London.[46]

WILSON'S LACK OF COMMUNICATION

President Wilson did not respond to any of the points or arguments Page made in his letters and telegrams for most of 1915. He was saying to House, Lansing, and others that Page had been too influenced by the British and was considering their interests more than those of America. For example, following the attack on the *Arabic*, on August 24, 1915, Page sent Lansing a cable stating that an unarmed liner that could not have been carrying contraband was deliberately destroyed and Englishmen "express the friendly grave fear lest delay in action should deepen the impression throughout Europe that the United States is seeking to maintain peace at the price of humiliation in the face of repeated offences." Wilson wrote on this message: "It is a little provoking to have Page do this kind of thing. Of course, that is the view over there, but we know how crazy they are to have us follow them. This makes one wish to order P. to visit his native land."[47]

When the President eventually replied to Page's letters on September 10, 1915, his short letter had almost no reference to the arguments Page had been putting forward. Inexplicably Wilson wrote the opposite of what he had been saying to those around him: "I do not often acknowledge your interesting letters, but that is not because they are not of vital interest to me but only because I have nothing to write in return which compares in interest with what you write to me." Wilson went on to say Page's letters were "of real service" to him and he hoped Page would "not leave out a single line or item which is interesting your own thought." While Wilson seemed to directly ask Page to keep writing his letters, which is the message Page obviously perceived, his closing paragraph could be interpreted as "cool off" until we can have a long talk. Using language similar to his letter of October 28, 1914, Wilson wrote that it would create a misapprehension if Page were to return home then, though Wilson did want to see him at a later time: "It would be jolly to see you and have a long talk with you, and I think it would refresh you to get into the freer and cooler mental atmosphere of this country of ours, where the majority are not half so much off their poise as a small minority seem to be, but we must postpone that pleasure for a little while." This was Wilson's real message, though it would have been much clearer if he had been more direct, asking Page to stop sending letters urging support for Britain and the Allies, maybe even explaining why it was not the time for such action.[48]

Lansing wrote such a message on July 11, 1915, just after becoming secretary of state, though it was in a personal memorandum. He believed America would eventually join the Allies in support of democracy: "I have come to the conclusion that the German Government is utterly hostile to all nations with democratic institutions because those who compose it see in democracy a menace to absolutism and the defeat of the German ambition for world domination." Despite this, Lansing felt "the time was not ripe" to join the Allies due to internal American opposition which would need to be turned around. This is exactly the guidance that should have been sent to Page. He would have known how America leaders were thinking at a pivotal point of the war and allowed him to tailor his own communications accordingly. Unfortunately, the atmosphere in the government was not conducive to constructive debate so Page was left in the dark.[49]

Page's arguments for democracy and liberty were consistent with what he and Wilson had been saying for many years. Page wrote in 1902: "A poor boy born in Connecticut may become an organizer of great industries in Minnesota, or an inventive lad born in North Carolina may revolutionize the warfare of the world—that any man anywhere in our democracy, if he have the mettle of the soil, is likely to win one of the capital prizes of his generation." This was the same argument Wilson put forward in a speech on October 27, 1913, stating freedom was more important than wealth; though freedom would lead to wealth as the citizens take advantage of the opportunities it provides: "I would rather belong to a poor nation that was free than to a rich nation that had ceased to be in love with liberty. But we shall not be poor if we love liberty, because the nation that loves liberty truly sets every man free to do his best and be his best, and that means the release of all the splendid energies of a great people who think for themselves." Page's letters were informal and often very long. Maybe he should have realized structured, concise correspondence was more appropriate to send to a busy president. At the same time, given their long relationship, likely often discussing these issues, and with positive feedback, it is not surprising Page kept sending Wilson his ideas.[50]

By the end of 1915, Page's confidence in Wilson's leadership had almost been lost as a result of both the trade disputes and what Page considered lack of action on the submarine attacks. On November 12, in a letter to House, Page expressed his frustration and disappointment regarding trade: "This job was botched: there's no doubt about that. We shall not recover for many a long, long year. The identical indictment could have been drawn with admirable temper and the way laid down for arbitration and for keeping our interpretation of the law and precedents intact—all done in a way that would have given no offense." At the same time Page had also lost a lot of faith in Lansing and House. In early December they told Page that a visit to London by House, which would occur in early 1916, was not about peace. Page knew otherwise and wrote on Lansing's message: "Why lie to me about it?" Then on December 28, he wrote in his diary that rumors of his resignation in American newspapers were "partly because of House's pussy-cat way of slipping about and of purring at the wrong times and in the wrong tones."[51]

As Page had warned in his Leadership Letter, threats do not work unless they are backed up by action, or the genuine prospect of action. As a result of its lack of action, the U.S. government had lost the respect of the warring nations, ending any chance it had as a serious peace negotiator or mediator. They only gave America begrudging respect due to its economic and industrial power, as well as its latent military power. The policies of key leaders in both Britain and Germany were to push America as far as they could without causing it to break relations: Britain pushed as far as it could on blockading trade, and Germany did the same with submarine attacks. Page knew all this; in reality it would have been the opportune time for him to have resigned the ambassadorship, gone home, and communicated directly to the people through his writing and speeches as he had for most of his life. He stayed due to his work ethic as well as loyalty to his nation and the office of the president.

\ 10 /
THE END OF THE RELATIONSHIP WITH WILSON
1916

PAGE'S DESPAIR—AND HOUSE'S PEACE PLAN

On January 5, 1916, Page wrote to Wilson and his despair in this letter is palpable. Believing he knew why America was being ignored, he tried to get his message across using the most neutral terms short of actually pleading with his president to take some action, for his nation to show leadership. He opened by stating, "I wish—an impossible thing, of course—that some sort of guidance could be given to the American correspondents of the English newspapers." He lamented that reports were being published almost daily about the Austrian chargé d'affaires or the German ambassador visiting the State Department in Washington to reassure Secretary of State Lansing regarding submarine attacks on civilian ships carrying U.S. citizens, causing American inaction: "The impression made upon the European mind is that the German and Austrian officials in Washington are leading the Administration on to endless discussion, endless notes, endless hesitation. Nobody in Europe regards their pledges or promises worth anything at all: the *Arabic* follows the *Lusitania*, the *Hesperian* follows the *Arabic*. The *Persia* follows the *Ancona*."

Page quoted from such reports, which also happened to be what he passionately believed: "'Still conferences and notes continue' these people say, 'proving that the American government, which took so proper and high a stand in the *Lusitania* notes, is paralysed—in a word, is hoodwinked and 'worked' by the Germans.'" Page believed this was a "restrained statement" of English and, as far as he could make out, European feeling. He then became more direct: "It has been said here that every important journal published in neutral or allied European countries, daily, weekly, or monthly, which deals with public affairs, has expressed a loss of respect for the U.S. Gov't and that most of them make continuous severe criticisms (with surprise and regret) of our failure by action to live up to the level of our *Lusitania* notes." He was confident that "practically all men of public influence" in those countries felt the same way. He then gave extensive anecdotal evidence from his experiences that opinions were the same across the classes, "governing," "middle," and "the Man in the Street." House,

Page wrote, had earlier dismissed these as "part and parcel of the continuous British criticism of their own Government" though Page remarked that House was living in an "atmosphere of illusion." Peace talks would not help America re-engage with the warring nations; the answer was to follow through on his *Lusitania* threats. Toward the end of the letter Page made it clear how he saw his own duty: "I do not know, Mr. President, who else, if anybody, puts these facts before you with this complete frankness. But I can do no less and do my duty." He was looking for some response and action from his nation's leader.[1]

On the same day Page wrote this letter to Wilson, House arrived in London on, as Page had realized, a peace mission. He had developed a scheme that involved speaking with the British leaders, indicating to them that Wilson was keen to mediate a peace, and working out terms that they would find favorable. He would then go to Berlin to see if the German leaders would agree to the terms. If so, America would be on the way to brokering a peace. If not, which was the likely outcome, Germany could then be accused of prolonging the war and it was probable America would enter the war on the side of the Allies. Remarkably Wilson, who was keen to re-engage with the warring nations as he felt America was being ignored, agreed to this plan which clearly favored Britain. This was inconsistent with his professed neutrality. House held talks in London, Berlin, Paris, and Le Havre, where the Belgian government was operating in exile, and then London again. Page declined to be involved in the second round of London meetings, believing they would be a waste of time as none of the British leaders had "any confidence in the strength of the President for action."[2]

Page believed House's peace plan lacked morality. He thought it would end up getting America into the war on issues about which it did not care, and it ignored the immediate issue which was Americans being killed by German submarines. If his country was to become directly involved in the war, Page wanted it to be for the right reasons because he still thought America could end it without becoming militarily involved. On February 17, he wrote to Wilson suggesting he follow through on his threat in the *Lusitania* notes, and "at once sever diplomatic relations with Germany and follow this action by a rigid embargo against the Central Powers." Page believed by doing this America could force Germany to surrender without having to "fire a gun or risk a man." Neutral countries bordering Germany were continuing to import levels of supplies well above what they needed, indicating they were being re-exported to Germany. Again, Wilson did not respond.[3]

House returned to New York on February 23, and Page was extremely pleased to see the back of his former friend and confidant. He had had enough of the deceptiveness of the man he had trusted for so long and had taken the trouble to involve in the Wilson campaign all those years ago. The day after House left, Page wrote despairingly in his diary that he would resign if House came to London again: "He cannot come again—or I go."[4]

Despite persistent American requests, Britain never responded to House's peace plan. Page knew the leaders were merely tolerating the president's representative, doing what was necessary to keep America onside. Even if the warring nations had been taking America seriously, House's plan would have failed as he and Wilson ignored the motivations of either side. The Allies did not want to reward Germany by ceding land and resources it had gained; nor did they believe America would do anything to enforce a peace if it became necessary. On the other side, the overwhelming ambition of Germany's powerful military leaders was, as Page had written before the war started and Lansing wrote in his memorandum of July 1915, to dominate the world and destroy democracy. Further, there had been a turning of British public opinion that made it impossible for the government to consider House's peace plan. Grey was battling political, press, and public agitation claiming that the blockade was too weak, allowing Germany to obtain valuable military supplies through neutral countries. Grey tried to defend the government's actions in the context of maintaining good relations with America, though to no avail. Consequently, there was a significant escalation in restrictive measures against Germany and neutrals under a new minister of blockade, Lord Robert Cecil.[5]

GERMANY'S SECOND SUBMARINE CAMPAIGN

On February 29, 1916, Germany started a new restricted submarine campaign. Until then Chancellor Bethmann-Hollweg's political maneuvering had been successful in stymieing the relentless internal push for a new campaign. A plan proposed by Lansing to disarm merchant ships had given Bethmann-Hollweg's political and military opponents the impetus they needed, arguing it had legitimized submarines and that America was less likely to retaliate by entering the war. While the new campaign was restricted to armed enemy merchant ships, there was a major tragedy less than a month after it started. On March 23, an unarmed French cross-channel ferry, the *Sussex*, was torpedoed drowning fifty passengers including three Americans. Two days later Page sent a telegram to Lansing reinforcing his message that breaking of diplomatic relations was the answer. The secretary of state agreed. "The time for writing notes [had] passed," as he wrote in a message drafted the next day for Wilson to use in formally breaking relations with Germany. On March 28 the German Reichstag voted for an unrestricted submarine campaign, to start immediately, and on March 30 the Russian hospital ship, *Portugal*, went down. House wrote in his diary that Wilson "was afraid if we broke off relations, the war would go on indefinitely and there would be no one to lead the way out." This was ignoring reality. Firstly, Germany was dependent on American supplies, which would halt if there was a break; and secondly, loss of neutral status would have had negligible impact as America's diplomatic efforts were not being taken seriously.[6]

Wilson's position changed following an investigation by the American military that found, as he wrote in a note to the German government, "that the *Sussex* was torpedoed without warning or summons to surrender." In this note of April 18 he stated "the Imperial Government has failed to appreciate the gravity of the situation which has resulted, not alone from the attack on the *Sussex* but from the whole method and character of submarine warfare as disclosed by the unrestrained practice of the commanders of German undersea craft during the past twelvemonth and more in the indiscriminate destruction of merchant vessels of all sorts, nationalities and destinations." This was correct as German policy remained to push America as far as it could without breaking relations. The note concluded with the statement Bethmann-Hollweg had been dreading: "Unless the Imperial Government should now immediately declare and effect an abandonment of its present methods of submarine warfare against passenger and freight-carrying vessels, the Government of the United States can have no choice but to sever diplomatic relations with the German Empire altogether." Bethmann-Hollweg tried hard to negotiate with U.S. ambassador Gerard, though he was told emphatically that Germany had to cease the submarine campaign totally and publicly. On May 4 the German government agreed to comply with America's request and end the campaign. For Bethmann-Hollweg it reinforced his belief that any future submarine campaign would lead to America entering the war.[7]

On April 13, 1916, Wilson wrote apologizing for not replying to Page's "admirable" letters and acknowledged their usefulness: "It must be a pretty dreary thing to you to send me letter after letter, upon which you spend so much thoughtful energy and in which you so conscientiously convey to me the things that it is useful for me to know in a way that enables me really to know them, and yet receive no adequate response from me." He was sure Page would understand it was due to lack of time. It's hard to know how Page interpreted this letter, though on May 8 his diary encapsulated his frustration with Wilson's "real lack of leadership" and poor communication. He restated his belief that "Americans would follow gladly if the President were to hold up his hand & say 'come on.'" Since the *Lusitania* a year and a day earlier, thirty-seven unarmed liners had been sunk by German submarines. On May 12 he wrote to Wilson reiterating his conviction the British were not interested in peace talks: "They are not going to get tired. Peace? Yes, on their terms. And, while they are fighting for their lives, they are the only nation that is not fighting also for booty." He tried to be positive in this letter, though it was more hope than reality: "The more I have thought of your last Note to Germany, the more admirable its content and especially its strategy appear." He was no longer being frank, telling Wilson what he thought he wanted to hear, and both were the poorer.[8]

Other ambassadors were being ignored by the president, as House noted in his diary six weeks later. He believed letters from ambassadors Gerard in Germany and Penfield in Austria-Hungary were unread. House was frustrated by Wilson's determination to ignore the war, writing that Wilson admitted to having "a one-track mind" in favor of domestic affairs. House lamented this was unsatisfactory, as the president had made statements in his speeches that reduced his influence internationally. Page had also made this point in his letters to Wilson.[9]

Page gave his president an insight to the personal relationship he had with Grey in a letter on July 21. When Page visited him on diplomatic matters, Grey was often too busy or distracted to talk, though "when I find him in the right mood, I linger in his office after my particular business is done and draw him into a general conversation." They discussed all manner of subjects: "We have gone over schemes of government, the general relations of our two countries, the future of the English-speaking peoples, Wordsworth, fishing (he wrote a book that is a sort of modern Izaak Walton)—every sort of thing that is big and interesting."[10]

"A COMPLETE BATH OF AMERICAN OPINION"

On July 18 Britain published a list of American individuals and companies with which British nationals were stopped from trading, as the government believed they had connections with the Central Powers. Although this "blacklist" was legal, it caused a political and public outcry in America. On July 23, Wilson wrote to House expressing his anger, saying he and Frank L. Polk, counselor for the State Department, were preparing a note which might be "as sharp and final as the one to Germany on the submarine." On July 26, Page was instructed by Polk, as acting secretary of state, to protest the blacklist using the "gravest terms" as the policy violated "true justice, sincere amity, and impartial fairness." Page did not dispute the legality of the blacklist, though he realized it was a major diplomatic blunder by Britain. On July 25 he wrote to Lansing: "I think they see they have made a bad tactical error and I expect a gradual correction of it." He therefore did not believe there was any need for American action. Polk agreed, though, as he wrote to House on July 22, the U.S. government had to do something to mollify public opinion.[11]

From American leaders' perspective, Page's attitude to the blacklist was another example of him being too pro-British, and Wilson and House thought they had the answer: bring him home to immerse him in American opinion. Naively they thought that spending time listening to Americans would change Page's mind because he did not understand how they were thinking. In May, House told Wilson that Page would "probably recover his equilibrium and there will be no further trouble with him" and in July wrote to Polk hoping Page would "be sent west to get a complete bath of American opinion." From early in the war Page had been keen to learn about American public opinion, writing to Alice on January 19, 1915, that he had asked "House to come here and stay with me. I'm eager to get into his mind & to see precisely how they look at it." By the time of House's comment, Page had gained an inkling of how Americans were thinking about the war, and he believed they had been shut off from reality. In a letter on July 21 to Wilson he wrote about how surprised Americans were when they arrived in Britain: "Every American who comes here straight from home remarks after a week or less, 'I didn't know it was this way. It seemed very different in the U.S.'"[12]

In this letter of July 21, Page excitedly wrote he had received a telegram from the State Department "asking if I think it advisable to go home for a personal conference." Eagerly grasping the opportunity, he wrote in this letter, "I do, decidedly—certainly for my own instruction and benefit." He concluded, "It will be a great pleasure, as well as a great benefit, to see you, Mr. President." Page's ship arrived in New York on August 11, 1916. A few days later he went to Washington, D.C., where he had lunch with Wilson, and others, twice in the first two weeks. Despite this, as Page later lamented, there was "not one word about foreign affairs." Page realized Wilson "had no idea of talking with me now, if ever."[13]

After these two lunches Page sent numerous requests for meetings, stating he had an urgent message from the British, though Wilson did not respond. Page was as frustrated about his treatment as he was determined. He wrote to Irwin B. Laughlin, first secretary of the embassy, who Page had left in charge:

THE END OF THE RELATIONSHIP WITH WILSON / 209

"I'm not going back to London till the President has said something to me or at least till I have said something to him." If Wilson did not send for him, Page was determined to go "to his house and sit on his front steps till he come out!" Page had no opportunity to meet with House, who had been in New Hampshire since he arrived. He wrote to House on August 26 accusing him of having "got off and hid."[14]

On the same day he wrote to Alice saying he had decided to resign at the end of Wilson's first term: "Of one thing I am sure. We wish to come home March 4th at midnight and to go about our proper business. There's nothing here that I would for the world be mixed up with. As soon as I can escape with dignity I shall make my bow and exit." Expressing his frustration at the lack of American leadership and how it would have been better for the nation and the world if they had broken off relations with Germany, he predicted: "They'll find out the truth some day, paying, I fear, a heavy penalty for delay." This along with the treatment by his leaders were the reasons for his decision.[15]

By coincidence the U.S. ambassador to France, William G. Sharp, was in Washington at the same time. Page and Sharp met with five members of Wilson's cabinet (Lansing, Franklin K. Lane, Thomas W. Gregory, Newton D. Baker, and Josephus Daniels) over lunch and none of their hosts wanted to discuss the war, the issue of greatest interest to their guests. Page was mystified: "Sharp and I might have come from Bungtown and Jonesville and not from France and England." Page later referred to it in his notebook as "the incident of 5 members of the Cabinet at lunch with me & no mention made of England or of our foreign relations."[16]

Page did eventually meet "several times" with Lansing, though it only added to his frustration. The secretary of state was not interested in American relations with Great Britain and, as Page noted later "the only remark he made was that I'd find a different atmosphere in Washington from the atmosphere in London. Truly. All the rest of his talk was about 'cases.' Would I see Senator Owen? Would I see Congressman Sherley? Would I take up this 'case' and that? His mind ran on 'cases.'" Page despaired, as he later wrote in a notebook: "I tried 6 times to talk about the general situation with Lansing. He saw nothing but 'cases.'" Lansing wrote in his memoirs that Page "ignored the fact that these 'cases' were, with few exceptions, founded on long recognized legal rights," though he actually agreed with Page. In a personal memorandum Lansing lamented Wilson's inability to "grasp the full significance of this war or the principles at issue," and, like Page, was frustrated that "the violations of American rights by both sides seem to interest him more than the vital interests as I see them." Using the same arguments as Page, he wrote, "That German imperialistic ambitions threaten free institutions everywhere apparently has not sunk very deeply into his mind." Lansing concluded with his "hope that the President will adopt the true policy which is 'Join the Allies as soon as possible, and crush down the German Autocrats.'"[17]

After later meeting with Polk, Page noted he was "as bad as the Prest. He can't get it out of his mind that Eng. is insulting us." Page's frustration came from his belief, held since the start of the war, that Britain was fighting for its very existence, so it was not a question of insulting any other country.[18]

At the time the presidential election campaign was under way and there was the threat of a massive, almost nationwide, rail strike, which may partly account for Page's difficulty in meeting with the president. Wilson's campaign was focused on domestic issues; in June he had extolled his fellow citizens to think of "America First." The Republican candidate was Charles E. Hughes, a Supreme Court judge who strongly advocated America entering the war. By contrast, Wilson's key message was that he had kept America out of the war. On September 1 the Wilsons went on their summer vacation at Shadow Lawn, a large white house with expansive secure grounds on the New Jersey coast. It had similarities to the one in Washington, including a semicircular portico, and became a focus of the president's re-election campaign as he delivered speeches from the front porch and met with cabinet members and other key people. It was here that Page, who had continued to send requests, would at last meet with the president to discuss relations between America and Britain.[19]

On September 21, just before he was due to return to London, Page wrote to Wilson that while the "situation between our government and Great Britain seems to me most alarming," he was convinced it was a misunderstanding that could be easily fixed. He referred to the atmosphere in Washington, though not in the way Wilson and House would have hoped: "I find here only an atmosphere of suspicion—unwarranted by facts and easily dissipated by straight and simple friendly methods." Page was referring to relations between America and Britain and his belief no one was listening to him. Wilson responded the same day with a telegram inviting Page to visit Shadow Lawn the following night. Page caught the train from New York and arrived at 10 p.m. on September 22. The next morning they had their meeting.[20]

While there is no official record of their conversation, Page made some scrawled notes full of abbreviations on his way back in the train.[21] He believed Wilson was still focused on the trade problems caused by England: "The P. said:

He started out as heartily in sympathy w.[ith the] Allies as any man c[d] be. But Eng. had gone on doing everything she wish[d], regardless of rights of others, & Am[erican] pride (*his* pride) was hurt." The President gave Page a message to pass onto the British leaders: "The P said Tell those gentlemen for me—and there followed a homily about a damage done to any Am.[erican] citizen is a damage done to himself. He described the war as a result of many causes—some of long origin. He spoke of England's having the earth, of Germany's wanting it." Page commented in his notebook: "Of course the German system is directly opposed to everything American. But this didn't seem to me to carry any very great moral reprehensibility."

The president told Page he wouldn't use the antiblacklist legislation recently granted by Congress until after the election, though he "hinted that if there were continued provocation afterward (in case he were elected) he would." Page noted that Wilson said "one of the worst provocations was the long English delay in answering our notes," and Wilson "evidently felt that such delays showed contempt." Page referred to the urgent message he had from the British: "When I delivered the private message of the B[ritish] Gv't that if the Germans ask[d] him to request an armistice, they w[d] not grant it, intimating that it w[d] be offensive if the P. proposed it—he said 'If an armistice no, that's a military matter & none of my business. If it be a proposal of an armistice looking towards peace,—yes, I shall be glad.'" One of his last notes was: "The P. remarked that at first everybody he met favored the Allies. Now he came across nobody who was not vexed with England." As he said goodbye, Page thought about how isolated Wilson had made himself. Seemingly trusting only his own thoughts, he could not see beyond them. Page later wrote to his son Frank: "I think he is the loneliest man I have ever known." This was the last time these two men, who had previously relished any opportunity for a discussion, were together.[22]

Wilson visited House the next day and, as House noted in his diary, they "spent several hours going over foreign affairs, principally our differences with Great Britain." House noted that "Page had left a mass of memoranda, which the President read aloud." According to House they agreed Britain was jealous of America's rapidly growing commerce and intention to build a navy larger than Britain's. House thought Britain would try to stop America if it tried.

On the following day House reluctantly met with Page, who vented the built-up frustration from the way he had been treated since arriving in Washington, to House's disappointment: "He is as pro-British as ever and cannot see the American point of view." House wrote, "He declares none of us understand the situation or the high purposes of the British in this war." House responded that Britain's actions had worsened relations between the two nations. To House's irritation, Page argued relations with Britain would have been better if America had acted differently.[23]

The irony was that while both House and Lansing agreed with Page, such was the atmosphere in the government there was not constructive debate on such issues. House's diary entry in November 1914, when he wrote his preferred outcome was an Allied victory, showed how he felt. Similarly, Lansing wrote in his memorandum: "For six months I have talked [to the President] about the struggle between Autocracy and Democracy, but do not see that I have made any great impression. However, I shall keep on talking." He had the advantage of being able to talk to Wilson and receive feedback, even if unspoken. Page had no such luxury and was left in the dark.[24]

PAGE'S ASSESSMENT OF WILSON AND HIS LEADERSHIP

On September 30, Page left America and recorded his thoughts in a perceptive and searching memorandum. Probably written on his return journey, it painted a picture of an atmosphere of a reluctance to be frank in the way Page was— dissenting ideas were not sought by the President: "Mr. Wilson shuts out the world and lives too much alone, feeding only on knowledge and subjects that he has already acquired and not getting new views or fresh suggestions from men and women." Page could not understand why such an intelligent man who was "a charming personality, an uncommonly good talker, a man who could easily make personal friends of all the world" would not engage with others and their ideas. Having seen how the gregarious Theodore Roosevelt operated, Page would have been shocked by the contrast. The consequence was unfortunate: "The influence of this lone-hand way of playing the game extends very far. The members of the Cabinet do not seem to have the habit of frankness with one another. Each lives and works in a water-tight compartment."[25]

Neutrality, Page wrote in his memorandum, had let American supporters of Germany dictate Wilson's policy on the war, losing him the support of many other Americans: "He has lost the silent confidence of many men upon whose conscience this great question weighs heavily." Page believed the consequence of this policy was to deal America "out of the game" in the "economic and political readjustment of the world" unless they were "forced into the war by Hughes's election or by the renewal of the indiscriminate use of submarines by the Germans."

This was not the 'atmosphere' Wilson, House, Lansing, and Polk wanted Page to soak up, though that had been an unrealistic expectation as they misunderstood Page. His focus was on the reality of the war, the future of democracy, and the need for America to show leadership. He believed public opinion had been influenced by the leaders not telling the people the truth about the war; being immersed in it would not have influenced him in the way they hoped. What he was looking for was the opportunity to discuss the government's policy regarding the war.

BACK TO THE BLACKLIST CRISIS

Page returned to the welcome of his embassy staff at Euston Station on October 9, then was back in the ongoing crisis around the blacklist. On October 10, Grey sent a negative reply to the American protest of July 26, and on the same day met with Page. In his report on this meeting, Page told Lansing that while the British government was trying to address American concerns, it also had to consider its own public opinion and the reactions of other neutrals: "There is no doubt they [Britain] now clearly see they had made a bad blunder and I think they will at least greatly reduce the list, but they are afraid of criticism in Parliament and in other neutral countries than ours. An American blacklist was sheer stupidity—they did not foresee the effect on American opinion." Page's assessment was correct. The British government had realized the extent of its mistake and was seeking to reduce the application of the blacklist.[26]

Throughout the crisis Page ensured America retained good relations with Britain by working closely with Grey. On November 16, Page wrote to Lansing advising that Grey and Cecil were prepared to go through the blacklist with a U.S. government member and reduce it as much as possible. He suggested Frank Polk would be a welcome choice. The secretary of state replied that while he was pleased with Britain's goodwill gesture, Polk could not be spared and he was not convinced about the suggestion. Page later wrote to Wilson that the language of the State Department had been so aggressive it had "provoked many a denial." Having Polk there personally might bypass this impediment to agreement. Despite this and the apparent anger of the U.S. government toward the blacklist, Lansing's lack of interest meant nothing happened.[27]

214 \ CHAPTER TEN

"ONLY AUTOCRACIES WAGE AGGRESSIVE WARS"

On November 24, 1916, Page presented his most eloquent argument in favor of America taking action to encourage the spread of democracy through Europe to end the war and prevent future wars. It was in a letter to Wilson, though it had the ingredients for a very persuasive article if he was back at the *World's Work*. After congratulating the president on his re-election earlier in the month and giving him credit for transforming the Democratic Party and American domestic policy, he ventured into foreign policy. He knew it would be difficult to raise Wilson's interest, though he tried anyway: "Now, if you will permit me to say so, from my somewhat distant view (four years make a long period of absence) the big party task is to build up a clearer and more positive foreign policy." He then returned to the argument he had put forward numerous times as ambassador, though it now had greater urgency: "We are in the world and we've got to choose what active part we shall play in it—I fear rather quickly."

Page suggested looking to the Founding Fathers for inspiration for America's international role postisolation: "If my long-term memory be good, they were sure that their establishment of a great free Republic would soon be imitated by European peoples—that democracies w^d take the place of autocracies in all so-called civilized countries; for that was the form that the fight took in their day against organized Privilege." This spread of democracy to Europe had occurred "with disappointing slowness," partly due to American isolationism. Page's key point was that America should not only look to encourage the spread of democracy for ideological reasons and to spread opportunity to all people, the main reason was that it would make the world a safer place: "It isn't, therefore, for merely doctrinal reasons that we are concerned for the spread of democracy nor merely because a democracy is the only scheme of organization yet wrought out that keeps the door of opportunity open and invites all men to their fullest development. But we are interested in it because under no other system can the world be made an even reasonably safe place to live in. For only autocracies wage aggressive wars. Aggressive autocracies, especially military autocracies, must be softened down by peace (and they have never been so softened) or destroyed by war."

Page compared the kaiser's rule with that of George III and his "Taxation—without—Representation," though "more virulent, stronger, and further-reaching." Ending it would free German people to "build-up their character" and take their place in the world. Defeating Germany would "make for the spread of the doctrine of our Fathers." Not wanting to criticize America directly, he blamed all democratic governments for not proactively encouraging the spread of freedom from autocracy: "For a century democracies and Liberal governments have kept themselves too much isolated, trusting prematurely and too simply to international law and treaties and Hague conventions." These had not been respected by the autocratic monarchies, so if they were to be effective it required the "outgrowing or the overthrow of the Divine Right" to govern. America's duty was clear: "Our championship of democracy must lead us to re-declare our faith and to show that we believe in our historic creed."

America needed to actively and openly identify with the Allies, by determinedly standing up to the military leaders of the autocracies: "This is the attitude surely that our fathers would have wished us to take—and would have expected us to take—and that our children will be proud of us for taking; for it is our proper historic attitude whether looked at from the past or looked back at from the future. There can be no historic approval of neutrality for years, while the world is bleeding to death." He then made another appeal for American action to end the war by the "complete severance of relations, diplomatic at first and later possibly economic as well, with the Turks and the Germans." This would "probably not cost us a man in battle nor any considerable treasure." Wilson did not reply.

In this letter Page followed through with his decision to tell Wilson he would resign at the end of his first presidential term, though was not as emphatic as he had decided in Washington. Referring to being "within sight of the early end of my services here," he equivocated by offering to resign, rather than making it definite: "When you call[d] me I answered, not only because you did me [a] great honor and laid a definite patriotic duty on me but because also of my personal loyalty to you and my pride in helping forward the great principles in which we both believe. But I understood then (and I am sure the subject lay in your mind in the same way) that my service would be for four years at the most. I made all my arrangements, professional and domestic, on this supposition. I shall, therefore, be ready to lay down my work here on March 4 or as soon thereafter as meets your pleasure." He went on to thank Wilson for the opportunity "to give such public service to my country" and "for the most profitable experience of my life."[28]

Wilson did not reply and discussed Page's position with House during December and January. They considered others for the role, though they could not make a decision. On December 30, Page wrote asking Wilson if he could advise "your wishes about the end of my service," though still he did not receive a response.[29]

Around this time Page wrote a memorandum to record the high opinion he had of two men. The first was Herbert Hoover, who, at Page's instigation, had done such sterling work leading the Commission for Relief in Belgium. He recommended Hoover, who later served as U.S. president (1929–33), for the State Department as he was "probably the only man living who has privately (i.e. without holding office) negotiated understandings with the British, French, German, Dutch, and Belgian Gov'ts." The other was Irwin B. Laughlin, "one of the best men" in the diplomatic service who he would make an ambassador if he was president. He had written to Wilson on July 5, 1914, recommending Laughlin be made an ambassador, even though Page would have missed him greatly in the embassy.[30]

AMERICAN PEACE OR GERMAN SUBMARINES?

On December 18, 1916, Secretary of State Lansing sent a notice on behalf of the president to the four Central Powers and the ten Allies. Wilson was attempting to get the warring nations to state as soon as possible their terms for peace and the arrangements they believed should be put in place to prevent future wars: "The President suggests that an early occasion be sought to call out from all the nations now at war such an avowal of their respective views as to the terms upon which the war might be concluded and the arrangements which would be deemed satisfactory as a guaranty against its renewal or the kindling of any similar conflict in the future as would make it possible frankly to compare them." The President was firmly convinced that the objects of both sides were "virtually the same." Page was instructed to advise the British foreign secretary that "it would be hard for the Government of the United States to understand a negative reply."[31]

On December 6 there had been a change in leadership of the British government, with David Lloyd George taking over as prime minister from Asquith, and Arthur Balfour replacing Grey as foreign secretary, though Cecil was acting in the position. Page gave Cecil the message, and Cecil asked Page for a comment. According to Cecil, Page replied "that the President . . . was an idealist by temperament, and this move . . . wise or not, was certainly dictated by the purest sentiment of humanity." Page's reply to Lansing, sent on December 22, indicated the message had not been received well in Britain. Both the public and the government were angry and distressed by Wilson's equating the war aims of Britain and Germany. Page sent a similar message to House, and in both letters told of the king's distraught reaction; to House he wrote: "A luncheon guest at the

Palace yesterday informs me that the King wept while he expressed his surprise and depression."[32]

Since late 1914, when Germany felt its submarines had become a potent weapon, senior civilian and military leaders had put relentless pressure on Chancellor Bethmann-Hollweg to ask the kaiser to allow the military to use them to their full capacity with an unrestricted campaign. This push had support from most of the Reichstag, many experts, academics, newspapers, and the public. In February 1915, Bethmann-Hollweg had relented, though in August 1915 forced suspension of the campaign out of conviction it would turn America against Germany. Using his power, along with skillful political and diplomatic maneuverings, he had been successful in outwitting his opponents, with the exception of the short campaign in early 1916. After October 1916 the pressure for an unrestricted campaign became too great and Bethmann-Hollweg's power ebbed away. By the end of December his political and military opponents knew they would get their way. There was just the formality of getting the kaiser's approval.[33]

\ 11 /

VINDICATION

1917 AND 1918

RETURN TO "RUTHLESS SUBMARINE WAR"

On January 6, 1917, German foreign minister Arthur Zimmermann and many other members of the government including senior public servants, as well as some German and American industry leaders, attended a dinner in U.S. ambassador Gerard's honor. Held by the American Association of Commerce and Trade at the Hotel Aldon, Gerard described it as "a sort of German-American love-feast." While the minister, the vice chancellor and the ambassador spoke about one another in the friendliest terms, Gerard knew it was a charade. Earlier, he had warned the State Department of reliable information that Germany would recommence its unrestricted submarine campaign: "Based not upon absolute facts but upon reports which seemed reliable and which had been collected through the able efforts of our very capable Naval Attaché, Commander Gherardi, and this information was confirmed by the hints given to me by various influential Germans."[1]

The decision to conduct the campaign was officially made by the kaiser at a conference with his military and civilian leaders on January 9. Bethmann-Hollweg saw he had been defeated and, against what he passionately believed, went along with the decision. Germany would use its submarines indiscriminately to sink ships approaching ports controlled by Germany's enemies in "a zone around Great Britain, France, Italy and in the Eastern Mediterranean." The campaign would start on February 1, though Germany decided not to inform America and other neutral countries until the day before. This meant they had to keep it secret for three weeks and Zimmermann had to string America along by pretending to talk peace. Gerard was continually "assured by Zimmermann and others in the [German] Foreign Office that nothing of the kind was contemplated."[2]

IGNORING REALITY

On January 3, Wilson and House commenced discussion of a speech that would clearly lay out how peace would be achieved and the role of America in ensuring it was maintained. Their planning continued despite negative responses to Wilson's notice of December 18, 1916, from both Germany and the Allies. On January 20, two days before the speech was to be given, House wrote to Wilson stating it was "possible" Germany was "maneuvering for position in regard to the resumption of their unbridled submarine warfare." He seemed to think such a campaign could be delayed "if we can tie up Germany in a conference." This strongly suggests he or Wilson had not seen or taken notice of Gerard's messages to the State Department and did not understand the political situation in Germany. Wilson made his speech to the Senate on January 22 and either deliberately or naively misrepresented reality when he ignored the negative responses to his notice of December 18 and repeatedly held out strong hopes of peace. He stated, "We are that much nearer a definite discussion of the peace which shall end the present war." More in hope than reality, he claimed, "The statesmen of both of the groups of nations now arrayed against one another have said, in terms that could not be misinterpreted, that it was no part of the purpose they had in mind to crush their antagonists."[3]

The opposite was true: Page and Gerard knew the aim of both sides actually was to "crush" the other. For the Allies the aim was to restore prewar borders and remove the military threat posed by Germany. Page had been saying this since the start of the war. In September 1914 he wrote to Wilson: "The English are not going to discuss peace except in Berlin. In other words, they will reject any terms that Germany will offer except on the basis of defeat. They are going to rid themselves and the rest of Europe of the menace that they have lived under for thirty years—a hostile military autocracy." Germany's aim was to take over as much territory as they could. As Gerard explained, they were aiming for "a German peace, a peace as outlined to me by the Chancellor; a peace impossible for the Allies and even for the world to accept; a peace which would leave Germany immensely powerful, and ready immediately after the war to take up a campaign against the nations of the Western Hemisphere; a peace which would compel every nation, so long as German autocracy remained in the saddle, to devote its best energies, the most fruitful period of each man's life, to preparations for war."[4]

Again, ignoring the true message from the warring nations, Wilson claimed their responses implied "that it must be a peace without victory." Lansing noted that several days before Wilson delivered his speech Page had a chance to comment on its content. He suggested this phrase, which became the most contentious in Britain, be replaced with "peace without conquest" or another phrase. Lansing agreed and suggested Wilson make this change, to which he responded,

"I'll consider it." In an undated memorandum, probably after America had entered the war, Page wrote the phrase was a "remote, academic deliverance while G't [Britain] & France were fighting for their very lives." He went on to lament that it "made a profoundly dejected feeling, & made my place more uncomfortable than ever. 'Peace without victory' brought us to the very depths of European disfavor."[5]

THE END OF RELATIONS WITH GERMANY

On February 3, 1917, Wilson reluctantly made another speech to Congress, very different to his one of twelve days earlier, announcing the end of diplomatic relations with Germany. By then he had been urged by Lansing, House, and his entire cabinet. On January 16, Zimmermann had sent a telegram from Bethmann-Hollweg to Bernstorff, German ambassador to America, advising him of the new submarine campaign. Then, as planned, Bernstorff had advised Secretary of State Lansing of Germany's decision on January 31. In his speech Wilson said this action by Germany was sudden and without warning, and went against the "solemn assurance" provided by Germany on May 4, 1916, which stated that merchant ships "shall not be sunk without warning and without saving human lives." The president stated he had directed the secretary of state to announce to the German ambassador that "all diplomatic relations between the United States and the German Empire are severed." Bernstorff was to immediately leave the country and Ambassador Gerard was to return home from Berlin. Wilson went on: "I refuse to believe that it is the intention of the German authorities to do in fact what they have warned us they will feel at liberty to do." He had such faith in the "ancient friendship" between the peoples that Wilson would only believe it if there were "overt acts on their part."[6]

Page sent a short telegram to Wilson saying what he didn't truly feel and trying to be positive about its implications: "Your prompt action after your patient efforts to avoid a rupture will strengthen our national character and build up our national unity at home. In Europe it will put us in the highest esteem of all nations, including even the people of the Central Powers; it will shorten the war; it will preserve to us our proper high place in the family of great powers; it will immeasurably advance the influence of democracy and it will give you the lead with your constructive programme in insuring peace hereafter."[7]

Wilson's speech again raises the question of whether he was aware of the political intrigues and agitation that had taken place in Germany since early 1915, combined with the power shift away from the Chancellor after October

1916 that had led to the decision by the German government. The decision to commence unrestricted submarine attacks had not been a last-minute whim that would only be implemented half-heartedly; it was backed by long-term strong and passionate support and planning from powerful civilian and military leaders.

A consequence of this ignorance was Wilson's stipulation that he needed evidence of "overt acts" before he would believe Germany would go ahead with its submarine campaign. Page interpreted this as saying he needed proof before America would declare war, which raised the question: Was Wilson prepared to sacrifice American lives from submarine attacks to get his proof, and if so how many? There were American casualties and rescues from numerous German submarine attacks and no word from the president. Page went from hope to despair, exclaiming on February 19, "I am now willing to record my conviction that we shall not get into the war at all. The P. is constitutionally unable to come to such a point of action." On February 25 the *Laconia* was sunk by a submarine and four Americans drowned. Page wrote in his diary that surely it was an "overt act." Wilson took no action, though the next day he requested Congress give him the authority to allow merchant ships to be armed. Congress went out of session on March 4 without the bill being passed, so five days later Wilson used his executive authority to arm merchant ships. Despite this, Germany kept sinking ships. Just over a week later an American steamship, the *Algonquin*, was sunk without warning, then another three went down in four days.[8]

The trade tension between America and Britain ended with the break in relations with Germany, as America stopped worrying about the outstanding cases. The 1914 American demand that Britain sign the Declaration of London was the start of more than two years of unnecessary and damaging trade tension over which Page was accused of being too pro-British. Lansing tentatively acknowledged the correctness of Page's position years later when he wrote, "As one looks back over the naval operations conducted by both sides in the Great War, there may appear a measure of justification for the British attitude and for the resentment which, according to Ambassador Page, was felt in Great Britain, because we proposed the adoption of the Declaration as a *modus vivendi* [agreement]." Kennan strongly supported Page's position when he wrote in 1952: "Looking backward today on these endless disputes between our government and the belligerents over neutral rights, it seems hard to understand how we could have attached so much importance to them. They irritated both belligerents and burdened our relations with them, and I find it hard to believe that they involved our national honor." Without the luxury of being able to look back, Page knew at the time that American insistence on neutral rights was based on a lack of perspective, not understanding what was really at stake. It was this naivety he had for years argued would be caused by isolationism. Greater involvement in international affairs would have provided the experience to better understand the implications of their actions, especially during such a crisis.[9]

On February 5, Wilson eventually got around to replying to Page's message regarding resigning. The secretary of state relayed the president's hope that Page remained "at the present time." In the euphoria following the breaking of relations, Page replied he was prepared to serve "at any sacrifice" and said he was putting arrangements in place to remain until the war ended.[10]

GERMANY'S PROPOSAL TO MEXICO

In his telegram of January 16, 1917, as well as Bethmann-Hollweg's telegram advising Bernstorff of the submarine decision, Zimmermann had attached another of his own that was to be forwarded to the German ambassador in Mexico, Heinrich von Eckhardt. Zimmermann proposed Germany and Mexico form an alliance. Germany would provide "generous financial support," and would declare war on the United States with the understanding that Mexico would "reconquer" its "lost territory in Texas, New Mexico, and Arizona." If Mexico was agreeable, Eckhardt was to suggest Mexico invite Japan to join the alliance.[11]

This telegram, which became known as the "Zimmermann Telegram," was intercepted by Britain on January 17. British Naval Intelligence spent five weeks deciphering the German code, using the full resources of their top-secret Room 40. On February 22 Rear-Admiral Sir William R. Hall, director of Naval Intelligence, discussed it with Edward Bell, U.S. secretary of embassy in charge of intelligence, in Room 40. Bell realized its significance, so they took it to the U.S. embassy where, with Page and Laughlin, they spent hours working out how it could be released publicly without revealing Britain had the ability to intercept Germany's messages and decipher Germany's code. The next day Foreign Secretary Balfour formally handed the telegram to Page.[12]

Page stayed up all night crafting the accompanying message to keep it in line with what they had agreed, and then at 1 p.m. on February 24 sent it to Polk, who was acting secretary of state as Lansing was on leave. Page's diary entry showed his lack of confidence in how the government would respond: "This would precipitate a war between any two nations. Heaven knows what effect it will have in Washington." Polk received Page's message with the Zimmermann Telegram attached at 8:30 that night and recognizing its importance took it straight to Wilson who, as Polk later related to Lansing, showed "much indignation." Then on February 27, Lansing returned from leave and gave Wilson evidence Polk had discovered that the Zimmermann Telegram had been forwarded to Mexico by Bernstorff from America over the State Department cable. Wilson was outraged, crying out "Good Lord!" two or three times as Lansing explained this to him, and angry at the gall of the German government. He asked Page to thank Balfour for the information and for the British government's "act of friendliness." The next day the U.S. government made the telegram public, and the following morning, on March 1, it was published in newspapers across the nation. Lansing believed it had a very significant impact on public opinion as it "created a profound sensation throughout the country" and its "effect on Congress was very marked."[13]

Despite this, there was no action from the government, and Page's frustration was evident in his diary on March 2: "I have never abandoned the belief that if the President were really to lead, all the people would follow. Whether he will even now lead remains to be seen." The next day Zimmermann confirmed he was the author of the telegram. On March 18, the State Department received reports that three American ships, *Vigilancia*, *Illinois*, and *City of Memphis*, had been sunk by German submarine torpedoes. The *Vigilancia* had been attacked without warning and fifteen Americans had died.[14]

If Wilson was waiting for public opinion to change so he could follow it, the time had come. The German government had made two decisions that when combined and brought to public attention, had turned the tide in America.

DECLARING WAR ON GERMANY

The morning after the submarine attack reports Wilson met with his secretary of state, and Lansing gave him the same message Page had been delivering: "I argued that war was inevitable, that I had felt so for months, and that the sooner we openly admitted the fact so much stronger our position would be with our own people and before the world." Then on the following afternoon, March 20, Wilson asked his cabinet their opinions about entering the war. There were mixed reactions, though all agreed America was already part of the war—they had no choice. The next day Wilson called an extraordinary session of Congress for April 2.[15]

224 \ CHAPTER ELEVEN

During this period Page frequently met with Balfour, smoothing the way for American entry into the war. This proved to be one of his most critical activities as, even with the military manpower and the industrial might America provided, without proper planning and coordination with the Allies, Germany could still have won the war. Page also prepared the embassy, as outlined in a letter to his son Arthur on March 25: "I have my staff of twenty-five good men getting all sorts of warlike information; and I have just organized twenty-five or thirty more—the best business Americans in London—who are also at work. I am trying to get the Government at Washington to send over a committee of conference—a General, an Admiral, a Reserve Board man, etc., etc." In this letter he accurately predicted what Wilson would say in his speech of April 2: "The impression becomes stronger here every day that we shall go into the war 'with both feet'—that the people have pushed the President over in spite of his vision of the Great Peacemaker, and that, being pushed over, his idea now will be to show how he led them into a glorious war in defense of democracy. That's my reading of the situation, and I hope I am not wrong." He was not wrong.[16]

On April 2, 1917, President Wilson gave a stirring and historic speech to an extraordinary session of Congress requesting America declare war on Germany. For Wilson, it was a critical speech: he had to convince the members of Congress of the merits of his argument, and he had to persuade the American people their country needed to go to war despite having repeatedly stated that it had nothing to do with them and they could blissfully remain neutral. He gave three reasons why America should declare war on Germany: submarine attacks on civilian ships; subterfuge against America; and the need to support democracy internationally. These arguments were not new; they were similar to those Ambassador Page had been putting to Wilson and House since before the war started, and for which he had been ostracized.

In his speech, Wilson stated the German government's indiscriminate submarine campaign had changed everything: "The new policy has swept every restriction aside. Vessels of every kind, whatever their flag, their character, their cargo, their destination, their errand, have been ruthlessly sent to the bottom: without warning and without thought of help or mercy for those on board, the vessels of friendly neutrals along with those of belligerents." Consequently, Wilson stated, Germany was waging "a war against all nations." Up to this point, America had tried to maintain friendly relations with Germany, though that was no longer possible: "We will not choose the path of submission and suffer the most sacred rights of our Nation and our people to be ignored or violated." Against its will, America had been thrust into the war and should "exert all its power and employ all its resources to bring the Government of the German Empire to terms and end the war."[17]

Page's predictions throughout the war that America would end up in this predicament if it didn't show leadership proved correct. Wilson's notes that ended the submarine campaigns of 1915 and 1916 merely put Germany in a holding pattern. The evidence was there; Germany was building submarines as fast as it could. It was only a matter of time before the attacks would recommence in earnest when Germany thought it could do it without drawing America into the war—or when it thought it had enough submarine strike power to defeat Britain so quickly it would not matter.

Wilson stated in his speech that the German government's subterfuge against the American people and their government started before the war began, as Germany had spies in America. Then when the war started, the German government "filled our unsuspecting communities and even our offices of government with spies and set criminal intrigues everywhere afoot against our national unity of counsel, our peace Within and without, our industries and our commerce." This culminated in the Zimmermann Telegram.

Page and Lansing knew the government and the people should not have been "unsuspecting." Page believed if Americans were unsuspecting, they had been lulled into a false sense of security by neutrality. On September 6, 1914, he had warned Wilson the German government could not be trusted because it had used diplomatic reassurances to undermined Britain's preparations for war. On July 11, 1915, Lansing wrote about German agents being active trying to generate anti-American feeling in Mexico, Haiti, San Domingo, and probably in other Latin American countries to distract America and keep it out of the war. It might have also been to facilitate "a future war" with America if Germany defeated the Allies. Lansing also chronicled in his memoirs a long list of illegal and anti-American activities by German and Austrian officials and agents that started early in the war, were known at the time to the U.S. government, including the president, and in some cases were made public.[18]

Wilson effectively conceded that the policy of neutrality was misguided: "Neutrality is no longer feasible or desirable where the peace of the world is involved and the freedom of its peoples, and the menace to that peace and freedom lies in the existence of autocratic governments backed by organized force which is controlled wholly by their will, not by the will of their people." Page's insight was that it was not sustainable for America to, on one hand, be a bastion of freedom and individual rights while, on the other, be neutral about an autocratic regime which repressed its citizens' freedom and rights and had launched an unprovoked attack on neutral Belgium. Germany was ruled by a military autocracy at the beginning of the war just as it was on April 2, 1917. Nothing had changed. Neutrality had failed.

Throughout his speech Wilson linked the behavior of the German government to it being an autocracy, not a democracy. For example: "Selfgoverned nations do not fill their neighbor states with spies or set the course of intrigue to bring about some critical posture of affairs which will give them an opportunity to strike and make conquest." Autocracies do not observe the principles of international peace or justice and therefore it was a war of democracy versus autocracy with the object of vindicating "the principles of peace and justice in the life of the world as against selfish and autocratic power." Page had made the same point in his letter to Wilson the previous November, stating that autocracies had never respected international laws, treaties, and the Hague convention, except when it suited them, "as springes to catch woodcock." This was the fundamental reason Page believed America should have supported Britain, and for which he was accused of being too pro-British.[19]

To maintain world peace, Wilson proposed the democratic nations work together: "A steadfast concert for peace can never be maintained except by a partnership of democratic nations. No autocratic government could be trusted to keep faith within it or observe its covenants." On January 2, 1914, Page had put forward a similar proposition in a letter to House. He raised the prospect of America forming an alliance with the democratic nations that would undertake work to benefit the whole world. Believing the English-speaking nations and Switzerland were the only countries with "permanent free government," Page wrote, "suppose there were—let us say for argument's sake—the tightest sort of an alliance, offensive and defensive, between all Britain, colonies and all, and the United States—what would happen? Anything we'd say would go, whether we should say, 'Come in out of the wet,' or, 'Disarm.' That might be the beginning of a real-world alliance and union to accomplish certain large results—disarmament, for instance, or arbitration—dozens of good things."[20]

We will never know the extent to which Wilson was influenced by his ambassador in London when drafting his historic speech, though in reality it is irrelevant: Page was vindicated. Despite being ostracized by his leaders for most of the war, and widely criticized in subsequent decades, his arguments were ultimately used by the president to justify American action.

On April 6, after four days of debate, Congress passed a joint resolution declaring war. On that day president Wilson signed the proclamation declaring war on the Imperial Government of Germany.[21]

VINDICATED THOUGH SIDELINED

Around the beginning of 1917 Wilson had begun to centralize war-related diplomacy and Page was sidelined, effectively ending his involvement. Communication was increasingly directly between House and the British government, bypassing Page and sometimes even the State Department. It put the British government in a quandary as they retained their high regard for Page. Balfour noted on a Foreign Office report in January: "The President is unjust to Page. Can we do anything to help the latter?" Unfortunately, they could not and by September the centralization was complete. Page's treatment was consistent with how Bryan had been treated, when he had been sidelined in favor of House, though on a greater scale. The British dealt directly with House, even bypassing the British ambassador. Even the secretary of state was on the outside, and Wilson and House considered ways of removing Lansing, including sending him to London to replace Page, though nothing eventuated.[22]

Page realized something was wrong, though he was typically philosophical, writing to Arthur, "My job is really done here. When I pulled thro' the neutrality period & won the confidence of this Gov't & people so that they understood &—saw us come in, *that* was really the end of my job." In November, House came to London with a group of experts to attend the Inter-Allied Conference in Paris and meet with British and French governments, though Page had no role of substance. He had been completely sidelined.[23]

AMERICA'S BLOCKADE

America's subsequent actions on trade vindicated Page's prediction during the Declaration of London dispute when, on October 22, 1914, he wrote to House, "England is going to keep war-materials out of Germany as far as she can. We'd do it in her place. Germany would do it. Any nation would do it." That is what happened. America enforced policies of blockade and blacklists even more widely and vigorously than Britain. It stopped the leaking of supplies from neutral countries that had been evading the British, only allowing these countries enough food to feed their populations. America blacklisted more than five thousand persons and organizations, far more than Britain.[24]

America was doing what Page had suggested in his Leadership Letter, though it was too late to work as he had envisaged. Back then, in October 1914, Page's idea was to work with the other neutrals to blockade Germany, forcing it to run out of supplies, then taking the lead in negotiations to end the war and demilitarize Europe. In 1917 America stopped supplies getting through to Germany, though tragically it was no longer enough to end the war as the positions of the three key nations had changed significantly:

- America was in a much weaker diplomatic position, having lost the respect of the German and British leaders, so would not be in a position to lead any negotiations.

- Britain was in a significantly weaker position, both financially and physically. Supplies were not getting through, and it was starting to experience food shortages. As Page noted in his diary on February 25: "We are practically blockaded—held up, held in, driven off the seas by the German threat!"

- Germany, by contrast, had improved its position. It had built enough submarines to stop supplies getting through to the Allies and pose a lethal military threat. It had significantly increased its agricultural output, including in its newly acquired territory in Northern France and Romania. Although Germany had strict rationing there was, as U.S. ambassador Gerard noted, "a far greater danger of the starvation of our Allies than of the starvation of the Germans."[25]

BRITAIN'S DEPENDENCE ON AMERICA

Germany's submarine campaign was devastatingly successful. More tonnage of British ships was sunk from February to April 1917 than the combined total of 1915 and 1916. There was a real danger of Allied defeat. On April 9, Admiral William S. Sims arrived from America and established himself in the embassy as the most senior U.S. Navy officer stationed in Britain. Realizing the dire situation, Sims sent urgent messages to the Navy Department in Washington, D.C., requesting ships be provided to combat the German submarines. Virtually ignored by the Department, Sims asked Page for assistance, though Lansing's response to Page's letter was noncommittal. Then on May 4 Page wrote to Wilson, stating, "The submarines have become a very grave danger." He went on to give statistics of the increasing volume of Allied ships being sunk, the great concern being Germany was building submarines faster than they could be destroyed. Consequently, "if merely the present situation continue, the war will pretty soon become a contest of endurance under hunger with an increasing proportion of starvation." Action was needed: "The greatest help, I hope, can come from us—our destroyers and similar armed craft,—provided we can send enough of them quickly." The sheer number of submarines meant that "the area to be watched is so big that many submarine-hunters are needed." Page also warned public discontent was so great there was "even talk of turning out the Government."

On June 29 Page emphasized to Wilson the urgency of the situation: "If the present rate of destruction of shipping goes on, the war will end before a victory is won." He pleaded: "The full available destroyer power that can by any method be made available must be concentrated in this area within weeks (not months)." And he concluded: "One sea-going tug now may be worth more than a dozen ships next year." When it became obvious the U.S. government was taking no notice, Page and Sims concluded they were considered so pro-British that their requests were not taken at face value. Page believed the Navy secretary, his former friend Josephus Daniels, and officials thought the British were protecting their own warships and wanted America to use their ships. Page and Sims decided the best option was for Foreign Secretary Balfour, who had high credibility among U.S. officials, to write directly to the president.[26]

Balfour's letter, sent on June 30, laid the situation bare: "The forces at present at the disposal of the British Admiralty are not adequate to protect shipping from submarine attack in the danger zone round the British Islands. Consequently, shipping is being sunk at a greater rate than it can be replaced by new tonnage of British origin." He went on to say it was inevitable that British ships would not be able to supply Britain with food and other essential supplies. Britain's Allies, France and Italy, were in a similar predicament. America was "the only allied country in a position to help" and the situation was critical: "Destroyers, submarines, gunboats, yachts, trawlers and tugs would all give invaluable help." Balfour pleaded: "But they are required now and in as great numbers as possible. There is no time for delay." A few days later Page reinforced Balfour's appeal with a letter to Wilson and Lansing. He pointed out the British leaders had publicly downplayed their nation's perilous position to keep Germany in the dark as much as possible, and if the public knew the true situation the government would probably fall. The appeal was successful, and, with much reluctance, the U.S. Navy's presence was boosted by August. In combination with other measures, especially convoys, the problems caused by the submarines were reduced. By December, when American battleships arrived, the volume of shipping lost to submarines was the lowest since the submarine campaign started.[27]

The Allies' financial position was dire. Britain was financing the Allied war effort, though in April 1917 its account with J. P. Morgan & Co. in America was overdrawn by $400 million. The situation continued to deteriorate, and on June 28 Page and Balfour sent separate messages to Lansing and House respectively requesting urgent financing for the debt. The next day Page wrote to Wilson with the same dire message, though he expressed frustration with the British for not raising the matter earlier: "Why on earth do the British drift along until they reach a precipice." With great reluctance the U.S. government provided the $400 million to take on Britain's debt using proceeds of the first Liberty Loan, which Treasury Secretary McAdoo had raised from the American public, then continued to provide the Allies with loans.[28]

By July 1917, American troops had started arriving in France, along with their leader General John J. Pershing. Over subsequent months thousands more arrived and went into action for the first time on November 2, though they would not have a significant impact until well into 1918.[29]

RESIGNATION AS HEALTH WORSENED

Although sidelined by his president, Page continued working at the embassy undertaking some significant diplomatic activities, hosting official American visitors, and considerable routine work. He remained highly sought after in London as a speaker and guest. In his letters Page continued to merely tell Wilson what he thought he wanted to hear, though he revealed his true thoughts to Arthur and in his diary, such as on February 3, 1918, when he wrote, "History will not give him the place of a real leader."[30]

In early 1918 Page's health, which had always caused him problems, rapidly deteriorated. Alice insisted he take a break and they spent the first two weeks of March in Cornwall. It seemed to rejuvenate him and an examination by his doctor, Sir William Osler, could find nothing wrong. After what Alice termed "three little break downs," in the middle of the year he took another break, this time for two months, though he never recovered. In reality, Page, who had been a heavy cigar smoker for forty years, was dying of emphysema and hypertension, both of which were untreatable. He refused to resign, playing down the seriousness of his condition. He may have also been subconsciously relying on the "hereditary robustness" he referred to in 1884 when writing obituaries for his uncle and great uncle in the *State Chronicle*. Friends and family were concerned about him, knowing he was failing. When Buttrick warned Page "you are going to lay down your life," Page responded, "I have only one life to lay down, I can't quit now." He even resisted extremely strong urgings from two worried sons. Major Frank, who was serving in France, and Arthur, who was in America, both went to England to convey their feelings. Still their father resisted, saying,

"No. It's quitting on the job. I must see the war through. I can't quit until it's over." It wasn't until Osler insisted in a professional capacity that Page relented. Even then it was with great regret, his work ethic and patriotism not letting him concede the inevitable.[31]

Page's actions are difficult to understand. He was not contributing to the war effort, largely doing the formalities of running the embassy. Uncharacteristically, he was concerned that if another ambassador took over, as he wrote to Arthur in March, he would "get much of the credit for my work and will be, in the popular mind, *the* war ambassador." If he wasn't so worried about his legacy, Page could have returned home and looked after his health. It was a sad end to his great adventure and certainly not what he would have wanted.[32]

In France, American soldiers were rapidly building in numbers. Their first involvement in offensive action on the western front was on February 13, 1918, though it was not until May 28 that a full-scale attack by American troops took place. By the start of July one million American troops and military personnel were in France. This included Frank and Katharine's husband, Charles G. Loring. By August, when America had deployed 1.3 million troops, they were having a significant impact and Germany was demoralized.[33]

On August 1, 1918, Page wrote a letter of resignation to Wilson, which commenced with the following lament: "I have been struggling for a number of months against the necessity to write you this note; for my doctors now advise me to give up all work for a period—my London doctor says for six months." He blamed his ill health on "a progressive digestive trouble which does not yield to the usual treatment" as well as "the war, five London winters, the monotony of English food and the unceasing labor w^h. is now the common lot." He was "ashamed" that such an affliction had brought him "to something near a breakdown." His doctors assured him he would recover following rest "in a dry, warm climate." Showing extreme reluctance, he wrote: "I see nothing else to do, then, but to bow to the inevitable and to ask you to be kind enough to relieve me and to accept my resignation to take effect as soon as I can go to Washington and make a somewhat extended report." His feelings were palpable: "I cannot tell you how great my disappointment is that this request has become necessary." Page had organized Laughlin, who had served first secretary of the embassy for his entire ambassadorship and for whom he had developed great respect, to be his interim successor. He concluded, "I send this, Mr. President, with more regret than I can express and only after a struggle of more than six months to avoid it."[34]

In his reply of August 24, Wilson indicated he understood why Page had resigned, saying, "It caused me great regret that the condition of your health makes it necessary for you to resign. Under the circumstances I do not feel I have the right to insist on such a sacrifice as your remaining in London. Your resignation is therefore accepted." Wilson did not realize the extent of Page's poor health, as he had played it down in his letter, and concluded by congratulating Page: "You can resign knowing that you have performed your difficult duties with distinguished success." On the same day German general Wrisberg was mocked by the Reichstag budget committee when he proclaimed the German high command was confident of victory. The Germans realized they were defeated, though they were not prepared to accept the Allies' conditions.[35]

"I LOVED THAT MAN"

Once his resignation had been made public Page received tributes expressing regret and respect from across Britain, including from people and newspapers that would not normally praise an American so effusively. Typical of the press was the headline in London's the *Times*: "A Great Ambassador." Prime Minister Lloyd George wrote highlighting the praise he had received from across the nation: "While you have always firmly presented the point of view of your own country, you have succeeded in winning, not only the respect and admiration of official circles, but the confidence, and I can say without hesitation, the affection of all sections of our people." Personal messages were also sent by the king, Grey, and almost all the senior members of the government. Plymouth granted him "freedom of the city," and the lord mayor and council came to London to confer the honor as Page's health did not permit travel. His speech at this ceremony was his last in England.[36]

Page became so ill that his doctors were reluctant to let him travel on a ship. Arthur took his father to Banff, Scotland, for a rest. From there on September 2 he wrote his last ever letter to his "dear Allie" and was desperately looking forward to retiring in his beloved South: "I find myself thinking of the winter down South—of a Thanksgiving Day dinner for the older folks of our family, of a Christmas tree for the kids, of frolics of all sorts, of Rest, of some writing (perhaps not much), going over my papers with Ralph—that's what he wants, you know; etc., etc., etc." On September 28, German General Erich Ludendorff advised Field Marshal Paul von Hindenburg an armistice was their only option, though Page's time in London was at an end as his doctors agreed he could travel home.[37]

It was a solemn occasion at Waterloo Station on October 2 when Page left

London. Sir Arthur Walsh represented the King, and senior ministers were there including Lord Robert Cecil and Balfour, who later recalled: "I loved that man, I almost wept when he left England." As the dignitaries stood respectfully with their hats removed, Page's train moved slowly from the platform. Despite his frailty, the man who had stood with them to defend democracy smiled and with great effort waved them farewell. He had done all he could.[38]

Page had always promised himself, his family, and his friends that he would spend his final days in his beloved North Carolina. When the *Olympic's* captain on Page's final voyage heard this, he went as fast as he could. Page was so ill for most of the trip that he was lucky to make it back to America. Arriving in New York on October 12, more than a day ahead of schedule, Page was critically ill and rushed to St. Luke's Hospital, where he rallied for a short period. While in hospital Page was able to see some old friends and was lively as he discussed international affairs. On October 17, Wilson sent a letter expressing distress about his condition, and that he would "wait patiently for your recovery in order that we may tell you how glad we are to have you safe on this side and how we have valued your services in your difficult post in London." Despite being in New York while Page was in hospital, Wilson did not visit, though, with his wife Edith, he sent a box of roses.[39]

Meanwhile, the Great War ended at 11 a.m. on November 11, 1918. About 5.1 million Allied and American soldiers had been killed, and about 3.5 million from the Central Powers. This was more than the known total of all other wars in history. The average daily toll was over 5,600 soldiers. More than one in three British and French men who were aged 19–22 in 1914 were killed. On top of this were the civilian deaths, including the massacre of more than one million Armenians and the deaths of 82,000 Serbians. Influenza killed 62,000 American soldiers in addition to the 48,000 who died fighting. The war devastated the lives of individuals and communities of the countries involved. Historian Martin Gilbert estimated that on top of the vast numbers of physically injured and maimed participants, more than 250,000 soldiers suffered psychological damage.[40]

FINAL DAYS

Page wrote his final letter to Wilson on November 23, 1918. Handwritten, as almost all his letters were, and with the scrawl clearly of someone very unwell, he lamented his position. Wilson was soon leaving for the Versailles Peace Conference in France, a trip that would include a stop in London. Page would have given anything to have been there to welcome his president and see the enthusiastic responses of the British people. His deep regret is clearly evident, though he was characteristically upbeat, generous, and full of optimism:

St. Luke's Hospital, New York
23 Nov, 1918

Dear Mr. President
The doctors continue to delay their permission for me to travel further, and (I fear) the chance lessens of my having the pleasure to see you and to report to you before you 'go'—on the most momentous journey a man ever took! My formal resignation therefore, is due—or past due, and I have sent it to Mr. Lansing.

I never wrote anything, my dear Mr. President, with such regret. What w^d I not give to be in England when you are there! But my regret is the measure also of my profound appreciation of your giving me the most interesting and (I hope also by far) the most useful experience of my life, an experience that I hope to turn to good use, and to your credit) as long as I live.—You will find the heart of England most grateful to us; and the admiration of your extraordinary management of the world's most extraordinary events—beyond bounds. It would be the greatest joy of my life to see them receive you. You have set the moral standard for the world to become a new world.

Great as my disappointment is in this detention here, I am assured that my illness is going well: my detention comes from minor causes. All my great doctors, English, Scotch, and American, assure me of a complete recovery within a reasonable period; and I am now undoubtedly making good *progress* in that slow process.

How gracious you and Mrs. Wilson were to have had sent to me the other day the beautiful box of roses that still brighten and perfume my prison here! So to be thought of is the happiest experience any prisoner could have.

I am my dear Mr. President, for your confidence and kindness, always most gratefully yours,

Walter H. Page

This is the first time I have held a pen since I wrote to you—perhaps 3 months ago.[41]

Wilson replied, in his final letter to Page, on November 26, writing, "It was good to see your handwriting and to see it so steady." Delighted that "the letter throughout speaks your old spirit," he was disappointed about Page's resignation: "You know with what sentiments and regrets I accept your resignation and how heartily sorry I am that you could not have been an active participant in the present all-important things that are going on on the other side," though he recognized Page had done the right thing for his health. He concluded, "I hope that the time is not far off when I can see you and catch up with things in a long talk."[42]

Page received invitations to speak from all over the nation, as many people were not aware of the extent of his illness. While his daughter Katharine replied to most, the last thing Page ever wrote was a reply to the mayor of Cleveland, Ohio, on the topic of American-British relations: "I deeply regret my health will not permit me to attend any public function for some time to come; for I deeply appreciate your invitation on behalf of the City of Cleveland for the meeting on December 7th, and have a profound sympathy with its purpose to bring the two great English-speaking worlds as close together as possible, so that each shall thoroughly understand the courage and sacrifice and ideals of the other. This is the greatest political task of the future."[43]

Very soon after, his health turned for the worse. His family acceded to his long-held desire and Alice and their son Frank traveled with him back home to Pinehurst, North Carolina. Arriving on December 12, Frank carried him from the train as he said smiling, "Well, Frank, I did get here after all, didn't I?" With him in his last days were Alice, his daughter Katharine, Frank, and another son Ralph, as well as brothers Henry, Chris, and Robert. His other son, Arthur, was serving in England. Walter Hines Page died several days later on December 21, 1918, at the age of just sixty-three.[44]

On December 4, the president had left for Europe on the *George Washington*. Visiting France, England, Italy, and Vatican City, everywhere he was received by the public as a hero and savior, as Page had expected. His trip ended in Paris and the Peace Conference was held in nearby Versailles. It commenced on January 12, 1919, and ended with the signing of the Treaty of Versailles on June 28, though from February 14 to March 13 Wilson returned to America for the closing of Congress.

At the conference Wilson had to fight every inch of the way for his proposed League of Nations and aspects of the Peace Treaty, to the extent that his health suffered tremendously. Wilson's difficulties were compounded by his loss of faith in House. Returning from America in March, he was devastated to learn that House had made significant concessions that were contrary to the instructions Wilson had given before leaving. He said to Edith, "House has given away everything I had won before we left Paris. He has compromised on every side, and so I have to start all over again and this time it will be harder, as he has given the impression that my delegates are not in sympathy with me." Wilson relied less and less on House and their last conversation was at the end of the conference. The ostracization was even more pronounced than Page's as Wilson completely shut House out of his life.[45]

While visiting London, on December 28, President Woodrow Wilson and King George V were photographed standing together at Buckingham Palace. This is the image Page so perceptively wanted his president to show "the old Earth" when war was brewing in mid-1913. Back then it could have made a difference. By the time it happened it was seven days too late for Page to see, and more than four years too late for the world. Page's idea was that if Germany thought America would support Britain the war might have been avoided. Without realizing it Wilson used the same logic during his break from the Peace Conference. On March 4, just before returning to Paris, he said in a speech in New York supporting the League of Nations that if Germany had realized Britain would have come in in support of France and Russia the war could have been avoided.[46]

Autocracy had been defeated but at enormous cost. Democracy had shown strength, but the Allied democracies were spent, except one. If democracy was to be spread it was up to America, though it had ended up in a position of profound diplomatic weakness and played itself out of the game. Wilson should have been in the box seat at Versailles as the European countries were completely dependent on America to avoid mass starvation and their own insolvency. It could have been very different if its leader had not ignored the prescient and perceptive advice of his ambassador to Great Britain.

"THE FRIEND OF BRITAIN IN HER SOREST NEED"

On June 16, 1923, Alice along with Arthur, Katharine, and four grandchildren, returned to England on the *Celtic* to attend a memorial service for her husband. After publication of his letters in two Pulitzer Prize–winning volumes by Burton Hendrick, there was a renewed interest in, and appreciation of, Page's efforts as ambassador. A letter was published in the *Times* of London by Asquith and Lloyd George, Grey and Balfour, prime ministers and foreign secretaries while Page was ambassador, as well as by A. Bonar Law, incumbent prime minister, calling for subscriptions to a memorial recognizing Page.[47]

The memorial service was held in Westminster Abbey on July 3. Joining Alice were Stanley Baldwin, Asquith, Winston Churchill, Lord Lansdowne, and many others. In a moving speech, Lord Grey paid heartfelt tribute to Page's character: "Walter Hines Page was an example of the truth that the strongest personalities are the outcome not so much of striving for personal success or fame, as of patriotism and of faith in an ideal. His patriotism was of the noblest kind; he loved his country both for what it was and for what he believed it could and would do for the benefit of mankind. His perception of the power of the United States, his belief in democracy, his absolute and never-faltering trust in the will of its people to do great things and good things for the world, were part of his very being." Grey captured why Page was so highly regarded and engendered such respect from others who sought to improve the South, the nation, and the world: strength, selflessness, and passionate beliefs. Grey went on to eulogize how he and his country felt about Page: "We in this country feel deep gratitude to him; we wish that there should be something to commemorate the sympathy and moral support that he gave us in the greatest crisis of our history. We wish his name to be remembered with regard, with honour, and with affection, as that of one who gave us invaluable help at a time when our liberty, our very independence even, seemed to be at stake."

Grey then unveiled the memorial plaque paid for with the subscriptions, which reads: "TO THE GLORY OF GOD AND IN MEMORY OF WALTER HINES PAGE 1855–1918. AMBASSADOR OF THE UNITED STATES OF AMERICA TO THE COURT OF ST JAMES'S 1913–1918. The friend of Britain in her sorest need."[48]

Six months later Page's successor as ambassador, John W. Davis, wrote: "I think it no exaggeration to say that no American Ambassador in London was ever nearer to the heart of the English people than was Mr. Page. He elicited not only their esteem and admiration, but their warm and lasting affection. I recognized constantly as his successor that I was the beneficiary of the good will which he did so much to create. He had the respect and something more of all ranks of society. Perhaps the instant widespread response in Great Britain to the suggestion of a memorial to him in Westminster Abbey is the most striking tribute ever paid to an American diplomat."[49]

Page's most significant contribution as ambassador was to maintain strong and robust relations between the two countries in anticipation of America eventually joining the war on the side of the Allies. His friend and ally Grey, in his farewell letter, summed up Page's contribution to the war effort and emphasized the great respect held by the British leaders: "If the United States had been represented here by any one less decided as to the right and wrong of the war and less firm and courageous than yourself, the whole of the relations between your country and ours would have been in peril. And if the two countries had gone apart instead of coming together the whole fate of the world would be very different from what I hope it will now be."[50]

It is hard to underestimate the extent of this achievement. In its insistence on being able to trade freely with Germany and neighboring neutral countries, not only was America hindering Britain's efforts to protect its independence, but it had also indirectly, and even directly, equated the blockade actions with Germany's submarine attacks on civilian ships. This had severely undermined British trust and confidence, the very characteristics essential between nations if they are to effectively fight together. Overcoming this, Page retained the trust and confidence of Britain's two wartime foreign secretaries, Grey and Balfour, ensuring strong relations continued between the two nations.

PART FIVE

THE MYTHMAKERS

\ 12 /

THE MYTH OF NEUTRALITY
A CASE STUDY IN POLITICAL LEADERSHIP

IGNORING REALITY

The myth of neutrality was that Americans could continue their existing way of life and ignore the threat to democracy posed by the war in Europe. It was uncannily similar to the situation Page had earlier encountered when myth-making Southern leaders convinced people not to face up to reality. The myth of neutrality lulled the people into a false sense of security and, as Page wrote in late 1916 after his visit to America, was exacerbated by the president's insistence on personal neutrality: "I can see it in no other way but this: the President suppressed free thought and free speech when he insisted upon personal neutrality. He held back the deliberate and spontaneous thought and speech of the people except the pro-Germans, who saw their chance and improved it! The mass of the American people found themselves forbidden to think or talk, and this forbidding had a sufficient effect to make them take refuge in indifference. It's the President's job. He's our leader. He'll attend to this matter. We must not embarrass him. On this easy cushion of non-responsibility the great masses fell back at their intellectual and moral ease—softened, isolated, lulled."[1]

During this 1916 visit, Page was horrified by the extent to which Americans had been lulled into a false sense of security by neutrality, as described later by Lord Cecil: "He said that it had been a shock to him, when he was in the United States recently, to find that, though his countrymen were fully aware of the facts of the war, they did not seem to appreciate what the German really was, or that Prussian militarism was, as he put it 'an organized crime.'" Cecil then wrote of an example Page had given: "Somehow or other, though the facts crossed the Atlantic the spirit of war did not; and he gave me an illustration drawn from his own experience at a private dinner party where, until he had explained at great length what was really going on on this side, his hearers, though men of the highest education and knowledge, had never really understood what was happening."[2]

242 \ CHAPTER TWELVE

NEUTRALITY THREATENED DEMOCRACY

After this visit home in 1916, Page summed up how neutrality had weakened American leadership and threatened the future of democracy: "There is a great lesson in this lamentable failure of the President really to lead the Nation. The United States stands for democracy and free opinion as it stands for nothing else and as no other nation stands for it. Now when democracy and free opinion are at stake as they have not before been, we take a 'neutral' stand—we throw away our very birthright. We may talk of 'humanity' all we like: we have missed the largest chance that ever came to help the large cause that brought us into being as a Nation."[3]

Britain and Germany saw it as a conflict for the superiority of democracy or autocracy. In his letter to Wilson on September 6, 1914, Page quoted Grey saying if Germany won Europe would be an unbearable place to live and that "the only place worth living will be the United States—till it attacks that, as it would." Germany believed it was a fight for the superiority of military autocracy. The military attaché to the German embassy in Washington, Captain Franz von Papen, stated to the German War Ministry on March 7, 1915, "It is above all pleasing to note how after 7 months of warfare, democratic heads begin at last to wonder whether the hated Prussian militarism has not borne a share in the marvelous blossoming of the German people and the marshaling of all moral and economic forces for the maintenance of our existence." In his letter, Page went on: "I see no hope of the world's going on towards ends and ideals that we value except on the hypothesis that Prussian militarism be utterly cut out, as surgeons cut out a cancer. And the Allies will do it—must do it, to live. It would dash our Monroe doctrine to the ground. It w^d even invade the U.S. in time."[4]

Other Americans also believed it was a fight for democracy. Secretary of State Lansing stated it in his personal memorandum of July 11, 1915. Gerard, the ambassador in Germany, wrote after he had been recalled in 1917: "If Germany wins this war it means the triumph of the autocratic system," and if that occurred "the whole world will be compelled to turn itself into an armed camp." Expanding on this he argued: "If we had stayed out and the war had been drawn or won by Germany we should have been attacked, and that while Europe stood grinning by: not directly at first, but through an attack on some Central or South American State to which it would be at least as difficult for us to send troops as for Germany. And what if this powerful nation, vowed to war, were once firmly established in South or Central America? What of our boasted isolation then?" As Kennan wrote almost four decades later: "Once in the war, we had no difficulty in discovering—and lost no time in doing so—that the issues involved in it were of the greatest significance to us." Wilson eventually recognized this in his 1917 speech to Congress, though never acknowledged that Page had been correct all along; to the contrary, he ostracized him.[5]

Neutrality meant America missed this opportunity to defend democracy, reinforcing Page's assessment over the decades before the war that it was not ready to take on the world-leadership role its economic and industrial power had thrust upon it. Page knew America needed free and democratic nations in Europe to ensure its own future; it could not realistically be neutral and it was mythmaking to pretend otherwise: "The President and the Government, in their insistence upon the moral quality of neutrality, missed the larger meaning of the war. It is at bottom nothing but the effort of the Berlin absolute monarch and his group to impose their will on as large a part of the world as they can overrun. The President started out with the idea that it was a war brought on by many obscure causes—economic and the like; and he thus missed its whole meaning. We have ever since been dealing with the chips which fly from the war machine and have missed the larger meaning of the conflict. Thus we have failed to render help to the side of Liberalism and Democracy, which are at stake in the world."[6]

EFFECTIVE POLITICAL LEADERSHIP

The myth of neutrality was the catalyst which led to the breakdown in the relationship between Page and Wilson. This was a result of their contrasting personalities. Page thrived on personal interaction and debate. He was interested in other people's ideas, practical solutions to problems, and communicating these as widely as possible. Consequently, he wrote regularly to his president offering his opinion on a wide range of issues. Wilson struggled with this as his decision-making process was based on internal reflection, not discussing matters with others, and he was seemingly reluctant to accept unsolicited advice. Further, when Wilson had a major disagreement with one of his team, he ostracized them, as he did with Bryan and Page, or cut them off, as he later did to House at the end of the Versailles Peace Conference.

Analyzing Wilson's ostracizing of his ambassador to Great Britain emphasizes three of the key characteristics of an effective political leader: not being blindly driven by idealism or ideology; the ability to hear, respect, evaluate, and possibly adopt other peoples' ideas; and bringing the people along when developing and implementing policies.

IDEALISM OR IDEOLOGY

Seeing past an ideal or ideology when it is not working is a key characteristic of a good political leader. Wilson was so determined not to get involved in the war that he actively denied reality until his country was in imminent danger and he had no choice. His inability to understand the reality of the war led him to charge Page with being too pro-British, anti-German, and indifferent to the interests of his own nation. This was incorrect; throughout the war Page advocated positions he thought were in the long-term interests of America and democracy. While Page had a deep affection for the British, it was in the context of their sense of unity with Americans; he believed America and Britain should unite as international upholders of democracy. Page's writing over the years made it clear he was not anti-German; he was pro-democracy.

OTHER PEOPLES' IDEAS

Effective political leaders accept that other peoples' ideas might be correct and their own might be incorrect. Rather than shut down anyone who disagrees, they will debate different ideas. Even if a leader is not comfortable with personal conflict, they need to accept it is inevitable. They have made the choice to put themselves forward for the leadership position, so their own discomfort is secondary to making correct decisions and governing in the best interests of the people. In Wilson's case he had the opportunity to at least consider a different opinion, especially from someone for whom he had such high respect. Accordingly, it would have been more productive for Wilson to have engaged with Page. Before the war and in its early months Wilson sent respectful replies to Page's letters and where he didn't agree explaining why he had decided against his suggestion. Therefore Page knew where he stood and could move on to other matters. As the war continued Wilson could have continued this practice, replying with his position and arguments for neutrality. This would have allowed Page to understand where the president was coming from, consider his position, and maybe respond. A productive debate may have ensued between these highly intelligent men.

Related to this, effective political leaders recognize when to set aside their personal preferences in the interests of their people. Wilson wanted to focus on domestic affairs and so he did not give the war his full attention. Page knew America's focus had to be foreign affairs as it was involved in the greatest international crisis in living memory.

CONVINCING THE PEOPLE

Once they have decided what is best for the nation, effective political leaders take it upon themselves to convince the people. Even though he supported democracy, Wilson pushed neutrality onto the nation to appease certain sections of the population. As Lansing noted in his memoirs, domestic opposition to America entering the war came "from several elements of the population which were inspired by different motives and influenced by different reasons." By far the largest number were those who thought it a "European quarrel with which we had nothing to do." Lansing went on to reflect on these people's motives: "They had not reasoned out the underlying principles at stake, nor were they disposed to consider them as important. They could see no reason for the United States becoming involved in what they believed did not concern this country." Page believed it was the president's role to explain these "underlying principles" and turn around public opinion. As he wrote on March 2, 1918: "If the Pres't were really to lead all the people w^d follow." Decades later, President Ronald Reagan referred to it as "the paradox of public office," which especially applied to the presidency: "One must serve the people but be willing to lead them, too—sometimes in new or controversial directions."[7]

Page believed the government needed to explain to the people that they could not ignore the war: if Americans wanted to continue to live with freedom and opportunity, their country needed to take on a leadership role in the crisis the world was facing. He wanted the president to ask the American people the critical questions, which were along the lines of:

- What type of a world do you want to live in?
- Do you want to live in a world where democracy is thriving?
- Or do you want to be the last bastion of democracy, clinging to your ideals of freedom and opportunity while Europe is ruled by an autocratic monarchy with the resources and determination to conquer the rest of the world?

If Page was back at the *World's Work,* he would have had the opportunity to put these questions to the people and present his arguments as why the answer to the last question should be an emphatic "*No.*" While Page's ethics and loyalty would have stopped him personally criticizing Wilson or revealing anything about his experiences as ambassador, this does suggest a reason why Wilson persisted with an ambassador to whom he felt he could not communicate. While the reasons will never be known, Wilson and House may have been concerned

246 \ CHAPTER TWELVE

about Page's opinions and giving him an opportunity to put his persuasive arguments before the people through his writing and speeches. On January 12, 1917, House wrote in his diary that Wilson had expressed concerns about a disgruntled Page expressing his feelings, though House did not believe Page would do such a thing. Wilson was already concerned about what was being written in the *World's Work* under Arthur's editorship. In August 1917 he expressed his displeasure in replying to a request from Arthur: "I do not feel that the World's Work has been at all fair in its criticism, particularly of the administration of the Navy Department, having permitted things to be published which were just as far as possible from the truth."[8]

INCONSISTENCIES OF NEUTRALITY

Page believed the policy of neutrality was riddled with inconsistencies. He summed up his feelings in a letter to Arthur on July 8, 1917. Writing from Salisbury where he was having a short vacation with his wife and the retired Grey, he expressed his frustration and bewilderment: "To save my life I don't see how the Washington crowd can look at themselves in a mirror and keep their faces straight. Yesterday they were bent on sending everything into European neutral states. The foundations of civilization would give way if neutral trade were interfered with. Now, nothing must go in except on a ration basis. Yesterday it must be a peace without victory. Now it must be a complete victory, every man and every dollar thrown in, else no peace is worth having." He made it clear he was not complaining, in fact he was rejoicing that his country was at last standing up for its beliefs, though he was confused that it could have been handled so badly. It was certainly not his style of leadership, as he went on to say: "I'm glad that kind of a rapid change is not a part of my record. The German was the same beast yesterday that he is to-day; and it makes a simple-minded, straight-minded man like me wonder which attitude was the (or is the) attitude of real conviction." Page hit the nail on the head. He knew the American people were also confused.[9]

The message from the president's speech to Congress on April 2, 1917, which was backed up by subsequent speeches and articles by himself and other leaders, was that it was necessary to enter the war as a result of Germany's subterfuge against America and to protect democracy. Wilson had the herculean task of convincing the people to stop believing in the myth of neutrality, which he had so conscientiously perpetuated for the first two and a half years of the war; though there was a fundamental weakness in his argument. America would have remained neutral and not acted to defend democracy if not triggered by Germany crossing the line with both the unrestricted submarine campaign and its proposal to Mexico. Congress and the public were not convinced the time had come for their nation to take on a world-leadership role; consequently, in subsequent decades America returned to isolationism.[10]

RESURRECTING THE MYTH OF NEUTRALITY

Wilson's peace speech to Congress on January 22, 1917, referred to America taking a leadership role in postwar Europe. Page would have been gratified by Wilson's allusion to a "new plan" which would be "the foundations of peace among the nations." He boldly claimed, "It is inconceivable that the people of the United States should play no part in that great enterprise." Unfortunately, the "inconceivable" became the conceivable. In March 1920 Congress rejected Wilson's extensive campaign to join the League of Nations, and later that year the people voted for an isolationist president, Warren G. Harding. With his confusing messages, Wilson had not persuaded them to do otherwise.[11]

The myth of neutrality was resurrected by President Harding in his inaugural address when he said, "The recorded progress of our Republic, materially and spiritually, in itself proves the wisdom of the inherited policy of noninvolvement in Old World affairs. Confident of our ability to work out our own destiny, and jealously guarding our right to do so, we seek no part in directing the destinies of the Old World. We do not mean to be entangled. We will accept no responsibility except as our own conscience and judgment, in each instance, may determine." Under Harding's and subsequent postwar administrations, America retreated further into isolation than ever before. Wilson's massive tariff reductions were replaced by the highest tariffs in the nation's history. Immigration was virtually halted, five neutrality statutes were passed by Congress prohibiting financial aid, arms sales, and most other commercial transactions with nations involved in a war, and deployment of the army was not permitted outside the Western Hemisphere. There was no world power keeping a check on Germany.[12]

Page knew the outcome of such decisions, of America failing to take on a world-leadership role, would be another world war. In a memorandum written for himself at the end of August 1913 he wrote an accurate analysis of the situation in Europe that predicted the advent of World War I, the diplomatic stagnation and military rebuilding of the interwar period, and the inevitability of World War II: "All the Europeans are spending their thought and money in watching and checkmating one another and in maintaining their armed and balanced *status quo*. A way must be found out of this stagnant watching. Else a way will have to be fought out of it; and a great European war would set the Old World, perhaps the whole world, back a long way; and thereafter, the present armed watching would recur; we should have gained nothing." He advised Wilson of this numerous times, including in his October 6, 1914 Leadership Letter and in his letter of May 4, 1917: "If we do not organize Europe and make another such catastrophe impossible, life will not be worth being born into except to the few whose days happen to fall between recurring devastations of the world."[13]

During the dark days of World War II, Henry R. Luce, founder of magazines which followed in the footsteps of the *World's Work*, wrote his seminal work "The American Century." He lamented that in the twentieth century Americans had "failed to play their part as a world power—a failure which has had disastrous consequences for themselves and for all mankind." This was particularly so after World War I: "In 1919 we had a golden opportunity, an opportunity unprecedented in all history, to assume the leadership of the world—a golden opportunity handed to us on the proverbial silver platter. We did not understand that opportunity. Wilson mishandled it. We rejected it. The opportunity persisted. We bungled it in the 1920's and in the confusion of the 1930's we killed it."[14]

Page had shown great foresight to see America's potential to demilitarize and democratize Europe; yet the opportunity had been squandered. He would have been appalled and disappointed.

MYTH OF NEUTRALITY FINALLY DEBUNKED

The myth of neutrality was finally debunked during World War II, using the strategy and arguments advocated by Page thirty years earlier. From the start of the war President Franklin D. Roosevelt, who had been Wilson's assistant secretary of the navy, showed explicit, strong, and unwavering support for democracy and the Allies. Just over six months into the war, on March 16, 1940, Roosevelt gave the speech Page believed Wilson should have given during World War I. He laid the foundation for the argument why America could not support an autocratic government, debunked the myth of neutrality, and conditioned the people to the reality that they needed to support democracies if they wanted their own to succeed: "Today we seek a moral basis for peace. It cannot be a real peace if it fails to recognize brotherhood. It cannot be a lasting peace if the fruit of it is oppression, or starvation, or cruelty, or human life dominated by armed

THE MYTH OF NEUTRALITY / 249

camps. It cannot be a sound peace if small nations must live in fear of powerful neighbors. It cannot be a moral peace if freedom from invasion is sold for tribute. It cannot be an intelligent peace if it denies free passage to that knowledge of those ideals which permit men to find common ground. It cannot be a righteous peace if worship of God is denied."[15]

Facing a high level of public opposition, Roosevelt led the people to understand that it was a fight for the future of democracy, not a far-away European war which could be ignored. Americans responded positively. In May and June 1940 nearly two-thirds thought it more important to stay out of the war than risk getting involved by aiding Britain. In mid-September opinion was evenly divided. Then by November, a significant majority supported helping Britain, even though their nation might end up at war. This emphasizes the correctness of Page's position: leaders arguing for what is right and will benefit society can change public opinion by showing leadership and bringing the people with them.[16]

Roosevelt's policy was to help Britain as much as possible without America going to war. On December 17, 1940, he stated that a significant number of Americans thought "the best immediate defense of the United States is the success of Great Britain in defending itself." He went on to say while it was important to ensure democracy survived, it was just as important to defend America, and to do that the nation should "do everything to help the British Empire to defend itself." This was the policy Page had advocated, including his proposal for an American-British alliance without America actually getting into the war.[17]

Roosevelt continued to take the people with him in a speech on March 15, 1941, four days after his controversial and widely debated Lend-Lease program to provide supplies to Britain had passed Congress and he had signed it into law: "Let not dictators of Europe or Asia doubt our unanimity now." This was a message to the waverers: either you are with the democratically elected Government of your country or are you with the dictators. Later in the speech he became even more inclusive: "We have just now engaged in a great debate. It was not limited to the halls of Congress. It was argued in every newspaper, on every wave length, over every cracker barrel in all the land; and it was finally settled and decided by the American people themselves." He went on to assert the decision had been proclaimed "with the voice of one hundred and thirty millions" and hence "It is binding on us all."[18]

By gradually turning around public opinion and standing up to those continuing to perpetuate the myth of neutrality, Roosevelt garnered support from others in the community and ensured when the time came to enter the war America was ready both physically and mentally. He was supported by other American leaders. Just as importantly, the nation was engaged in the international community during and after the war. This was exactly what Page had consistently encouraged Wilson to do in World War I.

\ 13 /

REMEMBERING WALTER HINES PAGE

"PROMOTING THE WELL-BEING OF MANKIND"

STANDING UP TO THE MYTHMAKERS

In many ways Page suited his times. The South needed to be awakened from its stupor, and he shook up the staid, conservative North Carolina newspapers, showing the residents what it meant to be a true progressive. He worked, primarily as a volunteer, with like-minded men to transform education and public health, and encouraged development to drag the South out of its dependence on an agrarian economy to catch up with the rest of the nation. He did all he could to bring the South back to the days of his grandfather, who would have been proud of what his grandson achieved.

The greatest challenges of Page's career, both professionally and as a volunteer, were standing up to, and trying to defeat, the mythmakers. It was often a great strain for him, causing conflicts with his fellow Southerners, sometimes with his friends, and ultimately with his president. His convictions about what was right, and what should be done to make things right, were so strong that he just kept going. Like his father, he made some great sacrifices, such as leaving the South and not returning, rather than compromise what he believed was right.

While the mythmakers saw him as a threat, the people embraced him as he tapped into a vein of discontent. His relentless positivity and his great foresight emanated from two sources: empathetic understanding of human nature and a desire for facts. Page did not accept that just because something was widely believed it was necessarily correct. He could articulate an alternative to what the people were being told by the leaders. Their myths were credible, often fitting in with what people wanted to believe, or maybe they thought they had no alternative. Despite this, Page often tapped into underlying concerns, questions people had, things that didn't seem quite right. He confronted head-on highly controversial issues such as lynching and racial disenfranchisement, yet his magazines were among the highest selling and most influential in the nation and he was a popular public speaker.

Echoes of Page's contribution to the information revolution reverberated through the 1920s "debate" between journalist Walter Lippmann and philosopher John Dewey, widely considered to be groundbreaking in their analysis of the media and public opinion in democracies. Like Page, Lippmann and Dewey believed that for a democracy to function the people needed to be educated about the issues facing society so that they would make informed choices when voting. The media had a crucial role in providing this information, though as society was becoming increasingly complex misinformation and information gaps were on the rise.

Consequently, Lippmann argued, the media could no longer fulfill its educational role and the general public's lack of knowledge would exclude them from the policy process. Policy decisions should be made by experts who had the information they needed to make informed decisions. Dewey responded by stating that democratic societies would always be complex because people are complex, and argued voters still had a role in government decision-making. He believed the media needed to have a new role presenting and analyzing complex issues to educate the public.

While this debate is still considered groundbreaking, decades earlier Page had already taken steps to address the increasing complexity of society, incorporating ideas Dewey and, to a lesser extent, Lippmann would later articulate. In 1902, Page emphasized the educational role of the media, stating it was critically important that journalistic writing be accessible by being direct, clear, accurate, informative, and relatable. His publications were full of facts obtained by research, expert opinion, surveys, and studies, usually commissioned by himself. In the *Forum*, for example, both sides of key debates were presented by experts, effectively democratizing the ideas of Lippmann. Page was the pioneer of investigative journalism that would later become part of the information revolution; though for Page it was a means to an end rather than a means of increasing circulation.[1]

While so many of Page's other ideas were also well ahead of his time, he was not aware of it, nor did he want to be so different from his contemporaries. A remarkable aspect of Page's ideas is that their foundations were fundamentally unchanged throughout his life. Four ideas particularly stand out for their legacy: racial equality, Southern development, universal public education, and American world leadership to promote democracy. To promote these, Page had to use all his writing, speaking and persuasive powers to try and defeat the three great myths of his time: the antebellum myth, the race-problem myth, and the myth of neutrality.

THE ANTEBELLUM MYTH

The antebellum myth had two phases. From the 1830s to the post–Civil War Reconstruction period, plantation owners and political and religious leaders entrenched their power by creating an image of the South as a perfect civilization. After the Compromise of 1877, the myth was revived primarily by Confederate leaders and perpetuated by politicians seeking power and influence by restoring the "Solid South." They portrayed the antebellum period as a way of life to which Southerners should aspire to return. It was the progressive New South leaders, with Page as their leading light, who recognized the danger of this way of thinking and pushed hard for public education and Southern development, with remarkable success both in their time and for future generations.

PUBLIC EDUCATION

The "unfulfilled ambition" of the South was one of Page's most powerful messages: By turning their back on education and training, Southerners had allowed themselves to be "disinherited" from the dramatic growth in their nation's wealth and prosperity. They needed to move beyond manual labor to be innovative, embrace technology and learn new ways of doing things. Page and his fellow education campaigners ushered in a new era for education in the South, both physically and culturally.

From 1900 to 1914 public school expenditure by Southern governments increased by more than 3½ times, from $23 million to $82 million. Per capita expenditure rose from $1.10 in 1900 to $2.75 in 1914, and the value of school property rose by almost 4½ times, from $40 million to $175 million. Teacher training became of greater importance, with summer schools and other courses conducted by the major tertiary education institutes across the South, as well as further professional training for school administrators, high school principals, and teachers. Their salaries increased significantly over the decade from 1900.[2]

All these reaped great rewards for the people of the South. Even though the campaign was forced to compromise its aim and accept segregation, both races benefited. Average illiteracy rates for both white and African American children were more than halved, and the average number of days in the annual school term increased by 24 percent (from 105 to 130). Importantly, this continued over subsequent decades. There were ongoing large increases in government expenditure for all areas of education, improvements in legislation, teaching standards, and equipment, and requirements for compulsory attendance. In the 1930s public school systems in Southern cities were comparable with those elsewhere in America.[3]

The cultural change was even more significant. As with the Watauga Club in the 1880s, the campaign's greatest achievement was turning around public opinion. Getting any public schools established in the Southern states was remarkable, given previously strong negative and apathetic attitudes among leaders and the public. Its successes were in three areas: bringing Northern and Southern educational workers together, encouraging the people supporting and working in education in the South, and gaining public support for a public school system through an extensive campaign. The farm-demonstration method transformed the rural South, and farmers' attitude to education.

The work of Page and his fellow campaigners was still being appreciated years later. At the end of the 1920s William F. Russell, dean of Columbia University's Teachers College, stated the campaign had rehabilitated education in the South due to "the presence of men of vision, the development of an economic base, the training of leaders, and the encouragement of their work of promotion at home." The remarkable turnaround in public opinion continued into the 1930s, as described by Dabney: "People, who were indifferent and antagonistic toward public education at public cost, have now come to look upon the education of all the children as the first duty of the people and the highest function of the democratic state." As Page said in standing up for the "forgotten man" and "woman": *We pay for schools not so much out of our purses as out of our state of mind.* Perceptive as ever, his passionate advocacy had been pivotal in transforming education in the South.[4]

In subsequent decades in America, public education became accepted as fundamental. In 1938 President Franklin D. Roosevelt, in his Message for American Education Week, included a statement which reflected Page's belief in the importance of education in a democracy: "Democracy cannot succeed unless those who express their choice are prepared to choose wisely. The real safeguard of democracy, therefore, is education . . . To prepare each citizen to choose wisely and to enable him to choose freely are paramount functions of the schools in a democracy." Public schools are now the foundation of education systems around the world, and their critical role in an individual's and a society's success is widely accepted.[5]

Hookworm disease eradication, the other major education campaign, also had great success. In 1931 Charles Stiles examined 18,649 Southern school children and less than forty were infected. Sanitation at the schools was of a high standard, unlike in 1902 when most were surrounded by infested soil. While complete eradication still has not been achieved today, as a few cases are discovered each year, the impact was tremendous in improving the lives, education, and working conditions of people living in the South.[6]

Similar campaigns were used against other major health problems, including malaria, yellow fever, typhoid fever, pellagra, and other infectious diseases. Southerners, both individually and as communities, changed the way they thought about controlling preventable health problems. They also looked to improve public health. In 1902 there were virtually no county health officers in 13 Southern states, in 1931 there were 339 full-time officers. These officers began regular medical examinations of school children, a practice which was non-existent in 1902. Over a similar period, public health expenditure rose from $230,496 to $4,217,997. In North Carolina, for example, state government expenditure in 1924 on a wide range of public education, health, and social work programs, as well as highways, was greater than total expenditure in the entire 30 years leading up to 1897 when Page had, as Connor wrote, "stirred the conscience of the state with his plea for 'The Forgotten Man.'"[7]

The sanitary commission's campaign was extended to other countries in the "hookworm belt," including India, Egypt, China, and Australia, and grew into the International Health Commission (IHC), of which Page was an original member. In August 1913 Ambassador Page facilitated a visit by Wickliffe Rose, by then director-general of the IHC, to London and with many medical experts developed a process to establish hookworm programs in specific British colonies. The IHC and its associated bodies became, as Dabney wrote in 1926, "the greatest health movement the world has ever known," and "no one rejoiced more in the stupendous success of this health movement than Walter Hines Page, who had been largely responsible for starting it."[8]

SOUTHERN DEVELOPMENT

By his own measure, Page's campaign for Southern development has been remarkably successful. In 1891 he explained that his focus was how the forgotten people would benefit: "What is the proper measure of this new awakening? The measure of the men it produces, and this only. It is not the measure of the wealth produced. Neither here nor elsewhere in this time nor ever is the value of industrial life the sum total of its concrete product, but only and always the sum total of its manhood." Page's great insight was that when given the opportunity, it is the people who will drive development. In the 1907 "Southern Number" of the *World's Work*, he wrote about the forgotten people at last starting to get the opportunities they had been denied: "For the most important change that is taking place is not the development of the wealth—great as that is—but the development of the people, the people who till now have been isolated, sidetracked, held back, kept out of the highways of life."[9]

It is highly likely Page's advocacy had a positive impact on North Carolina's long-term development, including industrialization, research, and technology. From 1883 he subjected the state to 1 1/2 years of relentless positivity encouraging the people to engage in entrepreneurship, improvement, investment, growth, and education or training. He exhorted them to move on from the antebellum period when most of them were forgotten, as the prospects of North Carolina and North Carolinians were never greater. The pinnacle of his efforts was the North Carolina Exposition of 1884, which he initiated and heavily promoted. In 1912 one of the exposition's organizers, Henry Fries, wrote to several of the state's leaders asking them to reflect on its role in industrial development over the subsequent twenty-eight years. In his response Page stated that the exposition "did have a tremendous influence on the development of North Carolina. There isn't the slightest doubt about that. I remember having heard of things being done and enterprises undertaken that date directly to it . . . a new spirit was manifest." The other replies were also very positive, including that by a Raleigh doctor, Richard Lewis, who believed the exposition was "practically the beginning of the great industrial growth" of the state. While it is generally difficult to prove cause and effect for such growth as there is rarely direct evidence, in 2023 North Carolina had the eleventh largest economy in the nation.[10]

A key factor in North Carolina's economic and industrial development—in 2008 the state had the nation's eighth largest manufacturing base—has been the Research Triangle Park (RTP). America's largest research park, the RTP was conceived in the mid-1950s when North Carolina's economy was dependent on three declining industries, tobacco, textiles, and furniture manufacturing. The state's per capita income was practically the nation's lowest, forty-eighth in 1952, and the "brain drain" that Page warned against in his "Forgotten Man" speech was still a serious problem. A research hub was proposed by business, educational, and government leaders to take advantage of the three research universities in the triangle comprising Raleigh (North Carolina State University), Durham (Duke University—formerly Trinity College), and Chapel Hill (University of North Carolina). Over his lifetime Page had significant connections to all three institutions, most significant being his role in establishing the North Carolina Agriculture and Mechanic Arts College, which is now North Carolina State University. Launched in 1959, the RTP's early growth was very slow, though with the three universities as its greatest asset supported by strong political, academic, and business leadership, as Page had advocated all those decades earlier, it eventually thrived. With a combination of multinational and small businesses mostly in high-technology industries, it is a world leader in technological development. The vast majority of employees have tertiary qualifications and work in research and development. The "brain drain" has ended, and North Carolina is no longer "a good State to be born in, but a poor State to live in."[11]

THE RACE-PROBLEM MYTH

The race-problem myth was the idea that African Americans living in the South, the freed slaves and their descendants, were a burden or danger to the rest of the population. Fanning the flames of existing racial prejudice, Southern politicians used the myth to disenfranchise African Americans. It replaced the antebellum myth and led to segregation, which meant the benefits of Southern development were lost to millions of people because of their race. Page believed this was a tragedy. People from both races would be disadvantaged because a divided South would suffer socially, industrially, economically, and educationally.

Of all the issues Page advocated for the South, racial equality was the most intractable. He appeared confused by the myth's potency. Perhaps he thought that just as it was obvious that the lifestyle of the antebellum period was not something to which Southerners should aspire, it was obvious that if everyone was treated equally regardless of race, they could all benefit from the advances in Southern prosperity. He eventually conceded that it would take one or more generations before African Americans would have equality, and he was correct.

Segregation became entrenched for many decades, resisting numerous attempts at the federal level to force its cessation. A decade after the 1954 *Brown v. Board of Education* Supreme Court decision declaring the unconstitutionality of segregation, less than 2 percent of Southern schools had complied. It was the same in the broader community. Even following the landmark 1964 Civil Rights and the 1965 Voting Rights acts, and further Supreme Court decisions in the late 1960s ordering desegregation, various forms of segregation and other types of discrimination continued throughout the South. It wasn't until the late 1970s and into the 1980s that desegregation was largely achieved. This vindicates Page's argument that by perpetuating the race-problem myth, Southern leaders entrenched a cultural change that would be extremely difficult to overcome.[12]

THE MYTH OF NEUTRALITY

The myth of neutrality was the idea that the United States could continue to base its foreign policy on the Monroe Doctrine, which declared noninvolvement in European affairs. Page's position on America taking on a world leadership role emanated from his desire for facts and his ability to understand their implications. He learned about America's enormous industrial power, as shown in the 1900 *World's Work* article by Frederic Emory, and knew that it meant the Monroe Doctrine was redundant.

Following President Franklin D. Roosevelt's actions during World War II that defeated the myth, America took on the military, diplomatic, and economic world leadership role no other nation could. It established an international system completely contrary to the colonial empires of the past based on openness, negotiations, alliances, and institutions. America used its military, economic, and industrial power to preserve and spread democracy and freedom. For four years from 1948, U.S. Congress, under the Marshall Plan, approved $13.3 billion to underwrite the rebuilding of Europe. Of the alliances established, the most important were the North Atlantic Treaty Organization to ensure peace in Europe, countering the Union of Soviet Socialist Republics (USSR) and its Warsaw Pact, and the U.S.-Japan alliance. America founded and became a member of the United Nations as a successor to Wilson's League of Nations, took in over 30 million immigrants before the end of the century, and with Britain initiated and developed the trade and financial institutions that underwrote unprecedented changes in the international economy.[13]

American world leadership laid the platform for the subsequent international spread of democracy, freedom, liberty, wealth, and peace. The Monroe Doctrine was replaced by the Truman Doctrine, articulated by Roosevelt's successor President Harry S. Truman in 1947: the United States would give democratic nations under threat from authoritarian forces political, military, and economic assistance. As Page advocated, America developed strong and enduring military alliances with Britain and its democratic former colonies to protect and promote freedom and democracy. Some of these alliances have been formalized. Out of World War II came the Five Eyes intelligence alliance with the United Kingdom, Canada, Australia, and New Zealand. Security arrangements include the 1951 ANZUS treaty with Australia and New Zealand, and the AUKUS pact formed in 2021 with Australia and the United Kingdom. President Barak Obama's letter to his successor in 2017 reiterated the importance of American leadership as the foundation of world peace and prosperity: "American leadership in this world really is indispensable. It's up to us, through action and example, to sustain the international order that's expanded steadily since the end of the Cold War, and upon which our own wealth and safety depend." These and many other examples of international leadership following World War II are the outcomes Walter Hines Page encouraged his nation's leaders to embrace over a century earlier.[14]

PAGE'S CHARACTER REMEMBERED

For most of his adult life Page was in close contact with past, current, and future American presidents. They asked him for advice, he offered unsolicited advice, and they wrote for his magazines and were extensively covered in his editorials. Given Page's low profile in presidential biographies and other historical works, most president's opinions of Page are unrecorded. Among the exceptions are Theodore Roosevelt and Herbert Hoover.

Following Page's death, Roosevelt, who had been Wilson's most persistent public critic for not entering the war earlier, wrote to Alice expressing his great admiration and respect for the former ambassador: "I have just come out of the hospital and am distressed to learn of the death of your husband. I could not overstate the admiration I feel for all that he has been and done during the term of his service at the Court of St. James's. I do not believe we have ever had in the diplomatic service a man who more typified what was best in American life, and who stood up more fearlessly for the right." Poignantly, Roosevelt died in his sleep just five days later.[15]

Hoover, in his memoirs published in 1951, attested to the greatness of Page's character in light of his extensive support for the Commission for Relief in Belgium: "He was one of those blossoms of American life which justify our civilization. When I put down that he was a great mind, a distinguished scholar, a great editor, the soul of intellectual honesty, a man of sympathy and kindness, unbreakable in friendship, almost fanatically devoted to the service of his country, I feel that I am writing the presentation paragraph for an honorary college degree. Yet this praise can be written of him with more fidelity than of any other American that I have ever known."[16]

While Page was respected by some who served in his nation's highest office, it was among the people that he gained the greatest respect. He was in high demand as a public speaker, and his publications were among the most widely circulated and influential in the nation. On two occasions he turned around failing national magazines, then started his own with great success. Page's special talent was to understand his readers and audiences, bringing them along with him in his writing and speaking. He remained positive, even in situations he knew were lost causes. He balanced empathy with leading, understanding his audience while trying to convince them when appropriate. Isaac Marcosson, who worked for him at the *World's Work* for three years, wrote about Page's concern for others: "Democracy was the supreme interest of his life, a kindling desire to uplift the plain man his ruling passion. Nor was it the usual emotional altruism for revenue or personal advancement. He incarnated sincerity and conviction."[17]

In remembering Page, fellow education campaigners including Mims, Dabney, Shaw and Buttrick looked back on the man they knew and reflected on his genuine interest in other people, what they did, their ideas, and if there was any way their lives could be improved.

In 1919 his friend Mims beautifully illustrated Page's contribution to developing the South and helping his fellow Southerners: "But neither his national nor international fame can obscure the thought in the minds of some that he was one of the great Southerners of his generation, and that no man had helped—positively helped—so many individuals, institutions, organizations, and movements that had as their primary aim the rebuilding of these old commonwealths." Mims was confident that "no one ever knew him who was not impressed with his cordiality, his enthusiasm, and his persistent and continuous interest in Southern development."[18]

Dabney, who knew Page very well, believed Page's dream was that "every man everywhere, of every race or land, rich or poor, black or white, was to have an opportunity to make the most of himself; and the great interest of his life was to give all men a chance to complete their lives." By referring to "man," Dabney was writing in the language of the time, but Page's ideal outcome would have been the same regardless of gender.[19]

In preparing his memorial address in 1924, Shaw, who remembered Page as "a man of physical and mental virility, cast by nature in a generous mold," asked Wallace Buttrick for his contribution. Buttrick, who campaigned more closely with Page than anyone and was a great friend and neighbor, gave a very perceptive and comprehensive summation of Page's character: "Page's interest was primarily in man as man . . . Page believed in democracy. His interest in education in all its phases centered about this great fact that he believed in man as man. From the beginning his influence in the work of the Southern Education Board, of the General Education Board, and of the International Health Board was of the highest character. We lunched together about once a week for years, and his conversation was always about what more we could do for the happiness and well-being of our fellow-men. Somehow or other, his whole great soul was wrapped up in this high purpose of promoting the well-being of mankind."[20]

Page combined the practical, action-oriented, fair-play character of his father with the thoughtful, scholarly, caring character of his mother. His actions were driven by his conviction that everyone should have the opportunity to reach their potential regardless of race, gender, or where they lived. While he had an ego like everyone else and appreciated praise, he was largely uninterested in his own advancement or status. Consequently, he tended to see past his own prejudices and beliefs to have a clear vision of what changes or decisions were needed to benefit people and their communities. He dedicated his life to this passion. The enormous respect with which he was held by his contemporaries, the widespread audiences he garnered for his ideas, his remarkable foresight, his strength in standing up to the people who perpetuated myths for their own ends, and most importantly the significant changes he facilitated for the forgotten men and women are all testament to the unforgettable life of Walter Hines Page.

The day I visited the little cemetery an ancient, rattle-trap Ford came banging into the church-yard . . . It contained a tall, lanky man, and seven children. He was a MacNeill from the next county—and was looking for Walter Hines Page's grave.

"It's been on my mind for a right smart time to bring my grandchildren here to see this grave. We're goin' to Southern Pines, so we just turned off here. They've seen Aycock's statue at the Capitol," he added proudly.

"I tell 'em them two men's the reason they done got a chance for a schoolin'—which their grandpap didn't have."

He removed his hat gravely and stood, paying tribute in his own way—as gracious and sincere a tribute as has ever been paid to the memory of a man.

CHARLOTTE HILTON GREEN, NOVEMBER 24, 1929[21]

NOTES

INTRODUCTION

1. Page, "Confederate Candidates," *State Chronicle*, December 1, 1883, p. 4.

2. Cooper, *Walter Hines Page*, pp. 206–7, 210–11.

3. Gregory, *Walter Hines Page*, p. 8.

4. Cooper, *Walter Hines Page*, pp. 144–49, 266–67; H. C. Bailey, *Liberalism in the New South*, pp. 106, 112–13; Goodman, *Republic of Words*, pp. 186–90, 194–95.

5. Baker and Dodd, *New Democracy*, vol. 1, p. xxi; A. S. Link, *Woodrow Wilson and the Progressive Era 1910–1917* (New York: Harper & Brothers, 1954), p. 199; Cooper, *Walter Hines Page*, p. xxviii; Heckscher, *Woodrow Wilson*, p. 374; Gregory, *Walter Hines Page*, pp. 109, 162; Jacobs, *Rogue Diplomats*, pp. 198–99.

CHAPTER 1. INFLUENCES AND EDUCATION

1. Hendrick, *Earlier Life and Letters*, pp. 13–15; Cooper, *Walter Hines Page*, p. 4.

2. "In Memoriam—Mrs. Esther Barclay Raboteau," *News and Observer*, April 6, 1901, p. 7; Hendrick, *Earlier Life and Letters*, pp. 11–13; F. L. Olmsted, quoted in Hendrick, p. 12; Cooper, *Walter Hines Page*, p. 7; C. E Beveridge, "Frederick Law Olmsted," Olmsted Network, https://olmsted.org/frederick-law-olmsted/life/, accessed March 24, 2024.

3. Hendrick, *Earlier Life and Letters*, pp. 12–13; Cooper, *Walter Hines Page*, p. 7; Hendrick, *Life and Letters*, vol. 1, pp. 7–8.

4. Daniels, *Tar Heel Editor*, p. 438.

5. "Married," *North Carolina Standard*, July 11, 1849, p. 3; Holland, "Page, Allison Francis (Frank)"; Hendrick, *Earlier Life and Letters*, p. 13; A. Kairis, "150 Years: Tales of Cary's Railroad Stop," *CaryCitizen.News*, April 8, 2021, https://carycitizen.news/2021/04/08/150-years-tales-of-the-railroad-stop/.

6. Hendrick, *Earlier Life and Letters*, pp. 14–15; Cooper, *Walter Hines Page*, pp. 6–7; Hendrick, *Life and Letters*, vol. 1, pp. 8–9; Page, letter to Kate, December 1876, quoted in Cooper, p. 6; Page, letter to Kate, 1893, quoted in Hendrick, *Life and Letters*, vol. 1, p. 9.

7. "Death of Mrs. A.F. Page," *News and Observer*, August 22, 1897, p. 5; "Sudden Death of Mrs. A.F. Page," *Semi-weekly Messenger*, August 24, 1897, p. 8; Cooper, *Walter Hines Page*, p. 152; Page, letter to H. E. Scudder, September 13, 1897, cited and quoted in Hendrick, *Earlier Life and Letters*, pp. 281–82.

8. Hendrick, *Earlier Life and Letters*, pp. 7, 30–31; Hendrick, *Life and Letters*, vol. 1, p. 4; advertisement, *North Carolina Standard*, January 30, 1839, p. 3; Arendell, "Busy Aberdeen"; Holland, "Page, Allison Francis (Frank)."

9. Hendrick, *Earlier Life and Letters*, p. 7; advertisements, *North Carolina Standard*, January 30 and July 3, 1839, p. 3; *North Carolina Standard*, January 9, 1850, p. 3; *Semi-weekly North Carolina Standard*, June 19, 1852, p. 3; *Semi-weekly Standard*, May 1, 1858, p. 3.

10. "Agricultural Society in Wake County," *Semi-weekly North Carolina Standard*, February 25, 1852, p. 3; "Report of Committee on Working of Reapers," *Weekly North Carolina Standard*, June 23, 1869, p. 5.

263

264 \ NOTES TO CHAPTER ONE

11. *Spirit of the Age*, Raleigh, North Carolina, October 12, 1853, p. 2 and July 12, 1854, p. 3.

12. Hendrick, *Earlier Life and Letters*, pp. 35–37; Page, quoted in Hendrick, p. 35; Page, "Obituary—Dr. John W. Page," *State Chronicle*, January 5, 1884, p. 1.

13. Hendrick, *Earlier Life and Letters*, pp. 28–30, 33–35, 37–41; Page, quoted in Hendrick, p. 35; Cooper, *Walter Hines Page*, p. 8; Page, letter to S. Jasper, quoted in Hendrick, pp. 40–41.

14. Hendrick, *Earlier Life and Letters*, p. 40; Page, "Death of Mr. Anderson Page," *State Chronicle*, October 11, 1884, p. 2; *Charlotte Democrat*, June 18, 1880, p. 3; "Agricultural Society in Wake County," *Semi-weekly North Carolina Standard*, February 25, 1852, p. 3; "Report of Committee on Working of Reapers," *Weekly North Carolina Standard*; *North Carolina Standard*, February 19, 1851, February 18, 1857, February 22, 1860 (all p. 3); *Observer*, reprinted in *Charlotte Home and Democrat*, September 5, 1884, p. 2; Page, quoted in Hendrick, p. 41.

15. Hendrick, *Earlier Life and Letters*, pp. 7–8; Page, quoted in Hendrick, p. 8; "Mr. A.F. Page Dead," *News and Observer*, October 17, 1899, sec. 1, p. 9.

16. Hendrick, *Earlier Life and Letters*, pp. 7, 10–11; Hendrick, *Life and Letters*, vol. 1, p. 4; Cooper, *Walter Hines Page*, pp. 5, 9; "Mr. A.F. Page Dead," *News and Observer*.

17. Hendrick, *Earlier Life and Letters*, pp. 9–10, 17; Cooper, *Walter Hines Page*, pp. 4–6, 11, 14.

18. Page, letter to House, November 24, 1916, quoted in Hendrick, *Life and Letters*, vol. 1, p. 6; Hendrick, *Earlier Life and Letters*, pp. 9–10, 16–17; Cooper, *Walter Hines Page*, pp. 5, 12–13; Hendrick, *Life and Letters*, vol. 1, p. 7.

19. Hendrick, *Life and Letters*, vol. 1, pp. 13–14; Cooper, *Walter Hines Page*, pp. 4, 9–10; Hendrick, *Earlier Life and Letters*, pp. 26–27. Cary is today a suburb of Raleigh.

20. "Mr. A.F. Page Dead," *News and Observer*; Hendrick, *Earlier Life and Letters*, p. 281; Arendell, "Busy Aberdeen."

21. Arendell, "Busy Aberdeen;" Daniels, *Tar Heel Editor*, pp. 437, 440.

22. Arendell, "Busy Aberdeen."

23. J. Daniels, "State Normal College Commencement and Mr. Walter H. Page's Address," *News and Observer*, May 20, 1897, p. 2; Daniels, *Tar Heel Editor*, pp. 440, 438. "Tar Heel" is the nickname of North Carolinians.

24. Augustus White Long, quoted in Cooper, *Walter Hines Page*, p. 9.

25. *News and Observer*, November 17, 1898, p. 8 and October 14, 1899, p. 5; *Semi-weekly Messenger*, November 22, 1898, p. 3 and October 17, 1899, p. 1; Page, letter to H. E. Scudder, November 4, 1899, quoted in Cooper, *Walter Hines Page*, p. 153; "Mr. A.F. Page Dead," *News and Observer*.

26. Hendrick, *Earlier Life and Letters*, pp. 20–21.

27. Hendrick, *Life and Letters*, vol. 1, p. 16; Cooper, *Walter Hines Page*, pp. 7–8, 15; Hendrick, *Earlier Life and Letters*, p. 23.

28. Hendrick, *Earlier Life and Letters*, pp. 23–24; Cooper, *Walter Hines Page*, p. 10; An Old Boy, "Bingham School—An Old Boy's Recollection of the School 15 Years Ago," *State Chronicle*, December 8, 1883, p. 1.

29. Cooper, *Walter Hines Page*, pp. 10–11; Page, "Address at the Inauguration."

30. Page, quoted in Hendrick, *Earlier Life and Letters*, p. 25.

NOTES TO CHAPTER ONE / 265

31. Hendrick, *Earlier Life and Letters*, pp. 27–28.

32. Hendrick, *Earlier Life and Letters*, pp. 42–44, 48–49; Cooper, *Walter Hines Page*, pp. 15–16. Trinity was the only Methodist higher education institution in North Carolina.

33. Dabney, *Universal Education in the South*, vol. 2, pp. 234–35.

34. Hendrick, *Earlier Life and Letters*, pp. 49–50; Hendrick, *Life and Letters*, vol. 1, pp. 20–21; Page, letter to Kate, quoted in Hendrick, *Life and Letters*, vol. 1, p. 20; Cooper, *Walter Hines Page*, pp. 16–18.

35. Campbell, "In Search of the New South," pp. 377–78; Hendrick, *Earlier Life and Letters*, pp. 56–59; J. H. Chamberlayne, quoted in Hendrick, p. 58.

36. Page, quoted in Hendrick, *Earlier Life and Letters*, p. 59.

37. Page, letter to Kate, April 12, 1874, quoted in Cooper, *Walter Hines Page*, p. 22; Cooper, pp. 23–24; Page, personal note, quoted in Cooper, p. 24.

38. Hendrick, *Life and Letters*, vol. 1, pp. 21–23; Hendrick, *Earlier Life and Letters*, pp. 63, 67; Cooper, *Walter Hines Page*, pp. 18, 21, 27; "Washington and Franklin Literary Societies," *Nashville Union and American*, Nashville, Tennessee, June 4, 1873, p. 3; "History of The Franklin Debating Society," Randolph-Macon College, https://www.rmc .edu/departments/communication-studies/franklin-debating-society/history, accessed December 28, 2018; "Randolph-Macon College—Commencement Celebration," *Daily Dispatch*, Richmond, Virginia, June 15, 1876, p. 1; "Randolph-Macon College," *Daily Dispatch*, June 16, 1876, p. 2.

39. Cooper, *Walter Hines Page*, pp. 18–19, 29–30; T. R. Price, quoted in Cooper, p. 19; Hendrick, *Life and Letters*, vol. 1, pp. 22–23.

40. Cooper, *Walter Hines Page*, pp. 31–34; Page, letter to S. Jasper, November 30, 1876, quoted in Hendrick, *Earlier Life and Letters*, p. 77.

41. Page, quoted in Hendrick, *Life and Letters*, vol. 1, p. 26; Page, quoted in Hendrick, *Earlier Life and Letters*, p. 73; Page, letter to D. C. Gilman, November 21, 1900, quoted in Hendrick, *Earlier Life and Letters*, p. 68.

42. Hendrick, *Earlier Life and Letters*, pp. 90–91; W. W. Jacques, quoted in Hendrick, p. 94; Page, letter, quoted in Hendrick, pp. 93–94.

43. Page, letter to Kate, July 2, 1877, quoted in Hendrick, *Earlier Life and Letters*, pp. 98–99.

44. Cooper, *Walter Hines Page*, p. 38; Page, *Observer*, October 3, 1887, quoted in Cooper, p. 38.

45. Page, letter, quoted in Hendrick, *Earlier Life and Letters*, p. 104.

46. Cooper, *Walter Hines Page*, p. 39; "Walter H. Page's Address at Johns Hopkins University," *Western Sentinel*, June 21, 1894, p. 3; Dabney, *Universal Education in the South*, vol. 2, p. 236.

47. Cooper, *Walter Hines Page*, p. 40; Page, quoted in Cooper, p. 40.

48. Battle, *University of North Carolina*, p. 157; Hendrick, *Earlier Life and Letters*, pp. 118–20, 121, 123; Cooper, *Walter Hines Page*, pp. 39–43.

49. Hendrick, *Earlier Life and Letters*, pp. 124–25; Cooper, *Walter Hines Page*, pp. 43–45; Page, letter to Frank, April 20, 1879, quoted in Cooper, p. 45.

50. Battle, *University of North Carolina*, p. 187; Cooper, *Walter Hines Page*, pp. 44–45; Page, quoted in Cooper, pp. 45, 44.

51. Hendrick, *Life and Letters*, vol. 1, p. 33; Page, quoted in Hendrick, *Earlier Life and Letters*, p. 130; Hendrick, *Earlier Life and Letters*, pp. 130–31; Cooper, *Walter Hines Page*, pp. 49–53; Page, *St. Joseph Daily Gazette*, quoted in *Lexington Weekly Intelligencer*, Missouri, April 10, 1880, p. 3; Page, editorial, *St. Joseph Daily Gazette*, November 7, 1880, quoted in Cooper, p. 53.

52. "Widow of Walter H. Page Dies at Age of 84," *Evening Star*, February 8, 1942, p. A14; Cooper, *Walter Hines Page*, pp. 48, 52; Hendrick, *Earlier Life and Letters*, pp. 133–34.

53. Hendrick, *Earlier Life and Letters*, pp. 134, 160; Cooper, *Walter Hines Page*, pp. 52, 90, 189; *Kansas City Times*, Missouri, quoted in *Phoenix Herald*, Arizona, December 24, 1880, p. 2.

54. Page, "Study of an Old Southern Borough"; *New York Tribune*, April 19, 1881, p. 6; e.g., *Orleans County Monitor*, Barton, Vermont, April 25, 1881, p. 2.

55. Hendrick, *Earlier Life and Letters*, pp. 134–35; Cooper, *Walter Hines Page*, p. 56; Page, quoted in Hendrick, *Life and Letters*, vol. 1, p. 34.

56. Mott, *History of American Magazines*, vol. 3, pp. 47–49; Cooper, *Walter Hines Page*, pp. 56–57; Hendrick, *Earlier Life and Letters*, pp. 136, 141–42.

57. Page, letter from Martin, Tennessee, July 2, 1881, quoted in Hendrick, *Earlier Life and Letters*, pp. 136–37 (Hendrick reprinted a selection of letters on pages 136–54); Cooper, *Walter Hines Page*, pp. 57, 60; "The Author of 'Uncle Remus,'" *Evening Star*, October 15, 1881, p. 6.

58. Cooper, *Walter Hines Page*, pp. 58–61.

59. Cooper, *Walter Hines Page*, pp. 61–62; *Memphis Daily Appeal*, Memphis, Tennessee, August 22, 1882, p. 1; *Salt Lake Daily Herald*, Salt Lake City, Utah, October 1, 1882, p. 4.

60. Cooper, *Walter Hines Page*, pp. 62–63; Cooper, *Woodrow Wilson*, pp. 39–41; Berg, *Wilson*, pp. 85–87.

61. Page, "North Carolina, Past and Present," *Boston Post*, reprinted in *Commonwealth*, September 20, 1883, p. 1; Page, "New South as Seen by a Southerner"; Cooper, *Walter Hines Page*, p. 64.

62. Hendrick, *Earlier Life and Letters*, pp. 158–59; Cooper, *Walter Hines Page*, pp. 64–65; Page, *State Chronicle*, January 5, 1884, p. 4.

CHAPTER 2. AMERICA'S "BEST EDITOR"

1. Cooper, *Walter Hines Page*, p. 65; Hendrick, *Earlier Life and Letters*, p. 162; Daniels, *Tar Heel Editor*, p. 439.

2. "Raleigh," *State Chronicle*, January 12, 1884, p. 4, and also pp. 2–5, 8.

3. "$250,000 Spent in Building during the Past Year" and "Stray Notes," *State Chronicle*, January 12, 1884, p. 1.

4. "Raleigh" and "Population and Death Rate," *State Chronicle*, January 12, 1884, pp. 4, 1; quote from Page, editorial, *State Chronicle*, November 8, 1884, p. 2; Sumner, "'Let Us Have a Big Fair,'" p. 77.

5. City of Raleigh, "Moore Square," https://raleighnc.gov/places/moore-square, accessed July 16, 2021; "The Well Ventilated and Conveniently Arranged Stables, Board-

NOTES TO CHAPTER TWO / 267

ing and Exchange Stables of Mr. W.E.V. Jackson," *State Chronicle*, January 12, 1884, p. 8; "Len. H. Adams—What he Has Done and Proposes to Do," *State Chronicle*, January 12, 1884, p. 2.

6. Editorial, *Salt Lake Daily Herald*, Salt Lake City, Utah, September 9, 1883, p. 4; *Commonwealth*, September 13, 1883, p. 3; Daniels, *Tar Heel Editor*, p. 94.

7. Daniels, *Tar Heel Editor*, pp. 79, 81; editorial, *Western Sentinel*, April 26, 1883, p. 2; *Western Sentinel*, July 12, 1883, p. 2; Cooper, *Walter Hines Page*, p. 67.

8. Page, "No Side Issues," *State Chronicle*, September 15, 1883, p. 2; "The State Chronicle," *State Chronicle*, October 6, 1883, p. 3; Cooper, *Walter Hines Page*, p. 86.

9. Woodward, *Origins of the New South*, pp. 145–46; Page, "Journalism in Raleigh," *State Chronicle*, March 1, 1884, p. 2.

10. Page, "The State Chronicle," *State Chronicle*, October 6, 1883, p. 3.

11. Page, "A Personal Letter—To Every Reader of The Chronicle," editorial, *State Chronicle*, March 15, 1884, p. 2.

12. Page, "No Side Issues," *State Chronicle*, September 15, 1883, p. 2; Page, "Journalism in Raleigh," editorial, *State Chronicle*, March 1, 1884, p. 2; Page, "Advertising," *State Chronicle*, October 20, 1883, p. 2.

13. Cooper, *Walter Hines Page*, pp. 74–77; Hendrick, *Earlier Life and Letters*, p. 173; "To Broaden the University," *State Chronicle*, June 14, 1884, p. 1; Daniels, "The News and Observer's Course," editorial, *Daily State Chronicle*, January 20, 1891, p. 2; Page, *State Chronicle*, February, 1885, quoted in H. C. Bailey, *Liberalism in the New South*, p. 135; Page, letter to Frank, quoted in Hendrick, p. 197.

14. Daniels, *Tar Heel Editor*, pp. 247–49; Daniels, "Announcement," *State Chronicle*, October 9, 1885, p. 2; Daniels, "A Change of Management in The Chronicle," *State Chronicle*, March 20, 1892, p. 2.

15. Cooper, *Walter Hines Page*, pp. 86, 90; *Western Sentinel*, August 2, 1888, p. 2; *State Chronicle*, November 2, 1888, p. 5.

16. Cooper, *Walter Hines Page*, pp. 86, 88, 91; "Personal Mention," *Indianapolis Journal*, September 11, 1887, p. 5.

17. Daniels, *Tar Heel Editor*, p. 256; Daniels, editorial, *Daily State Chronicle*, January 20, 1891, p. 2.

18. Campbell, "In Search of the New South," pp. 383–84; Mims, "Walter Hines Page," pp. 98–100; *Charlotte Home and Democrat*, October 10, 1884, p. 3; "N.C. Press Association," *Western Sentinel*, June 4, 1885, p. 2.

19. Mott, *History of American Magazines*, vol. 3, pp. 5, 25–26, 45–47 and vol. 4, pp. 1–8, 35 (quote); H. Cox and S. Mowatt, *Revolutions from Grub Street: A History of Magazine Publishing in Britain* (Oxford: Oxford University Press, 2014), pp. 26–28; Sedgwick, *History of the "Atlantic Monthly,"* pp. 246–47; Cooper, *Walter Hines Page*, pp. 91–92.

20. Cooper, *Walter Hines Page*, pp. 91, 99; Mott, *History of American Magazines*, vol. 3, p. 41.

21. Page, letter to L. S. Metcalf, October 23, 1887, quoted in Cooper, *Walter Hines Page*, p. 91; *Western Sentinel*, November 24, 1887, p. 2.

22. *Daily State Chronicle*, September 6, 1890, p. 1; *News and Observer*, September 6,

1890, p. 4; *Watauga Democrat*, Boone, North Carolina, September 11, 1890, p. 3; Cooper, *Walter Hines Page*, p. 90; "A Distinguished Visitor," *Daily State Chronicle*, March 5, 1891, p. 4.

23. Cooper, *Walter Hines Page*, pp. 91, 93–96; *News and Observer*, March 18, 1891, p. 4; "A Distinguished Honor to Mr. Page," *State Chronicle*, March 17, 1891, p. 2; *State Chronicle*, October 16, 1891, p. 1; *State Chronicle*, January 27, 1892, p. 8.

24. *Savannah Morning News*, March 1, 1892, p. 1; "A Great Agency for Southern Development," *State Chronicle*, March 3, 1892, p. 2; Cooper, *Walter Hines Page*, pp. 105–6; Woodward, *Origins of the New South*, pp. 144–45; *Wheeling Register*, Wheeling, West Virginia, March 4, 1892, p. 4; *Western Sentinel*, March 10, 1892, p. 2.

25. Page, letter to Dreher, April 3, 1893, and *Herald*, October 8, 1893, both quoted in Cooper, *Walter Hines Page*, pp. 95–96; Mott, *History of American Magazines*, vol. 4, pp. 649–50.

26. Page, quoted in Hendrick, *Earlier Life and Letters*, pp. 204–5; *Indianapolis Journal*, July 14, 1895, p. 12; Page letter to G. W. Cable, July 22, 1892, quoted in H. C. Bailey, *Liberalism in the New South*, p. 109.

27. Mott, *History of American Magazines*, vol. 4, pp. 515–16; Cooper, *Walter Hines Page*, p. 92; H. C. Bailey, *Liberalism in the New South*, p. 109; H. Holt, quoted in Mott, p. 515.

28. Page and *Herald*, both quoted in *News-Observer-Chronicle*, Raleigh, North Carolina, October 11, 1893, p. 2 and "Walter H. Page and the Forum," *Gold Leaf*, October 12, 1893, p. 2; e.g., "Making a Magazine," *Waterbury Evening Democrat*, Connecticut, October 20, 1893, p. 3.

29. *Jersey City News*, New Jersey, December 20, 1893, p. 2; and *Western Sentinel*, November 30, 1893, p. 2.

30. Hendrick, *Earlier Life and Letters*, p. 227; Cooper, *Walter Hines Page*, pp. 99–100.

31. P. Fry, *Birmingham Age-Herald*, Alabama, November 4, 1894, p. 2; "Literary Notes," *Capital Journal*, Salem, Oregon, May 18, 1894, p. 4; "Effects of a Force Bill," *Western Sentinel*, August 4, 1892, p. 1; "Two North Carolina Boys," *State Chronicle*, October 13, 1892, p. 2, quoting *Atlanta Journal* article by Hoke Smith; Woodward, *Origins of the New South*, pp. 265, 271, 375–76.

32. "Mr. Kennan's Serious Charge," *Pacific Commercial Advertiser*, Honolulu, Hawaii, August 17, 1893, p. 6; "Railroad Failures," *Morning Call*, San Francisco, California, March 10, 1894, p. 6.

33. Wilson, letters to Page, December 3, 1894 and July 4, 1895, Page Papers.

34. "Personal," *News and Observer*, January 9, 1895, p. 3 and January 22, p. 8; Arendell, "Busy Aberdeen."

35. Cooper, *Walter Hines Page*, pp. 110–12; Mott, *History of American Magazines*, vol. 4, p. 516; *News and Observer*, August 22, 1895, p. 4.

36. Wilson, letter to Page, July 4, 1895, Page Papers; *Indianapolis Journal*, July 14, 1895, p. 12; *News and Observer*, July 5, 1895, p. 4; *Outlook*, July 13, 1895, p. 51; *Review of Reviews*, August 1895, quoted in *News and Observer*, August 20, 1895, p. 4.

37. Sedgwick, *History of the "Atlantic Monthly,"* pp. 245, 252; Goodman, *Republic of Words*, p. 194; Hendrick, *Earlier Life and Letters*, p. 234.

NOTES TO CHAPTER TWO / 269

38. Page, letter to H. E. Scudder, July 20, 1895, quoted in Sedgwick, *History of the "Atlantic Monthly,"* pp. 250–51.

39. Cooper, *Walter Hines Page*, pp. 112–13, 120–21; Goodman, *Republic of Words*, p. 194; Sedgwick, *History of the "Atlantic Monthly,"* p. 252.

40. Sedgwick, *History of the "Atlantic Monthly,"* pp. 252–60; Cooper, *Walter Hines Page*, p. 121; Page, letter to B. Sharp, quoted in Hendrick, *Earlier Life and Letters*, p. 233; Goodman, *Republic of Words*, pp. 186–88, 195–97, 200–203; B. Perry, quoted in M. A. de Wolfe Howe, *The "Atlantic Monthly" and Its Makers* (Boston: Atlantic Monthly Press, 1919), p. 91.

41. J. Bryce, "The Essential Unity of Britain and America," *Atlantic Monthly*, July 1898, pp. 22–29; *American*, Omaha, Nebraska, July 22, 1898, p. 4.

42. Sedgwick, *History of the "Atlantic Monthly,"* p. 257; Scudder, correspondence to Page, September 7, 1897, quoted in Sedgwick, p. 257.

43. Cooper, *Walter Hines Page*, p. 122; *Arizona Republican*, Phoenix, Arizona, August 15, 1898, p. 2; *Herald*, Los Angeles, California, August 21, 1898, p. 22; *Kansas City Sunday Journal*, Missouri, September 4, 1898, p. 4; Boston *Herald* reprinted in *News and Observer*, July 31, 1898, p. 4.

44. *Semi-weekly Messenger*, September 16, 1898, p. 2; *News and Observer*, December 24, 1898, p. 4.

45. *News and Observer*, June 21, 1899, p. 4; *Charlotte Observer*, quoted in *News and Observer*, June 23, 1899, p. 4.

46. Cooper, *Walter Hines Page*, p. 127; Goodman, *Republic of Words*, p. 204; e.g., *Custer County Republican*, Broken Bow, Nebraska, January 11, 1900, p. 7; *Kansas City Sunday Journal*, Missouri, September 4, 1898, p. 4.

47. Cooper, *Walter Hines Page*, pp. 151–52.

48. Cooper, *Walter Hines Page*, pp. 153–58; Sedgwick, *History of the "Atlantic Monthly,"* pp. 270–72.

49. *Semi-weekly Messenger*, August 18, 1899, p. 2; *Saturday Review*, New York, quoted in *Semi-weekly Messenger*, August 18, 1899, p. 4; *Boston Transcript*, quoted in *Indianapolis Journal*, August 20, 1899, pt. 1, p. 2.

50. G. H. Mifflin, letter to Page, November 1, 1901, quoted in Cooper, *Walter Hines Page*, p. 117; Perry, letter to Page, quoted in Hendrick, *Earlier Life and Letters*, p. 234; Sedgwick, quoted in Cooper, p. 117.

51. Cooper, *Walter Hines Page*, pp. 156–59; S. McClure, letter to Page, July 7, 1899, quoted in Cooper, p. 157.

52. Cooper, *Walter Hines Page*, pp. 159–60; *News and Observer*, April 29, 1900, sec. 1, p. 6; *Indianapolis Journal*, December 19, 1899, p. 5.

53. Cooper, *Walter Hines Page*, pp. 126, 133, 162–64; H. C. Bailey, *Liberalism in the New South*, pp. 110–11; Page, *Publisher's Confession*, p. 55; Goodman, *Republic of Words*, pp. 195–96; Richards, *Ellen Glasgow's Development*, pp. 25, 68; *Atlantic Monthly*, December 1897, p. 796.

54. Page, letter to Glasgow, December 8, 1897, quoted in Hendrick, *Earlier Life and Letters*, pp. 336–37; Glasgow, letter to Page, 1897, quoted in Richards, *Ellen Glasgow's Development*, p. 157.

270 | NOTES TO CHAPTER TWO

55. Glasgow, quoted in Goodman, *Republic of Words*, p. 196; Cooper, *Walter Hines Page*, p. 133; Richards, *Ellen Glasgow's Development*, pp. 44–46; Glasgow, quoted in Inge, "Ellen Anderson Gholson Glasgow."

56. Richards, *Ellen Glasgow's Development*, p. 66; Cooper, *Walter Hines Page*, p. 163; Glasgow, quoted in H. C. Bailey, *Liberalism in the New South*, p. 110; Glasgow, letter to Page, January 4, 1902, quoted in Cooper, p. 193.

57. H. C. Bailey, *Liberalism in the New South*, p. 110; Glasgow, quoted in Wagner, *Ellen Glasgow*, p. 14; "Ellen Glasgow," *Virginia Changemakers*, Library of Virginia, https://edu .lva.virginia.gov/changemakers/items/show/93, accessed February 23, 2023; Inge, "Ellen Anderson Gholson Glasgow."

58. Page, "MoE—A word on a birthday," *World's Work*, November 1902, p. 2695; Hendrick, Life and Letters, vol. 1, pp. 66–70; Rusnak, *Walter Hines Page*, p. vii; Kipling and Page, quoted in Rusnak, p. 28.

59. Page, "MoE," *World's Work*, November 1900, p. 3.

60. Cooper, *Walter Hines Page*, pp. 179–81; Mott, *History of American Magazines*, vol. 3, pp. 34–35; Page, letter to W. R. Thayer, December 5, 1900, quoted in Hendrick, *Life and Letters*, vol. 1, p. 69; *Indianapolis Journal*, October 29, 1900, p. 5.

61. Cooper, *Walter Hines Page*, p. 177; Marcosson, *Adventures in Interviewing*, p. 42; Page, "Waterways and Schools," editorial, *State Chronicle*, March 1, 1884, p. 2.

62. Mott, *History of American Magazines*, vol. 3, pp. 40, 333, 342–43.

63. Page, "An Intimate View of Publishing," *World's Work*, September 1902, p. 2562.

64. Page, quoted in Marcosson, *Adventures in Interviewing*, pp. 40, 41; B. R. Newton, November 1903, quoted in Mott, *History of American Magazines*, vol. 4, p. 13.

65. Page, letter to R. S. Baker, July 14, 1908, quoted in Cooper, *Walter Hines Page*, p. 183; H. C. Bailey, *Liberalism in the New South*, p. 109; Page, letter to E. Mims, Spring 1911, quoted in Mims, "Walter Hines Page," pp. 108–9; Page, letter to Mims, November 1, 1911, quoted in Cooper, p. 183.

66. Page, *Publisher's Confession*, pp. 47–50, 53–58, 69.

67. Mott, *History of American Magazines*, vol. 4, p. 53; H. C. Bailey, "Heralds of Reform," p. 135; Cooper, *Walter Hines Page*, p. 176; N. W. Ayer and Son, *American Newspaper Annual and Directory*, cited in Rusnak, *Walter Hines Page*, pp. 30, 37. In 1903 the *Directory* noted advertisers valued *World's Work* "more for the class and quality of its circulation than for the mere number of copies printed," quoted in Rusnak, p. 37.

68. Page, "What *The World's Work* Is Trying to Do," *World's Work*, January 1913, pp. 265–68; Page, "MoE—A word on a birthday," *World's Work*, November 1902, p. 2696; Marcosson, *Adventures in Interviewing*, p. 39.

69. Mott, *History of American Magazines*, vol. 4, pp. 207–9.

70. Cooper, *Walter Hines Page*, pp. 98, 184–85; H. C. Bailey, *Liberalism in the New South*, p. 111; Rusnak, *Walter Hines Page*, pp. 42–43. Descriptions of Rice's series and examples of the *State Chronicle's* studies are in chap. 5.

71. Page, "MoE," *World's Work*, May 1906, p. 7469; Cooper, *Walter Hines Page*, pp. 184–85; "Editorial Notes," *Outlook*, July 13, 1895, p. 51.

72. Page, "On a Tenth Birthday," *World's Work*, January 1911, p. 13915; Rusnak, *Walter*

Hines Page, p. 13; "Courtesy between Journalists," *New York Tribune*, September 20, 1889, p. 1.

73. Rusnak, *Walter Hines Page*, pp. 43, 52.

74. Page, "What *The World's Work* Is Trying to Do," *World's Work*, January 1913, p. 265.

75. Cooper, *Walter Hines Page*, pp. 188–89; *Teaneck New Jersey Forty Years of Progress*, Township of Teaneck, 1935, pp. 5–7; Page, diary, March 31, 1907, Page Papers. Arthur had been working at the *World's Work* since 1905 (Rusnak, *Walter Hines Page*, p. 31).

76. Page, diary, May 14, 1907, Page Papers.

77. Marcosson, *Adventures in Interviewing*, p. 40; *Charlotte Observer*, quoted in "Prominent Men at the Winston-Salem Educational Conference," *Progressive Farmer*, April 30, 1901, p. 7.

CHAPTER 3. "WAKE UP, OLD LAND!"

1. Hendrick, *Earlier Life and Letters*, pp. 29–30; Sydnor, *Development of Southern Sectionalism*, pp. 1, 23.

2. Sydnor, *Development of Southern Sectionalism*, pp. 3, 5, 25, 29, 249–54; C. N. Degler, "American Negro Slavery," in Owens, *Perspectives and Irony*, pp. 4–7; S. L. Engerman, "Southern Slave Economy," in Owens, pp. 71–73. The slave trade from Africa had ended on January 1, 1808.

3. Sydnor, *Development of Southern Sectionalism*, p. 332; Page, "New South as Seen by a Southerner."

4. Sydnor, *Development of Southern Sectionalism*, pp. xi, 331–32.

5. Sydnor, *Development of Southern Sectionalism*, pp. 5–14, 335–36; W. S. Churchill, *A History of the English-Speaking Peoples: The Great Democracies*, vol. 4 (London: Cassell, 1958), p. 120.

6. Sydnor, *Development of Southern Sectionalism*, p. 336.

7. G. McDuffie, quoted in Sydnor, *Development of Southern Sectionalism*, p. 336; W. P. Miles, quoted in Sydnor, p. 337.

8. I. L. Brookes, quoted in Sydnor, *Development of Southern Sectionalism*, p. 338; J. H. Hammond, speech in U.S. Senate, *Congressional Globe*, March 4, 1858, p. 962; Syndor, p. 339.

9. Craven, *Coming of the Civil War*, pp. 280–81; E. Ingle, *Southern Sidelights: A Picture of Social and Economic Life in the South a Generation before the War* (New York: Thomas Y. Crowell and Company, 1896), pp. 85–86; Gregg, *Essays on Domestic Industry*, p. iii; R. S. Cotterill, *The Old South* (Glendale, Cal.: Arthur H. Clark Company, 1936), p. 197.

10. Gregg, *Essays on Domestic Industry*, pp. 7–8, 12–16, 21–22, 24–25.

11. J. F. Kvach, *"De Bow's Review": The Antebellum Vision of a New South* (Lexington: University Press of Kentucky, 2013), pp. 40–41; Memphis Commercial Convention's committee on manufacturing, quoted in Kvach, p. 40; Craven, *Coming of the Civil War*, pp. 272–80, 281–83.

12. Craven, *Coming of the Civil War*, pp. 281–83, 292; *De Bow's Review*, quoted in Craven, pp. 282–83.

272 \ NOTES TO CHAPTER THREE

13. *De Bow's Review*, January 1856, quoted in Craven, *Coming of the Civil War*, p. 286.

14. Craven, *Coming of the Civil War*, p. 288.

15. Craven, *Coming of the Civil War*, pp. 280–81; H. C. Nixon, "De Bow's Review," *Sewanee Review*, January–March 1931, p. 61.

16. Foner, "Reconstruction"; Thirty-Ninth Congress, "An Act to Protect All Persons in the United States in Their Civil Rights, and Furnish the Means of Their Vindication," April 9, 1866, Library of Congress, https://www.loc.gov/law/help/statutes-at-large/39th-congress/session-1/c39s1ch31.pdf, accessed July 30, 2020.

17. Foner, "Reconstruction."

18. Foner, "Reconstruction"; Woodward, *Origins of the New South*, pp. 3–11, 22.

19. Congress of the United States, Fifteenth Amendment to U.S. Constitution, March 30, 1870, Library of Congress, https://memory.loc.gov/cgi-bin/ampage?collId=llsl&fileName=016/llsl016.db&recNum=1166, accessed July 30, 2020; Woodward, *Origins of the New South*, pp. 23–44.

20. J. S. Mill, "Negro Suffrage—Letter from John Stuart Mill," *Chicago Tribune*, Chicago, Illinois, September 22, 1865, p. 2; G. McWhiney, "Reconstruction: Index of Americanism," in Sellers, *Southerner as American*, p. 97.

21. Woodward, *Origins of the New South*, p. 17; H. Savage, *Seeds of Time* (New York: Holt, 1959), quoted in Campbell, "In Search of the New South," p. 361; Campbell, p. 361; W. W. Braden, "Myths in a Rhetorical Context," *Southern Speech Communication Journal* 40, no. 2 (Winter 1975): 118.

22. Woodward, *Origins of the New South*, pp. 6, 145–48.

23. Woodward, *Origins of the New South*, pp. 11–22; H. C. Bailey, *Liberalism in the New South*, pp. 27–28, 53.

24. H. C. Bailey, *Liberalism in the New South*, pp. 12–13; Dabney, *Universal Education in the South*, vol. 2, p. 236; Marcosson, *Adventures in Interviewing*, pp. 43–44.

25. Campbell, "In Search of the New South," p. 362; J. H. Franklin, "As for Our History . . .," in Sellers, *Southerner as American*, pp. 8–11; J. S. Bassett, quoted in Franklin, p. 10; Connor, "Walter Hines Page," p. 167.

26. Page, "Confederate Candidates," *State Chronicle*, December 1, 1883, p. 4; Page, "Rebuilding of Old Commonwealths," p. 121.

27. Page, "To Our Northern Visitors," *State Chronicle*, November 17, 1883, p. 2; Page, "Penny by Penny," *State Chronicle*, December 1, 1883, p. 2.

28. Page, "The Farmers' Convention," *State Chronicle*, September 22, 1883, p. 2.

29. Page, "The State's Progress—The Boom that Exists in Almost Every Town in the State," *State Chronicle*, November 3, 1883, p. 3; "CATAWBA!—If This Isn't Progress Where Can You Find It?," *State Chronicle*, October 6, 1883, p. 3.

30. Page, "A Pleasant Suburb—Cary as a Desirable Place of Residence," *State Chronicle*, November 3, 1883, p. 1; Page, "Who We Are," editorial, *State Chronicle*, May 3, 1884, p. 2.

31. "North Carolina, Past and Present," *Boston Post*, reprinted in *Commonwealth*, September 20, 1883, p. 1; Sumner, "'Let Us Have a Big Fair," pp. 58–59; Page, "The Two Expositions," *State Chronicle*, September 15, 1883, p. 2; Page, "Special Raleigh Issue," *State Chronicle*, January 5, 1884, p. 2.

NOTES TO CHAPTERS THREE AND FOUR / 273

32. "Tobacco Production," "The Manufacture of It," and "What a Wonderful Story!," editorials, *State Chronicle*, May 31, 1884, pp. 3, 8; Woodward, *Origins of the New South*, p. 129.

33. *State Chronicle*, September 13, 1884, p. 1.

34. *State Chronicle*, September 15, 1883, p. 2, October 6, 1883, p. 1, October 13, 1883, p. 2; "We Have It—A Grand State Exposition to Be Held Here Next Year," November 10, 1883, p. 1; Sumner, "'Let Us Have a Big Fair,'" pp. 60, 70; "The State Exposition—Vance County," *Gold Leaf*, March 6, 1884, p. 3; "Forsyth County," *State Chronicle*, October 11, 1884, p. 1.

35. Sumner, "'Let Us Have a Big Fair,'" pp. 70, 78–80; S. Ashe, editorial, *News and Observer*, November 1, 1884, quoted in Sumner, p. 79; Daniels, *Tar Heel Editor*, p. 84; "The Closing Day," *State Chronicle*, November 8, 1884, p. 1.

36. *Boston Post*, quoted in *Eaton Democrat*, Ohio, May 14, 1885, p. 1; Sellers, "Walter Hines Page," pp. 492–93; Page, letter to E. Mims, ca. 1907, quoted in Mims, "Walter Hines Page," p. 105; Cooper, *Walter Hines Page*, p. 206.

37. Mims, "Walter Hines Page," p. 107; Page, "The Arisen South," *World's Work*, June 1907, p. 8925; Page, "A Journey through the Southern States," *World's Work*, June 1907, pp. 9003–38.

38. Page, "MoE": "The Secession of Senator McLaurin" and "Is the Solid South to Yield at Last?," *World's Work*, June 1901, pp. 797–98; "Page on the Preachers," *News and Observer*, June 16, 1901, sec. 1, p. 9, and "What Has Kept the South Back," July 7, 1901, sec. 1, p. 4; *Semi-weekly Messenger*, July 12, 1901, p. 2; Page, "MoE—The Southern Republican Elimination of the Negro," *World's Work*, October 1902, p. 2591.

39. Page, "MoE—'Commercialism' to Divide the South," *World's Work*, July 1901, pp. 910–11; Cooper, *Walter Hines Page*, pp. 108–9.

40. Page, "New South as Seen by a Southerner."

41. Page, quoted by Daniels, *News and Observer*, April 21, 1901, sec. 1, p. 1.

42. Page, diary, April 4, 1907, Page Papers.

43. Page, diary, May 16, 1907, Page Papers.

44. Inge, "Ellen Anderson Gholson Glasgow"; Glasgow, quoted in Wagner, *Ellen Glasgow*, p. 16.

45. Page, *Southerner*, pp. 108, 110, 112, 339, 389–91. In Page's time states were often referred to as "Commonwealths."

CHAPTER 4. RACIAL EQUALITY

1. B. R. Tillman, "The Race Problem," speech in U.S. Senate, February 23, 1903, Library of Congress; Woodward, *Origins of the New South*, p. 339; T. Heflin, quoted in *Official Proceedings of the Constitutional Convention of the State of Alabama*, May–September 1901, vol. 4, pp. 4302–3, Alabama Department of Archives and History.

2. Page, editorial, *St. Joseph Daily Gazette*, October 30, 1880, quoted in Cooper, *Walter Hines Page*, p. 53; Page, *World's Work*, "MoE—Is the Solid South to Yield at Last?," June 1901, p. 797, "MoE—Deep Waters of the Race Problem," January 1903, p. 2935; "MoE—The Only Way to Allay Race-Friction," August 1903, pp. 3720–21.

274 \ NOTES TO CHAPTER FOUR

3. H. C. Bailey, *Liberalism in the New South*, pp. 53, 62–63; Woodward, *Origins of the New South*, pp. 330, 334–35, 355, 402; Daniels, *Tar Heel Editor*, p. 258.

4. Page, letters to A. Shaw, August 11, 1892, and January 11, 1893, quoted in Cooper, *Walter Hines Page*, p. 107; H. C. Bailey, *Liberalism in the New South*, p. 84.

5. Page, editorials, *State Chronicle*, "The 'Independent' Game Ended," August 9, 1884, p. 2 and "Our Brother in Black," September 22, 1883, p. 2.

6. "They Are Welcome," *State Chronicle*, September 13, 1884, p. 2; "A Terrible Warning," *State Chronicle*, October 25, 1884, p. 2; Sedgwick, *History of the "Atlantic Monthly,"* p. 259; B. T. Washington, "The Awakenings of the Negro," *Atlantic Monthly*, September 1896, pp. 322–28; W. E. B. Du Bois, "Strivings of the Negro People," *Atlantic Monthly*, August 1897, pp. 194–98; Cooper, *Walter Hines Page*, p. 206; Sellers, "Walter Hines Page," pp. 492–93.

7. W. E. B. Du Bois, "The Negro As He Really Is," *World's Work*, May 1901, pp. 848–66.

8. Daniels, *Tar Heel Editor*, p. 258; B. T. Washington, letter to O. G. Villard, March 4, 1911, cited in H. C. Bailey, *Liberalism in the New South*, p. 88; Page, "N.H. College and New England Folks!," diary, Page Papers, undated though with entries for June 1907; Cooper, *Walter Hines Page*, pp. 116–17, 145; Marcosson, *Adventures in Interviewing*, p. 44.

9. Page, "Address at the Inauguration"; "University of North Carolina—A Chair of Sociology to Be Established—Investigation of the Negro Problem," *Charlotte Democrat*, January 15, 1892, p. 2; G. B. Johnson and R. L. Simpson, "Sociology at UNC—Chapel Hill," Department of Sociology, University of North Carolina, 1976, https://sociology .unc.edu/simpson-and-johnson/; "About," Department of Sociology," University of Chicago, https://sociology.uchicago.edu/about, accessed January 13, 2024.

10. Page, "MoE—Lynchings and the Color Line," *World's Work*, August 1903, pp. 3719–20.

11. Page, "The Last Hold of the Southern Bully," *Forum*, November 1893, pp. 303–14.

12. "The Southern Bully," *Richmond Dispatch*, Richmond, Virginia, October 29, 1893, p. 4; B. Arp, "We Have No Bully," *Atlanta Constitution,* reprinted in numerous newspapers including *Newberry Herald and News*, South Carolina, November 22, 1893, p. 1; "The Last Hold of the Southern Bully," *Indianapolis Journal*, November 1, 1893, p. 2.

13. Page, "MoE—Lynchings and the Color Line, August 1903, pp. 3719–20; "MoE— Barbarism and Heroism in the South," October 1901, pp. 1250–51, "MoE—The One Remedy for Mobs," September 1903, pp. 3829–30, *World's Work.*

14. Woodward, *Origins of the New South*, pp. 321, 331–35, 337–38; Page, "MoE—How Negro Disfranchisement Has Worked," February 1901, pp. 361–62, "MoE—The Supreme Court and Negro Suffrage," June 1903, p. 3491, *World's Work.*

15. Woodward, *Origins of the New South*, pp. 329–30, 338–41, 348–49; Page, "MoE— The Grim Humor of the Alabama Election," *World's Work*, January 1902, p. 1585.

16. Woodward, *Origins of the New South*, p. 355; H. C. Bailey, *Liberalism in the New South*, pp. 114–15; Cooper, *Walter Hines Page*, pp. 146–48; Page, quoted in Bailey, p. 115. Kashinath T. Telang was a highly respected Indian High Court judge who, around the same time as Page, was a pioneer in the campaign for greater equality in highly segregated Indian society; see V. N. Naik, *Kashinath Trimbak Telang, the Man and His Times* (Madras, India: G. A. Natesan & Co., ca. 1895).

NOTES TO CHAPTER FOUR / 275

17. Page, "MoE—How Negro Disfranchisement Has Worked," February 1901, pp. 361–62, "MoE—A 'Problem' that Thrives on Talk," December 1901, p. 1478, *World's Work*.

18. Page, "MoE—The Southern Republican Elimination of the Negro," October 1902, p. 2591, "MoE—A New Chapter in Southern Politics," December 1902, p. 2820, *World's Work*.

19. Page, "MoE—Deep Waters of the Race Problem," *World's Work*, January 1903, p. 2935.

20. Page, "MoE": "Larger Forces than Race Politics" and "How Race Politics Narrows the Horizon," *World's Work*, March 1903, pp. 3157–58.

21. Page, "MoE—The Supreme Court and Negro Suffrage," *World's Work*, June 1903, pp. 3491–92; Woodward, *Origins of the New South*, p. 321; J. S. Mill, "Negro Suffrage—Letter from John Stuart Mill," *Chicago Tribune*, Illinois, September 22, 1865, p. 2.

22. Page, letters to Alice, February 6 and 10, 1907, quoted in H. C. Bailey, *Liberalism in the New South*, p. 119; Page, "MoE—The Decline of Race Friction," *World's Work*, April 1909, p. 11421.

23. W. E. B. Du Bois, "Georgia Negroes and Their Fifty Millions of Savings," May 1909, pp. 11550–54, B. T. Washington, "How Denmark Has Taught Itself Prosperity and Happiness: The Rural High Schools Which Have Made Over a Nation," June 1911, pp. 14486–94, *World's Work*. In 1910 Washington visited Denmark as part of a trip to Europe.

24. Warnock, "Andrew Sledd," pp. 251–66; A. Sledd, quoted in Warnock, p. 254; Page, "MoE—The Shrieking Ghost of a Dead Era," *World's Work*, October 1902, p. 2597.

25. A. Sledd, quoted in Warnock, "Andrew Sledd," p. 269.

26. Page, "MoE—A Field for a Living Sociology," *World's Work*, October 1902, p. 2592.

27. J. S. Bassett, "Stirring Up the Fires of Race Antipathy," *South Atlantic Quarterly*, October 1903, pp. 297–305; H. C. Bailey, *Liberalism in the New South*, p. 118; Page, letter to B. N. Duke, November 26, 1903, quoted in H. C. Bailey, p. 118; S. Cohn, "Publisher's Forward: The Bassett Affair and SAQ's Centenary Anniversary," *South Atlantic Quarterly*, 101 no. 2 (Spring 2002): 245–46; Page "A Notable Victory for Academic Freedom," *World's Work*, January 1904, pp. 4284–87; Mims, "Walter Hines Page," p. 104; Page, memo to W. Wilson, November 24, 1912, quoted in Bailey, p. 211. By this time Page had ended his friendship with Daniels, partly due to his racist populism (Cooper, *Walter Hines Page*, p. 215), and attacks on the Rockefeller Sanitary Commission (see chap. 5, and Ettling, *Germ of Laziness*, p. 131).

28. Page, quoted in Cooper, *Walter Hines Page*, p. 59; Page, "Rebuilding of Old Commonwealths"; Dabney, *Universal Education in the South*, vol. 2, pp. 45–46; Page, *Southerner*, p. 385.

29. Page, letter to Alice, 1899, quoted in H. C. Bailey, *Liberalism in the New South*, p. 116; Page, letter to Francis J. Garrison after visiting Tuskegee in 1899, quoted in Bailey, p. 116; "An Appeal for Tuskegee—Meeting Held on Behalf of the Alabama Institute," *New York Tribune*, December 5, 1899, p. 7; Cooper, *Walter Hines Page*, p. 163; Bailey, pp. 83–84.

30. Sellers, "Walter Hines Page," pp. 492–93; B. T. Washington, "The Salvation of the Negro," *World's Work*, July 1901, pp. 961–71; Washington, "Educational Work at Hampton," *New York Tribune*, February 12, 1900, p. 5.

276 \ NOTES TO CHAPTERS FOUR AND FIVE

31. Page, "MoE—The Failure of Political Methods in the South," *World's Work*, June 1903, p. 3492.

32. Page, quoted in Lowrie, "Some Notes and Anecdotes," p. 336.

33. Page, "How the South May Regain Leadership."

CHAPTER 5. THE FORGOTTEN MAN AND WOMAN

1. Cooper, *Walter Hines Page*, pp. 58–60; *Connecticut Western News*, Salisbury, Connecticut, October 5, 1881, p. 2; *Charlotte Democrat*, September 30, 1881, p. 2.

2. "The Four Corners," *State Chronicle*, September 29, 1883, p. 1; "A Mediaeval Heresy," *State Chronicle*, December 8, 1883, p. 1; *Orange County Observer*, Hillsborough, North Carolina, May 24, 1884, p. 2; "The Banner County—How the People of Lenoir Make Their Schools Prosperous," *State Chronicle*, June 7, 1884, p. 1; Page, "Farming in Fact—Not the Fancy Article but the Genuine," *State Chronicle*, October 13, 1883, p. 1; Page, editorial, *State Chronicle*, October 13, 1883, p. 2.

3. Jenkins and Peck, "Blair Education Bill," p. 6; *Farmer and Mechanic*, April 9, 1884, p. 2.

4. Page, "North Carolina Favors It—County Superintendents on National Aid to Education," *State Chronicle*, April 26, 1884, p. 1.

5. "Private School-Work—Some Definite Facts about Our Institutions," *State Chronicle*, July 26, 1884, p. 1; Page, editorial, *State Chronicle*, July 26, 1884, p. 2.

6. H. E. Shepherd, "Prof. H.E. Shepherd—Writes His Observations of Educational Work in N.C.," *State Chronicle*, October 25, 1884, p. 3.

7. "The Negro Educational Bill," *Banner Enterprise*, Wilmington, North Carolina, April 10, 1884, p. 2; Page, "Let Us Go Forward," editorial, *State Chronicle*, June 7, 1884, p. 2.

8. Page, "Feel Proud and Go," *State Chronicle*, June 14, 1884, p. 2; "Closing Days of the Chautauqua," *State Chronicle*, July 5, 1884, p. 1; Page, "The Teachers' Assembly," editorial, *State Chronicle*, July 5, 1884, p. 2.

9. "North Carolina Favors It—County Superintendents on National Aid to Education—Normal and Technical Schools," *State Chronicle*, April 26, 1884, p. 1; "Labor and Wages Again," *State Chronicle*, 3 May 1884, p. 1; Dabney, *Universal Education in the South*, vol. 1, pp. 182, 185; "Constitution of the Watauga Club," Watauga Club Records.

10. Peele, "History of the Agricultural and Mechanical College," p. 2; Page, "Teachers' Prizes," editorial, *State Chronicle*, June 21, 1884, p. 2; Dabney, *Universal Education in the South*, vol. 1, pp. 186, 532–33; Thompson, "Pine Burr Society."

11. Thompson, "Pine Burr Society"; Peele, "History of the Agricultural and Mechanical College," pp. 4–6; "Raleigh and Wake News," *State Chronicle*, October 30, 1885, p. 3; "Important Meeting in Raleigh—The Query Shall We Have an Industrial School," *State Chronicle*, November 6, 1885, p. 3; Dabney, *Universal Education in the South*, vol. 1, pp. 186–87; "The Industrial School—The Board Decides to Indefinitely Postpone," *State Chronicle*, January 28, 1886, p. 1.

12. Page, "Is There Intellectual Freedom in North Carolina?—Mr. Page Writes Earnestly and Vigorously in Favor of Extirpation of What He Calls Mummies," *State Chronicle*, February 4, 1886, p. 2.

NOTES TO CHAPTER FIVE / 277

13. Daniels, "Patriotism Run Mad" and "The Chronicle in a New Role," *State Chronicle*, February 11, 1886, p. 2; Page, "Is There Intellectual Freedom in N.C.?—A Second Letter—Mr. Page Explains More Fully His Views and Writes as He Feels—Give Him a Hearing and Honest Criticism," *State Chronicle*, February 11, 1886, p. 3; C. B. Aycock, letter to Page, February 26, 1886, quoted in Hendrick, *Earlier Life and Letters*, p. 192.

14. Peele, "History of the Agricultural and Mechanical College," pp. 6–8; Dabney, *Universal Education in the South*, vol. 1, pp. 187–88; "The Agricultural and Mechanical College," *Asheville Citizen*, Asheville, North Carolina, February 20, 1887, p. 1; Thompson, "Pine Burr Society"; "The Agricultural and Mechanical College," *Progressive Farmer*, March 9, 1887, p. 1; W. J. Peele, "The Agricultural College," *State Chronicle*, August 31, 1888, p. 2.

15. "The A. & M. College," *State Chronicle*, October 4, 1889, p. 2; *Western Sentinel*, October 20, 1887, p. 1; "Watauga Hall," *News and Observer*, March 20, 1896, p. 5; examples included "Pride of the State," *Gold Leaf*, October 18, 1900, p. 1 and "Graduating Day at A.& M. College," *Farmer and Mechanic*, June 5, 1906, p. 8; D. H. Hill, "How Great Matter a Little Fire Kindleth," *Farmer and Mechanic*, October 6, 1914, p. 14; North Carolina State University, "The Watauga Medal," 2024, https://leadership.ncsu.edu/watauga/ and https://news.giving.ncsu.edu/2023/09/three-2023-watauga-medal-recipients-honored/.

16. "Inauguration of G.T. Winston," *Durham Daily Globe*, North Carolina, October 12, 1891, p. 1; Page, "Address at the Inauguration"; Battle, *University of North Carolina*, pp. 465–66.

17. *State Chronicle*, October 15, 1891, p. 1.

18. Page, quoted in Battle, *University of North Carolina*, p. 466.

19. "Intellectual Inspiration," *Charlotte Democrat*, January 15, 1892, p. 3.

20. Page, letters to C. D. McIver, March 29–30 and April 18, 1897, quoted in S. Romine, "Introduction," in *Southerner*, by W. H. Page, p. xv; Dabney, *Universal Education in the South*, vol. 1, p. 203.

21. Knight, *Public Education in the South*, pp. 415–24; Cubberley, *Public Education*, pp. 443–44; Woodward, *Origins of the New South*, pp. 398–400; Dabney, *Universal Education in the South*, vol. 1, p. 200; *Newberry Herald and News*, South Carolina, June 15, 1892, p. 3 and November 22, 1893, p. 1.

22. Examples include *Robesonian*, Lumberton, North Carolina, April 14, 1897, p. 3 and *Progressive Farmer*, April 20, 1897, p. 3; "State Normal Commencement," *News and Observer*, May 15, 1897, p. 5; "The Woman's College," *News and Observer*, May 18, 1897, p. 1; "The Normal College," *News and Observer*, May 19, 1897, p. 1.

23. "State Normal College Commencement and Mr. Walter H. Page's Address," *News and Observer*, May 20, 1897, p. 2; Dabney, *Universal Education in the South*, vol. 2, p. 236.

24. Unless otherwise noted, references in this section are from Page, "Forgotten Man."

25. Page, "Study of an Old Southern Borough," p. 649.

26. "State Normal College Commencement and Mr. Walter H. Page's Address," *News and Observer*, May 20, 1897, p. 2; "Dr. McIver's Address," *Western Sentinel*, May 27, 1897, pp. 2–3; "State News," *Progressive Farmer*, June 1, 1897, p. 3.

27. *Semi-weekly Messenger*, June 15, 1897, p. 2; "His Providence Speech," *Charlotte Democrat*, 17 June 1897, p. 3; *Semi-weekly Messenger*, June 25, 1897, p. 4.

278 | NOTES TO CHAPTER FIVE

28. "Mr. Page as Editor," *Progressive Farmer*, September 14, 1897, p. 2; *News and Observer*, October 7, 1897, p. 5.

29. R. Taylor, quoted in Campbell, "In Search of the New South," p. 361.

30. Daniels, "State Normal College Commencement," *News and Observer*, May 20, 1897, p. 2; C. D. McIver, letter to Page, July 22, 1897, quoted in Cooper, *Walter Hines Page*, p. 144; Dabney, *Universal Education in the South*, vol. 2, p. 238; Connor, "Walter Hines Page," p. 168.

31. Dabney, *Universal Education in the South*, vol. 2, pp. 3–12, 38; G. S. Dickerman, cited in Knight, *Public Education in the South*, p. 431.

32. Dabney, *Universal Education in the South*, vol. 2, pp. 11–12, 32; Page, diary, May 21, 1907, Page Papers.

33. Dabney, *Universal Education in the South*, vol. 2, p. 32; Daniels, "Educational Conference," *News and Observer*, April 21, 1901, sec. 1, pp. 1–2; *Birmingham Age-Herald*, Alabama, April 13, 1901, p. 3.

34. Dabney, *Universal Education in the South*, vol. 2, pp. 32, 39, 41–43; "Conference on Education—Campaign for Free Schools Resolved Upon," *Richmond Dispatch*, Richmond, Virginia, April 21, 1901, p. 23; Committee on Platform and Resolutions, quoted in Dabney, *Universal Education in the South*, vol. 2, p. 42.

35. E.g., *Atlanta Journal*, April 24, 1901, (quoted in Dabney, *Universal Education in the South*, vol. 2, p. 46), "Southern Educational Tour," *Waterbury Democrat*, Connecticut, April 25, 1901, p. 1 and *Appeal*, St. Paul, Minnesota, April 27, 1901, p. 2; Dabney, p. 46.

36. Dabney, *Universal Education in the South*, vol. 2, pp. 97–98, 100; Dickerman, quoted in Knight, *Public Education in the South*, p. 431.

37. Dabney, *Universal Education in the South*, vol. 2, p. 242; Page, "How the South May Regain Leadership"; Mims, "Walter Hines Page," p. 115.

38. Kirkland, letter to Page, May 2, 1904, and Baldwin, letter to Page, May 14, 1904, both quoted in H. C. Bailey, *Liberalism in the New South*, p. 141; Dabney, *Universal Education in the South*, vol. 2, pp. 242, 279; Lowrie, "Some Notes and Anecdotes," p. 335; *Progressive Farmer*, May 17, 1904, p. 8.

39. Dabney, *Universal Education in the South*, vol. 2, pp. 42–43, 58–59; Sellers, "Walter Hines Page," p. 494; Page and Shaw, quoted in "Dr. Frazer Gives Board's Plans," *Times*, Richmond, Virginia, March 13, 1902, p. 9.

40. Page, "The School that Built a Town," speech at the State Normal School, Athens, Georgia, 1901, in *Rebuilding of Old Commonwealths*, pp. 51–103; "The State Normal School," *Savannah Morning News*, December 13, 1901, p. 2.

41. Dabney, *Universal Education in the South*, vol. 2, pp. 123–24, 153, 513; Sellers, "Walter Hines Page," p. 494; GEB, *Account of Its Activities*, pp. 3, 11–14; J. D. Rockefeller Jr., letter to W. H. Baldwin (GEB Chairman), March 1, 1902, quoted in GEB, p. 216; Jenkins and Peck, "Blair Education Bill," p. 4.

42. Dabney, *Universal Education in the South*, vol. 2, pp. 46–47, 447–51; Ogden, letter to Page, quoted in Dabney, vol. 2, p. 46; H. C. Bailey, *Liberalism in the New South*, pp. 150–51; Cooper, *Walter Hines Page*, pp. 212–13.

NOTES TO CHAPTER FIVE / 279

43. Page, letter to Buttrick, April 11, 1902, quoted in Hendrick, *Earlier Life and Letters*, pp. 407–8.

44. "The Gospel of Work," *Progressive Farmer*, June 9, 1903, p. 9; "North Carolina Farming vs. Iowa Farming," *Progressive Farmer*, June 16, 1903, p. 2.

45. Page, "North Carolina Farming vs. Iowa Farming," *Progressive Farmer*, June 16, 1903, pp. 2–3.

46. Ogden, letter to Page, quoted in Hendrick, *Earlier Life and Letters*, p. 413; Dabney, *Universal Education in the South*, vol. 2, p. 243; Buttrick, quoted in H. C. Bailey, *Liberalism in the New South*, p. 139; Connor, "Walter Hines Page," p. 168; A. Flexner, letter to Hendrick, quoted in Hendrick, *Life and Letters*, vol. 1, p. 85.

47. Mims, "Walter Hines Page," p. 100.

48. GEB, *Account of Its Activities*, pp. 18–23.

49. GEB, *Account of Its Activities*, pp. 23, 27–28; *Sea Coast Echo*, Bay St. Louis, Mississippi, October 5, 1895, p. 3.

50. Hendrick, *Life and Letters*, vol. 1, p. 96; Page, "Farming in Fact," *State Chronicle*, October 13, 1883, p. 1; Page, editorial, *State Chronicle*, October 13, 1883, p. 2; Page, "MoE—The Most Direct Way to Build Up a People," *World's Work*, May 1903, pp. 3386–87; GEB, *Account of Its Activities*, pp. 24–27; H. C. Bailey, *Liberalism in the New South*, p. 144; Dabney, *Universal Education in the South*, vol. 2, p. 283.

51. S. A. Knapp, "An Agricultural Revolution," July 1906, pp. 7733–38, Page, "MoE—Making Rural Life Profitable," May 1908, pp. 10178–80, *World's Work*; H. C. Bailey, *Liberalism in the New South*, p. 144; Dabney, *Universal Education in the South*, vol. 2, pp. 179, 189–90.

52. Dabney, *Universal Education in the South*, vol. 2, pp. 191–93, 197; J. S. Lambert, letter, April 5, 1935, quoted in Dabney, p. 191.

53. Page, quoted in Hendrick, *Life and Letters*, vol. 1, p. 97; Dabney, *Universal Education in the South*, vol. 2, p. 189; Mims, "Walter Hines Page," pp. 114–15; Page, diary, April 1–11, 1912, Page Papers; *Columbia Herald*, Tennessee, March 22, 1912, p. 2.

54. Ettling, *Germ of Laziness*, pp. 98–99; Hendrick, *Earlier Life and Letters*, pp. 369–71; Stiles, quoted in Hendrick, p. 370; Dabney, *Universal Education in the South*, vol. 2, pp. 251–52; Cubberley, *Public Education*, pp. 676–78.

55. Ettling, *Germ of Laziness*, pp. 18, 20–23, 25–28, 33–34; Cubberley, *Public Education*, pp. 676–77; Dabney, *Universal Education in the South*, vol. 2, pp. 248–51.

56. Bleakley, "Disease and Development," pp. 76–77; Cubberley, *Public Education*, pp. 676–77; Ettling, *Germ of Laziness*, pp. 3–4.

57. Stiles, quoted in Cubberley, *Public Education*, p. 677; Ettling, *Germ of Laziness*, pp. 35–38.

58. Ettling, *Germ of Laziness*, pp. 99–100; Stiles, letter to Hendrick, May 22, 1922, quoted in Dabney, *Universal Education in the South*, vol. 2, p. 252.

59. Page, letters to Alice, quoted in H. C. Bailey, *Liberalism in the New South*, p. 115; Bleakley, "Disease and Development," pp. 103–4.

60. Hendrick, *Earlier Life and Letters*, p. 371; Cooper, *Walter Hines Page*, p. 227; Page, "MoE—A New Era in Health," *World's Work*, January 1908, pp. 9735–36.

61. Ettling, *Germ of Laziness*, pp. 100–107; Dabney, *Universal Education in the South*, vol. 2, pp. 252–53; Cooper, *Walter Hines Page*, p. 227.

62. Cooper, *Walter Hines Page*, p. 227; John D. Rockefeller Sr., letter to commission board members, October 26, 1909, quoted in Ettling, *Germ of Laziness*, pp. 107–8; Dabney, *Universal Education in the South*, vol. 2, pp. 253–55; Page, memoranda, October 26, 1909, quoted in Hendrick, *Earlier Life and Letters*, pp. 372–73; commission bylaws, quoted in Ettling, p. 110.

63. Ettling, *Germ of Laziness*, pp. 117–24, 129–51; Dabney, *Universal Education in the South*, vol. 2, pp. 254–58; Cubberley, *Public Education*, pp. 679–80; "Seaman A. Knapp Day," *Putnam County Herald*, Cookeville, Tennessee, December 5, 1912, p. 5; Haden, "Hookworm Eradication"; Bleakley, "Disease and Development," pp. 81–82.

64. F. M. Bjorkman, "The Cure for Two Million Sick," May 1909, pp. 11607–12, Page, "The Hookworm and Civilization," September 1912, pp. 504–18, *World's Work*; Ettling, *Germ of Laziness*, p. 135.

65. Dabney, *Universal Education in the South*, vol. 2, p. 257; Bleakley, "Disease and Development," pp. 74, 79, 85–90.

66. Page, "The Hookworm and Civilization," *World's Work*, September 1912, p. 505.

67. Haden, "Hookworm Eradication"; Bleakley, "Disease and Development," pp. 80, 82, 85; C. W. Eliot, quoted in Cubberley, *Public Education*, p. 680.

CHAPTER 6. POLITICS AND SOCIETY

1. Page, "Forgotten Man," pp. 4–5; Page, speech to the Conference for Education in the South, Nashville, Tennessee, April 1912, quoted in Dabney, *Universal Education in the South*, vol. 2, pp. 298–99.

2. Page, "MoE—Immigration and the Purity of the American Race," *World's Work*, August 1903, pp. 3716–17.

3. I. M. Ashby, "Child-Labor in Southern Cotton Mills," October 1901, pp. 1290–95, Page, "MoE—The Worst Crime of Civilization," September 1902, pp. 2475–76, "MoE—A Dark Side of Christmas," December 1906, p. 8264, *World's Work*.

4. Page, editorial, *St. Joseph Daily Gazette*, quoted in *Nebraska Advertiser*, Nemaha City, Nebraska, June 17, 1880, p. 2.

5. Cooper, *Walter Hines Page*, p. 224; H. C. Bailey, *Liberalism in the New South*, pp. 191–92; Page, "MoE—The Position of Mr. Cleveland," *World's Work*, January 1904, pp. 4278–79.

6. Hendrick, *Earlier Life and Letters*, p. 340; Page, "MoE," *World's Work*, December 1901, pp. 1463–64.

7. Cooper, *Walter Hines Page*, pp. 223–24; H. C. Bailey, *Liberalism in the New South*, p. 194.

8. Cooper, *Walter Hines Page*, pp. 231–35; H. C. Bailey, *Liberalism in the New South*, pp. 194, 196–200; Page, letter to H. Wallace, September 7, 1910, quoted in Bailey, p. 200.

9. Bureau of the Census, "M 56–67—Foreign Trade—Value of Merchandise Exports and Imports, by Economic Classes: 1821 to 1945," *Historical Statistics*, pp. 246–47. Tariffs

NOTES TO CHAPTER SIX / 281

are taxes on imported goods with the aim of making them more expensive, to "protect" local industries from international competition.

10. Page, "The Two Expositions," *State Chronicle*, September 15, 1883, p. 2; G. R. Hawke, "The United States Tariff and Industrial Protection in the Late Nineteenth Century," *Economic History Review*, February 1975, pp. 98–99; Page, "Speaker Carlisle—How His Election Has Given Democracy a New Start," p. 1 and "Sectional, of Course," p. 2, *State Chronicle*, December 8, 1883.

11. G. Cleveland, "Third Annual Message (first term)," December 6, 1887, in The American Presidency Project, Gerhard Peters and John T. Woolley, http://www .presidency.ucsb.edu/ws/?pid=29528, accessed September 16, 2017; "Aims of the Reform Club," *New York Times*, December 16, 1887; H. C. Bailey, *Liberalism in the New South*, p. 192.

12. "The Tariff Reform, *Indianapolis Journal*, February 22, 1889, p. 4; "Tariff Convention," *Barton County Democrat*, Great Bend, Kansas, March 7, 1889, p. 2; e.g., "An Important Inquiry," *Indiana State Sentinel*, Indianapolis, Indiana, June 5, 1889, p. 7 and "Questions for Farmers," *Hood River Glacier*, Oregon, June 22, 1889, p. 2.

13. W. R. Allen, "Issues in Congressional Tariff Debates, 1890–1930," *Southern Economic Journal*, April 1954, p. 341; examples of *Forum* articles are, N. W. Aldrich, "The McKinley Act and the Cost of Living," October 1892, pp. 242–54, Page, "Mr. Cleveland's —— Failure?," April 1894, pp. 129–38 (published anonymously, though according to Cooper, *Walter Hines Page*, pp. 108–9, it was written by Page), L. Windmuller, "The Dilatory Senate and Depression in Trade," June 1894, pp. 326–28; F. W Taussig, "The Tariff Act of 1894." *Political Science Quarterly* 9, no. 4 (December 1894): 587–88.

14. "Commercial Supremacy of the United States," *World's Work*, November 1900, p. 116; Bureau of the Census, "M 56–67—Foreign Trade—Value of Merchandise Exports and Imports, by Economic Classes: 1821 to 1945," *Historical Statistics*, pp. 246–47.

15. Page, "MoE—Three Views of the Tariff," *World's Work*, January 1908, pp. 9727–29.

16. "A Spicy Correspondence," *Charlotte Home and Democrat*, November 2, 1883, p. 2; Page, "A Farce or Not?," *State Chronicle*, November 3, 1883, p. 2; Page, "A Dead Letter— The Civil Service Act in North Carolina Politics," *State Chronicle*, November 10, 1883, p. 1.

17. Page, "The Kind of Man He Is," editorial, *State Chronicle*, July 26, 1884, p. 2.

18. Page, "Civil Service Reform—An Incident Showing How New Yorkers Believe in It," *State Chronicle*, November 19, 1885, p. 2; Page, "Civil Service Reform—Reply to Those Who Oppose Reform," *State Chronicle*, December 3, 1885, p. 1.

19. C. F. Adams, "What Mr. Cleveland Stands For," July 1892, pp. 662–70; L. B. Swift, "Civil-Service Reform: A Review of Two Administrations," October 1892, pp. 201–15; J. T. Doyle, "Civil-Service Reform: A Decade of the Merit System," October 1892, pp. 216–25, *Forum*.

20. Page, "MoE—What the Deitrich Case Shows," *World's Work*, January 1904, p. 4279.

21. Mott, *History of American Magazines*, vol. 4, pp. 216–19; Bureau of Labor Statistics, "Carroll D. Wright," https://www.bls.gov/bls/history/commissioners/wright.htm, accessed March 26, 2024; Department of Labor, "Hall of Honor Inductee: Carroll D.

282 \ NOTES TO CHAPTER SIX

Wright," https://www.dol.gov/general/aboutdol/hallofhonor/2015-wright, accessed March 26, 2024.

22. U.S. National Archives and Records Administration, "Sherman Anti-Trust Act (1890)," https://www.ourdocuments.gov/doc.php?flash=false&doc=51, accessed July 22, 2021; A. F. Walker, "Unregulated Competition Self-Destructive," *Forum*, December 1891, pp. 505–18; S. C. Dodd, "Ten Years of the Standard Oil Trust," *Forum*, May 1892, pp. 300–10; Archives at Yale, "Roger Sherman Papers—Biographical," http://hdl.handle .net/10079/fa/mssa.ms.0448, accessed March 26, 2024; R. Sherman, "The Standard Oil Trust: The Gospel of Greed," *Forum*, July 1892, pp. 602–15.

23. W. Z. Ripley, "The Labor Union Conquest of the United States," November 1903, pp. 4092–98, Page, "MoE—How Strikes Strengthen Great Corporations," October 1901, p. 1246, *World's Work*.

24. M. G. Cunniff, "A Mill Town in Strike Time," *World's Work*, October 1901, pp. 1326–31.

25. Page, "MoE—The Inherent Weakness of Labor Unions," *World's Work*, October 1901, pp. 1246–47.

26. Page, "MoE—The Moral and Political Effect of Restraints on Corporations," June 1903, p. 3488, "MoE—Corporation Publicity or a More Radical Measure," January 1904, p. 4278, *World's Work*.

27. Page, "MoE—Need to Amend the Sherman Law," January 1909, p. 11079, "MoE—The Doom of the Monopolizing Trust," July 1911, pp. 14547–49, *World's Work*.

28. Page, "MoE—A Strike in a Labor Utopia," July 1901, pp. 914–15, "MoE—The Steel Workers' and the Machinists' Strikes," September 1901, p. 1121, "MoE—The Ill-Advised Steel Strike," October 1901, pp. 1245–46, "MoE," January 1904, p. 4272, *World's Work*.

29. Page, "MoE—Decided Progress in Checking Strikes," May 1902, pp. 2038–39, "MoE—Strikes That Point to Hard Times," July 1903, pp. 3605–6, *World's Work*.

30. Page, "MoE—Contrasting Types of Labor Leaders," *World's Work*, September 1903, pp. 3835–36.

31. Page, "Writers in the June Forum," p. 520, J. M. Rice, "Need School Be a Blight to Child Life?," December 1891, pp. 529–35, Rice, "Evils in Baltimore," pp. 145–46, 148, Rice, "The Public-School System of New York City," January 1893, pp. 616, 621, *Forum*; *Herald*, quoted in Mott, *History of American Magazines*, vol. 4, p. 517.

32. Sedgwick, *History of the Atlantic Monthly*, p. 254; G. S. Hall, "The Case of the Public Schools—Part 1—The Witness of the Teacher," March 1896, pp. 402–13; Anonymous, "Confessions of Public School Teachers," July 1896, pp. 97–110, *Atlantic Monthly*; Advertisement in *Atlantic Monthly*, June 1896.

33. Page, "Study of an Old Southern Borough," pp. 654–55.

34. Page, "Extending Women's Work," editorial, *State Chronicle*, February 2, 1884, p. 2.

35. Page, "Real Usefulness," editorial, *State Chronicle*, October 11, 1884, p. 2.

36. *Charlotte Home-Democrat*, April 4, 1884, p. 1.

37. M. G. Van Rensselaer, "The Waste of Women's Intellectual Force," *Forum*, July 1892, pp. 616–28; C. D. Wright, "Why Women Are Paid Less than Men," *Forum*, July 1892, pp. 629–39.

38. "Among the World's Workers—Some Women at Work," June 1904, p. 4938; L.

Abbott, "The Advance of Women," July 1904, pp. 5033–38; J. M. Taylor, "Education of Women," August 1903, pp. 3751–53; Page, "MoE—The Hours of Women's Work," April 1908, pp. 10063–64, *World's Work*.

39. Page, "Extending Women's Work," editorial, *State Chronicle*, February 2, 1884, p. 2; Page, "MoE—What Woman Suffrage Does," *World's Work*, April 1909, pp. 11419–20; National Archives and Records Administration, "19th Amendment to the U.S. Constitution: Women's Right to Vote (1920)," www.ourdocuments.gov, http://www.ourdocuments.gov/doc.php?doc=63, accessed July 22, 2020.

40. "To Walk through the Mountains," *News and Observer*, June 2, 1901, sec. 1, p. 11.

41. Page, "MoE—The Greatest Enterprise of Our Time," *World's Work*, April 1908, pp. 10063.

42. "A Night Above Clouds—The Chronicle's Special Correspondent at Mt. Mitchell," *State Chronicle*, August 16, 1884, p. 1.

43. T. Roosevelt, "Big Game Disappearing in the West," *Forum*, August 1893, pp. 767–74.

44. "In the Path of an Avalanche," May 1910, pp. 12864–65, "MoE—The Increasing Class that Rests," June 1903, pp. 3497–98, *World's Work*.

45. J. W. Pinochet, "The Yale Summer School of Forestry," October 1904, pp. 5389–92, K. F. Geiser, "Forestry Results in Germany," March 1907, pp. 8642–50, R. Crandall, "The Riches of the Philippine Forests," May 1908, pp. 10228–35, *World's Work*.

46. Page, "MoE—'The Most Weighty Question,'" *World's Work*, January 1908, p. 9729; Cooper, *Walter Hines Page*, p. 224; "MoE—The Greatest Enterprise of Our Time," *World's Work*, April 1908, p. 10063.

47. Page, "MoE—The Calling of an International Conservation Congress," *World's Work*, April 1909, p. 114–16.

CHAPTER 7. "WATCH THAT MAN!"

1. Wilson, letter to Page, October 30, 1885, Page Papers; Berg, *Wilson*, pp. 98–99, 102–3.

2. Cooper, *Woodrow Wilson*, pp. 70, 78–79; "The Ambassadorship," Page Papers; Wilson letter to Page, May 20, 1895, Wilson letter to Page, June 7, 1899, Wilson letter to Page, October 4, 1899, Wilson letter to Page, June 17, 1902, Page Papers.

3. Page, quoted in Hendrick, *Life and Letters*, vol. 1, p. 104; H. C. Bailey, *Liberalism in the New South*, p. 202; R. Bridges, "President Woodrow Wilson and College Earnestness," *World's Work*, January 1908, pp. 9792–97.

4. Wilson to M. A. Peck, quoted in Berg, *Wilson*, p. 169; Berg, pp. 191–94; Wilson, letter to Page, March 18, 1910, Page Papers.

5. Berg, *Wilson*, pp. 199–203; Wilson, quoted in Berg, pp. 202–3; Wilson, letter to Page, November 7, 1910, Page Papers.

6. Berg, *Wilson*, p. 213; Page, letter to Wilson, February 8, 1911, quoted in H. C. Bailey, *Liberalism in the New South*, p. 204; Wilson, letter to Page, February 10, 1911, Page Papers.

7. Berg, *Wilson*, pp. 212–13; Wilson, (separate) letter to Page, February 10, 1911, Page Papers.

284 \ NOTES TO CHAPTER SEVEN

8. Cooper, *Walter Hines Page*, pp. 235–37; H. C. Bailey, *Liberalism in the New South*, p. 203; Cooper, *Woodrow Wilson*, p. 141; Wilson, letter to Page, March 23, 1911, Page Papers. The Aldine Club was the book publishers' social club (*New York Times*, March 24, 1889, p. 8).

9. Berg, *Wilson*, pp. 213, 217; H. C. Bailey, *Liberalism in the New South*, p. 203; Cooper, *Woodrow Wilson*, pp. 144–45; Cooper, *Walter Hines Page*, pp. 237–38; *New York Times*, quoted in Berg, p. 217.

10. H. C. Bailey, *Liberalism in the New South*, pp. 204, 207–8; Page, "MoE," May 1911, p. 14291, Hale, "Woodrow Wilson—Possible President," May 1911, pp. 14339–53, *World's Work*.

11. Page, "MoE—A Programme for the Democrats," *World's Work*, May 1911, pp. 14307–9.

12. Wilson, letter to Page, June 7, 1911, Page Papers.

13. Hendrick, *Life and Letters*, vol. 1, p. 107; H. C. Bailey, *Liberalism in the New South*, pp. 205–6; Seymour, *Intimate Papers of Colonel House*, vol. 1, pp. 28–39; Woodward, *Origins of the New South*, p. 471; Cooper, *Walter Hines Page*, p. 238.

14. H. C. Bailey, *Liberalism in the New South*, p. 207; Cooper, *Walter Hines Page*, p. 239; Wilson, letters to Page, July 5 and August 21, 1911, Page Papers; McAdoo, "Address," p. 39; Wilson, letters to Page, October 10, 1911, and January 25, 1912, Page Papers.

15. W. B. Hale, "Woodrow Wilson—A Biography—The Presidency Looms Up," *World's Work*, March 1912, pp. 522–34.

16. Berg, *Wilson*, pp. 231–33, 235–36; Stockbridge, quoted in Cooper, *Walter Hines Page*, p. 241; McAdoo, "Address," p. 40; Wilson, letters to Page, July 7 and 17, 1912, Page Papers.

17. Page, "MoE—A Programme for the Democrats," May 1911, pp. 14307–9, Wilson, "The New Freedom—Benevolence, or Justice," April 1913, pp. 628–40, *World's Work*. The similarity between Page's "Programme" and Wilson's "New Freedom" election policies was noted in H. C. Bailey, *Liberalism in the New South*, p. 205.

18. Page, letter to Wilson, November 5, 1912, quoted in Hendrick, *Life and Letters*, vol. 1, p. 108; Wilson, letter to Page, November 6, 1912, Page Papers.

19. Page, diary and (separate) memorandum, November 14, 1912, Page Papers (Wilson's quotes are from Page's account recorded in this memorandum, which Page incorrectly dated November 15. Wilson stayed in New York City on Friday, November 15, with most of his family before leaving for a four-week vacation in Bermuda (Berg, *Wilson*, p. 255). His diary has the correct date of November 14).

20. Cooper, *Walter Hines Page*, p. 243; H. C. Bailey, *Liberalism in the New South*, p. 212; Page, notebook, undated though likely to be November 1912, Page Papers.

21. Hendrick, *Life and Letters*, vol. 1, pp. 114–15; H. C. Bailey, *Liberalism in the New South*, p. 212; Dabney, *Universal Education in the South*, vol. 2, pp. 64, 253; Houston, *Eight Years with Wilson's Cabinet*, vol. 1, p. 16.

22. Wilson, letter to Page, December 23, 1912, Page Papers; Page, letter to E. A. Alderman, December 31, 1912, quoted in Hendrick, *Life and Letters*, vol. 1, pp. 122–23; Wilson, letter to Page, January 2, 1913, Page Papers.

23. House, quoted in Seymour, *Intimate Papers of Colonel House*, vol. 1, p. 47; Axson, quoted in Berg, *Wilson*, p. 253; Wilson, letter to E. B. Galt, August 28, 1915, quoted in Cooper, *Woodrow Wilson*, p. 193.

24. House, quoted in Seymour, *Intimate Papers of Colonel House*, vol. 1, p. 118; Daniels, letter to Newton D. Baker, February 3, 1936, quoted in Cooper, *Woodrow Wilson*, p. 193; Axson, quoted in Berg, *Wilson*, p. 253; Cooper, p. 52.

25. G. S. Viereck, *The Strangest Friendship in History: Woodrow Wilson and Colonel House*, Westport, Conn.: Greenwood Press, 1960, pp. 37–39; Cooper, *Woodrow Wilson*, pp. 189, 191; House, letter to Houston, February 1913, quoted in Houston, *Eight Years with Wilson's Cabinet*, vol. 1, p. 12; Houston, pp. 13, 14, 16; House, diary, quoted in Gregory, *Walter Hines Page*, p. 23; Cooper, *Walter Hines Page*, p. 246; Page, letter to Wallace, March 11, 1913, quoted in Hendrick, *Life and Letters*, vol. 1, p. 117.

26. Houston, *Eight Years with Wilson's Cabinet*, vol. 1, p. 18.

27. Gregory, *Walter Hines Page*, p. 23; Cooper, *Walter Hines Page*, pp. 243–46; Jacobs, *Rogue Diplomats*, p. 200; Page, notebook, undated though likely to be November 1912, Page Papers; Rusnak, *Walter Hines Page*, pp. 31, 62; A. W. Page, "The Cotton Growers," *World's Work*, January 1906, pp. 7049–59.

28. Page, diary, January 23–February 1, 1913, Page Papers; Page, letter to E. A. Alderman, January 26, 1913, quoted in Hendrick, *Life and Letters*, vol. 1, pp. 125–28; Page, letter to Wallace, March 11, 1913, quoted in Hendrick, p. 115.

29. Cooper, *Walter Hines Page*, pp. 244–45.

30. Cooper, *Woodrow Wilson*, pp. 191, 193–94, 198; Wilson, letter to E. B. Galt, August 28, 1915, quoted in Cooper, p. 193.

31. Page, letter to Wallace, March 11, 1913, quoted in Hendrick, *Life and Letters*, vol. 1, p. 117; Seymour, *Intimate Papers of Colonel House*, vol. 1, p. 114.

32. Page, diary, March 20, 1913, Page Papers.

33. Cooper, *Walter Hines Page*, p. 248; House, diary, March 24, 1913, quoted in Seymour, *Intimate Papers of Colonel House*, vol. 1, p. 185.

34. Page, "The Ambassadorship," Page Papers; Seymour, *Intimate Papers of Colonel House*, vol. 1, p. 186; Page, letter to Alderman, March 27, 1913, quoted in Hendrick, *Life and Letters*, vol. 3, p. 19. Page noted House's call was on April 1, though subsequent events and letters indicate that March 26, the date in House's diary, is correct.

35. Houston, *Eight Years with Wilson's Cabinet*, vol. 1, pp. 63–64.

36. Wilson, letter to Page, March 28, 1913, Page Papers.

37. Page, "MoE—The Way to a Better Diplomatic Corps," *World's Work*, November 1902, p. 2707; Page, "The Ambassadorship," Page Papers.

38. Page, "The Ambassadorship," Page Papers.

39. Wilson, letter to Page, April 2, 1913, Page Papers; Page, "The Ambassadorship," Page Papers; Department of State, "Biographies of the Secretaries of State: Richard Olney," https://history.state.gov/departmenthistory/people/olney-richard, accessed January 19, 2017; Harvard University, "Charles William Eliot," http://www.harvard.edu/about-harvard/harvard-glance/history-presidency/charles-william-eliot, accessed January 19, 2017; "Walter H. Page Is Made Ambassador to Great Britain," *World*, New York,

March 31, 1913, p. 1; Page, diary, April 4, 1913, Page Papers; U.S. National Park Service, "Hampton National Historic Site, Maryland—Henry White," https://www.nps.gov /hamp/learn/historyculture/henry-white.htm, accessed January 27, 2024; "Mr. Laughlin to London—Succeeds William Phillips as Secretary of Embassy," *New York Tribune*, September 20, 1912, p. 6.

40. Page, letter to Wilson, November 5, 1912, quoted in Hendrick, *Life and Letters*, vol. 1, pp. 108–9; Page, "The President's Message," *State Chronicle*, December 8, 1883, p. 3.

41. Berg, *Wilson*, pp. 293–94; Houston, *Eight Years with Wilson's Cabinet*, vol. 1, pp. 52–55; Wilson, "The Tariff," First Special Address to Congress, April 8, 1913, in Baker and Dodd, *New Democracy*, vol. 1, pp. 32–36.

42. Page, diary, April 12, 1913, and "The Ambassadorship," Page Papers.

43. Page, diary, April 16, 1913, Page Papers; Dabney, *Universal Education in the South*, vol. 2, pp. 306–10, 313, 513–14.

44. T. Iacobelli and B. Shubinski, "The General Education Board," Rockefeller Foundation, https://resource.rockarch.org/story/the-general-education-board-1903-1964/, 2013; H. C. Bailey, "Heralds of Reform," p. 136; Buttrick, letter to Page, January 19, 1914, quoted in H. C. Bailey, *Liberalism in the New South*, p. 139.

45. Page, "The Ambassadorship," Page Papers.

46. Page, diary, April 30, 1913, Page Papers; Page, "The Consecutive Story: The Ambassadorship," quoted in Gregory, *Walter Hines Page*, pp. 25–26; Page, letter to Wilson, March 18, 1914, Page Papers.

47. Houston, *Eight Years with Wilson's Cabinet*, vol. 1, pp. 62–63.

CHAPTER 8. STARTING HIS "GREAT ADVENTURE"

1. Cooper, *Walter Hines Page*, pp. 250, 256–57, 260–61; K. A. Page, quoted in *The Book of the Class of Nineteen-Thirteen* (Bryn Mawr College, Penn., 1913), pp. 76–77; Gregory, *Walter Hines Page*, p. 30; House, diary, June 29, 1913, quoted in Cooper, p. 256.

2. Emmerson, *1913*, p. 18; Page, letter to Wilson, May 21, 1914, Page Papers. (Page's letter was written at the start of the 1914 season, so it primarily describes the 1913 season.)

3. Emmerson, *1913*, pp. 15–16, 161; "The World's Financial Center," May 1902, pp. 2040–44 and "MoE—What New York Really Is," November 1903, p. 4045, *World's Work*; U.K. Government, "King Charles Street—A Brief History of the Foreign, Commonwealth & Development Office Main Building," https://www.gov.uk/government/history /king-charles-street, accessed October 8, 2021; U.K. Government, "Past Foreign Secretaries—Sir Edward Grey, Viscount Grey of Fallodon," https://www.gov.uk/government /history/past-foreign-secretaries/edward-grey, accessed October 8, 2021.

4. Gregory, *Walter Hines Page*, p. 30; "Yankees Abroad Celebrate Day of Thanksgiving," *Indianapolis Times*, November 25, 1926, sec. 2, p. 14; Page, letters to Wilson, June 5 and September 22, 1914, Page Papers; M. Bryant (Embassy Librarian), "A History of the American Embassy," ca.1953, U.S. Embassy in London, p. 3.

5. Page, letter to Wilson, December 21, 1913, Page Papers; Page, speech to Authors' Club, December 3, 1913, quoted in Hendrick, *Life and Letters*, vol. 3, pp. 97–100.

NOTES TO CHAPTER EIGHT / 287

6. Page, letter to Wilson, January 24, 1914, Page Papers.

7. Berg, *Wilson*, p. 314; Page, letter to Wilson, September 12 and Wilson, letter to Page, September 26, 1913, Page Papers.

8. Berg, *Wilson*, pp. 297, 314; Bureau of the Census, "M 68–74—Foreign Trade—Value of Merchandise Imports and Duties on Them: 1821 to 1945," *Historical Statistics*, pp. 247–48.

9. Page, letter to House, January 8, 1914, and E. Bell, letter to Arthur, April 23, 1920, both quoted in Cooper, *Walter Hines Page*, p. 259.

10. Page, letter to Wilson, December 21, 1913, Page Papers; Page, letter to House, November 23, 1913, quoted in Hendrick, *Life and Letters*, vol. 1, p. 212; Wilson, letter to Page, January 6, 1914, Page Papers.

11. Wilson, letters to Page, May 18, February 24 and September 14, 1914, Page Papers.

12. Wilson, letters to Page, December 6, 1913, and March 7, 1914, Page Papers.

13. Wilson, letter to Page, February 24, 1914, Page Papers.

14. Wilson, letter to Page, April 2, 1914, Page Papers.

15. Letter to Alice, February 1915, quoted in Hendrick, *Life and Letters*, vol. 2, p. 23; Houston, *Eight Years with Wilson's Cabinet*, vol. 2, pp. 182–83; Faith, "United Kingdom," p. 184.

16. Cooper, *Walter Hines Page*, p. 249; Page, "MoE—The Powers' Suspicion of Germany," May 1903, p. 3380. Other examples include "The Disruption of Nationalities in Austria," January 1902, p. 1590 and "The Danger to Holland from Germany," January 1902, pp. 3380–81, *World's Work*.

17. Gregory, *Walter Hines Page*, pp. 31–32; Page, letter to Wilson, November 2, 1913, Page Papers.

18. Page, "MoE—In Earnest About the Isthmian Canal" and "The New Canal Treaty with England," *World's Work*, December 1900, p. 135; Hay-Pauncefote Treaty 1901, Article 3, quoted in Berg, *Wilson*, p. 324; Berg, pp. 324–25.

19. Page, "MoE—Profitless Dishonor," *World's Work*, February 1913, pp. 385–86. Page believed it was also a poor law because it favored shipping over railroads: "MoE—The Two-Edged Panama Act," *World's Work*, October 1912, p. 610.

20. Houston, *Eight Years with Wilson's Cabinet*, vol. 1, pp. 59–60; Berg, *Wilson*, p. 325.

21. Gregory, *Walter Hines Page*, p. 39; Cooper, *Walter Hines Page*, pp. 261–62; Page, letter to House, August 28, 1913, quoted in Seymour, *Intimate Papers of Colonel House*, vol. 1, p. 199; Page, letter to Wilson, September 10, 1913, quoted in Gregory, p. 39.

22. Berg, *Wilson*, p. 325; Houston, *Eight Years with Wilson's Cabinet*, vol. 1, pp. 112–13; Wilson, address to Congress, "Panama Canal Tolls," March 5, 1914, in Baker and Dodd, *New Democracy*, vol. 1, pp. 92–93.

23. Hendrick, *Life and Letters*, vol. 1, pp. 259–60; Cooper, *Walter Hines Page*, p. 264; Page, letters to Wilson, March 13, 18, and 31, 1914, and Wilson, letters to Page, March 25 and April 2, 1914, Page Papers.

24. Cooper, *Walter Hines Page*, p. 264; Page, telegram to Wilson, June 12, 1914, quoted in Cooper, p. 264.

25. Berg, *Wilson*, p. 286; Cooper, *Walter Hines Page*, p. 262; Gregory, *Walter Hines*

Page, pp. 33–34, 36; Wilson, statement at cabinet meeting, March 7, 1913, quoted in Berg, p. 286.

26. Cooper, *Walter Hines Page*, pp. 262–63; Gregory, *Walter Hines Page*, pp. 36–37.

27. Page, letters to Wilson, November 2 and 22, 1913, Page Papers.

28. Cooper, *Walter Hines Page*, pp. 263; Wilson, letters to Page, December 6, 1913, and January 6, 1914, Page Papers; Page, letter to Doubleday et al., December 28, 1913, quoted in Henrick, *Life and Letters*, vol. 1, pp. 166–67.

29. Page, letter to Wilson, February 22 and Wilson, letter to Page, June 1, 1914, Page Papers.

30. Page, letter to Wilson, April 7, 1914, Page Papers. By comparison, Britain's ambassador to America had $85,000 a year; (Gregory, *Walter Hines Page*, p. 30).

31. Wilson, letter to Page, May 18, and Page, letter to Wilson, June 5, 1914, Page Papers.

32. Gregory, *Walter Hines Page*, p. 31; Page, letters to Wilson, November 4 and July 5, 1914, Page Papers; "MoE—The Selection of American Diplomatists," *World's Work*, July 1909, pp. 11748–49.

33. Page, "MoE," December 1900, p. 119 and October 1901, pp. 1239–40, "MoE—The Public Speeches of Two Presidents" October 1902, p. 2589, *World's Work*.

34. "American Exportation of Coal" and "Commercial Supremacy of the United States," *World's Work*, November 1900, pp. 115–16.

35. Page, "MoE—A Looking-Outward Number of 'The World's Work,'" November 1901, p. 1367, "MoE—The Ultimate 'Conquest' of Latin America," January 1904, p. 4275, *World's Work*. Page's comments were made in the context of the recently signed Panama Treaty, which he stated gave America control over the isthmus though was not "annexation" (p. 4276).

36. Page, "MoE—Our Part in the Asiatic Struggle" and "A New American National Deal," *World's Work*, March 1904, p. 4499.

37. D. H. Doyle, *The Cause of All Nations: An International History of the American Civil War* (New York: Basic Books, 2015), p. 8; E. Laboulaye, quoted in Doyle, p. 284; A. Lincoln, "Address at the Dedication of the National Cemetery at Gettysburg, Pennsylvania," November 19, 1863, in The American Presidency Project, Gerhard Peters and John T. Woolley, http://www.presidency.ucsb.edu/ws/?pid=73959, accessed September 16, 2017; F. Emory, "Our Growth as a World Power," *World's Work*, November 1900, pp. 65–72.

38. Page, "MoE—At the Century's End," *World's Work*, November 1900, p. 4; "Our Adopted Sons," *Ottumwa Tri-Weekly Courier*, Ottumwa, Iowa, February 18, 1905, p. 3; Wilson, speech at Steeplechase Pier, Atlantic City, October 13, 1910, quoted in Berg, *Wilson*, p. 201; Wilson, "The New Freedom—Benevolence, or Justice," *World's Work*, April 1913, p. 640.

39. Page, "MoE—The Secret of American Expansion," *World's Work*, January 1902, pp. 1575–76.

40. Page, quoted in Hendrick, *Life and Letters*, vol. 1, p. 275; Page, letter to House, August 25, 1913, quoted in Hendrick, p. 275.

41. Page, "MoE—Our Large Economic Place Among the Great Nations," *World's Work*, November 1901, pp. 1358–59.

NOTES TO CHAPTERS EIGHT AND NINE / 289

42. Wilson, letter to Page, September 11, 1913, Page Papers.

43. J. B. Boles, *Jefferson: Architect of American Liberty* (New York: Basic Books, 2017), pp. 506–7; Department of State, Office of the Historian, "Travels Abroad of the President," https://history.state.gov/departmenthistory/travels/president, accessed June 27, 2015; Page, letters to Wilson, March 18 and 31, 1914, Page Papers.

44. Wilson, letters to Page, December 6, 1913, and January 6, 1914, Page Papers.

45. Gilbert, *First World War*, p. 26; Gilbert quoting Grey (p. 26), Asquith (p. 22), and Lloyd George (p. 23).

46. May, *World War and American Isolation*, pp. 90–100; Keegan, *First World War*, pp. 28, 46–47.

47. House, letter to Page, December 13, 1913, in Hendrick, *Life and Letters*, vol. 1, p. 277; Hendrick, p. 279.

48. Hendrick, *Life and Letters*, vol. 1, pp. 279–82, 289–96; House, letter to Page, June 3, 1914, quoted in Hendrick, p. 297.

49. Page, letters to Wilson, July 5 (2 letters) and September 6, 1914, Page Papers.

50. Page, letter to Wilson, July 29, 1914, Page Papers.

CHAPTER 9. THE WARTIME CHALLENGE OF NEUTRALITY

1. Page, memorandum, August 2, 1914, quoted in Hendrick, *Life and Letters*, vol. 1, p. 301; Page, letters to Wilson, June 5, July 5, and August 2, 1914, Page Papers.

2. Gilbert, *First World War*, pp. 32–33; Grey, quoted in Gilbert, pp. 33–34.

3. Page, letter to Wilson, August 9, 1914, Page Papers; Faith, "United Kingdom," p. 188.

4. May, *World War and American Isolation*, pp. 34–36; Gregory, *Walter Hines Page*, p. 52.

5. Wilson, "American Neutrality—An Appeal from the President," presented in the Senate, August 19, 1914, in Baker and Dodd, *New Democracy*, vol. 1, pp. 157–58; Page, letter to H. A. Page, quoted in Hendrick, *Life and Letters*, vol. 1, p. 361; F. D. Roosevelt, "Fireside Chat on the War in Europe," September 3, 1939, in The American Presidency Project, Gerhard Peters and John T. Woolley, http://www.presidency.ucsb.edu/ws/?pid =15801, accessed September 18, 2017.

6. Page, letters to Wilson, September 22 and October 15, 1914, Page Papers.

7. Page, letter to Wilson, October 6, 1914, Page Papers.

8. Hoover, *Memoirs of Herbert Hoover*, pp. 152–57, 203; Berg, *Wilson*, pp. 447–48; Cooper, *Walter Hines Page*, p. 283.

9. Page, letter to Wilson, September 6, 1914, Page Papers.

10. Page, telegram to Wilson, September 11, 1914, quoted in Hendrick, *Life and Letters*, vol. 1, p. 325; Page, note to Wilson, September 8, 1914 (P.S. to letter of September 6), Page Papers.

11. Page, letter to Wilson, September 22, 1914, Page Papers.

12. Page, "MoE—Germany's Political Crisis," *World's Work*, March 1912, pp. 494–95.

13. Page, letter to Wilson, September 6, 1914, Page Papers.

14. May, *World War and American Isolation*, pp. 16–21, 53; Gilbert, *First World War*, p. 109; Hendrick, *Life and Letters*, vol. 1, pp. 375–77, 380; Page, letter to Wilson, September 22, 1914, Page Papers; Lansing, *War Memoirs of Robert Lansing*, p. 119; Keegan,

First World War, pp. 265–66; Siney, *Allied Blockade of Germany*, p. 124. "Contraband" referred to goods the British Navy would seize and not let through to Germany or any neutral ports that might be a conduit to Germany.

15. Page, letter to Wilson, October 15, 1914, Page Papers; Page, letter to House, October 22, 1914, quoted in Hendrick, *Life and Letters*, vol. 1, pp. 381–83; Lansing, *War Memoirs of Robert Lansing*, p. 119.

16. Page, letter to Wilson, October 28 and Wilson, letter to Page, November 10, 1914, Page Papers.

17. Page, letter to Wilson, October 6, 1914, Page Papers.

18. Keegan, *First World War*, pp. 28–31, 43–47; Gilbert, *First World War*, pp. 28–29, 39; Gerard, *My Four Years in Germany*, p. 258.

19. Lansing, *War Memoirs of Robert Lansing*, p. 120; Siney, *Allied Blockade of Germany*, p. 271 (data are for January to November); Gerard, *My Four Years in Germany*, p. 191. As noted by Siney (p. 126): "It was quite well known that cotton waste when properly treated with nitroglycerine became a basic substance for a large group of explosives."

20. Kennan, *American Diplomacy*, pp. 68–73. Kennan developed the containment policy that the United States followed throughout the Cold War, and was one of the State Department's most influential advisers (Department of State, "Kennan and Containment, 1947," Office of the Historian; H. A. Kissinger, "The Age of Kennan," *New York Times*, November 10, 2011).

21. Wilson, letter to Page, October 28, 1914, Page Papers.

22. House, letter to Page, December 4, 1914, quoted in Seymour, *Intimate Papers of Colonel House*, vol. 1, p. 318.

23. Page, letter to Wilson, October 29 and Wilson, letter to Page, November 10, 1914, Page Papers.

24. Page, letter to House, December 15, 1914, quoted in Seymour, *Intimate Papers of Colonel House*, vol. 1, pp. 318–19; "Lusitania Brings a Santa-Claus Cargo," *Las Vegas Optic*, East Las Vegas, New Mexico, December 23, 1914, p. 1; *Farmer and Mechanic*, December 29, 1914, p. 7.

25. Page, letter to Wilson, January 12, 1915, Page Papers.

26. Hendrick, *Life and Letters*, vol. 3, pp. 204–7; Page, letter to Wilson, January 12, 1915, Page Papers.

27. Page, letter to Wilson, January 12, 1915, Page Papers.

28. Gilbert, *First World War*, p. 102; Bryan, "Restraints on Commerce," telegram to Page, December 26, 1914, in Baker and Dodd, *New Democracy*, vol. 1, pp. 229–35.

29. Gregory, *Walter Hines Page*, pp. 130–31; Lansing, *War Memoirs of Robert Lansing*, pp. 121–22; Siney, *Allied Blockade of Germany*, pp. 123–24; Hendrick, *Life and Letters*, vol. 2, pp. 63–64, 67–68; Page, quoted in Hendrick, p. 65. The First Battle of Bull Run, July 21–22, 1861, resulted in a calamitous defeat for the Union army and indicated it would be a long and arduous war (J. Dunne, *The American Civil War: A Visual History* (London: Dorling Kindersley, 2015), pp. 60–61).

NOTES TO CHAPTER NINE / 291

30. Page, letter to Katharine, December 7, 1915, quoted in Gregory, *Walter Hines Page*, p. 138.

31. May, *World War and American Isolation*, p. 81; Cooper, *Walter Hines Page*, p. 299; House, letter to Page, January 18, 1915, and Page, letter to Alice, January 24, 1915, quoted in Cooper, p. 299.

32. House, diary, November 25 and December 14, 1914, quoted in May, *World War and American Isolation*, p. 77.

33. Cooper, *Walter Hines Page*, pp. 299–300; Page, diary, March 11, 1915, quoted in Gregory, *Walter Hines Page*, p. 130; Page, letter to Wilson, October 15, 1914, Page Papers.

34. May, *World War and American Isolation*, pp. 113–22.

35. Gregory, *Walter Hines Page*, p. 91; Bryan, "Solemn Warning to Germany," telegram to Gerard, February 10, 1915, in Baker and Dodd, *New Democracy*, vol. 1, pp. 280–83; May, *World War and American Isolation*, pp. 122–28.

36. Bernstorff, message to Jagow, April 6, 1915, quoted in May, *World War and American Isolation*, p. 129; Bethmann-Hollweg, session of the Bundesrat Committee on Foreign Affairs, April 7, 1915, quoted in May, p. 131.

37. Page, letter to Arthur, quoted in Gregory, *Walter Hines Page*, p. 95.

38. Gilbert, *First World War*, p. 157; House, telegram to Wilson, May 9, 1915, quoted in Berg, *Wilson*, p. 363; Page, telegram to Wilson, May 8, 1915, quoted in Hendrick, *Life and Letters*, vol. 3, p. 239.

39. Wilson, letter to Bryan, May 10, 1915, quoted in Hendrick, *Life and Letters*, vol. 3, p. 242.

40. Houston, *Eight Years with Wilson's Cabinet*, vol. 2, pp. 243–44.

41. Wilson, quoted in Berg, *Wilson*, p. 365; Bryan, "The First *Lusitania* Note," telegram to Gerard, May 13, 1915, in Baker and Dodd, *New Democracy*, vol. 1, pp. 323–28.

42. Heckscher, *Woodrow Wilson*, pp. 367–69; Berg, *Wilson*, pp. 367–68; Bryan, quoted in Berg, p. 368.

43. Page, letter to Arthur, May 1915, quoted in Hendrick, *Life and Letters*, vol. 2, p. 5.

44. Gilbert, *First World War*, p. 188; May, *World War and American Isolation*, pp. 218–27; Bernstorff, quoted in May, p. 218.

45. Page, letter to Wilson, August 19, 1915, Page Papers.

46. Cooper, *Walter Hines Page*, p. 321.

47. Gregory, *Walter Hines Page*, p. 108; Page, telegram to Lansing, August 24, 1915, quoted in Gregory, p. 109; Wilson, quoted in Gregory, p. 110.

48. Wilson, letter to Page, September 10, 1915, Page Papers.

49. Lansing, *War Memoirs of Robert Lansing*, pp. 19, 22–23.

50. Page, "MoE—The Secret of American Expansion," *World's Work*, January 1902, p. 1576; Wilson, "Speech to the Southern Commercial Congress," Mobile, Alabama, October 27, 1913, in Baker and Dodd, *New Democracy*, vol. 1, pp. 68–69.

51. Page, letter to House, November 12, 1915, quoted in Hendrick, *Life and Letters*, vol. 2, p. 79; Page, quoted in Gregory, *Walter Hines Page*, p. 140; Page, diary, December 28, 1915, quoted in Gregory, p. 134.

292 \ NOTES TO CHAPTER TEN

CHAPTER 10. THE END OF THE RELATIONSHIP WITH WILSON

1. Page, letter to Wilson, January 5, 1916, Page Papers.

2. Gregory, *Walter Hines Page*, pp. 140–41; Heckscher, *Woodrow Wilson*, pp. 370–73; Hendrick, *Life and Letters*, vol. 3, pp. 281–82, 289–90; Page, memorandum, February 9, 1916, quoted in Hendrick, p. 282.

3. Hendrick, *Life and Letters*, vol. 3, pp. 281–82, 285–86; Page, message to Wilson, February 15, 1916 (sent February 17), quoted in Gregory, *Walter Hines Page*, p. 153.

4. Page, diary, February 24, 1916, quoted in Gregory, *Walter Hines Page*, p. 145.

5. Gregory, *Walter Hines Page*, pp. 144–45; May, *World War and American Isolation*, pp. 309–18.

6. May, *World War and American Isolation*, pp. 228, 235–37; Gregory, *Walter Hines Page*, pp. 154–55; Gilbert, *First World War*, pp. 236–37; Lansing to Wilson, March 27, 1916, quoted in Gregory, p. 155; House, diary, March 30, 1916, quoted in Seymour, *Intimate Papers of Colonel House*, vol. 2, p. 228.

7. Lansing, "Submarine Warfare," message to Gerard, April 18, 1916, in Baker and Dodd, *New Democracy*, vol. 2, pp. 147–52; May, *World War and American Isolation*, pp. 250–52; Gregory, *Walter Hines Page*, p. 156.

8. Wilson, letter to Page, April 13, 1916, Page Papers; Page, diary, May 8, 1916, quoted in Gregory, *Walter Hines Page*, p. 156; Gilbert, *First World War*, p. 237; Page, letter to Wilson, May 12, 1916, Page Papers.

9. House, diary, June 23, 1916, Seymour, *Intimate Papers of Colonel House*, vol. 2, pp. 303–4; House, quoted in Seymour, p. 304.

10. Page, letter to Wilson, July 21, 1916, Page Papers.

11. T. A. Bailey, "United States and the Blacklist," pp. 15, 25; Wilson, letter to House, July 23, 1916, quoted in Gregory, *Walter Hines Page*, p. 163; Polk to Page, July 26, 1916, quoted in T. A. Bailey, pp. 24–25; Page, letter to Lansing, July 25, 1916, quoted in T. A. Bailey, p. 27; Polk, letter to House, Seymour, *Intimate Papers of Colonel House*, vol. 2, p. 313.

12. Gregory, *Walter Hines Page*, p. 163; House, letter to Wilson, May 18, 1916, quoted in Seymour, *Intimate Papers of Colonel House*, vol. 2, pp. 269–70; House, letter to Polk, July 25, 1916, quoted in Seymour, p. 315; Page, letter to Alice, January 17, 1915, quoted in Cooper, *Walter Hines Page*, p. 299; Page, letter to Wilson, July 21, 1916, Page Papers.

13. Page, letter to Wilson, July 21, 1916, Page Papers; Hendrick, *Life and Letters*, vol. 2, pp. 170–72; Gregory, *Walter Hines Page*, pp. 164–65; Page, memorandum of visit to Washington, D.C., quoted in Hendrick, p. 172.

14. Gregory, *Walter Hines Page*, pp. 164–65, 168; Page, letter to Laughlin, quoted in Hendrick, *Life and Letters*, vol. 2, p. 179; Page, letter to House, August 26, 1916, quoted in Gregory, p. 165.

15. Page, letter to Alice, August 26, 1916, quoted in Hendrick, *Life and Letters*, vol. 2, p. 189; Gregory, *Walter Hines Page*, p. 172.

16. Cooper, *Walter Hines Page*, p. 341; Page, memorandum of visit to Washington, D.C., quoted in Hendrick, *Life and Letters*, vol. 2, pp. 174–75; Page, notebook, Page Papers.

17. Page, memorandum of visit to Washington, D.C., quoted in Hendrick, *Life and*

Letters, vol. 2, p. 176; Page, notebook, Page Papers; Lansing, *War Memoirs of Robert Lansing*, pp. 168, 171–73.

18. Page, notebook, Page Papers.

19. Berg, *Wilson*, pp. 397–99, 404–8, 410–11; Hendrick, *Life and Letters*, vol. 2, p. 171.

20. Page, letter to Wilson, September 21, 1916, quoted in Hendrick, *Life and Letters*, vol. 2, p. 183; Hendrick, p. 184; Gregory, *Walter Hines Page*, p. 168; Cooper, *Walter Hines Page*, p. 345.

21. Gregory, *Walter Hines Page*, p. 169.

22. Page, notebook, Page Papers; Page, letter to Frank, quoted in Hendrick, *Life and Letters*, vol. 2, p. 188.

23. House, diary, quoted in Seymour, *Intimate Papers of Colonel House*, vol. 2, pp. 317, 319–20.

24. House, diary, December 14, 1914, quoted in May, *World War and American Isolation*, p. 77; Lansing, *War Memoirs of Robert Lansing*, p. 172.

25. Page, memorandum of visit to Washington, D.C., quoted in Hendrick, *Life and Letters*, vol. 2, pp. 171–79; Cooper, *Walter Hines Page*, pp. 349–51.

26. Cooper, *Walter Hines Page*, pp. 349–50; T. A. Bailey, "United States and the Blacklist," pp. 25–28; Page to Lansing, October 11, 1916, quoted in Bailey, p. 28.

27. T. A. Bailey, "United States and the Blacklist," pp. 29–30; Page, letter to Wilson, December 30, 1916, Page Papers.

28. Page, letter to Wilson, November 24, 1916, Page Papers.

29. Cooper, *Walter Hines Page*, pp. 354–55; Page, letter to Wilson, December 30, 1916, Page Papers.

30. Page, "Memoranda—Written, Not for the Sake of the Gentlemen Mentioned but for Possible Help to the President and the Service," undated though probably around the end of 1916, Page Papers; Page, letter to Wilson, July 5, 1914, Page Papers.

31. Lansing, "Note to the Belligerent Governments," December 18, 1916, in Baker and Dodd, *New Democracy*, vol. 2, pp. 402–6; "Note" covering telegram, quoted in Gregory, *Walter Hines Page*, p. 182.

32. National Library of Wales, "David Lloyd George the Prime Minister," https://www.llyfrgell.cymru/darganfod-dysgu/arddangosfeydd-arlein/david-lloyd-george/bywyd-a-gwaith-david-lloyd-george/david-lloyd-george-y-prif-weinidog, accessed April 4, 2024; Cecil to Spring-Rice, December 20, 1916, quoted in Gregory, *Walter Hines Page*, p. 182; Gregory, pp. 180–83; Page to House, December 1916, quoted in Seymour, *Intimate Papers of Colonel House*, vol. 2, p. 409.

33. May, *World War and American Isolation*, pp. 197–301, 404–13.

CHAPTER 11. VINDICATION

1. Gerard, *My Four Years in Germany*, pp. 262–64.

2. May, *World War and American Isolation*, pp. 413–15; Bethmann-Hollweg, telegram to Bernstorff, January 16, 1917, quoted in Lansing, *War Memoirs of Robert Lansing*, p. 209; Gregory, *Walter Hines Page*, p. 188; Keegan, *First World War*, p. 319; Gerard, *My Four Years in Germany*, pp. 264–65, 271–72.

3. Seymour, *Intimate Papers of Colonel House*, vol. 2, pp. 417–20; Keegan, *First World War*, p. 319; House, letter to Wilson, January 20, 1917, quoted in Seymour, pp. 429–30; Wilson, "Essential Terms of Peace in Europe," address to Senate, January 22, 1917, in Baker and Dodd, *New Democracy*, vol. 2, p. 407.

4. Page, letter to Wilson, September 22, 1914, quoted in Hendrick, *Life and Letters*, vol. 3, p. 141; Gerard, *My Four Years in Germany*, p. 271.

5. Page and Wilson, quoted in Lansing, *War Memoirs of Robert Lansing*, p. 195; Gregory, *Walter Hines Page*, pp. 186–87; Lansing, p. 195; Page, memorandum, quoted in Gregory, p. 187.

6. Gregory, *Walter Hines Page*, pp. 188–89; Tuchman, *Zimmermann Telegram*, p. 133; Lansing, *War Memoirs of Robert Lansing*, p. 210; Wilson, "Submarine Warfare and the Break with Germany," address to Congress, February 3, 1917, in Baker and Dodd, *New Democracy*, vol. 2, pp. 422–26.

7. Page, telegram to Wilson, February 4, 1917, quoted in Hendrick, *Life and Letters*, vol. 3, pp. 318–19.

8. Gregory, *Walter Hines Page*, p. 191; Page, diary, February 19, 1917, quoted in Gregory, p. 191; Gilbert, *First World War*, p. 314; Page, diary, February 27, 1917, quoted in Hendrick, *Life and Letters*, vol. 3, p. 324; Wilson, "Armed Merchant Ships," address to Congress, February 26, 1917, in Baker and Dodd, *New Democracy*, vol. 2, pp. 428–32; Lansing, *War Memoirs of Robert Lansing*, pp. 224–25; Tuchman, *Zimmermann Telegram*, p. 178.

9. Lansing, *War Memoirs of Robert Lansing*, p. 119; Kennan, *American Diplomacy*, p. 64.

10. Lansing to Page, February 5 and Page to Lansing, February 6, 1917, quoted in Gregory, *Walter Hines Page*, p. 190.

11. Zimmermann Telegram, quoted in Tuchman, *Zimmermann Telegram*, p. 133; Lansing, *War Memoirs of Robert Lansing*, pp. 225–26.

12. Tuchman, *Zimmermann Telegram*, pp. 3, 145, 148–49.

13. Tuchman, *Zimmermann Telegram*, pp. 151–52, 153–54, 157–58; Page, diary, quoted in Tuchman, p. 152; Polk, quoted in Tuchman, p. 154; Lansing, *War Memoirs of Robert Lansing*, pp. 226–29; Wilson, quoted in Lansing, p. 228; Wilson, quoted in Tuchman, pp. 157–58.

14. Page, diary, March 2, 1917, quoted in Hendrick, *Life and Letters*, vol. 3, p. 325; Lansing, *War Memoirs of Robert Lansing*, pp. 232–33.

15. Lansing, *War Memoirs of Robert Lansing*, pp. 233, 236–37; Gregory, *Walter Hines Page*, p. 195.

16. Gregory, *Walter Hines Page*, p. 195; Page, letter to Arthur, March 25, 1917, quoted in Hendrick, *Life and Letters*, vol. 2, p. 217.

17. Wilson, "Joint Address to Congress Leading to a Declaration of War against Germany," April 2, 1917, U.S. National Archives.

18. Page, letter to Wilson, September 6, 1914, Page Papers; Lansing, *War Memoirs of Robert Lansing*, pp. 19–20, 68–85.

19. Page, letter to Wilson, November 24, 1916, Page Papers.

NOTES TO CHAPTER ELEVEN / 295

20. Page, letter to House, January 2, 1914, quoted in Hendrick, *Life and Letters*, vol. 1, pp. 282–83.

21. Lansing, *War Memoirs of Robert Lansing*, p. 244.

22. Gregory, *Walter Hines Page*, p. 200; Cooper, *Walter Hines Page*, pp. 383–84; Balfour, quoted in Cooper, pp. 384.

23. Page, letter to Arthur, September 26, 1917, quoted in Cooper, *Walter Hines Page*, p. 383; Cooper, pp. 385–86.

24. Page, letter to House, October 22, 1914, quoted in Hendrick, *Life and Letters*, vol. 1, p. 381; Gregory, *Walter Hines Page*, p. 198; Hendrick, *Life and Letters*, vol. 2, pp. 264–66; T. A. Bailey, "United States and the Blacklist," pp. 32–33.

25. Page, diary, February 25, 1917, quoted in Hendrick, *Earlier Life and Letters*, p. 323; Gerard, *My Four Years in Germany*, pp. viii–ix.

26. Keegan, *First World War*, p. 353; Hendrick, *Life and Letters*, vol. 2, pp. 273–84; Page, letters to Wilson, May 4 and June 29, 1917, Page Papers.

27. Balfour, letter to Wilson, June 30, 1917, quoted in Hendrick, *Life and Letters*, vol. 2, p. 285; Hendrick, pp. 286–87, 294; Gregory, *Walter Hines Page*, pp. 198–99; Keegan, *First World War*, pp. 353–54; Gilbert, *First World War*, p. 387.

28. Hendrick, *Life and Letters*, vol. 2, pp. 272–73; Gregory, *Walter Hines Page*, pp. 199–200; Page, letter to Wilson, June 29, 1917, Page Papers; Berg, *Wilson*, pp. 475–76.

29. Keegan, *First World War*, p. 372; Gilbert, *First World War*, pp. 372, 399–400, 426–27.

30. Cooper, *Walter Hines Page*, pp. 388–89; Gregory, *Walter Hines Page*, pp. 200–201; Page, diary, February 3, 1918, quoted in Gregory, p. 201.

31. Cooper, *Walter Hines Page*, pp. 152, 390–92; Alice Page, quoted in Cooper, p. 391; Page, "Obituary—Williamson Page—Dr. John W. Page" *State Chronicle*, January 5, 1884, p. 1; Hendrick, *Life and Letters*, vol. 2, pp. 375–76, 393; Buttrick, quoted in Hendrick, p. 376; Page, quoted in Hendrick, pp. 376, 393.

32. Page, letter to Arthur, March 24, 1918, quoted in Cooper, *Walter Hines Page*, p. 388.

33. Gilbert, *First World War*, pp. 399–400, 426, 437; Keegan, *First World War*, pp. 372, 411–12; Gregory, *Walter Hines Page*, p. 204.

34. Page, letter to Wilson, August 1, 1918, Page Papers.

35. Wilson, letter to Page, August 24, 1918, quoted in Hendrick, *Life and Letters*, vol. 2, p. 396; Gilbert, *First World War*, p. 455.

36. Gregory, *Walter Hines Page*, p. 205; *Times*, quoted in Hendrick, *Life and Letters*, vol. 2, p. 396; Hendrick, pp. 396–402; Lloyd George, letter to Page, August 30, 1918, quoted in Hendrick, p. 399.

37. Gregory, *Walter Hines Page*, p. 205; Page, letter to Alice, September 2, 1918, quoted in Hendrick, *Life and Letters*, vol. 2, pp. 395–96; Gilbert, *First World War*, p. 466; Keegan, *First World War*, p. 412.

38. Cooper, *Walter Hines Page*, p. 394; Hendrick, *Life and Letters*, vol. 2, pp. 402–3; Balfour, quoted in Hendrick, p. 403.

39. Hendrick, *Life and Letters*, vol. 2, pp. 404–5; Cooper, *Walter Hines Page*, pp. 394–95; Wilson, letter to Page, October 17, 1918, Page Papers.

40. Gilbert, *First World War*, pp. 540–42; Keegan, *First World War*, p. 423.

41. Page letter to Wilson, November 23, 1918, Page Papers.

42. Wilson, letter to Page, November 26, 1918, Page Papers.

43. Page, letter to H. L. Davis, quoted in Hendrick, *Life and Letters*, vol. 2, p. 405.

44. Hendrick, *Life and Letters*, vol. 2, p. 406; Page, quoted in Hendrick, p. 406; Cooper, *Walter Hines Page*, p. 396; *Evening Star*, December 23, 1918, p. 2.

45. Berg, *Wilson*, pp. 520–21, 523–40, 555–601; Cooper, *Woodrow Wilson*, pp. 454–55; Wilson quoted in Berg, p. 556.

46. Berg, *Wilson*, pp. 551–52.

47. *Evening Star*, June 15, 1923, p. 9; "Propose Memorial to Walter H. Page," *Bozeman Courier*, Bozeman, Montana, February 28, 1923, p. 7.

48. Grey, July 3, 1923, quoted in Hendrick, *Life and Letters*, vol. 3, pp. 429–31; Westminster Abbey, "Walter Hines Page," https://www.westminster-abbey.org/abbey-commemorations/commemorations/walter-hinespage?_gl=1*1s2g13j*_up*MQ.*_ga*MTA2NjA5OTc5Ny4xNzA3MDM5NTE0*_ga_DHMS4WRT6Q*MTcwNzAzOTUxMy4xLjEuMTcwNzAzOTUyNy4wLjAuMA.#i12802, accessed February 4, 2024.

49. Davis, letter to Shaw, December 1923, quoted in Shaw, "Walter Hines Page," pp. 24–25.

50. Grey, letter to Page, September 2, 1918, quoted in Hendrick, *Life and Letters*, vol. 2, pp. 399–400.

CHAPTER 12. THE MYTH OF NEUTRALITY

1. Page, memorandum of visit to Washington, D.C., quoted in Hendrick, *Life and Letters*, vol. 2, p. 175.

2. Cecil to Spring-Rice, December 1916, quoted in Gregory, *Walter Hines Page*, p. 184.

3. Page, memorandum of visit to Washington, D.C., quoted in Hendrick, *Life and Letters*, vol. 2, p. 178.

4. Page, letter to Wilson, September 6, 1914, Page Papers; F. Papen, message to German War Ministry, March 7, 1915, quoted in May, *World War and American Isolation*, p. 129.

5. Gerard, *My Four Years in Germany*, pp. x–xi; Kennan, *American Diplomacy*, p. 65.

6. Page, quoted in Hendrick, *Life and Letters*, vol. 1, p. 361.

7. Lansing, *War Memoirs of Robert Lansing*, p. 22; Page, diary, 2 March 1917, quoted in Cooper, *Walter Hines Page*, p. 370; R. Reagan, "Foreword," in F. Freidel, *The Presidents of the United States of America* (Washington, D.C.: White House Historical Association, 1982).

8. House, diary, cited in Cooper, *Walter Hines Page*, p. 351; Wilson, letter to Arthur, August 16, 1917, Page Papers.

9. Hendrick, *Life and Letters*, vol. 2, pp. 287–88; Page, letter to Arthur, July 8, 1917, quoted in Hendrick, vol. 2, pp. 291–92.

10. E.g., Lansing, "America's Future at Stake," and L. F. Post (Assistant Secretary of Labor), "The German Attack," both in *A War of Self-Defense*, War Information Series

(Washington, D.C.: Committee on Public Information, August 1917); and Lansing, "Prussianism," address at Schenectady, New York, June 10, 1918.

11. Wilson, "Essential Terms of Peace in Europe," address to Senate, January 22, 1917, in Baker and Dodd, *New Democracy*, vol. 2, p. 408; "The League of Nations, 1920," Office of the Historian, Department of State, https://history.state.gov/milestones/1914-1920/league, accessed March 10, 2024.

12. W. G. Harding, "Inaugural Address," March 4, 1921, in The American Presidency Project, Gerhard Peters and John T. Woolley, http://www.presidency.ucsb.edu/ws/?pid=25833, accessed May 2, 2017; Kennedy, "Origins and Uses of American Hyperpower," pp. 17–18; Fullilove, *Rendezvous with Destiny*, p. 17.

13. Page, memorandum, August 1913, quoted in Hendrick, *Life and Letters*, vol. 1, p. 272; Page, letter to Wilson, May 4, 1917, Page Papers.

14. H. R. Luce, "The American Century," *Life*, February 17, 1941, pp. 61–65.

15. F. D. Roosevelt, "Radio Address for the Christian Foreign Service Convocation," March 16, 1940, in The American Presidency Project, Gerhard Peters and John T. Woolley, http://www.presidency.ucsb.edu/ws/?pid=15924, accessed January 28, 2017.

16. Fullilove, *Rendezvous with Destiny*, p. 98.

17. F. D. Roosevelt, "Press Conference," December 17, 1940, in The American Presidency Project, Gerhard Peters and John T. Woolley, http://www.presidency.ucsb.edu/ws/?pid=15913, accessed January 29, 2017.

18. F. D. Roosevelt, "Address at the Annual Dinner of White House Correspondents' Association," March 15, 1941, in The American Presidency Project, Gerhard Peters and John T. Woolley, http://www.presidency.ucsb.edu/ws/?pid=16089, accessed January 28, 2017.

CHAPTER 13. REMEMBERING WALTER HINES PAGE

1. J. Friedman, *Power without Knowledge: A Critique of Technocracy* (New York: Oxford University Press), 2019, pp. 81–83; C. D. Goodwin, "The Promise of Expertise: Walter Lippmann and the Policy Sciences," *Policy Sciences* 28 no. 4 (November 1995): 317–18, 324–28, 330–31; Page, "An Intimate View of Publishing," *World's Work*, September 1902, p. 2562.

2. Dabney, *Universal Education in the South*, vol. 2, pp. 510–11; Knight, *Public Education in the South*, p. 432.

3. Dabney, *Universal Education in the South*, vol. 2, p. 510; Knight, *Public Education in the South*, p. 437; Cubberley, *Public Education*, pp. 680–81.

4. W. F. Russell, Teachers College, Columbia University, New York, report 1928–29, quoted in Dabney, *Universal Education in the South*, vol. 2, p. 527; Dabney, p. 513; Page, "Forgotten Man," p. 30.

5. F. D. Roosevelt, Message for American Education Week, September 27, 1938, in The American Presidency Project, Peters and Woolley, https://www.presidency.ucsb.edu/documents/message-for-american-education-week, accessed February 5, 2024.

6. Bleakley, "Disease and Development," pp. 77–78; Dabney, *Universal Education in the South*, vol. 2, pp. 260–61; Haden, "Hookworm Eradication."

7. Dabney, *Universal Education in the South*, vol. 2, pp. 258–62; Connor, "Walter Hines Page," p. 168.

8. Etting, Germ of Laziness, pp. 186–90, 249; Hendrick, *Life and Letters*, vol. 1, pp. 100–101; Dabney, *Universal Education in the South*, vol. 2, pp. 237, 263–64.

9. Page, "Address at the Inauguration"; Page, "The Arisen South," *World's Work*, June 1907, p. 9040.

10. Sumner, "'Let Us Have a Big Fair,'" pp. 80–81; Letters to Fries from Page (November 30) and R. Lewis (December 6), quoted in Sumner, p. 81; Bureau of Economic Analysis, "Gross Domestic Product by State and Personal Income by State, 3rd Quarter 2023," U.S. Department of Commerce, December 22, 2023.

11. J. W. Hardin, "North Carolina's Research Triangle Park," in *Pathways to High-Tech Valleys and Research Triangles*, ed. W. Hulsink and H. Dons (Dordrecht, The Netherlands: Springer, 2008), pp. 27–28, 34–46.

12. T. J. Minchin and J. A. Salmond, *After the Dream: Black and White Southerners since 1965* (Lexington: University Press of Kentucky, 2011), pp. 1–4, 273–99; J. C. Cobb, *The "Brown" Decision, Jim Crow, and Southern Identity* (Athens: University of Georgia Press, 2005), pp. 8–11, 15–16.

13. Kennedy, "Origins and Uses of American Hyperpower," p. 19; G. J. Ikenberry, "Power and Liberal Order: America's Postwar World Order in Transition," *International Relations of the Asia-Pacific* vol. 5, no. 2, (2005): 133–52; Act of April 3, 1948, European Recovery Act [Marshall Plan], U.S. National Archives.

14. Department of State, Office of the Historian, "The Truman Doctrine, 1947," https://history.state.gov/milestones/1945-1952/truman-doctrine, accessed January 9, 2023; B. Obama, quoted in "Exclusive: Read the Inauguration Day Letter Obama Left for Trump," CNN website, https://edition.cnn.com/2017/09/03/politics/obama-trump-letter-inauguration-day/index.html, September 5, 2017.

15. T. Roosevelt, letter to Alice Page, January 1, 1919, quoted in *The Letters of Theodore Roosevelt: The Days of Armageddon*, ed. E. E. Morison (Cambridge, Mass.: Harvard University Press, 1954), vol. 8, p. 1421; Berg, *Wilson*, p. 522.

16. Hoover, *Memoirs of Herbert Hoover*, p. 203.

17. Marcosson, *Adventures in Interviewing*, p. 40.

18. Mims, "Walter Hines Page," pp. 97, 98.

19. Dabney, *Universal Education in the South*, vol. 2, p. 234.

20. Shaw, "Walter Hines Page," p. 23; Buttrick, quoted in Shaw, p. 24.

21. C. H. Green, "World Is Now Beating a Pathway to Tomb of Walter Hines Page," *News and Observer*, November 24, 1929, quoted in Sellers, "Walter Hines Page," p. 499.

BIBLIOGRAPHY

The following are items cited more than once; other items appear in the notes. (Newspapers are the only exception—see below.)

Arendell, F. B. "Busy Aberdeen." *News and Observer*, April 24, 1895, p. 2.

Bailey, H. C. "Heralds of Reform from the New South." *Social Science* 54, no. 3 (Summer 1979): 131–38.

———. *Liberalism in the New South: Southern Social Reformers and the Progressive Movement*. Coral Gables, Fla.: University of Miami Press, 1969.

Bailey, T. A. "The United States and the Blacklist during the Great War." *Journal of Modern History* 6, no. 1 (March 1934): 14–35.

Baker, R. S., and Dodd W. E., eds. *The New Democracy: The Public Papers of Woodrow Wilson*. Vols. 1 and 2. New York: Harper & Brothers, 1926.

Battle, K. P. *History of the University of North Carolina*. Vol. 2. Raleigh, N.C.: Edwards and Broughton Printing Co., 1912.

Berg, A. S. *Wilson*. New York: Putnam, 2013.

Bleakley, H. "Disease and Development: Evidence from Hookworm Eradication in the American South." *Quarterly Journal of Economics* 122, no. 1 (February 2007): 73–117.

Bureau of the Census. *Historical Statistics of The United States 1789-1945: A Supplement to the Statistical Abstract of the United States*. Washington, D.C.: United States Department of Commerce, 1949.

Campbell, J. L. "In Search of the New South." *Southern Speech Communication Journal* 47, no. 4 (1982): 361–88.

Connor, R. D. W. "Walter Hines Page: A Southern Nationalist." *Journal of Social Forces* 2, no. 2 (January 1924): 164–68.

Cooper, J. M. *Walter Hines Page: The Southerner as American 1855–1918*. Chapel Hill: University of North Carolina Press, 1977.

———. *Woodrow Wilson*. New York: Vintage, 2011.

Craven, A. *The Coming of the Civil War*. New York: Charles Scribner's Sons, 1950.

Cubberley, E. P. *Public Education in the United States*. Cambridge, Mass.: Houghton Mifflin Company, 1934.

Dabney C. W. *Universal Education in the South*. Vols. 1 and 2. Chapel Hill: University of North Carolina Press, 1936.

Daniels, J. *Tar Heel Editor*. Chapel Hill: University of North Carolina Press, 1939.

Emmerson, C. *1913: The World before the Great War*. London: Vintage, 2013.

Ettling, J. *The Germ of Laziness: Rockefeller Philanthropy and Public Health in the New South*. Cambridge, Mass.: Harvard University Press, 1981.

Faith, T. "The United Kingdom, 1914–1917: Washington's Nerve Center in Europe." In *War, Neutrality, and Humanitarian Relief: The Expansion of U.S. Diplomatic Activity during the Great War, 1914–1917*, pp. 182–216. N.p.: U.S. Department of State, Office of the Historian, Foreign Service Institute, 2020.

Foner, E. "Reconstruction—United States History." Encyclopedia Britannica. https://www.britannica.com/event/Reconstruction-United-States-history, accessed July 29, 2020.

Fullilove, M. *Rendezvous with Destiny*. Melbourne: Penguin, 2013.

General Education Board (GEB). *An Account of Its Activities: 1902–1914*. New York, 1915.

Gerard, J. W. *My Four Years in Germany*. New York: Hodder and Stoughton, 1917.

Gilbert, M. *The First World War: A Complete History*. New York: Henry Holt and Company, 1994.

Goodman, S. *Republic of Words: The "Atlantic Monthly" and Its Writers, 1857–1925*. Lebanon, N.H.: University Press of New England, 2011.

Gregg, W. *Essays on Domestic Industry: or, An Enquiry into the Expediency of Establishing Cotton Manufactures in South-Carolina*. Charleston, S.C.: Burges and James, 1845.

Gregory, R. *Walter Hines Page: Ambassador to the Court of St. James's*. Lexington: University Press of Kentucky, 1970.

Haden, R. "Hookworm Eradication." *The Encyclopedia of Arkansas History and Culture*. Central Arkansas Library System, updated July 15, 2022, http://www.encyclopediaofarkansas.net/encyclopedia/entry-detail.aspx?search=1&entryID=2233.

Heckscher, A. *Woodrow Wilson*. New York: Charles Scribner's Sons, 1991.

Hendrick, B. J. *The Earlier Life and Letters of Walter H. Page: The Training of an American*. London: William Heinemann, 1928.

————. *The Life and Letters of Walter H. Page*. Vols. 1 and 2. New York: Doubleday, Page & Company, 1922.

————. *The Life and Letters of Walter H. Page: Containing the Letters to Woodrow Wilson*. Vol. 3. London: William Heinemann, 1926.

Holland, I. R., "Page, Allison Frances (Frank)", NCpedia, 1994, https://www.ncpedia.org/biography/page-allison-francis.

Hoover, H. *The Memoirs of Herbert Hoover: Years of Adventure 1874–1920*. Vol. 1. New York: Macmillan, 1951.

Houston, D. F. *Eight Years with Wilson's Cabinet: 1913 to 1920*. Vols. 1 and 2. New York: Doubleday, Page & Company, 1926.

Inge, T. B. "Ellen Anderson Gholson Glasgow, 1873–1945." In *Encyclopedia of Southern Culture*, edited by C.R. Wilson and W. Ferris. Chapel Hill: University of North Carolina Press, 1989, accessed from "Documenting the American South", https://docsouth.unc.edu/southlit/glasgowbattle/bio.html.

Jacobs, S. *Rogue Diplomats: The Proud Tradition of Disobedience in American Foreign Policy*. Cambridge: Cambridge University Press, 2020.

Jenkins, J. A., and J. Peck. "The Blair Education Bill: A Lost Opportunity in American Public Education," September 27, 2016. Paper presented at the American, British, and Canadian Political Development Workshop, University of Toronto, ON, Canada, September 30–October 1, 2016.

Keegan, J. *The First World War*. New York: Alfred A. Knopf, 1999.

Kennan, G. F. *American Diplomacy, 1900–1950*. London: Secker and Warburg, 1952.

Kennedy, D. M. "The Origins and Uses of American Hyperpower." In *The Short Amer-*

ican Century, edited by A. J. Bacevich, 15–37. Cambridge, Mass.: Harvard University Press.

Knight, E. W. *Public Education in the South*. Boston: Ginn and Company, 1922. Reprint, London: Forgotten Books, 2015.

Lansing, R. *War Memoirs of Robert Lansing: Secretary of State*. Indianapolis: Bobbs-Merrill Company, 1935.

Lowrie, S. D., "Some Notes and Anecdotes of the Birmingham Conference." *Southern Workman* (Hampton Normal and Agricultural Institute, Virginia) 33, no. 6 (June 1904): 331–36.

Marcosson, I. F. *Adventures in Interviewing*. New York: John Lane Company, 1919.

May, E. R. *The World War and American Isolation, 1914–1917*. Cambridge, Mass.: Harvard University Press, 1959.

McAdoo, W. G. "Address." In *Memorial Meeting Walter Hines Page*, edited by E. A. Alderman, pp. 36–45. New York: Doubleday, Page & Company, 1920. Reprint, BiblioLife.

Mims, E. "Walter Hines Page: Friend of the South." *South Atlantic Quarterly* 18, no. 2 (April 1919): 97–115.

Mott, F. L. *A History of American Magazines, 1741–1930*. Vol. 3, *1865–1885*. Cambridge, Mass.: Harvard University Press, 1958.

———. *A History of American Magazines, 1741–1930*. Vol. 4, *1885–1905*. Cambridge, Mass.: Harvard University Press, 1958.

Owens, H. P., ed. *Perspectives and Irony in American Slavery*. Jackson, Miss.: University Press of Mississippi, 1976.

Page W. H. "Address at the Inauguration of President Winston." *North Carolina University Magazine* 11, no. 2, pp. 61–71, reproduced from the *State Chronicle*, 20 October 1891. Page gave the speech on October 14.

———. "The Forgotten Man" (speech at the State Normal and Industrial School for Women, Greensboro, N.C., 1897). In *The Rebuilding of Old Commonwealths: Being Essays Towards the Training of the Forgotten Man in the Southern states*, by W. H. Page, pp. 1–47. New York: Doubleday, Page & Company, 1902. Reprint, Kessinger Legacy Reprints.

———. "How the South May Regain Leadership in Industry and Politics—Address of Dr. Walter H. Page Editor of the World's Work, at the Conference for Education in the South, Birmingham, Ala., April 27, 1904." *Progressive Farmer*, May 10, 1904, pp. 4–5.

———. "The March of Events" (MoE), editorials in *World's Work*, various issues.

———. "The New South as Seen by a Southerner" (speech reported in *Boston Post*). Reprinted in *Savannah Morning News*, April 21, 1883, p. 1.

——— (published anonymously). *A Publisher's Confession*. New York: Doubleday, Page & Co., 1905.

———. "The Rebuilding of Old Commonwealths." Republished from *Atlantic Monthly*, May 1902, in *Rebuilding of Old Commonwealths*, pp. 107–53.

———. *The Southerner*. Columbia: University of South Carolina Press, 2008. Originally published under the name of Nicholas Worth, by Doubleday, Page and Co., New York, 1909.

———. "Study of an Old Southern Borough." *Atlantic Monthly*, May 1881, pp. 648–58.

Peele W. J. "A History of the Agricultural and Mechanical College." *North Carolina Teacher*, September 1888, pp. 1–14.

Peters, G., and J. T. Woolley. The American Presidency Project, https://www.presidency.ucsb.edu/.

Richards, M. K. *Ellen Glasgow's Development as a Novelist*. The Hague, the Netherlands: Mouton, 1971.

Rusnak, R. J. *Walter Hines Page and the "World's Work": 1900–1913*. Washington, D.C.: University Press of America, 1982.

Sedgwick, E. *A History of the "Atlantic Monthly," 1857–1909: Yankee Humanism at High Tide and Ebb*. Amherst: University of Massachusetts Press, 1994.

Sellers, C. G. ed. *The Southerner as American*. New York: E. P. Dutton, 1966.

———. "Walter Hines Page and the Spirit of the New South." *North Carolina Historical Review* 29, no. 4 (October 1952): 481–99.

Seymour, C. *The Intimate Papers of Colonel House: Behind the Political Curtain, 1912–1915*. Vol. 1. London: Ernest Benn Ltd., 1926.

———. *The Intimate Papers of Colonel House: From Neutrality to War, 1915–1917*. Vol 2. London: Ernest Benn Ltd., 1926.

Shaw, A. "Walter Hines Page: Memorial Address." *North Carolina Historical Review* 1, no. 1 (January 1924): 3–25.

Siney, M. C. *The Allied Blockade of Germany 1914–1916*. Ann Arbor: University of Michigan Press, 1957.

Sumner, J. L. "'Let Us Have a Big Fair': The North Carolina Exposition of 1884." *North Carolina Historical Review* 69, no. 1 (January 1992): 57–81.

Sydnor, C. S. *The Development of Southern Sectionalism, 1819–1848*. Baton Rouge: Louisiana State University Press, 1948.

Thompson J. W. Speech to the "Young Gentlemen of the Pine Burr Society." March 4, 1923, in Watauga Club Records.

Tuchman B. W. *The Zimmermann Telegram: America Enters the War, 1917–1918*. New York: Random House, 1958. Reprint, 2014.

Wagner L. W. *Ellen Glasgow: Beyond Convention*. Austin: University of Texas Press, 1982.

Warnock H. Y. "Andrew Sledd, Southern Methodists and the Negro: A Case History." *Journal of Southern History* 31, no. 3 (August 1965): 251–71.

Woodward, C. V. *Origins of the New South, 1877–1913*. Baton Rouge: Louisiana State University Press, 1971.

ARCHIVES

Walter Hines Page Papers, 1885–1918 (MS Am 1090.2–1090.13), Houghton Library, Harvard University. Includes letters to and from Page, as well as diaries that he kept intermittently.

Watauga Club Records, 1884–2011 (MC00229), Special Collections Research Center, North Carolina State University Libraries, Raleigh, N.C.

NEWSPAPERS

The following newspapers are cited more than twice; all others appear in the notes. Newspapers are accessed through Chronicling America, Library of Congress.

Charlotte Home and Democrat, Charlotte, N.C. (1884 to 1887 *Charlotte Home-Democrat*; 1887 to 1897 *Charlotte Democrat*).
Commonwealth, Scotland Neck, N.C.
Evening Star, Washington, D.C.
Farmer and Mechanic, Raleigh, N.C.
Gold Leaf, Henderson, N.C.
Indianapolis Journal, Indianapolis, Ind.
New York Times, New York, N.Y.
New York Tribune, New York, N.Y.
News and Observer, Raleigh, N.C.
North Carolina Standard, Raleigh, N.C. (also known as *Weekly North Carolina Standard*; *Semi-weekly North Carolina Standard*; and *Semi-weekly Standard*)
Progressive Farmer, Winston, N.C.
Savannah Morning News, Savannah, Ga.
Semi-weekly Messenger, Wilmington, N.C.
State Chronicle, Raleigh, N.C.
Western Sentinel, Winston-Salem, N.C.

INDEX

African American disenfranchisement: led to segregation, 83–84; Page believed only supported by a minority, 83; Page postulated about military intervention, 85; Page tried to be positive about ending of, 84; Page's opposition to, 83, 84. *See also* African Americans

African Americans: articles in the *World's Work* about, 79; in *Atlantic Monthly*, 79; education for, colleges for, 88; 88–89; equality for, 72–73, 79, 80–81, 123–24; equality rarely mentioned in the *State Chronicle*, 79; Page's jokes and 'stories' about, 80; Page's respect for, 80; predicament of, 84–85, 85–86; research to improve the lives of, 81; segregation of, 85, 86. *See also* African American disenfranchisement

agriculture-demonstration method: children's education, 113–14; described, 112–13; embraced by Page, 113; expansion financed by GEB, 113; importance for GEB, 112–14; success of, 113; transformed rural South, 113; widely promoted by Page, 113. *See also* GEB; Knapp, Seaman A.

Alderman, Edwin A.: accused of racism, 78; advocated Page for diplomatic position, 154–55; liberal progressive advocate for a New South, 67; mentioned, 150, 153, 155

Allies: accused by Wilson of damaging relations with America, 211; America's entry, 223–24, 228; blockade circumvented by Germany, 189; death toll from war, 233; dire financial position, 229–30; favored by House's peace proposal, 204; House supported, 195, 212; Houston criticized Page for encouraging America to join, 197; Lansing supported, 200, 210, 212; led by Britain, France, and Russia, 181; majority of Americans supported, 182; negative response to U.S. peace plan, 219; Page wanted America to stand with, 215; submarine threat to, 228; supplies depleted by submarine attacks, 229;

war aim of, 184, 188, 199, 205, 219, 242; Wilson's peace proposal, 216; mentioned, 186, 192, 225, 232, 236, 237

ambassadorship: accommodation not provided for, 163, 164; belated or no response to by Wilson to Page's communications, 190, 199, 200, 204, 206, 215; British tributes to Page, 232; no instructions given to Page by Wilson, 158–59; other ambassadors, 207; Page accused of being too pro-British, 199, 208, 211–12, 221, 226, 229, 244; Page acted neutrally, 185, 194; Page agreed not to resign from, 222; Page considered Wilson's offer, 155, 156; Page ignored when visited America, 208–10; Page indicated he would resign from, 173, 186, 191, 204–5, 209, 215; Page misunderstood by Wilson, House, Lansing and Polk, 213; Page's financial position, 163, 172–73; Page's research before starting, 156–57, 158; Page's farewell from London, 232–33; Page's resignation, 202, 231, 245; Page sidelined by Wilson and House, 227; Page thrived, 164–65; Page wrote prodigiously to House and Wilson, 167; tribute from Page's successor, 237; Wilson acted so Page wouldn't resign, 170, 173, 222; Wilson appreciated and encouraged Page's letters, 166, 167–68, 191, 200; Wilson offered position to Page, 154–55, 155, 156–57; Wilson's offer was against Page's beliefs, 156; Wilson wanted Page to spend time in America, 199, 200, 208. *See also* U.S. embassy in London; War, First World; Wilson, Woodrow, WWI

antebellum myth: creation of, 60–61; defined, 59, 60; New South advocates wanted to defeat, 66; perpetuated by restricting access to education, 91, 101; perpetuated by Southern leaders, 65–66, 67, 104, 116; replaced by race-problem myth, 78, 85, 257; Southern industrial development, 68, 72–73; two phases of,

antebellum myth (*continued*)
60, 65–66, 253; undermined and subtly
attacked in the *State Chronicle*, 92
Arendell, F. B., 15, 34, 42
Ashe, Samuel A., 33, 40, 70
Asquith, Herbert H., 179; advocated
memorial to Page in Westminster Abbey,
236; attended Katharine's wedding,
199; believed House's peace talks were
pointless, 195; lost prime ministership,
216; prime minister of Great Britain,
164
Atlantic Monthly: conflict between Page and
Scudder at, 44; Page as editor of, 43, 44;
Page advocated Southern development
in, 71; Page's resignation from, 45–46;
Page's success at, 44–45, 46; Page's writing
constrained at, 46, 104–5. *See also* African
Americans; education, public; Houghton,
Mifflin & Co.; Mifflin, George H.; Perry,
Bliss; public opinion; Scudder, Horace E.;
Sedgwick, Ellery; South
Aycock, Charles B.: liberal progressive advo-
cate for a New South, 67; racist, 78, 109;
support for Page, 97; supported education
campaign, 109; supported disenfranchise-
ment of African Americans, 78;

Balfour, Arthur, 222; advocated memorial
to Page in Westminster Abbey, 236;
concerned about Page's sidelining,
227; emotional farewell to Page, 233; as
foreign secretary, 216; Page retained good
relations with, 223–24, 238; pleaded for
assistance from U.S. government, 229–30;
mentioned, 223
Barclay, Esther Sr. (great-grandmother):
Confederacy supported by, 14; independent tavern proprietor, 9, 136
Bassett, John S., 67, 87–88
Bernstorff, Johann-Heinrich von: advised
Lansing of submarine campaign, 220;
forwarded "Zimmermann Telegram", 223;
German ambassador to America, 196; lost
respect for U.S. government, 196; ordered
to leave U.S., 220
Bethmann-Hollweg, Theobald von, 179;

German chancellor, 179; lost respect
for U.S. government, 196; submarine
campaigns, 195–96, 199, 205, 206, 217, 218,
220; mentioned, 222
Bingham School: conservative environment
at, 18; influence on Page, 17–18, 18; Walter
thrived at, 18; mentioned, 94
Blair, Henry W.: public education Senate bill
of, 93, 93–94, 109; mentioned, 95
Bryan, William J., 72, 166–67, 170, 193;
circumvented by direct communication
between Page and Wilson, 168; claimed
House was effectively secretary of state,
198; gave speech at dinner for Page, 158;
opposed Wilson on Panama Canal issue,
169; ostracized by Wilson, 198, 243; Page
discussed ambassadorship with, 157; Page's
dislike of, 126; resigned over First *Lusitania* Note, 198; told Wilson Page had been
unneutral, 190; U.S. secretary of state, 157;
Wilson's treatment of Page compared with
that of, 227; mentioned, 197
Buttrick, Wallace: GEB secretary and
executive officer, 109–10; concerned
about Page's health, 230; gave speech
at memorial to Knapp, 114; introduced
Knapp to Page, 113; met with President
Wilson, 154; P Page's impact on the
education campaign, 111; age instigated
Stiles discussing hookworm plan with,
117; Page remembered by, 260–61; praised
Page, 158; sought to improve agricultural
efficiency, 112; mentioned, 110, 153

Cable, George W.: interviewed by Page, 27;
liberal progressive advocate for a New
South, 67; mentioned, 40
career: developed editorial career in New
York, 35; first magazine article published,
23; first published writing, 22–23; interest
in teaching, 21, 23, 24; interest in writing,
23, 24; started as editor, 25; teaching at
University of North Carolina, 24; turning
point, 26
Cary, North Carolina: Cary Academy, 18, 25;
established by Frank Page, 14; originally
known as "Page's", 9; profiled in the *State*

Chronicle, 69; suburb of Raleigh, 69; mentioned, 100

Cecil, Robert, 213, 241; acting foreign secretary, 216; farewelled Page at Waterloo Station, 233; minister of blockade, 205

Central Powers: death toll from war, 233; Germany and Austria-Hungary, 181; Page advocated embargo against to end war, 204; Wilson's peace proposal sent to, 216; mentioned, 207

Chamberlayne, John H.: influence on Page, 19–20

child labor, 124

Churchill, Winston: attended Westminster Abbey memorial service, 236; described the antebellum South, 60; proposed "naval holiday," 179

civil service reform: articles supporting in the *Forum*, 130; Cleveland supported, 125, 130; Cleveland undertook as New York governor, 129; in the *State Chronicle*, 129, 129–30; Page's criticism of, 130.

classical liberal: Page as a, 123–24, 130–31, 132, 133; different to "liberal", 123. *See also* Mill, John S.

Cleveland, Grover, 130; advised by Page, 125; first president Page met, 125; mentioned, 35, 41, 54, 131. *See also* civil service reform; tariffs

Confederate veterans: Page's attitude toward, 18, 72

Conference for Education in the South, 105–8, 109; Page presided over final, 158; Page's 1904 speech at Birmingham, Alabama, 20, 90, 106–8; supported by most Southern governors, 106. *See also* education; GEB; Ogden, Robert C.; SEB

Connor, Robert D.: Page's impact on the education campaign, 111–12; Page's warning about the antebellum myth, 67; summed up impact of "Forgotten Man" speech, 104, 255

corporations, monopolistic. *See under* trusts

Craven, Braxton, 19

Dabney, Charles, 95, 97, 158; African American education, 109; described Page,

23; influence of Jefferson on Page, 19; liberal progressive advocate for a New South, 67; praised Page, 100, 104, 107, 111, 255, 260; summer school for teachers, 110; turnaround in public opinion on education, 254; mentioned, 88, 99, 106

Daniels, Josephus, 39, 70, 99, 209, 229; belief in white superiority, 78; criticized for publishing Page's "Mummy Letter", 96; described how House ingratiated himself with Wilson, 151; led campaign against J. S. Bassett, 87–88; liberal progressive advocate for a New South, 67; newspaper attacked Page over hookworm claims, 116; on Page, 10, 15–16, 32, 35, 80, 99–100, 103; Page's strong criticism of, 88; *State Chronicle* owner and editor, 34; supported by Aycock, 97; mentioned, 30, 34, 74

De Bow, James D. B., 62–63, 64

Declaration of London, 185, 186–87. *See also* trade dispute, U.S.-Britain

Dewey, John: role of the media in a democracy, 252

Doubleday, Frank N.: partnership with Page, 47; partnership with Samuel McClure, 46

Doubleday, Page & Co., 47, 49, 53, 71; published B. T. Washington's autobiography, 89. *See also* Glasgow, Ellen

Du Bois, W. E. Burghart: article in the *Atlantic Monthly*, 79; articles in the *World's Work*, 79, 86, 89; predicament of African Americans, 79–80; research on African Americans, 87; resigned to reality of disenfranchisement and segregation, 86

education: in *Forum*, 134; Page on, 90, 92–93, 98, 100, 105, 106–8, 109–10, 113; significant coverage in the *State Chronicle*, 92–93. *See also* Conference for Education in the South; education, public; education, technical and industrial; GEB; SEB; teacher training

education, public: advocated by New South liberal progressives, 66; dominant issue for Page, 91; *Forum* exposed serious problems in schools, 135; gave independence and opportunity to women and girls, 102, 136;

308 \ INDEX

education, public (*continued*)
important for a town's development, 108; important in a democracy, 101; lack of in North Carolina, 100–1; lack of in the South, 91, 99; major series in the *Atlantic Monthly*, 135–36; new era in the South, 253–54; North Carolinian's attitude to, 93–94, 98, 102; opportunity lost in the South due to Page's ambassadorship, 158; Page advocated revolutionary approach to, 103; Page tried to galvanize campaign for, 104; Page's criticism of North Carolina's leaders, 101; Page's support for, 88, 90; Southerners attitude to, 91; three interrelated benefits of, 91; training was essential for Southern development, 107, 110–11. *See also* Conference for Education in the South; education; GEB; SEB

education, technical and industrial: 95, 96–97. *See also* education; North Carolina Agriculture and Mechanic Arts College

environment: articles in the *Atlantic Monthly*, 140; articles in the *Forum*, 139–40; extensive coverage of in the *World's Work*, 140–41; Kate influenced Page's love of, 138–39; mentioned in the *State Chronicle*, 139; Page encouraged appreciation and conservation of, 139, 140–41

Flexner, Abraham: Page's impact on the education campaign, 112

Forum, 37; influence of, 41–42; Page business manager of, 37–38, 39; Page editor of, 38, 39; Page praised, 40, 42; Page sought to foster change in society at, 134–35; Page stimulated debate while editor, 40, 137; Page's advocacy of Southern development in, 71; Page's editorial style at, 39–40; Page's ethics at, 53–54; Page's resignation from, 42; Wilson and, 40, 42. See also African Americans; civil service reform; education; environment; great strike periods; investigative journalism; public opinion; South; tariffs; trusts; women

Garfield, James A.: Page reported Southern reaction to assassination of, 27; Page supported candidacy of, 124–25

Gates, Frederick T.: and Page met with President Wilson, 154; manager of Rockefeller philanthropies, 117

General Education Board (GEB), 154; accepted reality of segregation, 109; funded children's agriculture clubs, 113; hookworm campaign integral to success of, 119; Page's contribution to, 109–10, 111–12, 153, 260; rural poverty was biggest impediment to operation of, 112; wound up in 1964, 158. *See also* Buttrick, Wallace; education; agriculture–demonstration method; SEB; Rockefeller, John D. Sr.; Rockefeller Sanitation Commission

George V: British ceremonial head of state, 164; Page considered underrated, 165; Page wanted Wilson to stand with, 177; photographed standing with Wilson, 236; reaction to war starting, 182; represented at Page's farewell, 233; tribute to Ambassador Page, 232; wept when received U.S. peace proposal, 216–17; mentioned, 163, 179, 199

Gerard, James W.: Allies faced greater danger of starvation than Germany, 228; believed Germany was fighting for autocracy, 242; Bethmann-Hollweg tried to negotiate with, 206; confirmed Page's Leadership Letter argument, 189; dinner held in honor of, 218; ignored by Wilson, 207; instructed by Wilson to communicate neutrally, 190; made preparations to be recalled, 197; outlined Germany's war aim, 218, 219; recalled, 220;; U.S. ambassador in Germany, 183, 189; warned U.S. State Department of 1917 submarine campaign, 218; mentioned, 196

German government: aim was to push U.S. without breaking relations, 201–2, 206; American neutrality ended due to actions of, 246–47; believed war was a fight for autocracy, 242; kept 1917 submarine campaign plan secret, 218; lost respect for U.S. government, 196; negative response to U.S. peace plan, 219; Page critical of, 184–85, 188, 211, 214, 225–26, 242; submarine campaigns of, 195–96, 198–99, 205–6, 206, 217, 218, 228–29; U.S. ended relations with, 220; U.S. sent three *Lusitania* notes to, 198

Germany: encouraged by Page to embrace democracy, 185; essentially an autocracy, 179; management of forests in, 140; manufacturing volume well below U.S., 128; no world power keeping check on, 247; Page had a soft spot for the people, 184–85; Page visited as a university student, 22–23; still could have won war after America's entry, 223–24

Gildersleeve, Basil: influence on Page, 21

Glasgow, Ellen: Page's publishing relationship with, 47–49; rejected the antebellum myth, 74–75; success as an author, 49

Great Britain: classical liberals in, 123; manufacturing volume well below U.S., 128; Page believed America should uphold democracy with, 244; Page encouraged good relationship between America and, 44; supported by President Roosevelt in World War II, 249–50

Great Britain government: aim was to push U.S. without breaking relations, 193–94, 201–2; believed the war was a fight for democracy, 242; negative reaction to U.S. peace proposal, 216–17; Page retained good relations with, 213, 223–24, 237–38; Page's sidelining caused quandary for, 227; policy of good relations with U.S., 168; war aim of, 219

great strike periods: in the *Forum*, 131; voluntary conciliation and arbitration proposed, 134; period covered in the *World's Work*, 132

Gregg, William, 61–62, 63, 64

Grey, Edward, 179, 180, 182, 232; advocated memorial to Page in Westminster Abbey, 236; attended Katharine's wedding, 199; battled public opinion on blockade, 205; believed the war was a fight for democracy, 242; British foreign secretary, 164; changed Britain's policy on western

hemisphere, 171; inevitability of Britain's involvement in war, 181; and Page, 169, 171, 183, 194, 207, 213, 237–38, 238, 246; pushed U.S. without breaking relations, 193–94; replaced by Balfour as foreign secretary, 216; unveiled Page's plaque in Westminster Abbey, 237; mentioned, 186

Hale, William B., 144, 146, 147–48

Hampton Normal and Agricultural Institute, 89, 107

Harding, Warren G., 247

Hatcher, B. W., 93, 95

Hayes, Mary (grandmother), 11

hookworm disease: existence in the South, 115; relatively easily cured and prevented, 115–16; would have been a relief for Page, 116–17. *See also* Rockefeller Sanitation Commission; Stiles, Charles W.

Hoover, Herbert C.: gratitude to Ambassador Page, 183; praised by Page, 216; successful humanitarian activities, 183; tribute to Page, 259

Houghton, Mifflin & Co., 43, 45–46, 80

House, Edward M.: accused Page of being too pro-British, 208, 211–12; had advised Texan governors, 147; ingratiated himself with Wilson, 151–52; ironically agreed with Page, 212; Page influenced to support Wilson, 147; Page's loss of faith in, 201, 204–5; Page's reaction to peace proposals of, 180, 195, 205; Page's response to Wilson's neutrality edict, 191; peace proposals unsuccessful, 179–80, 194–95, 204–5; reaction to *Lusitania* sinking, 197; suggested Page for British ambassadorship, 154–55; wanted Page to understand American public opinion, 208; and Wilson, 147, 151, 152, 153–54, 167, 190, 236, 243

Houston, David F., 106; and Page met with President Wilson, 154; concerned about Wilson's people skills, 152, 155; misunderstood Page's response to *Lusitania* sinking, 197; Page advocated similar policies to, 152, 154; Page helped to become secretary

Houston, David F. (*continued*)
  of agriculture, 152; Page suggested to
  Wilson for secretary of agriculture, 150;
  shared a joke with Page, 159; turned down
  secretary of agriculture position, 152;
  wanted Page to be secretary of agriculture,
  152; Wilson decided to offer cabinet
  position to, 152; mentioned, 167–68, 169

immigration: Page's pragmatism regarding,
  124
international relations: America a beacon
  of freedom, 175–76; America formed
  military alliances after WWII, 258; American indifference to, 173, 189–90, 220,
  221–22, 247, 248; American leadership
  after WWII, 258–59; American leadership
  during WWII, 249, 250; Page advocated
  American leadership in, 173–74, 175, 177,
  178, 185, 247–48; Wilson conscious of
  American inexperience in, 178
investigative journalism: defined, 52–53; Page
  pioneered the use of in magazines, 40, 53,
  252; Page used, 40, 53, 134–35; undermined
  by sensationalist "muckraking", 52–53

Jacques, William W.: Page's visit to Germany
  as student, 22
Jasper, Sarah (mother's cousin): mentioned,
  12, 21
Jeanes Fund board: Page agreed to be
  member of, 74; Page and Taft became
  acquainted serving on, 126
Jefferson, Thomas, 177; influence on Page, 19;
  mentioned, 130
Johns Hopkins University, 115; Page elected
  president of New York alumni of, 23; Page
  ended time as student at, 23; influence on
  Page, 21–23; Wilson applied to study at,
  28; mentioned, 74, 106, 184

Kennan, George F., 221, 242–43, 189–90
Kirkland, James H., 106, 107
Knapp, Seaman A., 112, 113, 114, 149. *See also*
  agriculture-demonstration method

labor unions, 132, 133–34
Lansing, Robert, 209, 228; American
  reaction to British contraband list, 194;
  caused Page to despair, 209; confirmed
  Page's Leadership Letter argument, 189;
  described American's attitude to the
  war, 245; knew of German subterfuge,
  225; lack of interest in Page's plan to end
  trade dispute, 213; Page's loss of faith in,
  201; replaced Bryan as secretary of state,
  198; surreptitiously agreed with Page that
  the war was a fight for democracy, 200,
  209–10, 212, 242; told Wilson Page had
  been unneutral, 190; Wilson and House
  considered dismissing, 227. *See also* trade
  dispute, U.S.–Britain
Laughlin, Irwin B., 222, 231; Page praised,
  215–16; mentioned, 208
Leadership Letter, 195, 197, 198, 201, 227, 248;
  America could dictate the terms of peace
  without joining the war, 187–90. *See also*
  Gerard, James W.; Lansing, Robert
Lincoln, Abraham, 176
Lippmann, Walter, 252
Lloyd George, David, 179; advocated
  memorial to Page in Westminster Abbey,
  236; became prime minister, 216; tribute
  to Ambassador Page, 232
London: description of in 1913/14, 163–64
Loring, Charles G.: marriage to Katharine,
  199; serving in France, 231
Luce, Henry R., 248
Lusitania: Alice traveled home on, Decem-
  ber 1914, 191; Page wanted Wilson to enact
  threats he made in notes, 203–04, 204;
  Page's reaction to sinking of, 197; sunk by
  German submarine, 197; U.S. government
  notes to German government, 197–98;
  mentioned, 194
Lynching, 81–82, 251

magazines, 36–37, 38. *See also* investigative
  journalism
Manufacturers' Record, 39
Marcosson, Isaac: described Page, 50–51, 52,
  55, 67, 80, 260
McAdoo, Willliam G., 155; involved in

INDEX | 311

Wilson's presidential campaign, 147; praised Page's campaign advice, 147, 148; treasury secretary, 230

McClure, Samuel: *McClure's Magazine*, 37; offered Page job at Harper & Brothers, 46, 47; partnership with F. N. Doubleday, 46

McCombs, William F., 145, 147

McCorkle, William, 145

McIver, Charles D., 101; accused of racism by Page, 78; invited Page to give commencement address, 99; liberal progressive advocate for a New South, 67; praised Page's "Forgotten Man" speech, 103, 104; State Normal and Industrial College for Girls, 99

McKinley, William, 174. *See also* tariffs

Metcalf, Lorettus S., 37, 38, 40

Mexico, 170, 171

Mifflin, George H., 43, 46

Mill, John S.: classical liberal philosopher, 123; stated that Southern culture would be difficult to change, 65, 85

Mims, Edwin, 106; articles in the *World's Work*, 89; legacy of "Forgotten Man" speech, 112; Page asked to write articles on the South, 51; Page remembered by, 260; praised Page's 1904 Birmingham speech, 107; praised the *World's Work* "Southern Number", 71

Monroe Doctrine, 242; key aspect defined, 177; Page knew it was redundant, 258; replaced by Truman Doctrine, 258

"muckraking." *See under* investigative journalism

Murphy, Edgar G., 67, 124

neutrality, American, 181; claimed neutral trade should be unimpeded, 185–86; failure of, 225–26; lulled Americans into false sense of security, 241; missed opportunity to defend democracy, 243; Page believed disadvantaged America, 212–13; Page predicted failure of, 225–26; riddled with inconsistencies, 246; weakened American leadership, 242; Wilson's confusing messages about, 246–47. *See also* myth of neutrality

myth of neutrality: catalyst for breakdown in relationship between Page and Wilson, 190–91, 243; debunked by Franklin D. Roosevelt in WWII, 248–49; defined, 241; resurrected in the inter-war period, 247; Wilson's insistence on personal neutrality exacerbated problems caused by, 241. *See also* neutrality, American

New South: conservative progressive advocates for, 66; liberal progressive advocates for, 66–67; Page criticized conservative progressives, 66; Page wanted more fundamental change than other advocates, 67, 123; racism of most advocates for, 78

New York *World*: Page worked for, 27–28; Page's resignation from, 29

North: Page's networks in, 74; racism common in, 78. *See also* South

North Carolina: at the *State Chronicle* the major topic was development of, 68; illiteracy rate, 94; industrial development held back by antebellum myth, 68; Page encouraged Northern investment in, 69–70; Page relentlessly encouraged local entrepreneurship in, 68–69; Page wanted to spend final days in, 233; Page's advocacy likely had positive impact on development, 256–57; Research Triangle Park, 256–57; state of public education in, 93–94, 100–1. *See also* North Carolina Exposition 1884

North Carolina Agriculture and Mechanic Arts College, 256; established, 97; now North Carolina State University, 97; Page's commencement address at, 110–11; success of, 97. *See also* Watauga Club

North Carolina Exposition 1884, 70, 256

North Carolina State University: part of North Carolina's Research Triangle Park, 256; Watauga Medal, 97. *See also* North Carolina Agriculture and Mechanic Arts College

Northerners: Page's attitude to, 74

Obama, Barak: American world leadership, 258–59

Ogden, Robert C.: accepted reality of

Ogden, Robert C. (*continued*)
segregation for education campaign, 109; death of, 158; leadership of Conference for Education in the South, 105, 158; organized SEB, 108; Page's contribution to the education campaign, 111; transported Northerners to Conference for Education in the South, 105, 106

Oldham, Edward A.: influence on Page, 32; praised Page, 38; *State Chronicle* assistant editor, 32

Page, Allison Francis 'Frank' (father), 9, 11, 13–16, 17, 35, 42; advertised in the *State Chronicle*, 30; built their home, 10; death of, 16; desire for Walter to enter the ministry, 17, 20; established Cary Academy, 18; founder of Cary, 14, 69; influence on Walter, 14, 15–16, 30, 32, 42, 251, 261; married Kate Raboteau, 10; relationship with Walter, 15–16, 100; mentioned, 116

Page, Anderson (grandfather), 11–13; death of, 13; influence on Walter, 59, 75–76, 92–93, 107, 113, 251; mentioned, 116

Page, Arthur Wilson (son), 26, 149, 191; birth of, 32; concerned about Walter's health, 230; North Carolina mountain hike with Walter, 139; not in favor of Walter accepting ambassadorship, 155; took Walter to Scotland for a rest, 232; traveled with Alice to memorial service in London, 236; unable to be with Walter for his final days, 235; Walter considered impact of ambassadorship on, 156; Walter showed pride in, 55; Wilson displeased with the *World's Work*, 246; working at the *World's Work*, 55; *World's Work* managing editor, 153; mentioned, 166, 197, 198, 224, 227, 231, 246

Page, Catherine 'Kate' Raboteau (mother), 9–11, 13, 14, 35, 42; death of, 11; desire for Walter to enter the ministry, 17, 20; influence on Walter, 10, 16, 17, 136, 138–39, 261; marriage to Frank Page, 10; undertook Walter's early schooling, 17; mentioned, 19, 21, 22

Page, Frank Copeland (son), 26, 55, 191; birth of, 35; concerned about Walter's health, 230; serving in France, 231; supported Walter accepting ambassadorship, 155; traveled with Walter to London, 163; with Walter for his final days, 235; mentioned, 211

Page, Katharine Alice (daughter), 26; as a child, 55; birth of, 38; husband serving in France, 231; journey to London on the *Adriatic*, 163; marriage to C. G. Loring, 199; replied to the final letters received by Walter, 235; traveled with Alice to memorial service in London, 236; Walter considered impact of ambassadorship on, 156; with Walter for his final days, 235; mentioned, 142, 194

Page, Ralph Walter (son), 26, 232; birth of, 27; North Carolina mountain hike with Walter, 139; Walter showed pride in, 55; with Walter for his final days, 235

Page, Walter Hines: academic success, 18, 20; achieved career goal, 47, 49; advocated or used research to improve understanding, 39, 53, 81, 87, 90, 93–94, 128, 135, 135–36, 137–38, 174; appearance described, 55; argument with parents over entering ministry, 20; attitude to journalism, 25; birth of, 9; character of, 17, 55, 159, 183, 237, 259–61; death of, 235; desire for editorial independence, 24, 32, 34, 42; disappointment with presidents he supported, 145; earned widespread respect, 259–60; embraced by the people, 251; error in accepting Harper & Brothers job, 47; family was important to, 54; featured on North Carolina State University Watauga Medal, 97; final letter to Wilson, 233–34; honorary doctorate, 45; ideas consistent throughout life, 252; impressive public speaker, 20, 100, 106–7; influenced by educated and independent women, 136; love of literature, 21; memorial and plaque at Westminster Abbey, 236–37; mythmakers presented his greatest challenges, 251; not professional "Southern reformer," 74; philosophy, 123–24; planning to semire-

INDEX / 313

tire, 152–53, 153; policies for Democrats for 1912 elections, 146; poor health of, 10, 23, 45, 105, 230–31, 232, 233; role of the media in a democracy, 252; tired of being criticized, 74

Page, Willia Alice Wilson (wife), 25–26, 27, 32, 35, 38, 39, 105, 142; admiration for sons, 55; attended Westminster Abbey memorial service, 236; concerned about Walter's health, 230; horrified when arrived in London, 163; importance in Walter's life of, 26; Katharine's wedding, 199; marriage to Walter, 25–26; met Wilson for first time, 157; traveled to London on the *Adriatic*, 163; traveled home on *Lusitania*, 191; traveled home with Walter for the last time, 235; Walter considered impact of ambassadorship on, 156; Walter discussed ambassadorship offer with, 155; Walter lamented racism of, 78; Walter's last letter to, 232; with Walter for his last days, 235; mentioned, 85, 89, 116, 125, 167, 181, 195, 208, 209, 246, 259

Panama Canal, 168, 169–70

Peele, William J.: chairman of Watauga Club, 95; featured on North Carolina State University Watauga Medal, 97; praised Page, 97

Perry, Bliss, 44, 46

Pinehurst, North Carolina: Page planned to semiretire at, 152, 153; Page returned to for final days, 235

Poe, Clarence H.: advocated segregation of farming, 78; articles in the *World's Work*, 89; gave speech at memorial to Knapp, 114; praised Page's speeches, 107–8, 110; pushed for Page to be secretary of agriculture, 149; report on "Forgotten Man" speech, 103–4

politics: Page considered entering, 21, 29; Page supported candidates and policies rather than parties, 124

Polk, Frank L., 207, 208, 210, 213, 222–23

Polk, Leonidas L., 97

Price, Thomas R., 21

public opinion: Page tried to use the *Atlantic Monthly* to influence, 44; Page tried to use

the *Forum* to influence, 39–40, 134–35; Page tried to use the *State Chronicle* to influence, 33; Page tried to use the *World's Work* to influence, 49–50

public opinion, American: converted by German submarine attacks and "Zimmermann Telegram", 223; Page's understanding of, 208, 213; U.S. government had to take account of, 208

Raboteau, Kate (mother). *See* Page, Catherine 'Kate' Raboteau

Race-problem myth: academic freedom undermined by, 86–88; defined, 77–78, 257; Page underestimated pervasiveness of, 78–79, 79, 82, 84, 85; perpetuated by Southern leaders, 77–78, 106; replaced the antebellum myth, 78, 85, 257; turned public opinion against African American education, 109

Raleigh, North Carolina: description of in 1883, 30–32; Page grew up near, 9; Page started the *State Chronicle* in, 30; Page's grandfather established home near, 11; Page's mother went to school in, 9; *State Chronicle* "Special Raleigh Edition", 69–70; three other newspapers in, 33; Watauga Club formed in, 95

Randolph-Macon College, 19, 20, 21

Rockefeller Sanitary Commission for the Eradication of Hookworm Disease (Rockefeller Sanitary Commission): eradication campaign developed after Page's intervention, 117; establishment and description of, 117–18; integral to work of SEB and GEB, 119; Page enjoyed working on, 153; Page's influential promotion of campaign, 119; Southern communities embraced public health, 118–19; success of campaign, 120, 254–55. *See also* hookworm disease; Rockefeller Foundation; Rockefeller, John D. Sr.; Rose, Wickliffe; Stiles, Charles W.

Rockefeller Foundation: funding for GEB, 158; provided Rockefeller Sanitary Commission funding for five years, 117, 120

314 \ INDEX

Rockefeller, John D. Sr.: Page thought of to fund hookworm campaign, 117; GEB proposed and funded by, 108–9. *See also* SEB

Roosevelt, Franklin D., 178; attitude to neutrality was the same as Page's, 182; debunked myth of neutrality, 248–49, 258; showed the leadership Page had advocated, 248–50; support for public education, 254; turned around public opinion, 249

Roosevelt, Theodore, 113, 178; admiration for Page as ambassador, 259; advised by Page, 125; contrast with Wilson, 212; controversial appointment of African American to government position, 84; criticisms of Sherman Antitrust Act, 133; death of, 259; dined with Washington at White House, 78, 125; Ellen Glasgow compared Page with, 48; supported by Page, 125–26; supported tariffs, 128; wrote for the *Forum*, 40, 139–40; mentioned, 140. *See also* environment; tariffs

Rose, Wickliffe, 106, 119, 153, 255; responsible for running Rockefeller Sanitary Commission, 118; mentioned, 114

Sazonoff, Sergius, 178–79, 181

schools, public. *See under* education, public

Scudder, Horace E., 46; conflict with Page, 43–44; discussed employment offer with Page, 43; editor of the *Atlantic Monthly*, 43; major series on public schools, 135–36; resigned as editor, 44

Sedgwick, Ellery, 46

Shaw, Albert: explained role of SEB, 108; Page remembered by, 260

slavery: Southern inertia and other problems caused by attitude to, 67, 68, 77, 98, 111, 112. *See also* race-problem myth

Sledd, Andrew: academic freedom and, 86–87

South: antebellum aristocracy, 60; articles in the *Atlantic Monthly*, 71; articles in the *Forum*, 71; articles in the *World's Work*, 71; Page better off living and working in the North, 34, 35, 36, 73, 76, 87; Page wanted to change the culture of, 34, 72–73, 73, 76, 123, 251; Page's attitude towards, 27, 72–73, 74, 75–76; period of national prominence, 59; politics dominated by Democratic Party "bosses", 129; racial inequality was the most intractable problem, 257. *See also* Southerner, The; Southern development; Southerners

Southern development: development of the people was Page's priority, 255–56; fell behind North during antebellum period, 59–60; inefficiency of agriculture in, 112; needed education and training for development, 107; Page encouraged industrialization in, 29, 34, 39, 66, 69, 71–72, 251; pre–Civil War growth in manufacturing, 63; used Doubleday Page & Co. and the *World's Work* to promote, 71. *See also* South; tariffs

Southern Education Board (SEB): aimed for equality in education, 109; hookworm campaign integral to success of, 119; Page enjoyed working on, 153; Page gave speeches supporting, 108; Page's impact on, 111–12, 260; realized funding and building of schools was needed, 108; Rockefellers impressed with work of, 108; wound up in 1914, 158. *See also* Conference for Education in the South; education; GEB; Rockefeller, John D. Sr.; Rockefeller Sanitary Commission

Southerner, The: Page's feelings towards the South shown in, 75–76; Page's position on equality in education shown in, 89; published by Page in 1909, 75

Southerners: criticized Page, 34, 35, 38, 72, 91–92, 96, 103–4; Page believed should consider themselves Americans first, 72–73, 74, 76; praised Page, 38, 40, 42, 45, 98, 103. *See also* education, public

State Chronicle: established, 30; first edition of, 32; Page sent articles from New York to, 35; Page's editorial style at, 33, 92; Page's ethics at, 33–34; Page's resignation from, 34. *See also* African Americans; antebellum myth; civil service reform; education; environment; lynching; investigative journalism; North Carolina; North Carolina Exposition 1884; public opinion; tariffs; women

Stiles, Charles W.: assessed success of hookworm campaign, 254; vindicated by North Carolina health official, 116; on hookworm disease, 114, 115, 116, 117; criticized by North Carolina governor, 116; Page praised the work of, 119. *See also* hookworm disease; Rockefeller Sanitary Commission

Stockbridge, Frank P.: Page's pride at Wilson's nomination recalled by, 148; Wilson's campaign publicity manager, 145, 146

Taft, William H., 144, 169, 170, 178; and Page, 126

tariffs: articles supporting reform in the *Forum*, 128; classical liberals generally oppose, 126; Cleveland strongly supported reform, 127, 128, 174; Congressman McKinley's bill raised tariffs to record levels, 128; controversial national policy, 126–27; data supported Page's reform argument, 127, 128; need for reform raised extensively in the *State Chronicle*, 127; need for reform raised as a major issue in the *World's Work*, 128; Page on, 28, 126–27, 128, 165; reform advocated by Page, 72, 127–28, 146, 157, 174; reform advocated by Wilson, 28, 144, 157; reform opposed by T. Roosevelt, 128

teacher training: GEB funded, 110; importance of, 253; lack of in the South, 136; Page's support for, 94–95; SEB planned to promote, 108

trade dispute, U.S.-Britain, 193–94: ended upon U.S. break with Germany, 221; Page vindicated over, 221–22, 227–28. *See also* Declaration of London

Trinity College: now Duke University and part of North Carolina's Research Triangle Park, 256; Page planned to dedicate new library at, 110; Page studied at, 18–19;

supported academic freedom, 87–88; mentioned, 67, 106

Truman Doctrine, 258

trusts: in *Forum*, 131–32; Page advocated control of monopolistic corporations, 130–31, 133; Roosevelt tried to control growth of, 133; Wilson enacted antitrust legislation in New Jersey, 145; in *World's Work*, 132

Tuskegee Normal and Industrial Institute, 87, 89

University of North Carolina: Page at, 24, 81; Page's advocacy of role in industrialization, 98, 256–57; Page's speech at inauguration of President Winston, 98; part of North Carolina's Research Triangle Park, 256; mentioned, 17, 18, 106, 145

U.S. embassy in London: Page inspired great loyalty amongst staff, 166; Page moved to "dignified offices", 164; poor condition of, 163, 164; represented embassies of most warring nations, 182; short walk from Foreign Office, 164. *See also* ambassadorship

U.S. government: confidence of British in was undermined, 238; declared war on Germany, 226; reaction to British blacklist, 207–8; reaction to the first German submarine campaign, 196; reluctantly assisted the Allies, 229, 230; sent three *Lusitania* notes to German government, 198; weak diplomatic position of, 79–80, 194–95, 204, 205, 235–36, 236. *See also* German government; Great Britain government

U.S. State Department, 166–67, 208

Wallace, Henry D.: Page encouraged not to criticize Houston, 152; traveled with Page and Stiles, 114; mentioned, 153, 154

War, First World: centralization of U.S. diplomacy, 227; conflict between democracy and autocracy, 173, 188, 212, 226, 236, 242–43; inevitability of Britain's involvement in, 181; Page believed American

War, First World (*continued*)
leadership could peacefully end, 187–89, 193, 195, 196–97, 198, 199, 201–2, 203–4, 206–7, 209, 215; Page advocated American leadership to prevent, 177, 180, 236; Page believed American peace efforts pointless without showing leadership, 184, 199, 204; Page disagreed with Wilson's personal neutrality instruction to Americans, 182–83; Page lamented inevitability of, 184; Page described the first week of, 181–82; Page's arguments vindicated in Wilson's speech to Congress, 224, 225, 226; Page's despair at Wilson's inaction, 221; U.S. colonel G. O. Squire's first-hand description of, 192–93; U.S. government tried to prevent, 179–80; U.S. not expected to join, 182; Wilson blamed Britain for decline in relations, 211; Wilson did not respond to Page's ideas to peacefully end, 190, 204, 215; Wilson equated aims of both sides, 216, 219, 238; Wilson focused on domestic issues, 190, 207, 210; Wilson told Americans to be personally neutral, 182–83. See also Allies, ambassadorship; German government; Great Britain government; Wilson, Woodrow, WWI

Wardlaw, Jack B., 19–20

Washington, Booker T., 80, 83, 90, 125; Alderman and McIver refused to eat with, 78; article in the *Atlantic Monthly*, 79; articles in the *World's Work*, 79, 86, 89; autobiography published by Page, 89, 110; declared great man by J. S. Bassett, 87; dined with President Roosevelt at White House, 78; invited to dinner with Page in Boston, 78; liberal progressive advocate for a New South, 67; praised Hampton Institute, 89; principal of Tuskegee Institute, 89

Watauga Club, 254; advocacy for industrial school, 95, 97; formed in Raleigh, 95; public meeting held by, 96; turned around public opinion, 97. *See also* North Carolina Agriculture and Mechanic Arts College

Wilhelm II, 179, 185, 217; meeting with House, 180; officially approved submarine campaign, 218, mentioned, 214

"Wilson doctrine," 171

Wilson, Woodrow: considered Page for a cabinet position, 152, 153; did not visit Page in hospital, 233; final meeting with Page, 210–11; first meeting with Page, 28; nature of pre-war relationship with Page, 28, 142–43, 165; Page believed Wilson had potential for high office, 143; Page sought unofficial presidential advisory role, 149, 150–51, 151, 152–53, 154; Page suggested Houston for secretary of agriculture, 150; Page's concern about people skills of, 150–51, 155; stood up to corrupt Democratic Party bosses, 145, 147–48. *See also* ambassadorship; *Forum*; House, Edward M.; Houston, David F.; tariffs; trusts; War, First World

Wilson, Woodrow, political campaigns: decided on path to presidency, 143; Democratic candidate for 1912 election, 148; gratitude to Page for support, 148, 149; Page's advice during nomination campaign, 145, 146, 147; Page's influence on gubernatorial campaign, 144; Page's influence on presidential campaign, 148; Page's pride and excitement at election win, 148, 149; presidential nomination campaign supported in the *World's Work*, 145–46; sought New Jersey governorship, 143–44; won 1912 presidential election, 149; won New Jersey election, 144

Wilson, Woodrow, WWI: advised by cabinet and Lansing to join war, 223; afraid to break relations with Germany, 206; announced end of relations with Germany, 220; British blacklist equated with German submarines, 207, 238; not respected at the Versailles Peace Conference, 235, 235–36; Page lost confidence in, 201, 207, 220, 230; Page's assessment of Wilson's leadership, 212–13; peace proposals unsuccessful, 179–80, 194–95, 204–5, 216, 219; reluctance to enter the war, 197; speech requesting Congress declare war on Germany, 224–26; three reasons to declare war on Germany, 224; T. Roosevelt persistently critical of, 259; vindicated Page's argument on how war could have been avoided, 236; world leadership role not taken during war, 248. *See also* ambassadorship; neutrality, American; U.S. government; War, First World

women: *Forum* debated wide range of topics, 137; Page advocated for, 72–73, 123–24, 136–38, 260, 261; *State Chronicle*, 136–37; *World's Work* 137–38

World's Work: focus of, 49–50; Page achieved career goal at, 54; advocacy of Southern development, 71–72; Page's at, 50–51, 52, 53–54; supported Woodrow Wilson, 143, 144, 145–46, 147–48. *See also* African Americans; environment; great strike periods; investigative journalism; labor unions; public opinion; South; Southern development; tariffs; trusts; women

Wright, Carroll D., 131, 137

Zimmermann, Arthur, 218, 220. *See also* "Zimmermann Telegram"

"Zimmermann Telegram", 222, 223, 225

Printed in the United States
by Baker & Taylor Publisher Services